COLLECTING OBJECTS/
EXCLUDING PEOPLE

COLLECTING OBJECTS/
EXCLUDING PEOPLE

Chinese Subjects and
American Visual Culture, 1830–1900

LENORE METRICK-CHEN

STATE UNIVERSITY OF NEW YORK PRESS

cover art: Phillip Chen, "Flower Water," 2002, relief etching, 21" × 32"

Published by
State University of New York Press, Albany

© 2012 State University of New York

All rights reserved

Printed in the United States of America

No part of this book may be used or reproduced in any manner whatsoever without written permission. No part of this book may be stored in a retrieval system or transmitted in any form or by any means including electronic, electrostatic, magnetic tape, mechanical, photocopying, recording, or otherwise without the prior permission in writing of the publisher.

For information, contact
State University of New York Press, Albany, NY
www.sunypress.edu

Production, Laurie D. Searl
Marketing, Michael Campochiaro

Library of Congress Cataloging-in-Publication Data

Metrick-Chen, Lenore.
    Collecting objects/excluding people : Chinese subjects and American visual culture, 1830–1900 / Lenore Metrick-Chen.
        p. cm.
    Includes bibliographical references and index.
    ISBN 978-1-4384-4325-6 (hardcover : alk. paper)
    ISBN 978-1-4384-4326-3 (paperback : alk. paper)
    1. Art, Chinese—Collectors and collecting—United States.   2. Art museums—Social aspects—United States   3. Art and race.   4. China—Foreign public opinion, American—History—19th century.   5. China—Foreign public opinion, American—History—20th century.   I. Title.   II. Title: Chinese subjects and American visual culture, 1830–1900.

N7340.M47 2012
709.51'0973—dc23   2011037741

10 9 8 7 6 5 4 3 2 1

CONTENTS

ILLUSTRATIONS AND CREDITS

CHAPTER ONE

CHAPTER TWO

ACKNOWLEDGMENTS

I have been very fortunate in relationships, with mentors whose wisdom and compassion have been seemingly limitless, and with a loving and supportive family. My research could not have started without the initial support of the Committee of Social Thought at the University of Chicago. I was accepted into this PhD program, although I had not been granted a bachelor's degree and had a very unorthodox and nonlinear roster of coursework. Besides contributing their knowledge, my mentors demonstrated the connections between lived circumstances and scholarly thought.

My loving gratitude goes to Professor Arnaldo Momigliano, now deceased, who met with me weekly to discuss life, including family history and scholarship. With his modest self-disclaimer "Of course I do not know much about this, but . . ." he would then proceed to insights and critiques that went to the heart of every issue. I deeply miss his insights and affection.

Professor Stephen Toulmin, who died in 2009, showed me that all aspects of culture can become a place for the mind to play and learn, and that hierarchies of "high" and "low" do not apply to how objects and things actually mix in the world. The idea for this book emerged during a discussion at his home. He helped imagine the project when in its inception; I would have valued his comments on its completion.

My warm thanks and esteem go to Professor Wendy Doniger, my exemplar as a scholar and a mentor. She has assisted and guided my research in every aspect: from the bare bones of the thesis to aiding in its final publication. Every stage of this book has been touched with her intelligence and kindness.

Professor Wu Hung has been generous with his time and knowledge, especially in discussing the extent to which America imagined a China. And my gratitude goes to Professor Reinhold Heller, who showed me what art history could be. His insights in reading art as objects of discourse within cultural and political contexts are an inspiration, and his perception in reading visual language continues to be a goal I strive for.

My thanks to Drake University, especially the Center for the Humanities at Drake University for its generous support of my work through course reassignments and grants. My thanks also to my colleagues at Drake University for their continuing support and enthusiasm for my endeavors. As with all scholarly publications, so many people have helped bring this book to publication. I am indebted to Jennifer Riley, Manager of Image Licensing Ventures, and Paul McAlpine, librarian, at the Museum of Fine Arts, Boston, for their help in locating and obtaining obscure photographs.

Individuals at SUNY Press have been extremely helpful in bringing this book to fruition. I am most grateful to Nancy Ellegate for her encouragement and direction and to Laurie Searl for her careful editing. I also thank Leonard Rosenbaum for his meticulous indexing and careful reading of my text.

My debt and gratitude to my friends and family are immeasurable. My parents, gave me a love of learning. They conveyed the knowledge that intelligence is not elitist, that history is available for everyone, and that difficult thoughts can often be expressed in clear words.

I can only begin to express the impact my children, Cora and Shaye, have on my work. Their candor challenged me to pursue elusive ideas; frequently their thoughts and questions on race and its visual manifestations have entered these textual discussions. They created a daily life that integrated the life of the mind with the joy of everyday activities. They are both inspiration and distraction, and always a source of renewal.

My husband, Phillip Chen, has provided observations and insight that have added subtlety to the discussions in the text. His support through everything that came our way has made these solitary thoughts become lived experiences. This book is lovingly dedicated to him.

INTRODUCTION

You cannot escape from the world more certainly than through art; and you cannot bind yourself to it more certainly than through art.

—Goethe

This book explores the cultural consequences of politicized imagery of Chinese people in the mid- to late nineteenth century. American political policy and cultural orientations intersected, interpenetrated, and were transformed when Chinese people, and not just Chinese objects, arrived on American shores. The four chapters that follow address a critical question that engrossed mid-nineteenth-century American society, but went unspoken: What happens when the exotic refuses to remain our fantasy, our abstraction, and instead intrudes into our space? When the exotic other is too close for comfort, what more is then at stake?

Since Edward Said's groundbreaking postcolonial analysis of the West's conception of the East in his 1978 work *Orientalism*, and equally in his *Culture and Imperialism* (1993), Orientalism—the West's idea of the East created through a mixture of knowledge and projection—has been a topic of scholarly study. In this work I diverge from classic Orientalist studies in several ways, but especially, rather than presuming the formation of Western ideas of Eastern peoples through the journey of Western peoples to the East, I look at movement in the opposite direction, considering the influence of Eastern people's travel to the West.[1] Other scholars, notably James Clifford and Anne McClintock, have discussed the nineteenth century's radical reassignment of spatial geography and its resulting cultural tensions. Political and social anxieties rippled through (white) America as a consequence of such interpenetration.[2] James Clifford describes the impact occurring "whenever marginal peoples come into historical or ethnographic space that has been defined by the Western imagination. . . . [G]eopolitical questions must now be asked of ever inventive poetics of reality . . . Whose reality? Whose new world?"[3] These questions form the crux of this book. By examining resonances of Chinese immigration within American culture, we discover the far-reaching cultural consequences when the exotic Orient is no longer only a place "over there," but has its emissaries arriving over here.

The four essays in this book developed from my unease resulting from a nagging incongruity: throughout the nineteenth century the United States imported large quantities of luxury items from China, and millions of Americans became acquainted with an abundance of Chinese material culture through its display at American world's fairs. Later in the century, Americans began to appreciate Chinese objects as art, and placed them in newly made art museums as international signs of American aesthetic acumen and refinement. Yet over the century, incidents of both physical and legal hostility against Chinese immigrants increased, both physically and legally. Despite America's foundational description of itself as a nation with open immigration, and despite the fact that few Chinese people lived outside of California—that in 1870, New York's population of 63,254 reportedly included only 58 Chinese people—Congress voted to exclude Chinese people. In 1882 the US government passed the Federal Exclusion Act prohibiting Chinese from immigrating and forbidding those already in the country from naturalizing.[4] How did America imagine Chinese and Chinese-ness in such a way that, on the one hand, it justified barring an entire people, while, on the other hand, it encouraged coveting objects redolent of Chinese culture? What relationships does this imply about *high versus low*: between classes, between fine art and popular culture, between citizens and alien? How were Chinese objects considered, and how did Americans visualize Chinese people during this half century? In short, what did *Chinese* signify to Victorian Americans in the eastern states?

CHINESE IMPORTS AND MUSEUM CULTURE

Nineteenth-century America's relationships with Chinese people and objects were neither simple nor unilateral; quite the opposite: they were interwoven, complex, and reciprocal. (Re)connecting China's immigration and American visual culture exposes their dramatic frisson, startling in its implications for both museum and vernacular cultures. Probing this tension, one discovers that the meaning of *Chinese* became one of the sites at which competing ideas of ethics and power struggled for hegemony. The profusion of images of Chinese people found in nineteenth-century America reveals the range of portrayals of Chinese vying for predominance within American culture.

Art and politics are generally relegated to separate histories, but (re)united they form a powerful alliance. In these essays political history converges with the history of images and aesthetic objects, linked by their shared subject: nineteenth-century American constructions of "Chinese." Consequent to reuniting of art and political history, reciprocities are restored, countermanding assumed dualities: fine art reveals its mercantile bent, while issues of race and ethnicity are shown to penetrate the museums and influence curatorial decisions. On nineteenth-century trade card images, racial tolerance collides with xenophobia, and representations of cultural groups become profuse and contradictory. Confusions arise between defining self and representing others.

Although Chinese objects were displayed in American art museums almost since their foundation, the museums presumed a wide gap between Chinese objects and American art standards. John Ruskin (1819–1900), an English art and social critic, had equated artistic excellence with moral content and a realistic style. Ruskin's works resonated with an American audiences because by connecting good art with truth to nature he presented art in familiar categories and, even more, because his style, tone, and moral rhetoric paralleled that of evangelical preachers popular with mass audiences throughout America. No art books were more influential, and an American paradigm of fine art emerged based on Ruskin's writings that judged the quality of artworks by their facility in reproducing nature and their clarity as moral narratives. Yet by the 1880s the American art world had become more sophisticated, showing the relations in Ruskin's theory to be unfeasibly simplistic. Aestheticism, asserting art for art's sake rather than art as morality, began to supplant Ruskinianism.

A nation's art historical narrative reflects its official cultural memory. Every received history has its authorized version, and the standardized American art history never speaks of Chinese things, neither as objects in their own right nor as influences on American works. Our traditional art history does not demonstrate an understanding of Chinese art within American culture but rather our *lack of understanding;* even the suppression of an understanding. Studies about the America–China trade and the shiploads of fine Chinese import wares—inlaid tables, fine porcelains, painted wallpapers—have not been included in the history of American art. Similarly, very little has been said about interactions between Chinese and Japanese art within the United States or complications regarding their relative status. Instead, America's art historical narrative portrays its relation to Chinese art as mediated through European art history, duplicating its account that Chinese and Japanese objects entered Western art awareness in two separate waves: the Chinese wave in the 1700s that produced Chinoiserie and Rococo and the Japanese wave in the 1800s that produced Japonisme, Impressionism, and Post-Impression. From that premise, errors are compounded, accrediting a history of American art in which, without the Rococo movement, Chinese objects had no presence, and appreciation of Japanese objects were mediated through French taste. Consequently, American art history has marginalized the influence of Chinese objects. Rather than perpetuate the misperception, begun in the nineteenth century, that imported Chinese objects stand outside the American art scene, these chapters place them in the midst of a changing art and social culture, and show how their interaction from within the museum aided the transition to the newly forming paradigm of Aestheticism. Such unexpected shifts of meaning occur with radical cultural change. In her discussion of the contemporary visual issues, N. Katherine Hayles perceived that "material objects are penetrated by information patterns."[5] Some of these patterns emerge only with a shift in vision, a cultural transformation.

While certainly not the intention of museum curators, nevertheless the cumulative presence of Chinese objects and the changing aesthetic strategies gradually surmounted the uncomfortable lack of coincidence with the Ruskinian moral understanding of aesthetics. Asserting qualities not contained within any previous Western art theory, they helped transform Western art, both in objects and in theory. With its highly patterned surface decoration, appearing as if created "for art's sake," Chinese art within the United States contributed to this radical reworking of American perceptions and categories of art late in the nineteenth century.

The lack of reference to Chinese art's presence and influence on American art persisting in our art history is an indirect consequence of the legacy of the negative portrayal of Chinese people. Indeed, the decades surrounding the Federal Exclusion Law of 1882 saw the inauguration of both the Metropolitan Museum of Art and the Museum of Fine Arts, Boston. And while Exclusion Laws were tightened in the 1890s, these museums greatly increased their collections and display of Chinese art. Issues and transformations affecting the political arena spill over into and affect social relationships and structures in the art world. The idea that ethnicity falls away completely in one area of culture while its presence is heightened and dramatized in another flies in the face of the interconnectivity that we recognize between all social strata.

Race and ethnicity were not the only political issues impacting the nineteenth-century art world. Indeed, America's overarching goal for its art was itself political: the nation's pressing desire was determining what art could appropriately signify a democratic nation. Echoing the dilemma in France after the Revolution, America asked, "What *is* art for the people?" Philip Fisher's insight about museums describes a fundamental aspect of the American for that century: he wrote that such institutions display and stabilize "the idea of a national culture, an identifiable *Geist*, or spirit, that can be illustrated by objects and set in contrast to other national cultures."[6]

Political and business leaders constructed museums in part as a means to culturally display democracy. For them, the museum was a temple: like its religious counterpart, it would lead its populace toward better values. Yet, the museums inadvertently revealed more about American democracy than their trustees had desired. Even as the art museums signified democracy, and created a broad art public, the museums also displayed the existing power hierarchy.

Industrial capitalists gained control over business and politics, and the populace became a consumer market. As much as civic leaders wanted museums to provide a refuge from capitalism, a sanctuary from the materialism of their business world, nevertheless the paradigm based on consumption played out in the art world. Despite their longing for art to attest to and verify their spiritual sensibilities, and provide a balm for mercantile competition, as the nation's manufacture became increasingly mass-produced, art also changed in all aspects, from production to sales. Art's process, its subject, its theory, and its marketing all now were part of the mercantile system. For instance, new techniques of mass-production, such as the steam-powered rotary printing press and chromolithography, revolutionized publishing and printing, generating seemingly unlimited visual prints quickly with great ease. American painting began to include industry in their canon of subjects, seen in paintings by J. Alden Weir, such as *Willimantic Thread Factory* (1893), or Fritz Thaulow's *The Smokey City* (1895). And stylistic innovations, coincident to the new art theory of Aestheticism, no longer imagined a painted object as a single and completely integrated entity. Rather, each figure was painted to demonstrate that it was assembled from discrete parts, even the formal components appeared as discrete entities. In works by William Merritt Chase, as in those by Whistler, each pattern on clothing, every limb, all facial features existed independently, creating a painting of relatable pieces, rather than a seamless unity. Interestingly, this way of seeing was unintentionally yet intrinsically visually analogous to assembly-line production. And Whistler, well known for championing separation of art from all lesser concerns, advocating the idea of "art for art's sake" ("art should be independent of all claptrap"), was among the first to use strategies from the marketplace to generate higher-priced prints. The result was that the art arena was not a separation from commodity culture but, as Walter Benjamin suggested a half century later, another aspect of it.[7]

CHINESE IMMIGRATION

But this book is not only about the impact of objects on other objects; rather, it reconnects art theory with social change. Besides examining the impact of objects on objects—Chinese things on American art—the book also attests to the significance of Chinese *people* on American visual *culture*.

Since its inception, America took pride in its distinction of being a nation of immigrants. Most immigration had occurred primarily from

European nations, but with a shortage of laborers in the nineteenth century, entrepreneurs began to recruit heavily in China. Despite enticing descriptions of America as the "golden mountain," most Chinese people were not eager to emigrate. Only the dire circumstances of famine and poverty, the result in part from the havoc caused by the West's decades of war with the Qing empire, led to a sizable exodus.

Prior to the mid-nineteenth century, the balance of trade between China and England leaned heavily in China's favor. Determined to change this, England began to import opium into China. When the Qing government protested this illegal activity, Britain used its military to force the trade's continuation. The Opium Wars resulted in huge financial, military, cultural, and humanitarian losses for China. Poverty forced many people, mainly young men, to risk the truly wretched conditions of the ocean journey to America.

While at first Americans welcomed the much-needed Chinese workers with curiosity and affability, within a decade small groups of antagonistic and aggressive Americans demanded that "the Chinese must go." The fact that many of the most aggressive groups were in California exacerbated what might have remained a localized vendetta. Both American political parties coveted the electoral votes in the western states, particularly California's (six in the 1870s and nine by the 1880s), and they courted them by joining the polemic against the Chinese. But how to turn a group of once-desired, industrious group of people into a negative presence?

The question about whether or not to reject Chinese immigrants impelled the manufacture of Chinese "traits." Dynamics such as Chinese immigration are complex nebulae. Imagery is a way to get hold of something too enormous to be grasped, or as fugitive as an idea. Picturing provides particulars: generating something tangible and legible, rather than an abstraction, allows some measure of control over destabilizing concepts. For two decades, from the 1860s to 1882, Americans described, fabricated, analyzed, debated, and eventually voted, in essence stipulating what characteristics would be (permanently) relegated to Chinese people. Imaging Chinese people became a way to signify what they could mean, what they *would* mean, within the United States.

With no direct encounter between most Americans and Chinese immigrants, attitudes toward the Chinese were formed primarily through representations. Examining the ways diverse media imagined qualities of Chinese-ness reveals the multiplicity of narratives pinned to the meaning of "Chinese" in the nineteenth century.

AMERICAN MEDIA VISUALIZES CHINESE

Communication in a complex society occurs through various forms of media, which uses images to translate phenomenon into recognizable traits. Media communication disseminates information and provides a sense of control, especially over the unknown, mapping out attitudes and alternative viewpoints. Imagery is the heart of communication.

Such imaging is not merely descriptive, it's also prescriptive. This becomes evident throughout these chapters. Each essay addresses images of Chinese people characteristic to a major institution that that helped create the nineteenth-century body politic. The first two chapters examine Chinese objects and their display in museums and world's fairs, set against the background of America's political and economic engagements with China. The last two chapters examine America's imaging of Chinese people in pictorial and in written media, as the nation persuaded itself toward legalizing exclusion.

Because this volume does not focus on a single medium but examines several, no medium dominates as a sole authoritative voice, but is corrected, amplified, corroborated, and contradicted by each of the others. Chapters 1 and 2 look at art museums—specifically the Dunn Museum, the Peter's Museum, the Museum of Fine Arts, Boston, and the Metropolitan Museum of New York. Chapter 3 discusses newspapers—specifically the *New York Times*; while chapter 4 focuses on visual prints—the free advertising cards that were the major form of advertising at the time.

Each examination relies on distinct archival sources. And, as Marshall McLuhan famously pronounced, each medium becomes part of its message: therefore, as primary sources for each chapter varies, so do their narratives. Together the chapters form a kind of symphony, comprised of the confusion and harmonies, selections and omissions in lived experience. The book achieves something of the effect described by Edward Said, who spoke against the artifice of symmetry in historical narrative and advocated acknowledging the more authentic quality of inconclusiveness.[8]

Although the four chapters can function independently, read in tandem they build on each other, explicating and complicating the study of images and objects, and their political consequences. Each chapter reveals a component of the varied, hitherto largely unrecognized cultural consequences resulting from the interaction between Chinese images and objects and people, on the one hand, and American aesthetic culture, on the other hand. Each shows effects of political ideology on art judgments, and reciprocally, discloses the power of imagery to affect the lives of the people they purportedly represent.

THE CHAPTERS

The chapters adhere to a roughly chronological order. Chapter 1 provides the prologue to the narratives of political history and art history in the last third of the century. Beginning with the first American ship launched to trade with China, it broadly traces the general history of trade relationships between Americans and Chinese in the early nineteenth century. This provides a context for its discussion of subsequent changes in American understanding of art during the 1870s. These ephemeral changes are perceived through examining changes in its material culture, and specifically in the reception of Chinese things.

This chapter, as well as the next, dovetails a study of the reception of Chinese objects with a sociopolitical historical narrative. Due to the negative associations of Chinese immigration, the immense presence of Chinese material culture in America became problematic for American people. Americans' political reception of the Chinese framed how Chinese objects were understood and therefore categorized and ranked.

Critically located between the emerging respect for Chinese objects as art and its abrupt subordination to often similar Japanese products, the Philadelphia Centennial Exposition of 1876 presents a significant turning point in attitudes toward Chinese objects, providing an opportune contrast between American's vociferous new enthusiasm for the "Japanese aesthetic" with its increasingly circumspect regard of similar Chinese ware. In fact, the awareness of the Chinese origin of thousands of objects in the United States became obscured, even erased, as many Chinese objects became subsumed into the Japanese aesthetic: Americans celebrated the *Japanese* aesthetic, known colloquially as the "Japanese craze." Participating within this same political ideology, museums also showed very little interest in understanding their Chinese objects, satisfied by referring only to China's great age, rather than providing any information; occasionally they misclassified Chinese objects as Japanese. Erasure of Chinese influence, or even presence, were not restricted to the nineteenth century; its legacy of absence continues into current chronicles of American art history.

While the first chapter discussed the effects of politics on the American response to Chinese art, the second chapter investigates the art and politics of the transformation in the definition of "fine art" in America between 1870 and 1900 through the mediation of Chinese objects in the newly established art museums.

The second chapter picks up the relation to Chinese imports where the first chapter ended, focusing on the dissonance between Chinese objects and American art standards, within the Museum of Fine Arts, Boston, and the Metropolitan Museum of Art in New York, both founded in 1870.

The museum communicates ideology and hierarchies through the arrangement of objects in exhibition space, analogous to words on a page or images on paper. Philip Fisher expresses this clearly: "The museum is more than a location. It is a script that makes certain acts possible and others unthinkable. . . . When we think of an object as having a fixed set of traits we leave out the fact that only within social scripts are those traits, and not others, visible or real."[9] Because the museum is so solid a building, it seems fixed, allowing its messages to appear as timeless truths. Museums inevitably assume the voice of authority: informed, wise and powerful, often benevolent, disseminating knowledge to a less knowing mass audience. Art museums helped place Chinese art into a hierarchical worldview, which validated the Western racialized order of civilizations.

From their earliest years both museums exhibited Chinese objects along with American and European oil paintings, plaster casts of European sculpture, but then struggled to understand them as art. Chinese objects neither fit into the prevailing Ruskinian aesthetic paradigm nor were they appreciated for their own cultural integrity: Chinese art history was virtually unknown in the West. Art museum displays dehistoricized Chinese art as they reframed it within American cultural values.

The Chinese objects became reconfigured within a new paradigm of art that unfolded other meanings, aiding in transforming Americans' understanding of art from a paradigm of morality and narrative, to one in which art is seen as inhabiting a world composed of forms and patterns.

The marginalized status of both Chinese people and Aesthetes, their whiff of decadence to the dominant culture, their proposal of alternatives to the respected classic world and its art, and through all that, their suggestion of alternative social relationships, posed similar threats to the status quo and consequently received similar suspicion and scorn. Chapter 2 explores this alliance between Chinese objects and this incipient stage of artistic modernism known as the Aesthetic movement.

Unlike the first two chapters, and their examination of Chinese objects, the third chapter examines written imagery of Chinese people through a textual exegesis of articles written in the *New York Times* over the twelve-year period from 1870 through 1882.

Several different opinions of Chinese people appeared in the *New York Times* over the twelve-year period. The fundamental issue in the chapter is discerning the underlying voices speaking about the Chinese people. What were their underlying agendas? Most of the articles have no byline, as if they are not a person's point of view. Yet opinions are woven into the descriptive text: the voice of the *Times* can be discerned through its adjectives as well as its articles. The *Times* also printed transcripts and commentary on the congressional debates on exclusion in 1882. Voices are heard, both pro- and anti-exclusion. And in just a few exceptional articles, Chinese immigrants are quoted in the paper. At stake is the question posed by James Clifford: "Who has the authority to speak for a group's identity or authenticity?"[10]

I selected the *New York Times* for its reputation as a moderate paper with considerable political influence.[11] While its circulation was not quite as large as that of other penny newspapers, such as the *New York Herald* and the *New York Tribune*, the *New York Times* strove for balanced reporting.

It consciously avoided the extreme partisanship and sensationalism of the *Herald* and the *Tribune*: the former was considered a platform for the Republican and Whig parties, the later described its mission as "not to instruct but to startle."[12] In its attempt to reflect the middle ground of opinions and images circulating in the culture, the *Times* provides a more representative cross-section of the general public.

A close reading of the *New York Times* articles reveals the chronological attributions of negative qualities gradually fastened to Chinese people and disseminated to an East Coast readership. Distinguishing the ten most frequently used adjectives or characteristics, all of them adverse, I document the transformation in the depiction of Chinese people from a relatively affirmative description in the earlier years, to an increasingly antagonistic portrayal, noting the attendant decrease in the number of articles expressing opposition to legislating exclusion. The articles exhibit the complexities and contradictions in the eastern states' effort to create a definitive definition of *Chinese*.

The subject of the last chapter is cultural coding: the significance of the iconographic visual characterizations of Chinese people found on the widely disseminated advertising trade cards. These small, palm-sized cards were the main form of advertising between the 1870s and 1880s, and continued into the early twentieth century. Tens, if not hundreds of thousands of images were printed and, although only a small percentage of the total, a considerable number depict Chinese people or themes. The Chinese image is generally not at all related to the product advertised.

The trade card images complicate our understanding of the significance of the image of the Chinese to American culture. Unlike the more programmatic use of "Chinese" in the *New York Times*, where one meaning gradually dominated, the trade card images did not adhere to the chronological rhythm of newspaper articles, produced and discarded daily. Instead, the visual images remained in circulation over a longer period and the medium held multiple meanings simultaneously. Their various portrayals—some idealized, some demonic, some painterly—exist together all at once, rather than sequentially. And most images contained more ambiguous, and therefore a wider, range of meanings than those found in the increasingly polemical newspaper descriptions.

Trade cards also served as an object lesson, helping educate the American populace in the increasingly controlling idiom of symbolic capital and reflecting the fluid exchange now prevalent in American culture. They provided material objects for rehearsing both the physical and the mental manipulations necessary for the emerging fluid market economy. Following Jean Baudrillard's "floatation" of signs and Jackson Lear's "disembodied signifiers," I use the term *floating signifiers* to indicate the multiple readings contained within one image.[13] Representations of Chinese people functioned as floating signifiers within nineteenth-century American culture; they became the repository for symbolic engagement with contradictions and surprises in the new and still unstable democracy.

Three consequences immediately can be seen from this study: the chapters convey a sense of the complex media networks linking material culture and politics; confirming that political actions interact with and affect the world of high art. Ultimately, they demonstrate the continuing implications of the effects of Chinese subjects on American art history and theory.

The book articulates the consequences of attempts at institutionalizing otherness. Each chapter establishes the permeability of another boundary: geographical, social, and personal. At the moment the unknown is first noticed, in some sense it merges with the self. We see each other and we are changed through that process of envisioning.

Finally, I show how actions performed under one set of political and theoretical conditions can lead to unintended consequences that in turn, *mutatis mutandis*, modify and transform the originating conditions.

Although the topic of all four chapters is the image of Chinese in America, its correlative emerges throughout this study, insistently demanding that we notice that America cannot define Chinese without also defining itself. Each way it distinguished itself from China helped construct its meaning.

ONE

THE POLITICS OF CHINOISERIE

The Disappearance of Chinese Objects

"Is there any point to which you would wish to draw my attention?"
"To the curious incident of the dog in the night-time."
"The dog did nothing in the night-time."
"That was the curious incident," remarked Sherlock Holmes.

—Arthur Conan Doyle, "Silver Blaze"

This chapter explores an absence, or more accurately, an erasure. It is an attempt to understand why Chinese art disappeared from an American art discourse in the 1870s. This remains a critical question still, because despite the reemergence of Chinese objects in the art discourse of the 1890s, that almost twenty-year silence has shaped subsequent discussion concerning American art of that time. The significance of Americans' reluctance to acknowledge the Chinese origin of import ware during this period cannot be seen fully by examining the isolated Chinese object. Rather, such an investigation requires a more oblique look, one capable of incorporating the surrounding political as well as the aesthetic context. Reconstructing the surrounding positive space gives shape to the missing discourse: seeing Chinese material culture through the mediating histories of the earlier decades of commerce between China and the United States, through American attitudes toward Chinese people, and, finally, through the contrasting American reception of Japanese people and things.

The juxtaposition of social/political history with the study of material culture assumes a relationship between politics and art. Connections between the two have been elaborated throughout the modern period at least as early as 1798, when William Blake wrote: "The Foundation of Empire is Art and Science. Remove them or Degrade them and the Empire is No more. Empire follows Art and not vice versa as Englishmen suppose."[1] Blake's statement asserts a relationship that is familiar to us from the Modernist relation of art to politics; art as an "avant-garde," anticipating and leading social and political change by breaking from societal authority as well as from artistic tradition.[2] According to art historian Richard Shiff, modernist artists "assume the role of revolutionaries either by introducing change, returning to values long lost . . . or representing truths in personalized, perhaps deviant, expressive form."[3] In the mid- and late nineteenth century, the use of Japanese motifs often signaled Western artists' membership in progressive, innovative art movements. For instance, in 1880 New York art critic Clarence Cook spoke derisively of previous American arts who "blindly" accepted English standards and conventions, compared to the current "reclaiming of artistic freedom." For Cook, this revived "freedom" derived in large part from the discovery of the "far more artistic art of the Japanese with freedom and naturalness equally its characteristics."[4] Was there a relationship between innovative nineteenth-century art and political advancement? Did this proto-avant-garde art equally signal and promote social change?

And why, then, was there an emphasis on Japanese objects only, and not also on the Chinese things that were also present in the country at the same time? What associations connected Japanese art with freedom that did not apply similarly to the alternatives offered by Chinese art, which would be equally available for scrutiny? After all, Chinese objects had a long history in the United States. They were admired and collected in the colonies in the seventeenth century and exhibited in Salem in 1799; before 1850 two museums were created exclusively for Chinese objects.[5] The types of objects imported ranged from decorative doodads to exquisitely crafted furniture and vases. While consumable items formed the bulk of Chinese exports to America—silks and tea were the main exports—ivories, fans, clothing, and porcelains were also exported in great quantities. A smaller component of the trade were specialty items such as paintings and furniture and wallpaper, generally of excellent craftsmanship.[6] But in the 1870s, when Americans first began to discuss Asian objects as fine art, they focused almost exclusively on Japanese objects.

As Arjun Appadurai points out, "Commodities represent very complex social forms and distributions of knowledge."[7] Objects are seen in this book to be more than singular things; they are understood as social signs. Each object can be seen as a nexus of encounters, a focal point for societal values. The desirability and significance of Chinese and Japanese objects derived from their social meaning and the social relationships they promised. This chapter looks at these meanings and how they attached to the objects; it examines what associations Americans were buying when they purchased Chinese or Japanese art.

The chapter extends the investigation of objects into a study of the social networks constellating around them. In doing so, it reframes the relationship between art and politics, encountering more complexity than the general assumption of a politically precocious artistic avant-garde. This investigation of the disappearance of Chinese art from America's art historical canon mandates the need for another look at *how* the art world functions as an instigator, or even a barometer, of social change.[8] If indeed art is such an indicator, this study suggests that the social change augured by the art might not always be one we hope to find.

The earlier decades in the century are critical in informing both the art and politics of the later decades. Consequently, the investigation of the decades from 1800 to 1870 serve as introduction to the later period and as an investigation in its own right. The second section concentrates on a smaller time period, from 1870 to the Centennial Exposition in 1876. While American relationships to Chinese art and people differ significantly throughout the century, nevertheless both periods were characterized by resistance to accepting Chinese objects or imagery as art.

SECTION I. THE EARLY NINETEENTH CENTURY

1. The Presence of Chinese Objects in the United States

By the 1870s and increasing through the last two decades of the century, collecting and imitating Japanese art was an enthusiasm shared by all classes, and promoted heavily by the print media.

Chinese objects excited no comparable response, although they were equally available and affordable.[9] Because most American art historians do not perceive the presence, even omnipresence, of Chinese objects, they perpetuate a history in which Japanese art presents a sudden revelation of aesthetic possibilities. Historians have meticulously documented and interpreted America's overwhelming enthusiasm for Japanese objects in the early 1870s that continued through the end of the nineteenth century.[10] This concentration on Japanese art exclusively interprets the excitement over Japanese objects as an immediate—and unmediated—appreciation of Japanese aesthetics, without prior foundation.

For instance, William Hosley's perceptive analysis of the Japanese display at the Philadelphia Centennial Exhibition in 1876 interprets the Japanese government's approach to its bazaar as both a commercial and a political enterprise. Hosley reports that the Japanese government viewed the Fair as an international trade competition, and he identifies the strategies used to enhance Japanese sales.[11] A key factor in marketing and sales was the Japanese government's stipulation that a consortium of its own merchants, rather than foreigners, select the merchandise; further, its expenditure of $600,000 on its exhibition, was more than twice the investment of any other foreign country, and more than the expenditures of Great Britain, France, Italy, and Germany combined.[12] Japan's investment strategies proved profitable; all its exhibited items sold. Given Hosley's subtle analysis of the business acumen involved in merchandising the Japanese objects, it is then surprising that, like other historians, he too, attributes the impact of the Japanese style completely to its freshness to Western eyes. In Hosley's words:

> With the West anxious to enlarge its vocabulary of naturalistic ornament, Japanese art was a revelation that provided a new visual language of birds, animals, sea creatures, and flowers. Monkeys and dragons, cranes and chickens, elephants and eagles, chrysanthemums and cherry blossoms; these are just a few of the motifs that Americans discovered at the Japanese display.[13]

Yet some of these motifs had already appeared in familiar Chinese objects, which also were displayed at the fair.[14] But although few Americans could differentiate between Chinese and Japanese art, comparatively little mention was made of "Chinese" objects journal articles. Not until the last decade of the century did Chinese objects receive the high artistic regard earlier ascribed to Japanese objects, and secure a place of pride within newly created American art museums. And then, unlike Japonisme, they rarely entered into popular awareness of art, but were discussed mainly by Chinese experts and connoisseurs.

The absence of a vernacular appreciation of Chinese objects paralleling Japonisme does not denote their lack of consequence in nineteenth-century American culture. On the contrary, the question why the mania embraced only Japanese things, rather than including Chinese things as well, indicates that these objects resonated with political and cultural concerns.

Most Americans today do not realize how eagerly the United States anticipated the American–China trade, as a source for individual wealth and, perhaps just as much the expectation of material profits, as an international gesture to verify America's independence and nationhood. While a British colony and subject to the monopoly rights of the East India Company, American speculators rankled at England's prohibition of their trade with China, believing that it might be a pathway toward enormous wealth. Within a year of signing the Treaty of Paris, acknowledging the United States as an independent nation, Americans quickly inaugurated direct China trading, launching their first trade ship, the *Empress of China*, with raw goods from America to trade for manufactured goods in Canton.[15]

As early as 1765, Americans brought soybeans from China for cultivation with the anticipation of further trade, and ginseng grown in the United States became the first market export traded to China.[16] Furs and Spanish silver dollars supplemented American exports. Contemporary shipping records report that Americans received in exchange:

> tea along with textiles, porcelain, furniture, and fireworks. . . . mandarin heads, umbrellas, ciphered fans, flower seeds, bamboo washstands, sweetmeats, tea waiters, boxes of paints, ivorywork caskets, sugar, cassia, clay images, paper hangings, furniture, satin, lacquerware, bamboo blinds, floor mats, fans, and whangee canes.[17]

Subsequently, the U.S. government created special tariffs and duties designed to favor China traders.[18]

The ready availability of Chinese goods by midcentury for consumption by moderate income households is borne out by advertisements found in broadsides and in newspapers announcing the presence of Chinese merchants and merchandise. (See fig. 1.1) One such advertisement appeared in the *New York Times*, Friday, December 8, 1854, under the title CHINA TEA STORE:

> I, TSUNG ZEQUAY, issue my proclamation to the inhabitants of the city of Brooklyn, situated on the beautiful bay of New York, on whose waters sail the great ships bringing the produce of far off lands, that I, TSUNG ZE-QUAY having left my kindred and my nation, and having been led to your goodly land, proclaim my design of offering for sale the products of the Celestial Empire. I have with me much Tea, Coffee, Cocoa, Chocolate, &c. of the choicest gatherings which I will give you for your smallest pieces of gold and silver; and may health, joy and length of day attend you. All you who want the finest, choicest flavored Teas, come to me, and you shall have the purest that China can produce. Also, a beautiful assortment of Lacquer-ware work tables, Lacquer-ware centre tables, Lacquer-ware work boxes, Lacquer-ware Tea-Caddies, Lacquer-ware checkerboards, Lacquer-ware writing desks, flower Vases of every size & elegance, Chinese Pipes for tobacco, Chinese Pipes for Opium, Flowered Fans, Sandal wood Fans, Sandal wood Boxes, Chinese Lanterns, Ornamental Stone figures, Fairies & Toys, Stuffed Birds, Ivory Fans, Pomatum Jars, Buddhist Rosaries, Chinese Shawls,

Teapots, Teacups, Chinese chop-sticks, Wrought silver bracelets, Feather Fans ALL FROM CHINA!—My place of traffic is at the corner of Schermerhorn and Court Sts., Brooklyn.[19]

And, twenty-two years before that, in New York, an auction was held consisting entirely of hundreds of fans from Canton, listed as:

500 Palm Leaf Fans, 500 painted Silk fans, 500 embroidered do do, 500 Rice fans [?pith paper], 600 cut and painted bone fans {?ivory}. 400 imitation sandal wood Fans, 400 do do do painted, 100 real camphor wood do, 500 palm leaf Fans, ivory mounted . . .[20]

Estimating the vast numbers of goods imported during those years, in his dissertation Thomas Schlotterback referred to it as a "flood" and

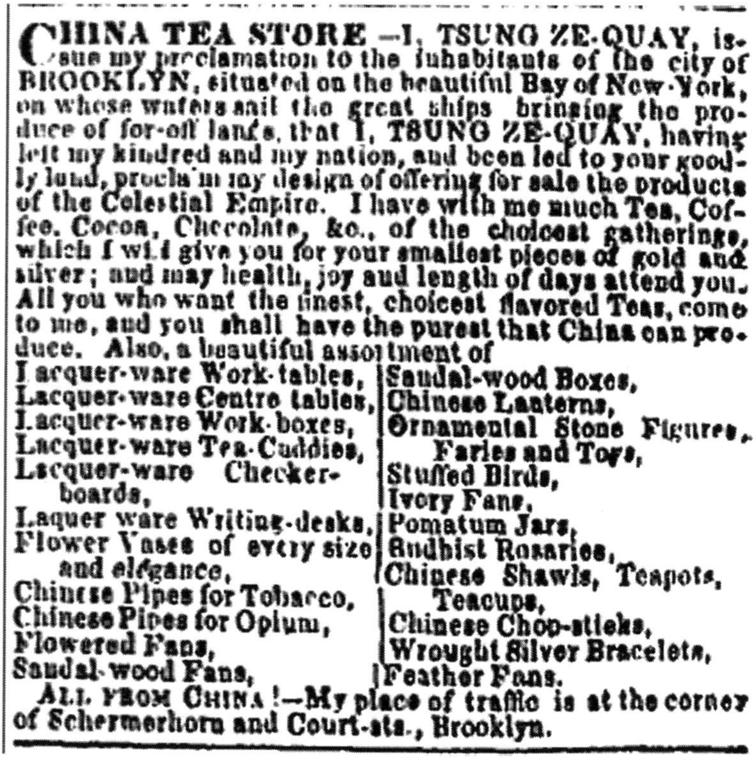

CHINA TEA STORE —I, TSUNG ZE-QUAY, is-sue my proclamation to the inhabitants of the city of BROOKLYN, situated on the beautiful Bay of New-York, on whose waters sail the great ships bringing the produce of far-off lands, that I, TSUNG ZE-QUAY, having left my kindred and my nation, and been led to your goodly land, proclaim my design of offering for sale the products of the Celestial Empire. I have with me much Tea, Coffee, Cocoa, Chocolate, &c., of the choicest gatherings, which I will give you for your smallest pieces of gold and silver; and may health, joy and length of days attend you. All you who want the finest, choicest flavored Teas, come to me, and you shall have the purest that China can produce. Also, a beautiful assortment of

Lacquer-ware Work-tables, Lacquer-ware Centre tables, Lacquer-ware Work-boxes, Lacquer-ware Tea-Caddies, Lacquer-ware Checker-boards, Laquer ware Writing-desks, Flower Vases of every size and elegance, Chinese Pipes for Tobacco, Chinese Pipes for Opium, Flowered Fans, Sandal-wood Fans, Sandal-wood Boxes, Chinese Lanterns, Ornamental Stone Figures, Fairies and Toys, Stuffed Birds, Ivory Fans, Pomatum Jars, Budhist Rosaries, Chinese Shawls, Teapots, Teacups, Chinese Chop-sticks, Wrought Silver Bracelets, Feather Fans.

ALL FROM CHINA!—My place of traffic is at the corner of Schermerhorn and Court-sts., Brooklyn.

Fig. 1.1. *New York Times*, December 8, 1854, CHINA TEA STORE.

speaking just of chinaware, stated that "it is possible to conjecture that during the first half of the nineteenth century several hundred, perhaps even thousands, of tons of chinaware were brought into America."[21] Because of their participation in the China trade, by 1800 citizens of Salam had the highest per capita income in the country.[22]

2. Opium, Politics, and American Perceptions of the Chinese

Chinese people had an initially affirmative relationship with the United States.[23] The predominant American view of China in the eighteenth century had been laudatory. With its agricultural economy, and its question of how to feed a large nation, America admired, indeed was envious, of China's agronomic management, capable of sustaining a population of awesome proportions. A representative positive description is found in the *New Haven Gazette* on June 21, 1787, synopsizing or, more accurately, plagiarizing a French author:

> Turn your eyes, to the eastern extremity of the Asiatic continent inhabited by the Chinese, and there you will conceive a ravishing idea of the happiness the world might enjoy, were the laws of this empire the model of other countries. This great nation unites under the shade of agriculture, founded on liberty and reason, all the advantages possessed by whatever nation, civilized or savage. The blessing pronounced on man, at the moment of his creation, seems not to have had its full effect, but in favour of this people, who have multiplied as the sands on the shore. Princes, who rule over nations! arbiters of their fate! view well this perspective: it is worthy your attention. Would you wish abundance to flourish in your dominions, would you favor population, and make your people happy; behold those innumerable multitudes which cover the territories of China, who leave not a shred of ground uncultivated; it is liberty, it is their undisturbed right of property that has established a cultivation so flourishing, under the auspices of which this people have increased as the grains which cover their fields.[24]

And the scant information Americans had about China served them better than a tabula rasa, providing a (mythic) ideal of a proto-democracy in China. An article in *North American Review* is typical in its admiration, commending the Chinese form of government especially for its system of examinations which it compared to American democracy.[25] Such favorable comparisons of American and Chinese governments had antecedents in America's early nationhood and were perceived by other countries as well.

In the late 1700s, the merchant Andreas Everardus van Braam Houckgeest (1739–1801) published a book in Dutch; his dedication to George Washington equated the Chinese government "that makes its Chief the Father of the National Family" with the American government "in which everything bespeaks the love of the First Magistrate for the People."[26] In 1852, California's Governor John McDougal praised Chinese immigrants; addressing the California legislature, he called the Chinese: "one of the most worthy classes of our newly adopted citizens."[27]

Yet by 1882 the U.S. federal government enacted the Chinese Exclusion Law, effectively banning Chinese from immigrating to the United States and refusing naturalization to those who had already immigrated here. What accounted for this extreme shift?

Throughout the eighteenth century Americans had admired the Chinese and had been eager to engage in trade, but because of trade disagreements in the last decade of that century, two cultures saw a change in this cordiality. In the late eighteenth century a negative portrayal of Chinese people was first constructed; disapproving comments began to appear as early as 1786: Americans directly involved in the China Trade were among the first to malign the Chinese, followed shortly by diplomats.[28] The first American appointed as consul general to China, Boston merchant Samuel Shaw, previously the supercargo on the *Empress of China* (an executive position responsible for the sale and purchase of cargo on board a ship), was among the earliest Americans to denigrate the Chinese, and he readily acknowledged his opinion as a radical departure from previous views: "Notwithstanding the encomiums which are generally bestowed on the excellence of the Chinese government, it may, perhaps, be questioned, whether there is a more oppressive one to be found in any civilized nation upon earth."[29] By the mid-nineteenth century the two nations had rapidly reached a relationship best characterized as mutual disdain.[30] According to Jean McClure Mudge, "Both nations met mainly for trade, with the aggressiveness of the Americans only increasing the restraint of the Chinese. Commerce was carried on in an atmosphere of suspicion and contempt."[31]

Prefiguring remarks that would become widespread in the last third of the century, in 1827, M. Malte-Brun's *Universal Geography, or a Description of All the Parts of the World on a New Plan, According to the Great Natural Division of the Globe* . . . , published in Philadelphia, described the Chinese as "a set of subjugated and disciplined barbarians. Seldom do they lay aside the humble insinuating air of a slave anxious to please." His critique included castigating the Chinese language as: "composed of monosyllables, and scarcely contains 350 terms which a European can distinguish from one another . . . perpetuates that eternal infantine imbecility of intellect by which the Chinese are degraded, and almost rendered inferior to nations immersed in the savage state."[32]

But behind the negativity was the friction over the trade of opium that eventually exploding as the Opium War (1839–1842). Although Miller does not attribute the change of attitude entirely to this commerce, nevertheless his chronology suggests that American opinion changed initially and was voiced loudest by Americans who probably trafficked in opium.[33] Orientalist Edward D. Graham traces the beginning of America's involvement in selling opium to a small shipment in 1805, which proved so lucrative that opium sales rapidly increased, in the next few decades becoming one of the most important of American trades. Graham writes that "so far as the American merchant community was concerned opium had become a part of the commercial landscape by the 1820's."[34] A large number of American merchants covertly added to their fortunes by flaunting their disdain for Chinese legislation, joining the British in forcing opium into China. In *Philadelphia and the China Trade*, Jonathan Goldstein cites profits derived from opium: "In the single season of 1837–38, foreign opium sales in China reached a record high of 28,307 chests worth $19.8 million." In 1848, Western traders imported about 50,000 chests of opium, increasing to 85,000 by 1860, all in violation of Chinese law.

Yet the illegality of the trade in China and the disapproval that pushing drugs occasioned in America led the American merchants to obscure the realities of their activities for the American public. At the same time that American merchants were trading opium and describing it as a "legitimate business," without censure from the American government, the majority of American people believed that U.S. merchants remained uninvolved and were not complicit in the illegal traffic.[36] In fact, many Americans imagined a special relationship between the United States and China, in part based on the erroneous assumption that China preferred Americans to all other Westerners since they had taken a moral stand against the Opium trade![37]

In the wake of the Opium War, by 1839 as public awareness of their involvement grew, American opium traders tried to vindicate themselves, fabricating various fictional histories. To disguise American complicity, traders publicly insinuated their lack of participation in dealing opium (the 1840 *Democratic Review* is one of the journals whose coverage of the opium problem never mentioned America's involvement). Simultaneously, they shifted the blame for the opium problem onto the Chinese, contending that China was at fault for tolerating a trade which Britain, less guilty, merely supplied.[38] American statesmen also reinvented events to shift culpability. Edmund Roberts was a merchant/trader who became part of the American embassy of 1832 and was considered quite successful by Americans, negotiating lower duties in Bangkok and influencing Bangkok policies almost to the point of legalizing opium. His journal of his Asian tour scathingly criticized China's politics, religion, and customs:

> The Chinese of the present day are grossly superstitious. . . . In their habits, they are most depraved and vicious: gambling is universal and is carried to a most ruinous and criminal extent; they use pernicious drugs as well as the most intoxicating liquors . . . ; they are also gross gluttons; everything that runs, walks, creeps or flies or swims . . . and articles most disgusting to other people, are by them greedily devoured. The government has a code of laws, written in blood; the most horrid tortures are used to force confessions and the judges are noted for being grossly corrupt; the variety and ingenuity displayed in prolonging the tortures of miserable criminals . . . can only be conceived by a people refined in cruelty, blood-thirsty and inhuman."[39]

Even dignitaries such as former President John Quincy Adams sanctioned the merchants' opinions and blamed the war on China. In 1842, *Niles's* newspaper printed Adams's remarks, declaring "The cause of the war is the Ko-tou!—the arrogant and insupportable pretensions of China, that she will hold commercial intercourse with the rest of mankind, not upon terms of equal reciprocity, but upon the insulting and degrading forms of relation between lord and vassal."[40]

As the United States steadily increased its economic, mercantile, and military capacities, realizing its idea of progress, it had correspondingly begun to judge the worth of other countries exclusively by American goals and standards. Kevin Walsh describes that Americans saw themselves as participants in a modern world of "rational advancement through increments of perpetual improvement."[41] America's expansionist policy of Manifest Destiny clashed with the Chinese policy of isolation, and journal articles reflected and helped manufacture a new, negative portrayal of the Chinese. China's worth and integrity diminished in American eyes as chauvinism increased.

Even as long as two decades after the end of the Opium War, some Americans still argued for the trade's renewal. An article by Emanuel Weiss titled "Hints as to the Development of our California-China Trade," appeared in *Hunt's* magazine in 1862. It did not hint at but explicitly advocated opium dealing:

> One-third of the Chinese export goes to the United States. Why should the citizens of this country not plant this much in opium on the Pacific shores, as long as the article sells, and sells well—

better than our cotton ever did in its best days? This cultivation is monopolized not only by the British, but also by the Dutch and Spanish colonial authorities in India. Much has been said by our Anglo-phobic and Puritan press of the immorality of this trade, yet it has been studiously ignored that our Boston houses in the Chinese ports indulge as largely in this contraband trade as their rivals, the English and Parsee.[42]

The end of the Opium Wars did not improve the American circulation of negative imagery of Chinese people. In fact, new dimensions were added to the negative portrayal by religious Americans' frustration at Chinese people's reluctance to undergo Christian conversion.

Prior to 1840 only twenty Protestants missionaries were allowed to proselytize in China, but agreements made at the end of the Opium War allowed Americans to immediately double that number, with an increase every year thereafter. American trade ships gave missionaries free passage. This aggressively ambitious group became instrumental in disseminating a negative view of Chinese people. Miller explains how the missionaries enlarged tales of Chinese villainy for their own didactic purposes: in their attempts to persuade Americans to be against China some even construed the entire culture as a creation of Satan. Typical of such diatribes is the opinion voiced by Rev. Maclay, admonishing how immoral behavior was everywhere in China:

> Its corrupting and debasing influences pervade all classes of society. . . . Forms of this vice which in other lands skulk in dark places, or appear only in the midnight orgies of the bacchanalian revelers, in China blanch not at the light of noon-day. . . . this lust funds ready access to the precincts of the family, the forum, and the temple.[43]

Such lurid descriptions of Chinese culture found ready ears in the flush of new religious enthusiasm brought on by a Christian revival movement in America.[44]

The success of these strategies can easily be seen: the once-marginal negative opinion began supplanting the older one: Americans retaining a favorable view of China were now considered traditionalists, while the most inflammatory rhetoric gained greater credibility and appeared more frequently in print. Newspapers such as the *Democratic Review* and the *National Intelligencer* disseminated vicious accounts of Chinese people, stating: "bigoted, intolerant, incommunicative, and selfish, the Chinese have kept apart from the people of the world, have resisted the power of civilization spreading itself so effectively through all other nations."[45]

3. The Chinese in the United States

Immigration from China to the United States began in earnest with the discovery of gold in California in 1848, the main immigration occurring between 1850 and 1880, when the Chinese population in the United States increased from 7,520 to 105,465.[46] The influx of thousands of Chinese people into the United States provided fuel for those with an anti-Chinese attitude. But the Chinese population was small and localized, and this attitude remained confined to fringe groups.

Due to the labor shortage in the early nineteenth century, the western states needed and appreciated the assistance of skilled Chinese craftspeople: for its first stone buildings, San Francisco imported both the stones and the stonemasons from Guandong.[47] Chinese labor was part of the grand scheme conceived by several American industrialists, most notably Aaron H. Palmer, to assist construction of a transcontinental railroad across the United States. Palmer envisioned Chinese people as ideally suited for transforming the wild regions of California into cropland, writing, in 1848 that: "No people in all the East are so well adapted for clearing wild lands and raising every species of agricultural product . . . as the Chinese."[48]

American merchants advertised in China, enticingly portraying America as a land of gold and plentiful employment, a land that desired Chinese workers. Yet the three-month sea voyage between China and America was arduous, often deadly. Chinese travelers were confined to the hold below decks, crammed in as cargo, dependent on their own supplies for food and sometimes even for water. The death toll for the Chinese on American ships commonly was 350 to 450 persons per voyage, and reaching as high as 600 persons.[49]

Peter Parker, the US consul in Canton, reported that between January 1, 1851, and January 1, 1852, 14,000 Chinese arrived in California. The following year the number reached 20,025, and throughout the next decade approximated an average of 4,000 immigrants per year.[50] While the majority of the Chinese worked on the railroads or in the mines, a number of others brought or acquired skills in a wide variety of businesses and professions, becoming merchants, tradesmen, doctors, carpenters, cigar makers, restaurateurs, and farmers.

Only dire circumstances, those directly resulting from the Opium Wars, could prompt so many thousands to leave their homeland for an uncertain future. The wars had devastated China, producing chaos and famine: food shortages and disease resulted in 20 million to 60 million deaths. By 1860 China had become so debilitated that, on its resistance to the British demand for further concessions, it could not prevent Anglo-French troops from burning the Forbidden City's palaces and gardens, destroying the structures they had so recently marveled at and replicated as chinoiserie.

By 1864, 10,000 Chinese men, nicknamed "Crocker's Pets" by Americans, were recruited by the railroad mogul Chester Crocker. Allegedly, when challenged about the suitability of Chinese men for this purpose, Crocker had responded, "the Chinese built the great wall, didn't they?"[51] Many of the Chinese workers came as sojourners, not immigrants, planning to return to China after achieving their financial goals.[52]

As the number of Chinese laborers increased they became viewed as rivals to other laborers, and over time increasingly became a target for aggressive, even violent behavior. Nonetheless, many others maintained their high regard for the Chinese immigrants: in 1852 the governor of California John McDougal responded to the Chinese immigrants' skill and general civility by recommending land grants to encourage further Chinese immigration and settlement in California.[53] For several decades in the mid-century goodwill and antipathy existed simultaneously. An example of this schizophrenia is easily found: in the same year that Governor McDougal commended the Chinese, a California newspaper reported a violent incident against a Chinese man: "An American yesterday attacked a Chinaman, beating him shamefully. The Chinamen in the neighborhood were afraid to interfere and the Americans, of whom there was a large crowd, stood by and saw the poor Chinaman abused."[54] As such hostility became more common, leaders of California's Chinese community began to warn people in China about the increasing hostility in that state, cautioning them not to make the journey.[55]

The violence that began as physical and illegal acts quickly spilled over into areas in which it could be legitimated. Throughout the 1850s and in the decades that followed, the California government increasingly used the legal system in a similarly brutal manner. In *Tea That Burns* Edward Bruce Hall enumerates the legislated atrocities:

Flouting the 1868 Burlingame Treaty, which promised the Chinese civil rights equal to any other foreign residents, local laws were passed to prevent Chinese from owning real estate, attending white schools or even fishing whether commercially or for pleasure. There was even a California law enacted threatening jail for people who slept in a space of less than 800 cubic feet—an obvious attack on the notoriously crowded Chinese neighborhoods. This measure backfired, however, when it was realized not only that tens of thousands of Chinese would have to be incarcerated, but also that the space allotted to them in jail was considerably less than that prescribed by law. Chinese immigrants were baselessly accused of spreading leprosy and bubonic plague. . . . And since Asians did not technically fall into the categories of "white persons, Africans, or those of African descent" specified by the 14th Amendment to the Constitution, Chinese people were denied naturalization. Since they couldn't become citizens, they couldn't vote. Since they couldn't vote, politicians ignored them.[56]

From 1852 to 1870, the list of legalized infringements of Chinese rights in California escalated in quantity and in intensity, including:

1850 (1853, 1853, 1855) The foreign Miners Tax was initially enacted to force forcing Chinese out of the mines.

1852 The Columbia District Mining Regulations prohibited Asians from mining.

1852 The Bond Act required all arriving Chinese to post a $500 bond.

1854 A California Supreme Court Decision decreed Chinese ineligible to testify in court against whites.

1860 The Fishing Tax restricted Chinese access to fishing.

1870 The Act to Prevent Kidnapping and Importing of Mongolian, Chinese and Japanese Females for Criminal Purposes prevented the entry of Chinese women into the United States without a special certificate.

1870 The Act to Prevent Importing of Chinese Criminals prohibited entry of Chinese males without proof of good character.[57]

Newspapers added their own form of hostility. Finding that disseminating "humorously" derogative stories of Chinese people bolstered their sales, they published sensationalized stories alleging to reveal Chinese life in America. A typical example: in 1852, *Frank Leslie's Illustrated Newspaper*, published in New York, printed an article by P. B. Doesticks titled "Among the China-men." Purporting to be a factual account of his visit to China Lodging House, Number 61 Cherry Street, in New York, Doesticks's bias was never far from the surface, beginning with his opening sentences: "Where do the Celestials roost? Do they hang themselves up by their unctuous pigtails; do they roll themselves into balls to sleep; as they do in the streets to beg; or do they make unto themselves beds, like respectable human animals, wherein they slumber in like fashion with other men?" He ended the article with an inevitable account of the opium smoke.[58]

Western aggression intensified against the Chinese in China as well. After the renewal of the 1858 Treaty of Peking (the Sino-American Treaty of Tientsin, aka the Burlingame Treaty), Raphael Pumpelly (1837–1923), a geologist who traveled extensively throughout Asia, described how he witnessed Western ships deliberately mowing down Chinese junks, and the parallel practice of some Western pedestrians in China striking Chinese in their path with walking sticks.[59]

4. Americans Assess China's Artistic Ability

The hostilities between China and the West threatened the China trade, while at the same time the previous century's delight with Chinese art and philosophy gave way to derision. This connection, however, went un-noticed. Rather than attribute the changes in esteem of Chinese culture to their own frustration in commerce, Westerners transferred accountability, claiming that their changed regard stemmed from new information about the Chinese personality. A member of an unsuccessful British trade embassy to China belittled the Chinese, alleging: "[what] was not *then* so generally known as *now* . . . the proneness to falsehood, the duplicity and knavery of the Chinese."[60]

Not surprisingly, the same people instrumental in disparaging the Chinese people also were the first to disparage the art. In his survey of the writings of American traders on Chinese art the early 1800s, A. Owen Aldridge concludes that, in concert with their negative opinions on the Chinese people, many Americans actively involved in the Chinese trade equally disdained Chinese art.[61]

Robert Waln Jr., supercargo on the Caledonia in 1819–1820, ridiculed Chinese artists with what was to become the archetypal complaint. "The Chinese are excellent copyists," he wrote, "but possess little or no inventive faculties."[62] In an essay of 1823 titled "Painters of Canton," Waln itemized the faults of Chinese art:

> Chinese painters offend against every rule of perspective, which, with the effects produced by the proper disposition of light and shade, they affect to consider unnatural. Always taking a horizontal view of their subject, they place themselves alternately in front of the objects, whatever may be their position or extent; thus, in their paintings, houses are placed one on top of another, and the method which they have imagined to express objects at a distance, is to represent clouds intersecting tress, buildings and men. They absurdly contend that it is proper to represent the objects in the back, of the same size as those in the fore ground, because they

are so in nature. . . . Having no idea of demi-tints, or softening shades, or indeed of any shades at all, and no variety of colouring being commonly used, a Chinese landscape appears at first to be a mass of black marks, representing nothing; and a closer examination only discovers the bare outline of an unsuccessful and rude attempt to imitate nature."[63]

But on what objects did these Americans base their assessment of Chinese artistry? While in earlier centuries European countries had imported chinaware made to European form, the painted designs remained traditional to Chinese decoration. However in the first half of the 1800s, emulating the European fashion, Americans bought their dinnerware from China but instructed Chinese artisans to copy Western motifs and designs.[64] Consul General Shaw was typical in his commission of a large set of commemorative porcelain. Conforming to the prevailing American aesthetic preference for allegory, he designed a scene incorporating the insignia of Cincinnati as the central motif.[65] This motif was quite popular—apparently George Washington purchased 302 pieces of the set[66] (fig. 1.2). Shaw's design exemplifies the American fashion of combining classical iconography with specifically American motifs. His order was for an "American Cincinnatus, under the conduct of Minerva, regarding Fame, who, having received from them the emblem of the order, was proclaiming it to the world." To familiarize the Chinese artist with this iconography, Shaw provided him with two engravings of the Roman goddess Minerva, a sketch of the figure of the Count d'Estaing to represent the military, and the medal of the order of Cincinnatus: he instructed the artist to duplicate them as an ensemble. But to his dismay, Shaw discovered that the artist "was unable to combine the figures with the least propriety; though there was not one of them which singly he could not copy with greatest exactness."[67]

Shaw's opinion typifies the cultural chauvinism leading most Americans into twofold error in assessing Chinese art. First, as did Shaw, many Americans mistook the export work from China as Chinese art. And then, judging this "Chinese" art by Western standards they, not surprisingly, found it lacking. Shaw's comments replicated a Western view of Chinese art circulating since Matteo Ricci first visited China, stating: "there are many painters in Canton, but I was informed that not one of them possesses a genius for design. . . . It is a general remark, that the Chinese, though they can imitate most of the fine arts, do not possess any large portion of original genius."[68]

Yet not all traders and diplomats disdained Chinese culture. During the first half of the nineteenth century, two Americans separately established museums of Chinese objects, directed toward the American public. Nathan Dunn, a Philadelphia merchant who resided in China for over twelve years,

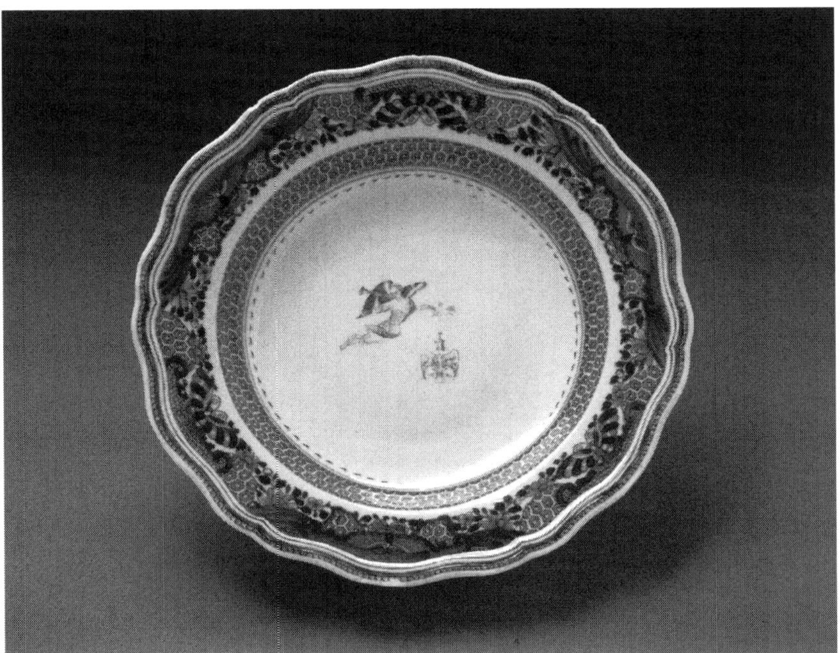

Fig. 1.2. Soup plate from the Society of Cincinnati china set, used by George Washington. Courtesy of Mount Vernon Ladies' Association.

collected innumerable objects and established the first such museum. Dunn paid the considerable sum of $20,000 to buy land for a museum site and leased the ground floor of the building constructed there for his Chinese museum. Charles Wilson Peales's more famous museum occupied the next two floors of the same building.[69] Dunn modeled the building's entrance on a Chinese summerhouse, and placed life-sized mannequins of Chinese people throughout the displays. The collection and its installation are estimated to have cost nearly $58,000.[70] Between 1838 and 1850, Dunn traveled his collection, exhibiting the Chinese objects in Philadelphia, Boston, and New York. His primary intention was in heightening American recognition of the high quality of Chinese culture.[71] And Americans responded: in Philadelphia alone, the exhibition reportedly attracted 100,000 visitors in three years.[72]

Within a year of the museum's opening, a catalog had been created to accompany the exhibition. Titled *Ten Thousand Chinese Things: A Descriptive Catalogue of the Chinese Collection in Philadelphia* . . . it sold over 65,000 copies, further disseminating Chinese culture and aesthetics (fig. 1.3). In it,

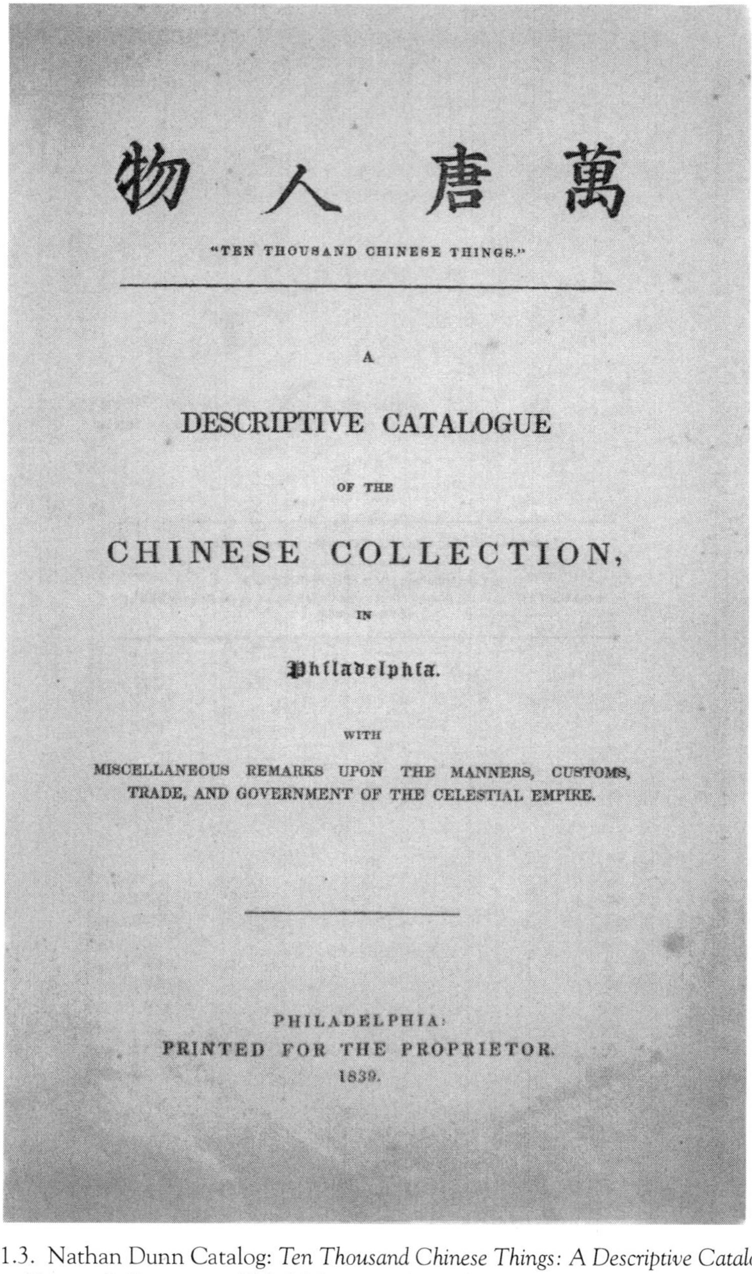

物　人　唐　萬

"TEN THOUSAND CHINESE THINGS."

A

DESCRIPTIVE CATALOGUE

OF THE

CHINESE COLLECTION,

IN

Philadelphia.

WITH

MISCELLANEOUS REMARKS UPON THE MANNERS, CUSTOMS,
TRADE, AND GOVERNMENT OF THE CELESTIAL EMPIRE.

PHILADELPHIA:
PRINTED FOR THE PROPRIETOR.
1839.

Fig. 1.3. Nathan Dunn Catalog: *Ten Thousand Chinese Things: A Descriptive Catalogue of the Chinese Collection, in Philadelphia . . .* (1839).

descriptions of the objects counterpointed a discourse on Chinese people and politics. While the objects were generally not discussed as art, and in fact the mannequins of Chinese people receive a great share of Dunn's commentary, occasionally an object or motif would be admired and regarded artistically. Floral designs were singled out for their exemplary aesthetics. For instance, apropos of a Chinese screen:

> The silk inserted in the panels is as gay as it can be rendered by a profusion of exquisitely executed paintings of the most delicate and magnificent of eastern flowers. The whole view is redolent of the spirit and beauty of spring. The drawings and colouring of the flowers are admirable, and show the perfection which has been attained in these branches of their art by Chinese painters.[73]

The catalog listed the items contained in the various cases, including elastic pillows of bamboo covered in glazed leather, pewter vessels for wine, bronzed copper hand-furnaces for keeping the fingers warm when walking in cold weather, a curious root resembling a beggar, an enameled vase, grotesque lions, lamps, and much more.[74]

The Dunn collection left Philadelphia after three years, traveling both in America and abroad. After its tenure in London the collection was dismantled and a part of the original collection returned to the United States, acquired by P. T. Barnum in 1850, who integrated the Chinese Museum, as well as an assemblage of Chinese people, purportedly a family, into his American Museum.[75]

During this same period, a second Museum of Chinese things was constructed. John R. Peters had served with the Cushing mission responsible for negotiating the first official agreement between China and the United States—the Treaty of Wang-hsia in 1844. He organized a Chinese museum in Boston filled with the prodigious number of Chinese objects he had collected. Peters arranged his museum's cases didactically; each case intended to illustrate one facet of Chinese life: a particular employment, status, or daily activity. The museum exhibited not only Chinese paintings, decorative arts, and wax Chinese mannequins but also two Chinese homes, complete with two Chinese attendants.[76] The museum's entryway reproduced a Chinese temple.[77]

After a year of display in Boston, the exhibition traveled to Philadelphia. Like Dunn, Peters had a catalog printed in conjunction with the museum collection, *Miscellaneous Remarks upon the Government, History, Religions, Literature, Agriculture, Arts, Trades, Manners and Customs of the Chinese: As Suggested by an Examination of the Articles Comprising the Chinese Museum in Marlboro' Chapel, Boston* (fig. 1.4).

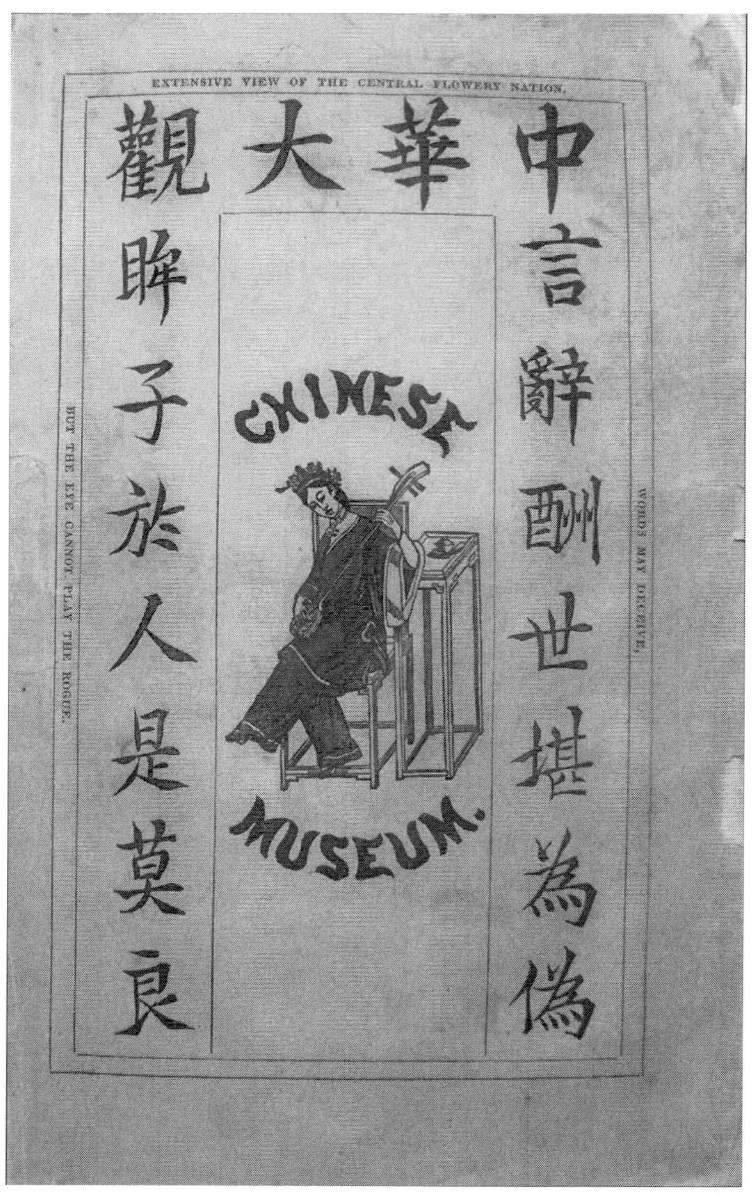

Fig. 1.4. John R. Peters Catalog: Miscellaneous Remarks upon the *Government, History, Religions, Literature, Agriculture, Arts, Trades, Manners and Customs of the Chinese: As Suggested by an Examination of the Articles Comprising the Chinese Museum, in the Marlboro' Chapel, Boston* (1845).

While there was a material motivation for creating these museums—an interest in boosting sales of Chinese objects—the overarching intention for both Peters and Dunn was their appreciation of China and their concern about the adverse opinion gaining ascendancy in America. In creating their museums, Dunn and Peters hoped that the impact created by the remarkable and diverse Chinese objects would challenge the negativity and persuade Americans of the worth of Chinese culture. This desire was built into the very architecture of Peters's museum: in two panels suspended on either side of the entry door, Chinese characters composed an aphorism which, roughly translated, stated: "Words may deceive, but the eye cannot play the rogue."[78] Even more explicitly, the museum catalogs communicated the stance both men took against the denigration of Chinese people. Both texts confronting politics directly. For instance, toward the end of his 120-page catalog, Dunn speaks bluntly about the ongoing Opium War (1838–1842) and the duplicity of Western policy toward China. Dunn's company had been one of the few Western business ventures in Canton that resisted participating in opium traffic.[79] Noting how lucrative the trade had become—bringing in nearly $20,000,000 annually—he referred both to the dependency of Britain on this commerce and to its monetary value for the United States. In spite of that, he heatedly condemned the trade, saying:

> Yet if the sum were ten times as great as it is, it could not affect the question of its moral bearings. No amount of pecuniary advantage can make that right which is wrong in itself. . . . The introduction of opium into China is contrary to the laws of the land, and consequently can be effected only by an act of public and gross dishonesty. And this injustice is committed against a heathen country, which the countrymen of the offending individuals are seeking to convert to Christianity. . . . The opium smuggled into the Celestial Empire is for the most part raised on the lands of the British East India Company in India; and the whole trade is winked at, if not directly encouraged, by the British government. . . . But it is not England alone that is to blame in this matter; most of our own merchants at Canton are guilty in the same way, and to an equal extent.[80]

Peters's candid remarks took a different route, defending China's ancient integrity against American's modern bombastic judgments:

> The Chinese have been ridiculed for assuming to be the only civilized nation in the world. This assumption is probably owing to their peculiar institutions. They live in the past, we in the future, and

consequently they are not to be judged by our standard. . . . Other great empires and kingdoms have risen and flourished for a season, but where are they? . . . The most powerful modern kingdoms of Europe are but of yesterday compared with China. While they count their existence by hundreds, she reckons hers by thousands of years and is now in the enjoyment of a green old age under the administration of laws founded upon the precepts of her sages.[81]

But despite Dunn's and Peters's efforts, art proved ineffective as a means of political persuasion. While the museums received great praise, exemplified by a comment from a visitor who exclaimed, "I had no idea that the Chinese were so luxurious and refined," still the Chinese collections could not defeat Americans' increasing arrogance toward Chinese culture.[82]

Just as the Dunn and the Peters museums and catalogs failed to dissuade Americans to abandon their negative view of Chinese people, they similarly failed to persuade them of the artistry of Chinese objects. In various manners, each critic expressed a resistance to the Chinese aesthetic. One critic who admired what he saw, seemed to need to reassure himself about the hierarchy between Chinese and Western arts by expressing loyalty to his nation's artistic superiority. Writing about the paintings in Dunn's collection guardedly praised the works:

> We do not meant to compare Chinese panting with the works of European Masters, or the productions of our own artists, for the purpose of claiming equality for them. This would be preposterous. All we desire is to render justice where it has been hitherto denied. We do not exaggerate the truth, when we assert that many of the paintings in Mr. Dunn's collection are highly respectable as works of art, and some of them would not discredit our own eminent artists. There is one large landscape paintings of very high merit, and several miniature likenesses furnished with the most elaborate care, and in very beautiful style.[83]

The publisher of the Dunn catalog, who commended the Chinese artisans for their correctness in line and for the beauty and brilliance of color in painting all aspects of nature, concluded nevertheless that the Chinese could not attain the perfection in the fine arts achieved by enlightened Christians. And most viewers would have agreed with Philip Hone, one of the wealthiest New Yorkers, who was impressed by the Dunn exhibition in but regarded the objects only as "an immense collection of curious things."

Only a few observers, such as Benjamin Silliman, were astonished by the extraordinary quality of the works and allowed themselves to express it. Silliman's surprise at the mastery displayed especially in ceramics caused him to speculate correctly that the more beautiful Chinese objects were rarely exported.

But cultural imperialism cut both ways. As Silliman had suspected, few Americans had ever seen indigenous Chinese art; disdaining American ignorance of their art, the Chinese deliberately withheld the finer pieces. The range and quality of Chinese art remained largely unknown in the United States. Chinese indifference in hiding their scorn for Western ignorance provoked American contempt all the more.[84]

5. The Influence of the Chinese Aesthetic on American Art

That Chinese imported objects caused a sensation in Europe in the eighteenth century is well known. The exotic European fantasy of "Cathay" provided some respite from the complexities and anxieties of Europe's own visually bleak and disorienting industrialization.[85] This oriental dreamland became the basis for the Rococo and for chinoiserie; a style based on the European idea of the Eastern exotic.[86]

With so many Chinese objects imported to America by mid-nineteenth century, it is logical to ask if they effected a similar influence on American arts. Despite the negative comments by traders about the Chinese aesthetic, the abundance of Chinese things valued both as essentials and as luxuries by Americans suggests that their aesthetic might have inspired American artists. Remarkably, few scholars have explored this subject; rather, they have essentially ignored the vast presence of Chinese objects.

The few scholars to explore the possibility of the influence of Chinese objects, specifically the painted representation on Chinese imports, on American artists, agree that, despite the enormous amount of things imported from China, they made no artistic impact. For instance, Ellen Denker comments: "So far, however, only a small number of scholars have examined the evidence of Chinese influence in American life and material culture. . . . For the most part the subject of Chinese influence in American life has been neglected." Her own catalog essay, however, touches on the subject of Chinese influence on the American aesthetic only to dismiss the idea. She concludes that because of its bias toward European arts, America never appreciably attended to the aesthetic of these Chinese things.[87]

Despite its title, even as comprehensive a compilation of Chinese influence Thomas Schlotterback's 1972 dissertation "The Basis for Chinese Influence in American Art, 1784–1850," ultimately corroborates Denker's claim that Chinese art lacked influence in America. Schlotterback particular analyzes the relationship between Thomas Cole and Chinese things in America. His study is thorough and evocative, detailing how "not only subject matter but more subtle formal qualities in Thomas Cole's landscape paintings parallel those in Chinese paintings."[88] But after six pages itemizing persuasive instances of visual affinities between Cole's work and Chinese painting, Schlotterback arrives at the exasperating determination that, since Cole never attested to even the slightest awareness of Chinese imagery, there is no hard evidence to support its influence on him. The numerous parallels between Cole's and Chinese landscapes and are attributed to "nothing more than [an] interesting coincidence."[89]

What is common to both Denker and Schlotterback is that they search for overt influences only. With Chinese objects in so many households, their lack of influence on American taste and culture would be truly remarkable. The sheer number of Chinese objects in America points toward some connection. If, rather than stipulate that Chinese influence on American art must derive from an unequivocally direct influence, a more implicit relationship is permitted, then the same data now suggests the possibility of an enormous, albeit indirect influence of Chinese art, through imported household objects, on American artists. Understood in this manner, the influence of Chinese household items does not require any explicit remarks to correlate them to American visual iconography. Affinities noted between Thomas Cole's artworks and landscapes on imported Chinese wallpaper, between James Audubon or Titian Ramsay Peale and Chinese animal motifs found on furniture, vases, as well as on wallpaper, can be perceived as arising from familiarity, rather than formal study. And the fact that the Peale museum was housed in the same building as the Dunn museum, corroborates this idea of familiarity and indirect influence.

However, while recontextualizing the issue of influence, the supposition of familiarity raises a more critical one: given the many Chinese items that were available as source material for American artists, why didn't any artist mention them? What were the reasons for suppressing acknowledgment of their influence?

Three related possibilities occur: either American artists remained unconscious of their impressionability; or they did not choose to recognize it; or both—they remained unaware because they did not choose to recognize the influence of Chinese art. Certainly a propensity toward Eurocentricism heightened American's reluctance to accredit Chinese art as an influence in their artistic endeavors. In the early years of nationhood, the American art world feared accusations of provinciality. Americans desiring to appear artistically sophisticated aspired to the European art aesthetic. Chinese aesthetics arrived in the nation at a time when Americans defensively affirmed their artistic proficiency by denigrating art other than European.[90]

Yet, the relationship we have discussed between animosity toward Chinese people and animosity toward their art suggests another, less ingenuous reason for downplaying Chinese influence. All objects are embedded within their specific historical and cultural contexts and those receiving the status of art are further coded with cultural agendas. More was gained socially by discounting admiration for Chinese aesthetics than in admitting it. The low regard for the Chinese would certainly dissuade Americans from acknowledging learning anything from the Chinese or their culture. Visual ideas derived from Chinese things would at best pass unstated, relegated to the background rather than forwarded as an influence.

We have in this relationship between art and politics, then, a correlation which does not affirm the model ascribed in Western accounts, of its artistic avant-garde leading political and social awareness. While American art did respond to Chinese influence, the negative political atmosphere shaped its lack of recognition of that art, whether through timidity or oversight; the inverse of our Western paradigm, and of Dunn's and Peters's desire.

SECTION II. THE LATE NINETEENTH CENTURY

1. Regarding "Oriental": Whose Aesthetic Is It?

CHINESE OBJECTS IN THE UNITED STATES

As we have seen, the material evidence substantiates the presence of great numbers of Chinese things in the United States by the early 1870s. Through numerous exhibitions throughout the nineteenth century, Americans were brought in contact with Chinese objects and avidly sought them out for purchase.[91]

For a short time in the 1870s, Americans began to look enthusiastically at both Chinese and Japanese things, but as the decade drew on the approval voiced for Chinese things diminished. The lack of acclaim for Chinese objects during the seventies and eighties becomes even more striking when examined in the context of the simultaneous celebration of a "Japanese aesthetic." By the end of the 1870s, Japanese culture (or rather, the American idea of Japanese culture) became widely popular. The acceptance of Japanese goods was so notable that, along with the European and American styles such as Renaissance, Colonial, and Federal, they were praised as exemplary, and the Japanese style was credited when imitated by American artisans. Chinese art, on the other hand, was rarely mentioned, subsumed in the phrase "Japanese-style."[92]

Surprisingly, this disparity persists even among scholars today. Ellen Denker's catalog is one of the few that reflects on this practice of identifying a Japanese influence, but rarely a Chinese influence, on art made in the United States:

Historians and critics more often than not have credited Japan as the most important Asian source in American arts. Also because of the tendency of writers in the West to lump Persia, India, China and Japan together as "The Orient," scholars have only recently begun to examine the contributions of each of these distinct cultural areas.[93]

In part, this disparity between Chinese and Japanese receptions in the United States results from timing.

In the 1870s when Japanese objects arrived en masse in the United States, the American idea of art was no longer restricted to the European perspectival oil paintings. Especially through the influence of Ruskin, in the four or five decades between the beginning of America's China trade and its newer trade with Japan, taste in art had changed considerably from the early 1800s, when Waln faulted Chinese artists for having "no mind to convey the idea of distance, solidity, expression, and magnitude of objects, by fore-shortening, perspective, and a due proportion of light and shade"; in short, for not painting according to Western standards. A new artistic climate had been cultivated for an earlier period of European art, a pre-Renaissance art, considered to be "primitive." Connections between this new "pre-Raphaelite" art and characteristics found in Asian art—flatness, patterns of decorative color, less emphasis on one-point perspective—were noted as early as 1862. Impressed by the Japanese display at the London International Exhibition, a visitor stated, "To realize the real Middle Ages [one] must visit the Japanese Court."[94] In 1875 James Jackson Jarves (1818–1888), a Boston art writer and world art collector, expressed his enjoyment of the differences between Western and Japanese art:

> In entering the new world, familiar ideals and ordinary rules must be cast aside. Instead we must accept new ideals and rules, and try to enjoy everything good in its principle and sound in its manifesta-tion after its kind, however much it varies from the forms and laws which we have been trained to esteem as the only correct ones.[95]

Chinese style was included in this new standard and, for a short time, it seemed that Chinese art would finally come into its own. The art critique that appeared in *Harper's Magazine* on August 1870 exemplifies this admira-tion, situating Chinese art on the cusp of the changing American aesthetic. It begins with great compliments:

> The works of art of the Chinese are well known for their great beauty of color, and the extraordinary fineness as well as originality

in design in carvings of wood and ivory; while the bronze objects which represent the antique art of China are often most remarkable for the skill and fancy with which the forms of natural objects, plants, and animals have been treated in composing the ornament. The grotesques, for which they have an especial liking, are also far beyond any that European artists have ever designed.[96]

At this early date, the writer felt optimistic about the Chinese ability to progress in industry and his article ends on the note that, in doing so, the Chinese people will eventually produce an even better art.[97]

By the time the United States began to welcome Asian arts, Chinese subjects of all sorts pervaded American media. A single edition of *Harper's* shows the extent to which Chinese themes had penetrated into American culture: the sixteen-page issue had eight specific references to Chinese people or things. Besides the art critique already cited, the magazine devoted a full page to a political drawing on the subject of Chinese immigration by Thomas Nast. A smaller Nast cartoon on the last page also had a Chinese theme; three items under the heading "Home and Foreign Gossip" referred to Chinese people; and in the ads one could purchase "The New Chinese Target Pistols" (fig. 1.5).

But the frequency of Chinese referents can veil the fundamental changes occurring in the attitude toward Chinese things. The magazine as a whole exhibited a negative approach counterpointing the critique's nascent appreciation of Chinese objects. A closer look at the contributions shows the unease about Chinese, specifically about Chinese immigration. In particular, the large Nast cartoon, titled "The Comet of Chinese Labor" and captioned "The New Comet—A Phenomenon Now Visible in All Parts of the United States," characterized this uneasiness (fig. 1.6). It coupled the emotion involved in the spectacle of a comet streaking across the night sky with the controversy of Chinese people entering the country. Nast gave the comet the face of a Chinese man, his queue the comet's tail. In glaring letters the comet beams "Cheap Labor," as it arches into its descent, toward a crowd of Americans. Giant telescopes tracking the comet are variously labeled "the press," and "capitalist." A group of angry, gesticulating men stand on a tall platform with a sign advertising a meeting of "Know Nothings on the Chinese Labor Question." Nast's smaller cartoon also deals with the question of Chinese immigration, featuring a Chinese shoemaker pestered by a giant fly representing his adversary—the labor organization of the Knights of St. Crispin.

And in the article on Chinese art: although Chinese art received high praise, ultimately it fell short of Japanese:

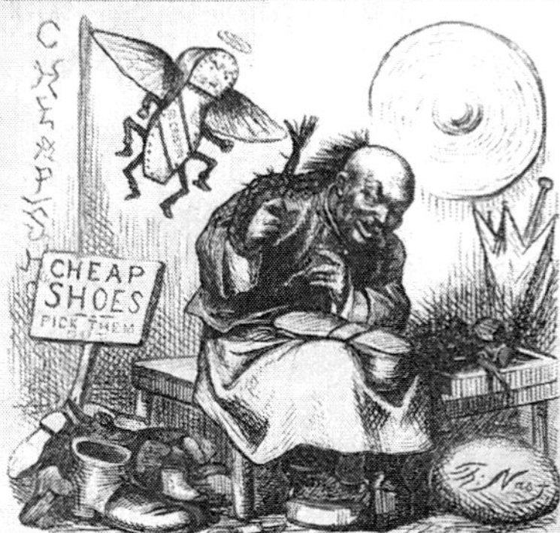

THE LATEST EDITION OF "SHOO, FLY!"

ARMORY OF THE 22d REGIMENT.

WOOD BROTHERS

have removed their entire stock of fine

Pleasure Carriages,

embracing every variety for City, Park, and Road driving, to the Armory of the Twenty-second Regiment,

14th Street, between 6th and 7th Avs.

Attention is called to the fact that these Carriages are fresh stock, exclusively of their own manufacture, of the newest designs and most perfect finish, made for the present season to stock their new warerooms, No. 740 Broadway, but, owing to the late accident that necessitates the rebuilding of their warehouse, have been removed to the above Armory, on 14th Street, and are to be

Sold at Cost of Production.

Elegant Close Coaches - - - - - $1000 | Clarences - - - - - - - $1400 to $1650
Landaus - - - - - - - $1500 to 1650 | Wagons - - - - - - - 200 to 400

These Carriages have no superior in Elegance, Durability, or Finish.

Prices fixed, and every Carriage offered for sale is equal in quality to those built to order.

GUARANTEES MADE GOOD IN EVERY CITY OF THE UNION.

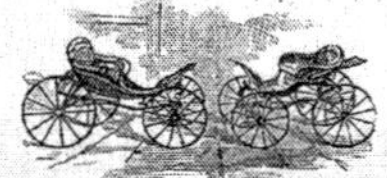

PONY CARRIAGES, New Designs, for $150.   PONY CARRIAGES, New Designs, for $150.

IF WE WERE TO PURCHASE

A Sewing Machine,

WE SHOULD GET A

FLORENCE;

not solely because it took the highest prizes at the New England Fair at Providence, at New York State Fair, Maryland State Fair, or because the Judges at the American Institute say, "This is better than any of its class known to the Judges"—and these, not all together, but because we like it best, as a woman would say. It works like a charm; we can sew anything we please with it; the children can't get it out of order; and it is put at most reasonable terms.

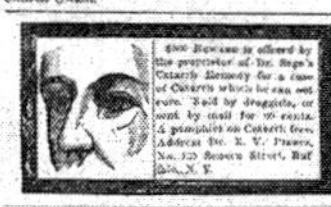

$500 Reward is offered by the proprietor of Dr. Sage's Catarrh Remedy for a case of Catarrh which he can not cure. Sold by druggists, or sent by mail for 60 cents. A pamphlet on Catarrh free. Address Dr. R. V. Pierce, No. 133 Seneca Street, Buffalo, N. Y.

FISHERMEN!

TWINES and NETTING,

MANUFACTURED BY

WM. E. HOOPER & SONS,

Send for Price-List.]   Baltimore, Md.

$2000 A YEAR AND EXPENSES

To Agents, to sell the celebrated WILSON SEWING MACHINES. The best machine in the world. Stitch alike on both sides. One Machine Without Money. For further particulars, address

THE WILSON SEWING MACHINE CO.,
Cleveland, Ohio; Boston, Mass.; or St. Louis, Mo.

What Did It?—Lyon's Kathairon made my hair soft, luxuriant, and thick; and Hagan's Magnolia Balm changed that sallow complexion into the marble beauty you now see. This is emphatically the language of all who use these articles. A fine head of hair and a refined complexion are the greatest attractions a woman can possess. The Kathairon and Magnolia Balm are just what will give them to you, and nothing else will. The Balm is the bloom of youth. It makes a lady of thirty appear but twenty. Both articles are entirely harmless, and very pleasant. They should be in every lady's possession.

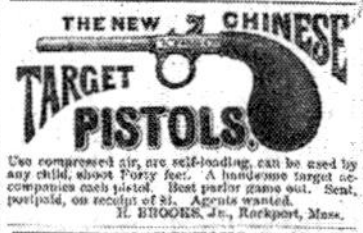

Use compressed air, are self-loading, can be used by any child, shoot Forty feet. Best parlor game out. Sent, postpaid, on receipt of $1. Agents wanted.

H. BROOKS, JR., Rockport, Mass.

PATENTS—INVENTORS who wish to take out Letters Patent are advised to counsel with MUNN & CO., Editors of the Scientific American, who have prosecuted claims before the Patent Office for Twenty-three Years. Their American and European Patent Agency is the most extensive in the world. Charges less than any other reliable agency. A pamphlet, containing full instructions in Inventors, is sent gratis. Address MUNN & CO., 37 Park Row, N.Y.

Mann's Improved Double Trolling Spoon

Unequaled for catching Pike, Pickerel, Bass, Trout, &c. Price, by mail, $1 00. JOHN H. MANN, Syracuse, N.Y.

One Million Acres of Choice Iowa Lands

FOR SALE, at $2 per acre and upward for cash, or on credit by the Iowa Railroad Land Co. Railroads already built through the Lands, and on all sides of them. Great inducement to settlers. Send for our free Pamphlet. It gives prices, terms, location; tells who should come West, what they should bring, what it will cost; gives plans and elevations of 36 different styles of ready-made houses, which the Company furnish at from $350 to $4000, ready to set up. Maps sent if desired. Address

W. W. WALKER, Vice-President,
Cedar Rapids, Iowa.

BISHOP & REIN,

JEWELERS,

Under the Fifth Avenue Hotel,
NEW YORK.

MISSISQUOI SPRING.

The water of this world-renowned spring is a specific for Cancer, Scrofula, and all Diseases of the Kidneys. Thousands have been cured. The most eminent physicians prescribe it.

N. B.—The Missisquoi Springs Hotel, adjacent thereto, is first class. Board from $15 to $28 a week, or $56 a month. Route via the Albany, Vt.

J. W. SUBLETT, Proprietor.

YALE LOCKS.

SECURITY

FULL SIZE OF KEY.

BEST & CHEAPEST.

FOR SALE BY THE HARDWARE TRADE.

YALE LOCK MFG. CO. N11 BARCLAY St. N.Y.

SOZODONT

Perfumes the breath, hardens the gums, preserves the teeth.

Newspaper Advertising.

A Book of 125 pages, contains a list of the best American Advertising Mediums, giving the names, circulations, and full particulars concerning the leading Daily and Weekly Political and Family Newspapers, together with all those having large circulations, published in the interest of Religion, Agriculture, Literature, &c., &c. Every advertiser, and every person who contemplates becoming such, will find this book of great value. Mailed free to any address on receipt of fifteen cents. GEO. P. ROWELL & CO., 40 Park Row, New York.

Farnham, Gilbert, & Co.,

BANKERS,

No. 8 Wall Street, New York.

Prang's Chromos.

Cut Paper Patterns

OF SUITS IN

HARPER'S BAZAR.

Arrangements have been made to furnish CUT PAPER PATTERNS of the beautiful Paris Costumes which it is intended shall appear fortnightly in Harper's Bazar. These Patterns are Graded to Fit any Figure, from 30 to 46 inches Bust Measure, and are fitted with the greatest accuracy, the names and directions for putting together being printed on each separate piece of the pattern, so as to be adjusted by the most inexperienced.

The following patterns are now ready:

WATTEAU STREET SUIT ....No. 22
TRAINED CARRIAGE SUIT 24
WALKING SUIT 24
COUNTRY WALKING SUIT 23
TRAINED HOUSE DRESS 20
SEA-SIDE COSTUME 22

The Publishers will send either Pattern by mail, prepaid, on receipt of TWENTY-FIVE CENTS and BUST MEASURE. The same Patterns cost sixty cents in gold in Paris. The whole set of Nine Sizes will be sent for $2 00.

In ordering, please specify the Number of pattern containing Suit and send Bust Measure. Dealers supplied at the usual discount.

HARPER & BROTHERS, New York.

JANES & KIRTLAND, 10 READE ST., New York.

FOUNTAINS, VASES, SETTEES, &c., for Gardens and Lawns. Send for a Catalogue.

ENGINEERS and MACHINISTS.

Who can spare an hour a day, can earn from $25 to $100 a week. Address S. BISSELL, Treasurer, Hartford, Conn.

NEW BOOKS OF THE SEASON,

PUBLISHED BY

HARPER & BROTHERS, NEW YORK.

Sent by Mail, postage prepaid, to any part of the United States, on receipt of the price.

ROBERTSON'S LIFE, LETTERS, &c. Life, Letters, Lectures, and Addresses of Frederick W. Robertson, M.A., Incumbent of Trinity Chapel, Brighton, 1847-1853. With Portrait on Steel. Complete in One Volume. 840 pages, large 12mo, Cloth, $4 00.

ROBERTSON'S SERMONS. Sermons preached at Brighton by the late Rev. Frederick W. Robertson, the Incumbent of Trinity Chapel. New Edition. With Portrait on Steel. Complete in One Volume. 752 pages, large 12mo, Cloth, $2 50.

DICKENS'S SPEECHES, LETTERS, and SAYINGS. Speeches, Letters, and Sayings of Charles Dickens. To which is added a Sketch of the Author by George Augustus Sala, and Dean Stanley's Sermon. 8vo, Paper, 50 cents.

HARPER'S HAND-BOOK FOR TRAVELLERS IN EUROPE AND THE EAST. Being a Guide through France, Belgium, Holland, Germany, Austria, Italy, Egypt, Syria, Turkey, Greece, Switzerland, Tyrol, Russia, Denmark, Sweden, Spain, and Great Britain and Ireland. With 45 Maps and Plans of Cities. By W. Pembroke Fetridge. Revised Edition. Sixth Year. Large 12mo, Leather, Pocket-Book Form, $7 00.

THE ROB BOY ON THE JORDAN, Nile, Red Sea, and Gennesareth, &c. A Canoe Cruise in Palestine and Egypt, and the Waters of Damascus. By J. Macgregor, M.A. With Maps and Illustrations. Crown 8vo, Cloth, $2 50.

FREE RUSSIA. By W. Hepworth Dixon, Author of "Her Majesty's Tower," &c. With Two Illustrations. Crown 8vo, Cloth, $2 00.

THE HISTORY OF HORTENSE, Daughter of Josephine, Queen of Holland, Mother of Napoleon III. By Joan S. C. Abbott, Author of "The French Revolution," "History of Napoleon Bonaparte," &c. With Engravings. 12mo, Cloth, $1 50. Uniform with Abbott's Illustrated Histories.

THE BAZAR BOOK OF DECORUM. The Care of the Person, Manners, Etiquette, and Ceremonials. 16mo, Toned Paper, Cloth, Beveled Edges, $1 00.

CHRISTIANITY AND GREEK PHILOSOPHY; or, the Relation between Spontaneous and Reflective Thought in Greece and Positive Teaching of Christ and His Apostles. By B. F. Cocker, D.D., Professor of Moral and Mental Philosophy in the University of Michigan. Crown 8vo, Cloth, $2 75.

THE LIFE OF COUNT BISMARCK, Private and Political. With Descriptive Notices of his Ancestry. By Dr. George Hesekiel. Translated and Edited, with an Introduction, Explanatory Notes, and Appendices, by Kenneth R. H. Mackenzie, F.S.A., F.A.S.L. With upward of 100 Illustrations. 8vo, Cloth, $3 00.

MEMOIR OF THE REV. JOHN SCUDDER, M.D., Thirty-six Years Missionary in India. By Rev. J. B. Waterbury, D.D. With Portrait of Dr. Scudder. 12mo, Cloth, $1 75.

SELF-HELP; with Illustrations of Character, Conduct, and Perseverance. By Samuel Smiles, Author of "The Life of the Stephensons," "History of the Huguenots," &c. A Revised and Enlarged Edition. 12mo, Cloth, $1 00.

HISTORY OF THE AMERICAN CIVIL WAR. By John W. Draper, M.D., LL.D., Professor of Chemistry and Physiology in the University of New York. In Three Vols., 8vo, Cloth, $3 50 per vol.

FRESH NOVELS,

PUBLISHED BY

HARPER & BROTHERS, NEW YORK.

JOHN: A Love Story. By Mrs. Oliphant, Author of "Agnes," "Chronicles of Carlingford," "The Minister's Wife," "Life of Edward Irving," "Brownlows," &c. 8vo, Paper, 50 cents.

MAN AND WIFE. By Wilkie Collins, Author of "Armadale," "Moonstone," "No Name," "The Woman in White," &c. With Illustrations. 8vo, Paper, $1 00; Cloth, $1 50.

MISS THACKERAY'S WRITINGS, COMPLETE. The Writings of Anne Isabella Thackeray. Illustrated. 8vo, Paper, $1 75; Cloth, $1 75.

KILMENY. By William Black, Author of "In Silk Attire," "Love or Marriage?" &c. 8vo, Paper, 90 cents.

STERN NECESSITY. By F. W. Robinson, Author of "Poor Humanity," "Mattie: a Stray," "For Her Sake," "Carry's Confession," "No Man's Friend," &c. 8vo, Paper, 50 cents.

GWENDOLINE'S HARVEST. By the Author of "Carlyon's Year," "One of the Family," "Found Dead," "A Beggar on Horseback," &c. 8vo, Paper, 75 cents.

PUT YOURSELF IN HIS PLACE. By Charles Reade, Author of "Hard Cash," "Griffith Gaunt," &c., &c. From the Author's early sheets.

HARPER'S OCTAVO EDITION of "Put Yourself in His Place." With all the Illustrations, including the characteristic Vignettes not to be found in any other American edition. Paper, 75 cents; bound in Cloth, $1 25.

HARPER'S DUODECIMO EDITION of "Put Yourself in His Place." Uniform with the Boston Household Edition of Charles Reade's Novels, and bound in Green-Morocco English Cloth, to match that edition. Illustrated. Price $1 00.

THE VICAR OF BULLHAMPTON. By Anthony Trollope, Author of "The Bertrams," "Castle Richmond," "Framley Parsonage," "Orley Farm," "Small House at Allington," &c. With Illustrations. 8vo, Paper, $1 00; Cloth, $1 50.

MISS VAN KORTLAND. A Novel of American Society. By the Author of "My Daughter Elinor." 8vo, Paper, $1 00.

Fig. 1.5. *Harper's Weekly* 1870, back page, Thomas Nast Chinese shoemaker cartoon.

In painting they are great imitators; and having perfect colors, they succeed in painting birds, flowers, fruit, animals, and figures of men and women in the brightest and finest colors, but without any idea of very correct drawing or placing the object in perspective. In this respect they are behind the Japanese, who show a much more artistic feeling for natural beauty and picturesque arrangement.[98]

JAPANESE OBJECTS IN THE UNITED STATES

As early as 1799, under the command of captain James Devereux, the American ship the *Franklin* brought back a cargo filled with goods from Japan. However, it was actually chartered by the Dutch East India Company, which, due to European wars, had no ships of its own for its annual Japan voyage; Japanese things did not appear in large quantities in the United States until the last third of the nineteenth century.[99]

The 1870s saw Japanese art emerge into a collecting fad so prolific it was referred to as a "mania." Japanese objects became omnipresent as American homemakers tried to achieve the "Japanese style," following descriptions in numerous magazine articles and "how-to" books. Throughout American

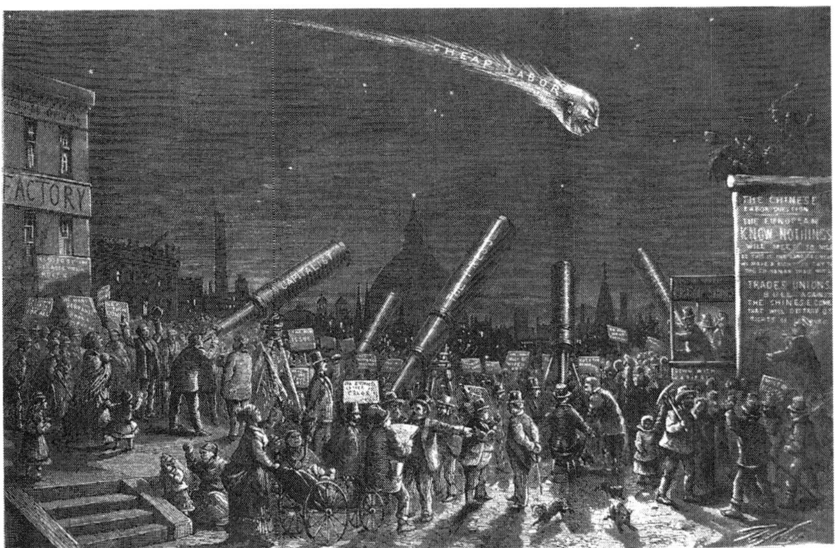

Fig. 1.6. Thomas Nast cartoon, "The Comet of Chinese Labor," *Harper's Magazine*, 1870.

culture, vernacular and elite, Japan was presented as a nation embodying the idea of art. And the Japanese versions of crafts and design influenced their American counterparts, together becoming the proponents of the "art idea."[100] In fact, the Japanese face and figure, generally female, signifying an artistic appreciation beyond the mainstream, itself became an American decorative motif adorning all sorts of American-made objects from teapots to buttons, and even a wonderfully intricate hardware set for doorways, with geisha faces engraved on the doorknobs and full-length Japanese figures on the hinges[101] (fig. 1.7). Contrastingly, it was the male Chinese figure that became a motif in American objects, and, unlike its Japanese counterpart, it generally was not a graceful adornment but served more as a vernacular icon, appearing as the shape for bottles, buttons, and even as a mold for barley sugar candies (figs. 1.8 and 1.9).

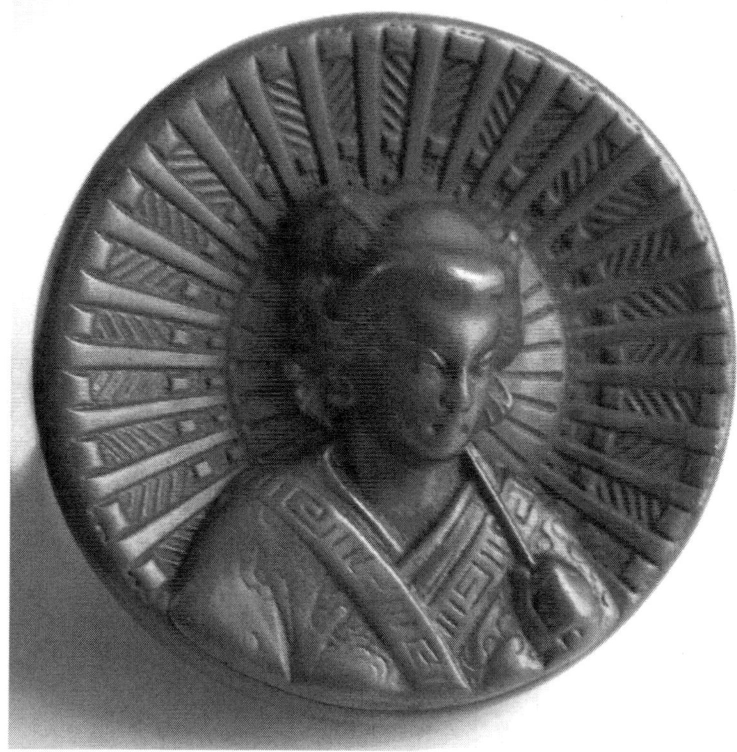

Fig. 1.7. Geisha, cast metal doorknob, Russell & Erwin Co.

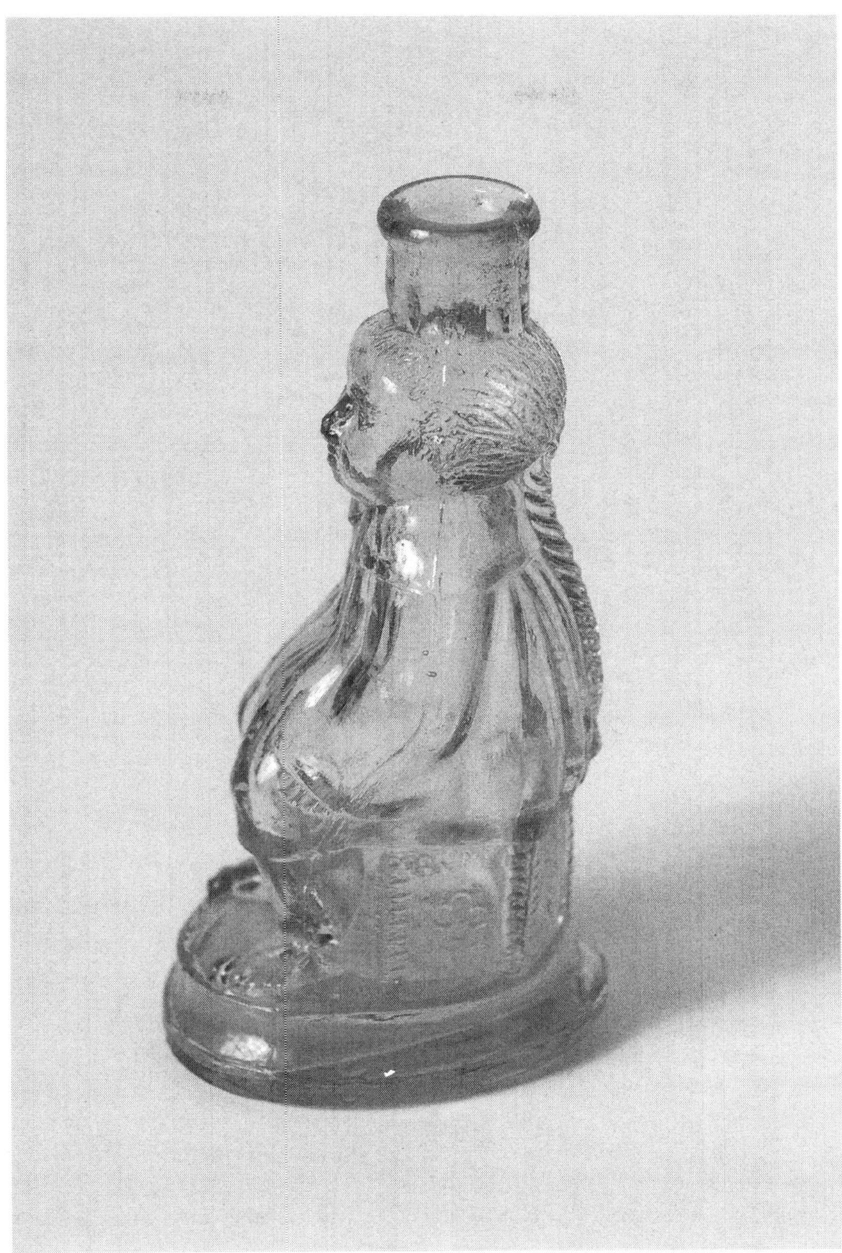

Fig. 1.8. Clear glass bottle shaped as Chinese man. The base is embossed. C. F. Knapp, Philadelphia.

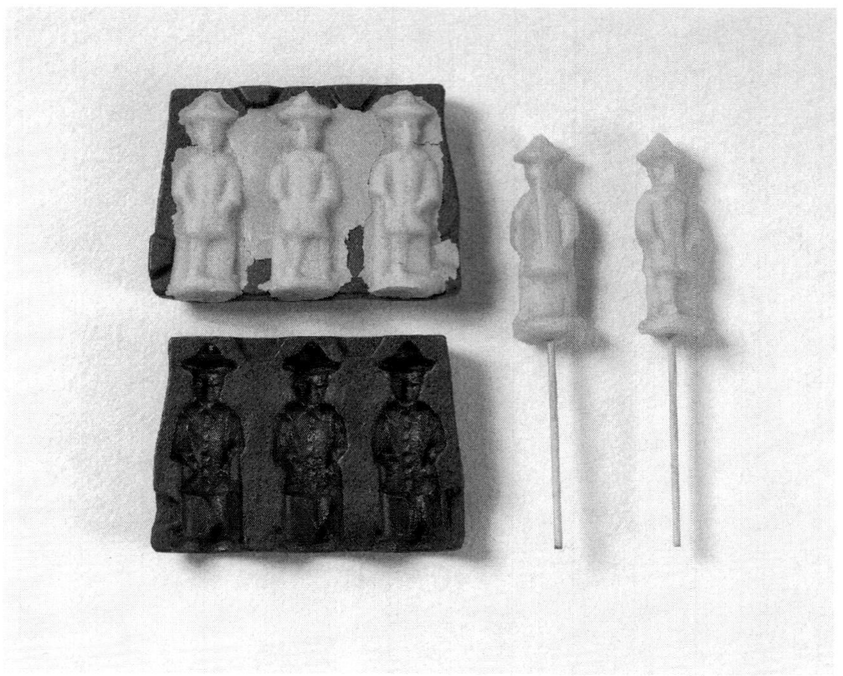

Fig. 1.9. Nineteenth-century mold for barley candies. The figures shown here are molded in wax.

The excitement created by Japanese objects in America and its profound consequences for American fine art and industry have been examined in detail. Many scholars unhesitatingly date the visual impact of Japanese things to the Philadelphia Centennial Exhibition of 1876.[102]

However, other starting dates have been proposed. In *Japonisme Comes to America: The Japanese Impact on the Graphic Arts 1876–1925*, Julia Meech and Gabriel P. Weisberg offer evidence of a more reluctant American reception to the first European dealers in Asian materials. In particular, they discuss Parisian dealer Siegfried S. Bing's endeavor to create an American audience for his Asian inventory. Arriving in New York in 1887, he tried to promote sales by exhibiting the Japanese objects in a gallery, with preliminary viewing available in an apartment rented for that purpose. The poor sales of Bing's merchandise lead Meech and Weisberg to conclude that the amounts of objects and their relatively high prices discouraged American consumers.[103] They describe a climate exhibiting little fervor toward Asian arts until significantly later than the Centennial, beginning only when Americans became aware of the lively European interest validating these objects.[104] And even with that, greater interest was stimulated only through tenacious advertising. Meech and Weisberg state, "By 1900 so many books and articles had been published on the Far East that few with any interest in culture could have remained totally oblivious to the seduction of Japanese civilization."[105]

Alternatively, Christine Wallace Laidlaw's 1996 dissertation. "The American Reaction to Japanese Art, 1853–1876." offers extensive evidence that the change in taste occurred earlier, prior to the Centennial exhibition: "even before 1876, Americans were increasingly familiar with Japanese art and were coming to admire the Japanese portrayal of nature more and more." She theorizes that "the Japanese influence on American art, decorative arts, and architecture during the 1860s and 1870s was much more important than has been realized." Her research proposes that the immense popularity of Japanese goods at the Centennial was not the beginning of American interest but a response conditioned by the already existent climate of receptivity to Japanese art.[106]

And in *Chinoiserie*, Dawn Jacobson contradicts Meech and Weinberg's contention that America's Japonisme occurred only via the route of Europe. In fact, she states definitively that "America was not indebted to Europe for Japonisme's genesis. The style arrived in the two continents simultaneously, and America would incorporate Japonisme into architecture and interiors in more subtle, profound and long-lasting ways than Europe."[107]

The discrepancy between these various dates and estimations of Europe as an influence seems to be more a difference in definition than in observation. As early as the mid-1860s two New York stores had sold Japanese goods along with Chinese and Indian stock. Stores such as Foutains & Co. on Broadway held special annual sales of such merchandise. And not only objects; by the end of the decade Japanese prints also were standard items in the shops.[108] However, although Americans seem to have become interested in Japanese things in the 1850s, immediately after the United States' major role compelling Japan to admit Western diplomats and open trade with Western countries, the widespread interest known as the "Japan craze" or "Japanosime" did not start until two decades later. By the 1870s Japanese merchandise was available in countless American shops. And certainly the Centennial made Japanese things available to a much larger audience. Despite some contention over the date and route of the initial enthusiasm, all the research agrees that by the end of the 1870s Japanese objects exerted an enormous influence on home furnishings and taste in Victorian America.[109]

By the end of the 1800s, the different receptions of Japanese and Chinese objects were pronounced.

2. American Confusion of Japanese and Chinese Objects

This leads to a fundamental issue. How much of the mania for Japanese things was also a convenient deflection, obscuring the Chinese origin of many of these admired objects? Were the objects fundamentally different in appearance? On what basis did Americans distinguish them?

If differences in appearance resulted in the preference for Japanese objects over Chinese, these differences could arise from only two alternatives: either the workmanship from the two nations differed appreciably, or their aestheticism and artistry substantially differed. Were either (or both) of these the criteria used in Americans' differentiation of the two Asian nations' manufactures?

The Centennial Exposition of 1876 provides an opportunity to closely compare the seminal American art discussions about objects from Asia. Great quantities of Chinese and Japanese merchandise were available for purchase, some booths literally side by side (and across the aisle from Great Britain) and they drew equally large crowds.[110] While both received generally positive reviews, a few critics became quite impassioned about the Japanese display and their critiques proclaimed their preference:

> After the Japanese collection everything looks in a measure commonplace, almost vulgar. The English embroidery and china in imitation of their models are either pitiably weak or like feverish fancies, quite disordered and unnatural . . . the whole nearer East looks dim and rough after the splendor and sheen of Japan. China strikes one as elaborately ugly and grotesque, Egypt as poor and semi-civilized.[111]

In the Centennial catalogue, *The Centennial Exposition Described and Illustrated*, 1876, J. S. Ingram included a chapter headed "The Japanese Exhibits." He described the Japanese department as one of the main attractions of the fair, "the delight of lovers of the curious and the bizarre, and at the same time of the delicate and intricate workmanship."[112] Ingram's admiration of the display derived in part from his surprise and pleasure in discovering an unknown nation, yet he did not hesitate proclaiming that the display showed Japan's "characteristic art."

Significantly, the Chinese display did not figure prominently in Ingram's catalog. Rather, it was somewhat incongruously placed within the chapter titled "Japanese Exhibits"; appearing after a discussion of Japanese art, under the smaller subheading "China."

Such critiques created the assumption of a discrepancy in the quality of the workmanship between Japanese and Chinese objects, implying that the interest in Japanese merchandise predominating later in the century stemmed from its superior quality. Subsequent historians generally take these critiques at face value, and accordingly have based their research on the premise of the general excellence in the Japanese objects and an inferior quality in the Chinese. This premise, in turn, has led to further speculation, that the different receptions resulted from the fact that the Japanese themselves selected the objects they displayed, while an American government official chose the Chinese objects. Based on these speculations, the inferiority of the Chinese to the Japanese exhibition in both the quality of the art and in the aesthetics of the display has been rationalized and perpetuated.[113]

But, although recent scholarship concludes that the diminished regard of the Chinese exhibition rested on China's lackluster engagement with its own art and display, examining the exhibition records of the time show these conclusions are based on a false premise: the premise, in fact, justified the predetermined conclusion. Examination of both Ingram's and Norton's Centennial texts finds that, rather than an indifference on China's part, both texts refer to a Chinese curator by name. They describe that many of the more precious objects came from the collection of one Chinese man in particular. Ingram described him as a "rich millionaire" named Hu Quang Yung, "otherwise known as Hu Tuen Tzen (Great Man)."[114] To familiarize the West with more than Chinese export art, Hu Quang Yung sent quality examples of Chinese antiquities in cloisonné, bronzes, and ceramics in the charge of his nephew Wu Ying Ding, who was described as intelligent, and very fluent in English. Norton's catalog similarly spoke of the curator in equally admiring terms. In his introduction of the Chinese exhibition, Norton affirmed that: "This section owes much of its importance and value to Ha-Quang-Yung, of Shanghai, an eminent Chinese, a pink-button mandarin, and said to be the wealthiest banker in the Empire . . . He has a reputation both throughout Europe and Asia as a collector of ancient and valuable specimens of Chinese art."[115] The participation of this Chinese art expert and his nephew contradicts Cohen's contention that a disaffected China yielded the choice of the Chinese display entirely to American officials.

Equally erroneous is the contention that the Chinese objects were overlooked in the face of the Japanese sensation. On the contrary, while the Japanese display generated a buzz of excitement, the critical response to the Chinese display was resoundingly enthusiastic as well. For instance, despite the uneven treatment of some of the cataloging of Japanese and Chinese exhibitions, Ingram's catalog praised the collection of ancient Chinese art. Although Ingram gave the perfunctorily disclaimer, describing the objects through the lens of Western art, "artistically beautiful though aesthetically grotesque ornamentation," he then proceeded to praise them quite extravagantly: "taken as a whole, the display was one of the most choice and elegant collections ever seen, whether at any of the great world's fairs or in the art cabinets of the crowned heads of Europe,"[116] and admiringly concluded that "even the most ordinary articles of household use have been transformed into visions of unique beauty."[117]

Similarly, in his account of the fair, Frank B. Norton, editor of *The Illustrated Historical Register of the United States Centennial Exposition 1876*, endorsed the Chinese exhibit, writing: "The Chinese section in the Main Building has proved to be one of the most attractive in the entire exhibition, and compares favorably with that of Japan in the curiosity and interest."[118] (fig. 1.10). He singled out a miniature pagoda, four and a half feet high and made of ivory, set in an ivory base representing the ground, completed by forty fruit trees and miniature Chinese people, which he pronounced "exquisite," and he found the heady price of $600 "certainly not unreasonable"[119] (fig. 1.11).

Looking more closely at the perception of quality in the Japanese and Chinese objects available in the United States reveals that the original critics often exaggerated the merits of Japanese art: after all, it was the largest quantity of Japanese art ever seen outside of Japan, and it was intended

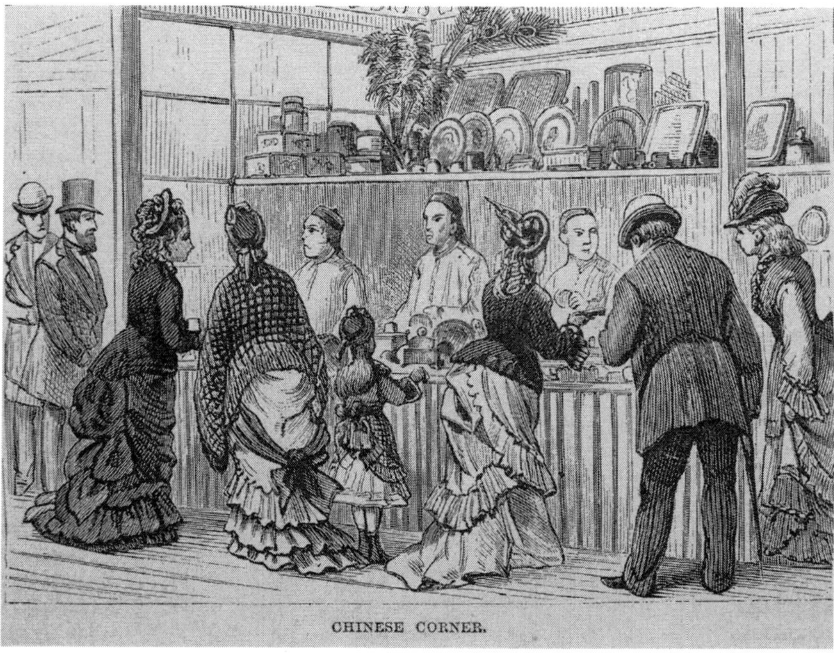

Fig. 1.10. "Chinese Corner," *The Illustrated Historical Register of the United States Centennial Exposition 1876*.

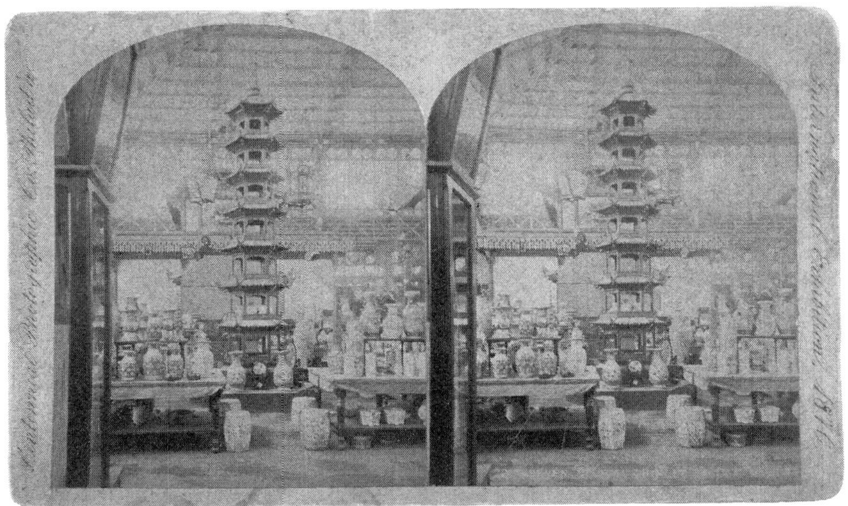

Fig. 1.11. Chinese pagoda model at Centennial World's Fair, stereoview.

for purchase as well as viewing. To an extent, the flurry about Japan was an interest in the novel. But the prevailing explanation that Japanese art achieved sudden popularity at the Centennial because of its intrinsic merits—its superior craftsmanship compared to Chinese objects—has not proved valid, since the audience of the time noted no such difference. The decline in valuation of Chinese objects, then, requires an alternative explanation.

Having ruled out the quality of workmanship, the remaining alternative is that the different receptions of Chinese and Japanese objects were based on aesthetics. Were there conspicuous differences in the aesthetics of the objects being imported? And, equally important, did Americans in the 1870s perceive them?

A number of American critics had not been impressed by previous encounters with Japanese objects in shops in Philadelphia, New York, Boston, and even in Cincinnati over the twenty-five years preceding the Centennial. But the impact of the fair's display caused some opinions to change radically. As the critic for *Lippincott's* declared:

> We have been accustomed to relegate Japanese art to the domain of the hopelessly grotesque . . . Such prepossessions disappear as we stand before the fountain that occupies the vestibule of the Japanese section, inlaid with silver, covered with raised figures, and more crowded with embellishments than a Gothic shrine.[120]

But the object glimpsed through this praise—an inlaid silver fountain crowded with embellishments—seems woefully un-Japanese. Were such hybrid items as this typical of Japanese things at the Centennial? Did the same hybridization hold true for Chinese things? In short, what types of objects were being imported from Japan and China?

The answer is incontrovertible. In her dissertation, *A True Japanese Taste*, Hina Hirayama testifies to the lack of distinction between the newly arriving Japanese objects and the long-available Chinese ones, stating unequivocally that "American merchants were exporting from Japan goods that were similar to those from China, rather than items specific to Japan."[121] The mania for Japan suppressed recognition of China's simultaneous and prior manufacture of similar objects.

And even as Jarves lamented the general decline in quality of exported Chinese objects during the year of the Centennial, and feared that the West's demands for cheap and plentiful goods would cheapen the still pure Japanese art, his contemporaries described this as already accomplished.[122] Pumpelly made just this point in his *Reminiscences*, lamenting how "the West had already begun to commercialize Japanese art," and he observes that, on the advice of the Germans at the Vienna World's Fair in 1873, the Japanese had embellished their Centennial bronzes with extra ornamentation.[123]

Even more clearly than the written text, the visual evidence demonstrates a shared aesthetic in the imports from the two Asian nations; an aesthetic owing more to Victorian taste than to either Asian culture. Norton's *Historical Register* includes an almost full-page etching of just such a composite form, captioned "Mammoth Japanese Bronze Vase" (fig. 1.12). The object has three discrete parts: the base which resembles a root structure, with gnarled, thick, and writhing branches; above that the vase itself, a wide engraved box with four attenuated curving legs that perch on the base; and above that, a round conical lid surmounted by an eagle. The eagle's wings are spread wide and its body is twisted as it gazes downward, balancing on one leg on the ball of the lid. Such decoration has more to do with the tradition of European baroque and romanticism than the more sparse line, angular geometry and serenity associated with traditional Japanese sculpture. A second Japanese vase is also pictured; an even more complicated affair, with a central element like a pillar comprised of four parts, including a tangle of serpents near the top and, ringing the midsection, alternating carvings of eagles and elephant heads. A root structure again forms the base and a wide, shallow ornamented basin surmounts the entire mountainous form (fig. 1.13).

In his catalog review of the exhibition, Ingram pronounced the bronzes superlative, remarking with satisfaction that the bronzes not only were "finer than the one made by Japan at Vienna," but, even more significantly, that "the wonderful creations we saw here hav[e] been nearly all produced ex-

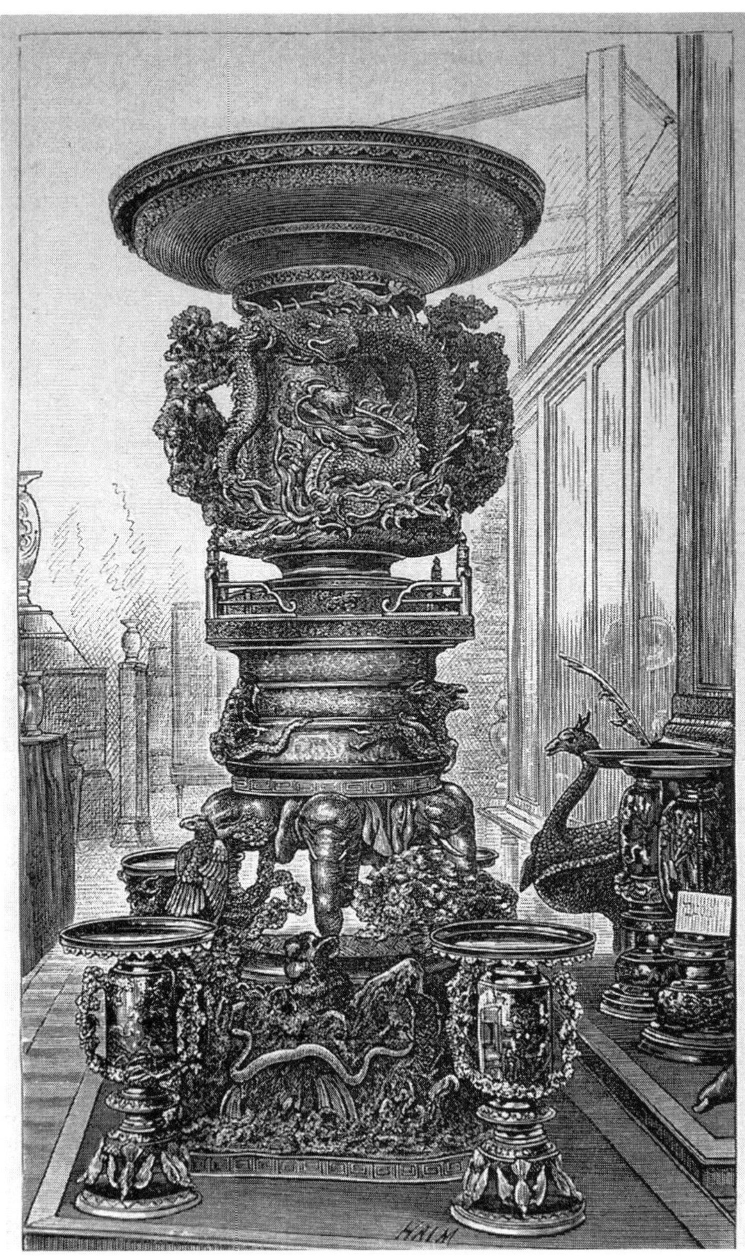

Fig. 1.12. Japanese vase, shown at the Centennial Exposition, illustrated in *The Illustrated Historical Register of the United States Centennial Exposition 1876*.

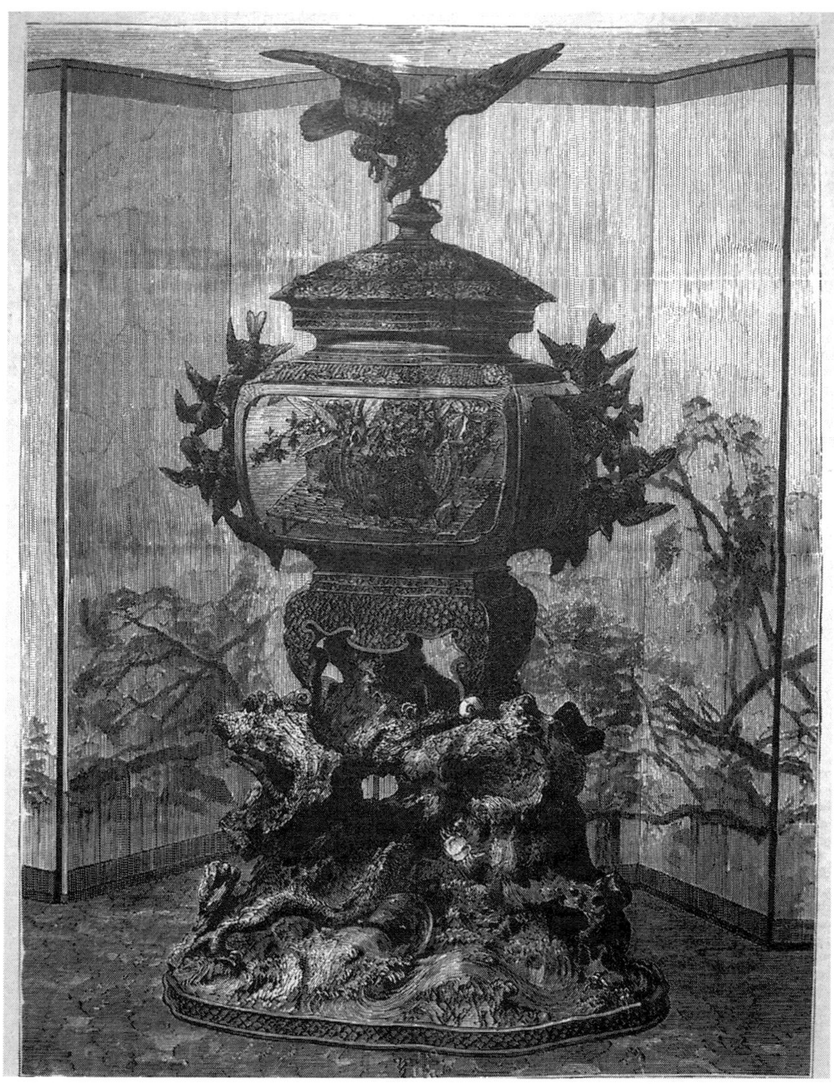

Fig. 1.13. Mammoth Japanese bronze vase, shown at the Centennial Exposition, illustrated in *The Illustrated Historical Register of the United States Centennial Exposition 1876*.

pressly for our Centennial Exhibition."[124] Both countries created such objects specifically for the export trade.

Turning to the catalog illustrations of Chinese pottery finds lidded urns in abundance. While several pieces seem more traditional in form than the Japanese sculpture, many others are equally garish, if less conspicuous in size and ambition. One illustration of a dozen Chinese ceramics shows extravagantly ornamented ceramic vessels dressed in rows of tiny raised balls, wreaths, and eagles, or stars, and shaped into composite forms sporting necks of concentric rings or resembling upright clarinets with wavy rims (fig. 1.14).

Crossman's book on *The Decorative Arts of the China Trade* addresses both the issue of quality and that of hybridization, documenting and discussing the types and the quality of hundreds of objects brought to America during the China trade.[125] Unlike most other historians studying Chinese and Japanese exports, Crossman's assessment of the Chinese objects is not based on period writing about the works; rather, he has located many of the actual pieces. He describes an overall decline in the quality of Chinese merchandise in America in general since midcentury:

> [T]he objects made for Chinese export changed as the century progressed, quality declined and decoration became gaudier; and by the 1860s, workmanship left much to be desired. The porcelains of the earlier periods, decorated to the western taste, were no longer in demand since the English and continental porcelain factories could make a comparable, if not better product for less money. By the time of the United States Centennial Exhibition of 1876, the China trade as it had been known in the 18th and early 19th

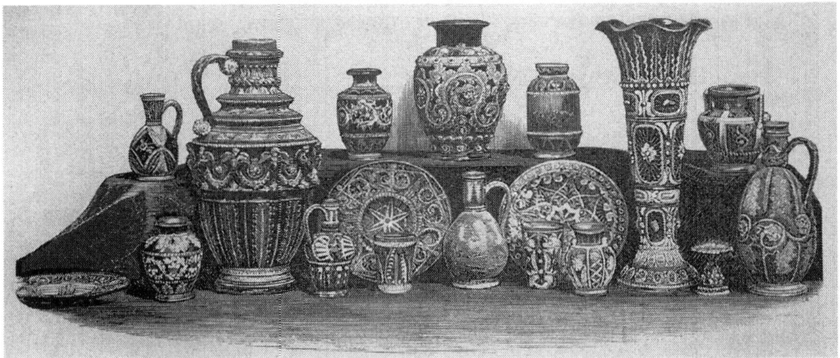

Fig. 1.14. The Chinese Pottery Exhibit at the Centennial, illustrated in *The Illustrated Historical Register of the United States Centennial Exposition 1876*.

centuries was virtually over. Steamers and advanced transportation brought on a period of tourist travel, and the items made for this market were much inferior to those which had been so carefully produced during the previous one hundred and fifty years.[126]

But this general decline of excellence was not found in the Chinese goods at the Centennial. Quite the contrary: Crossman commended the Chinese section, remarking: "the objects exhibited at the Centennial Exhibition of 1876, however, were made by the finest Chinese craftsmen in the ports still catering to a Western market, and were some of the last quality objects of the 19th century."[127] He describes several items, among them items from a dealer named Hoaching (the same Ho A Ching listed in the Centennial records) who, Crossman states, "was unquestionably the finest dealer in ivories, gold, silver and lacquer in Canton." Crossman finds the Chinese work of consistently high quality, albeit much more complex in design than were Chinese objects not intended for export. Of interest to our question on quality is his statement that it is "typical of many designs throughout time that the longer they are in vogue the more ornate and less well conceived they become; and this, despite the splendid workmanship, would certainly appear to be true of the lacquerware exhibited at Philadelphia."[128] The objects in the Chinese section can be seen as nontraditional forms, somewhat gaudy and of excellent quality.

In the catalogs and journals, comparisons between the two nations' objects were de rigueur. But perhaps the comparisons were in fact the consequence of not being able to clearly discern differences. Even when consciously intending to distinguish Japanese from Chinese objects, many Americans nevertheless confused them. In an article published in the *Art Journal* in 1876 on "The Porcelain of Japan," Charles Elliott, manager of the Household-Art Company in Boston, attempted to articulate several key differences between Chinese and Japanese ceramics. After asserting that Chinese porcelain showed more invention and variety, while Japanese often had a better glaze, Elliot confessed the difficulty of correctly attributing the works to their country of origin. And he inadvertently proved his point, attributing Japanese manufacture to a teapot that a contemporary claimed to be Chinese.[129] Many of these errors of "Japanese-style" attributions still survive today.[130]

In fact, writing on Japanese and Chinese things shows that they were not easily distinguished, and authors often elided one into another. Indeed, this phenomenon provoked the twentieth-century art historian Henry Adams to comment on the frequency with which "Chinese" or "Japanese" were substituted for each other in both Europe and America. In discussing the Victorian World's Fairs, historian Paul Greenhalgh bettered this observation, stating: "When discussing Asian, Arabic, or African design, commentators had little difficulty in comparing them to European design as though the latter were an amorphous whole, the individual nuances of the national styles apparently being less important than the numerous qualities they had in common."[131]

In the 1870s, even the art professionals often spoke of Chinese and Japanese as a single unit. For instance, the painter John La Farge, the only mid-century American artist to declare his own work's debt to Japanese compositions, nevertheless described his endeavor as wanting "to take a Chinese subject and make it absolutely Chinese in character and design and yet to carry it out in the programme of a certain Western accuracy of drawing. . . ."[132]

Walter Smith, an expert on the industrial arts, wrote the second volume in the three volume series *Masterpieces of the Centennial International Exhibition*, in which he discussed Asian objects at the Centennial. Smith attributed their impact to their novelty in the West, and in this he merged Chinese and Japanese goods:

> It is the novelty that makes Japanese and Chinese goods so popular with us and Europeans. In form, construction, ornamentation, and decoration, the products of these nations are different from anything produced elsewhere. Particularly are their pictorial representations interesting, because they illustrate costumes, custom and a life that might belong to a different world, so opposed are they to our notions of the fitness of things.[133]

The historical evidence, then, supports a conclusion that a distinction between Japanese and Chinese objects at the Centennial based on aesthetics was also unlikely. Although differences existed, and the Japanese trumped the Chinese with their large and elaborate bronzes, apparently neither workmanship nor aesthetics were the main factors in the Victorian distinction between Chinese and Japanese things.

3. Politicized Perceptions of the Chinese

Beginning in the 1870s, although Americans increasingly referred to "Japanese" style, adding China perhaps as an afterthought, yet Americans often mistook, substituted or synthesized the two nations' aesthetics. The emphatic contrast in response to the art of the two nations, therefore, was not predicated on either aesthetic or qualitative considerations of characteristics found within the objects. Consequently, we must look now to criteria based on distinctions located exterior to the objects, exploring the objects' horizon of associations and examining the meanings attached to them.

Understanding how Americans discriminated between the two nations' objects necessitates recovering these external associations. What did Americans see when they looked at Asian objects? Or, more specifically, what values were attached to Japanese and not Chinese items that would account for the increasing favor of Japanese things?

In his essay "All the World a Melting Pot?" Harris contends that, for most Americans in the 1870s, the Japanese were a "tabula rasa," and the 1876 World's Fair provided their first, and most likely, only glimpse into the culture. Harris states that "visitors to the fairs would have little with which to correct or supplement the official displays, for almost everything they saw or learned at the fairs was new."[134] The Japanese government understood the politics of their appearance and composed the presentation of their art and of their skill at the Fair to create a strongly favorable first impression.

Harris structures his arguments on the premise that Americans' assessment of the Japanese artwork occurred prior to the judgment on the people. Cohen, following Harris, enhances this premise in which admiration of art preceded and led to admiration of the people who created the art:

> Harris suggests that Americans who first saw the Japanese display and who ransacked the Japanese bazaar at the exposition came away with a heightened respect and admiration for the Japanese: the people who created such sensitive work had to be sensitive themselves. There may not have been any more *understanding* of Japanese culture, but there was greater respect for and interest in that culture in art circles and, conceivably, among the millions who visited the fair.[135]

But these versions of history postulating that American attitudes toward the Japanese people arose as a direct response to their favorable impression of the art are not borne out by the evidence. Rather than the artwork creating a first impression on a tabula rasa, the reaction to the art occurred in a climate of excitement on American's already existing perception of the Japanese people.

Americans certainly had an opinion of Japan before the Centennial. After all, Commodore Matthew Calbraith Perry had just recently brought glory to America by "opening" Japan, a country perceived as hermetically sealed and out of reach to other nations.[136] With the United States' leadership role in Japan since 1854, its first leadership role in world affairs, even while most people would not have seen Japanese art, they would have had a positive reception toward the people America had "discovered." The idea of "Japanese" clustering around objects from that country was be both exotic and approachable.

Since the 1850s, the Japanese had been described in the American press and in books in idealized, albeit miniature, terms, rather like newfound playthings for the American imagination. Speaking of Japan congenially as "our nearest neighbor across the Pacific," America imagined Japan as a treasure box, imagining its opening with excitement and curiosity.[137] Numerous newspaper articles, journal articles, and an illustrated three-volume book were immediately published on the subject of the voyage. In fact, in an attempt to ensure the popularity of his book on his voyage to Japan, Perry asked Nathaniel Hawthorne to help prepare the manuscript; Hawthorne declined.[138]

The first Japanese embassy arrived in the United States in 1860 to great fanfare, a source of great excitement to the nation. After three weeks of feting in Washington they visited New York, where they paraded up Broadway escorted by seven thousand troops and cheered by a crowd in the hundreds of thousands. Throughout the 1870s more Japanese visited the United States. All were Samurai, the upper classes, and royalty, and they were addressed with the title of prince. Their high social status delighted the American public; the *New York Times* described one party as "all very young and intelligent looking"[139] (fig. 1.15). The press celebrated the Japanese for their aristocratic manners and their progressive attitude. With very few Japanese people living in the eastern states—only five residing in

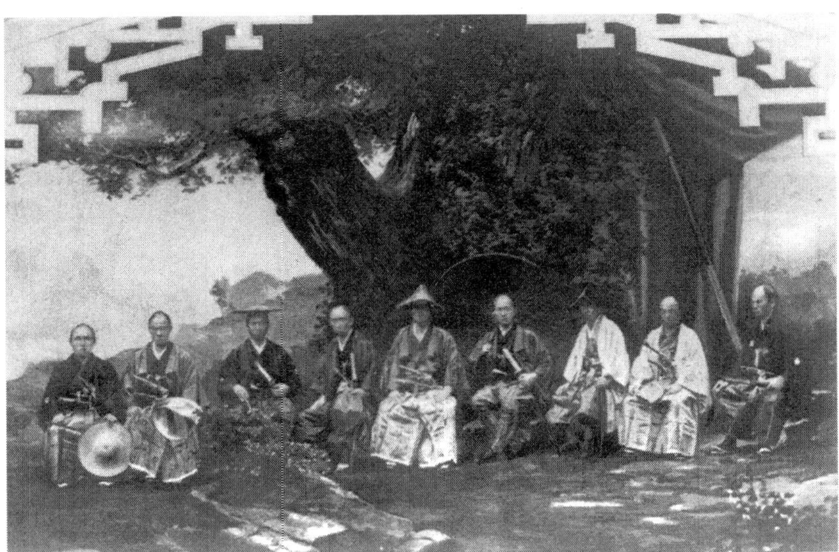

Fig. 1.15. The Japanese Embassy. Photo: Mathew Brady, New York.

Boston—the idea of "Japanese" was provided mainly by enthusiastic articles about these prestigious visitors and their nation's eagerness to Westernize.[140]

Notably, one word appearing repeatedly throughout the 1870s in conjunction with Japan was "progress," used both as a verb and a noun. For example, an 1870 *New York Times* review of a book on Japan by Pumpelly relished the idea of Japan as a potential market for American goods and encouraged respect toward the Japanese as an advancing civilization. Although the reviewer cited Pumpelly's opinion that American notions about both the Chinese and Japanese people must be changed, the *Times* reporter focused exclusively on the Japanese when he wrote:

> we must change altogether the notions we are acting on: that we are dealing with a people on whom we are far more dependent than they on us, and yet are hoping to create among them the principal markets for the products of our industry. . . . Our traditional notions of the Japanese . . . are based on what we have read in childhood, and are as inaccurate as were the sources whence we derived our information.[141]

The article noted that the business sentiment also drove the American vision of the Japanese. It also advised the West against encouraging revolution in Japan or forcing opium on the country's people.[142]

Later that month, a second article, entitled "Modern Improvements in Japan," praised the Japanese for their rapid advancement in such a short time.[143] Similar accolades such as "Japan: Extraordinary Advances Toward Civilization," "Progress in Japan," continued throughout the decade (fig. 1.16).

Japanese art certainly profited by its association with the upper class. Indeed, the rapid transformation from its undifferentiated grouping with Chinese art to its higher status occurred at the same time as the arrival of these distinguished guests. American critics went to great lengths to assign favorable attributes to Japanese objects, even attempting a positive spin on objects whose aesthetic merits remained elusive—leading to some preposterous claims. When confronted with "grotesque" Japanese wooden masks, an American enthusiast defended them, saying that they "represent the Japanese idea of prehistoric men. . . . Some ideas of evolution—of Darwinism, so to speak—have always existed in the Japanese mind, and these masks practically illustrate them."[144]

While the popular press repeatedly declared the Japanese to be "intelligent," "refined," and "clean," it frequently derided Chinese immigrants as "plodding, and viewless" and as "benighted heathens."[145] Japan was aggrandized both on its associations with progressive attitudes and as a foil, a counterbalance to American's increasingly negative view of China. But this

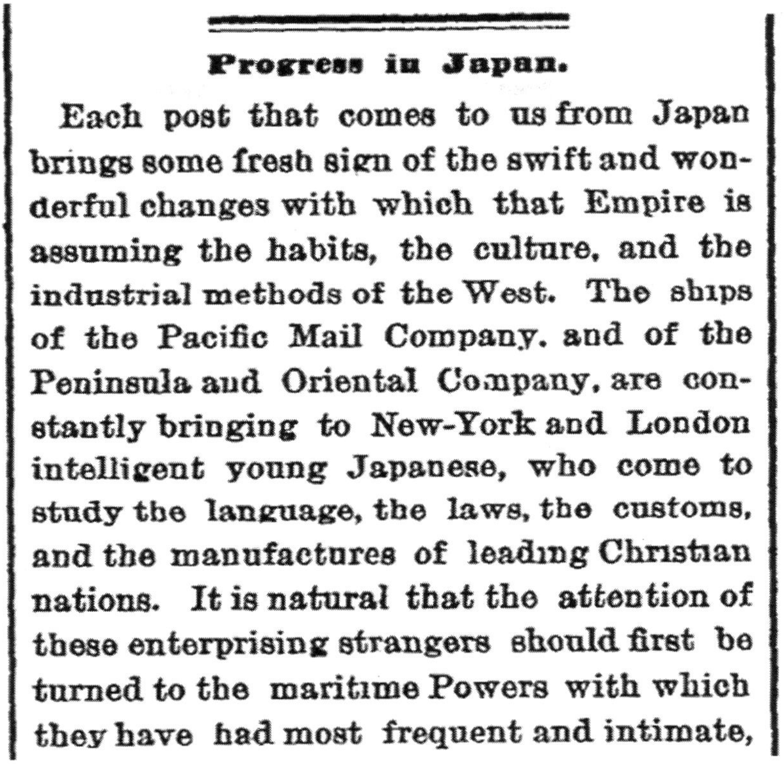

> ## Progress in Japan.
>
> Each post that comes to us from Japan brings some fresh sign of the swift and wonderful changes with which that Empire is assuming the habits, the culture, and the industrial methods of the West. The ships of the Pacific Mail Company, and of the Peninsula and Oriental Company, are constantly bringing to New-York and London intelligent young Japanese, who come to study the language, the laws, the customs, and the manufactures of leading Christian nations. It is natural that the attention of these enterprising strangers should first be turned to the maritime Powers with which they have had most frequent and intimate,

Fig. 1.16. "Progress in Japan," *New York Times*, February 23, 1873.

associative influence has passed unnoticed; Japanese art was hyperbolized as if on artistic merits alone.

Conversely, America's relationship with Chinese people had few of the delights surrounding the Japanese encounter. China continued to rebuff America's commercial advances while Japan, unlike China, was making itself available. And by the Centennial Chinese immigration and naturalization had become a subject of anxiety for Americans.

Over the 1870s, the anti-Chinese violence, both physical and legal, previously seen primarily in California and a few other western states, proliferated and moved eastward. This animosity becomes quite striking when placed in conjunction with the statistics: Chinese immigrants in California accounted for 10 percent of the state's population in 1880, but in the United States as a whole Chinese inhabitants reached only 105,000, around .002

percent of the entire population.[146] The census of 1870 showed only 200 Chinese people living in New York.[147] Nevertheless, as the western states began to wield influence on the outcome of federal elections, their constituency acquired prominence and authority and anti-Chinese attitudes spread to the eastern states.

In June 1870 the first Chinese immigrants brought to the east coast specifically as a laborer group arrived in North Adams, Massachusetts, employed by shoe manufacturer, Calvin T. Sampson. Seventy-five Chinese men and boys journeyed from the West Coast to replace the striking members of a labor organization, the Knights of St. Crispin. The strike was not widely supported, and though the Chinese occasioned some antagonism, they caused even more amazement and received copious press coverage as novelties. "Whoever goes to . . . North Adams," declared the editor of *Harper's Magazine*, "wishes to see the celestial shoemakers"[148] (figs. 1.17 and 1.18). Two other eastern employers quickly followed suit: in 1870, sixty-eight Chinese men were hired to work in a steam laundry near Belleville, New Jersey, and in 1872, 165 were employed in a cutlery factory in Beaver Falls, Pennsylvania.[149] But even this limited relocation provided an impetus for racism and the anti-Chinese faction in the eastern states received its first direct targets. Throughout the 1870s, newspapers reported conflicting attitudes toward the East Coast Chinese, printing articles about rallies against the Chinese shoemakers as well as articles and letters supporting the Chinese declaring the experiment of hiring the Chinese as shoemakers to be "quite successful."[150]

But the specter of a Chinese invasion conjured up by anti-Chinese factions had greater impact than did the actual facts or statistics. Responding

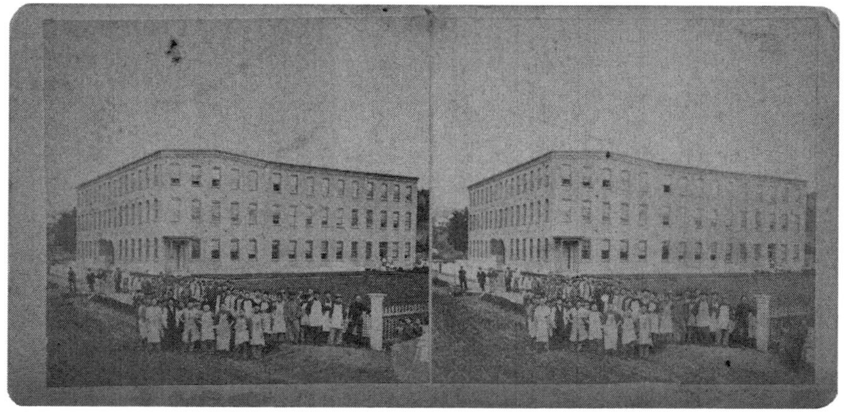

Fig. 1.17. Chinese Shoemakers, North Adams Massachusetts, stereoview, c. 1870.

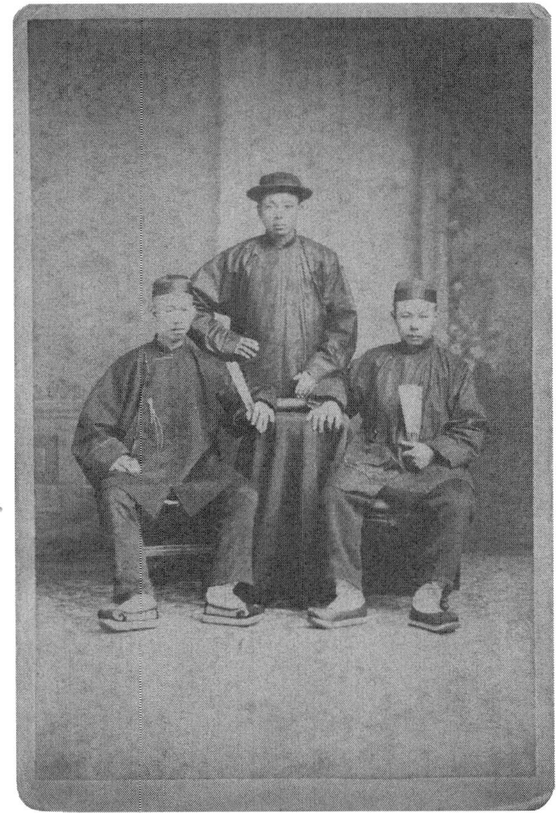

Fig. 1.18. Three Chinese Shoemakers, North Adams Massachusetts, carte de visite, c. 1870.

to the clamor from angry labor groups, the New York legislature discussed banning Chinese laborers from the state. And rapidly reactionary, two parties in Massachusetts, the Democratic and Labor Reform parties, passed anti-Chinese resolutions by the mid-1870s.[151]

In response, the Chinese also organized, predominantly through their existing association called the Six Companies, which petitioned for tolerance in San Francisco: "We hoped you would by knowing us, learn to like us, and be willing to protect us from some evils we now suffer."[152] But a newspaper retorted: "[the Chinese man] is a slave, reduced to the lowest forms of beggarly economy, and is no fit competitor for an American freeman. . . . his sister is a prostitute from instinct, religion, education, and interest, and degrading to all around her . . . . they defy the law."[153] In 1875, legal constraints against the Chinese, initially localized in the western states, also moved eastward, becoming national laws. The Page Law, sponsored by California Congressman Horace F. Page, was the first law to nationalize oppression, restricting Chinese immigration and essentially abolishing any possible immigration of Chinese women.[154]

The increasingly threatening political climate throughout the next decade, in which Chinese men became demonized as deviants, Chinese women as prostitutes, and New York's Chinese community as an exotic world of vice and depravity, will be discussed fully in chapter 3. By the Centennial, the racism expressed in the western states had affected the East Coast, precipitating increased agitation against the Chinese there as well.

Objects are not valued in their own right; that value is a social relationship between things and states of affairs. America's response to Chinese material culture was joined to its social and political response to China. In her discussion of American objects styled on Asian ware, Denker's remark regarding the low status of Chinese workers in America is illuminating. Citing mistaken attributions in which American nineteenth-century objects valued as "Japanese-style," have recently been authoritatively confirmed to be based on Chinese models, her analysis recognizes a political component to that error:

> "Anglo-Japanese" was a favorite expression of designers, and Japanese rooms began to appear in some fashionable houses. It was often a misnomer: the craze for things Japanese and *the menial position of Chinese workers in Western society at that time led writers in this field to ignore the influence of the Chinese.* Today's observers, taking the original identifications on trust, often fail to correctly identify pieces that have decidedly Chinese inspiration. Take, for example, the wardrobes made by Herter Brothers about 1880. The wonderfully innovative design for a well-known form was decorated with exquisite inlay. Often pronounced to be Japanese in inspiration, the shape is, in fact, taken from Ming furniture; the decoration can be attributed only generally to "the Orient" ([emphasis added).][155]

Her observation concerning the menial position of Chinese people in the United States and its effect on the perception of Chinese goods illustrates that an object serves as an embodiment for housing associated ideas, thoughts, and impressions. American ideas of China and Chinese were located within the objects, not just in the surrounding context, and, although not perceived identically, nevertheless response to one shaped response to the other.

Interestingly—perhaps inadvertently—Cohen arrived at a similar correlation. Although his premise asserted that art was valued on its physical qualities, and that valuation led to admiration of the society that created the art, in one paragraph he toyed with the opposite insight. Remarking that Americans perceived Japanese people as more advanced than Chinese prior to looking at their art, Cohen wrote:

> Americans also had a sense of the Japanese as a people with not only a glorious past, but a promising future. Unlike the Chinese, who seemed unresponsive to the ideas of the West, who seemed satisfied to bask in the glories of their history, the Japanese seemed eager to learn, eager for progress. As the Japanese government might have hoped, the art it displayed in Philadelphia contributed to the growing vision of the Japanese leading East Asia toward Westernization.[156]

In this statement Cohen suggests that the positive impression Americans *already* had about the Japanese would be reinforced by the artwork.

4. Politics Become Aesthetic Criteria

Looked at afresh, the Centennial catalogs now demonstrate an unequivocal juxtaposition of objects and attitude, lacing aesthetic with political judgments. A glance at the descriptions of peoples and nations reveals the extent to which Centennial catalogs depended on stereotype. For example, in describing various ethnic groups in the main exhibition hall, McCabe noted that the "stalwart Indian stalks through the hall, as emotionless as a stone."[157] Similarly, McCabe's characterization of Chinese people did not stem from his observations but relied almost entirely on conventionalized images. Many came directly from Bret Harte's still popular poem from 1871, including the epitaph "Heathen Chinee," and a description of Chinese habits as "ways that are dark and tricks that are vain."[158] McCabe maintained the facetious tone of the poem in caricaturing Chinese physical traits, referring to "almond-eyes and long pig-tails, his comical dress." This same negativity shaded descriptions of the Chinese objects. Although he commended objects in the Chinese exhibition, McCabe undercut his own favorable judgments with slurs against the same items' makers; after praising Chinese bedsteads as "very Handsome," McCabe derisively remarked that this signified "that John Chinaman has an eye to solid comfort in the midst of all his love of gaudy colors and gingerbread ornaments." Describing Chinese household objects, his greatest compliment was to equate them with similar objects made by the Japanese! "They are as handsome and as well executed as anything of the kind in the Japanese section, which is saying a great deal."

By contrast, in what appears to be direct observation, McCabe characterized a Japanese man as "small but alert," and limited his remarks on physique to an indeterminate comment about Japanese clothing: "his loose dress caught up as if it were an obstacle rather than a convenience."[159] The catalog does not comment further.

In one paragraph, McCabe's observations at first seem to support the idea that art can alter political views. For McCabe, Japanese things validated the modern perception that Japan was not barbaric:

> The visitor who made even a hasty inspection of the display . . . could but amend his ideas of Japan. We have been accustomed to regard that country as uncivilized, or half-civilized at best, but we found here abundant evidences that it outshines the most cultivated nations of Europe in arts which are their pride and glory, and which are regarded as among the proudest tokens of their high civilization.[160]

However, this opinion resulted not from a look at Japanese art but from a display of the Japanese educational system, exhibiting student compositions written in English, French, and German, as well as in Japanese. McCabe complimented the Japanese on their progress in introducing the "learning and civilization of Europe."[161]

Often illustrations also displayed a partiality: deprecating the Chinese, while portraying the Japanese more respectfully. A drawing in *Norton's Centennial Catalogue* documenting the construction of a Japanese house depicts the Japanese craftsmen industriously engaged in building, their facial features represented without exaggeration or caricature[162] (fig. 1.19). Contrastingly, in the illustration *Celestial Exhibitors Explaining Their Wares*, found in the same catalog, Chinese men appear servile. They are not shown busily working, but bowing their heads: there is no eye contact with the Caucasian gentleman and lady who appraise the ceramic vessel[163] (fig. 1.20). In an illustration of the Chinese department of the Mineral Annex, the living Chinese man is scrutinized by a young white gentleman, as much an objects as the Chinese wares and figurines (fig. 1.21). Even in the depiction *Interior of the Japanese Workmen's Temporary Quarters*, which is obviously modeled after familiar images of Chinese opium dens, the Japanese are not indolent. They are shown as alert and engaged in intellectual pursuits, reading and discussing various Japanese books, even if they are also smoking opium[164] (fig. 1.22).

The subtle influence of prejudice against Chinese people in American judgments about Chinese art becomes apparent when we return to the catalogs' discussions of objects. At times the preference is conveyed in the tone more than in the words themselves. For example, compare Norton's descriptions of similar objects made by the Chinese and by the Japanese. Norton adopts an even, dry expression as he exhaustively enumerates all the Chinese collectors and lists the multiple categories of Chinese ware: native iron, chemicals, and then teacups and porcelain. His laconic comments

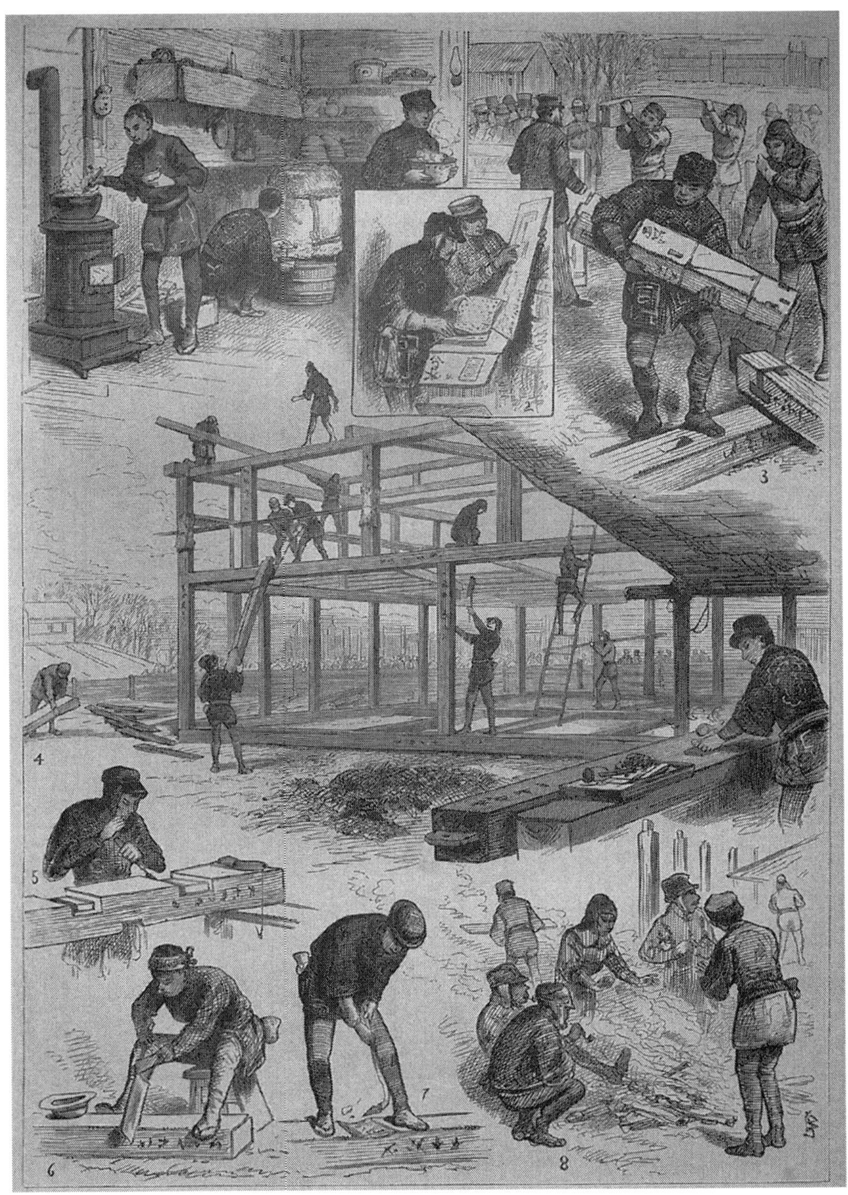

Fig. 1.19. Japanese workmen constructing the Japanese pavilion at the Centennial, illustrated in *The Illustrated Historical Register of the United States Centennial Exposition 1876*.

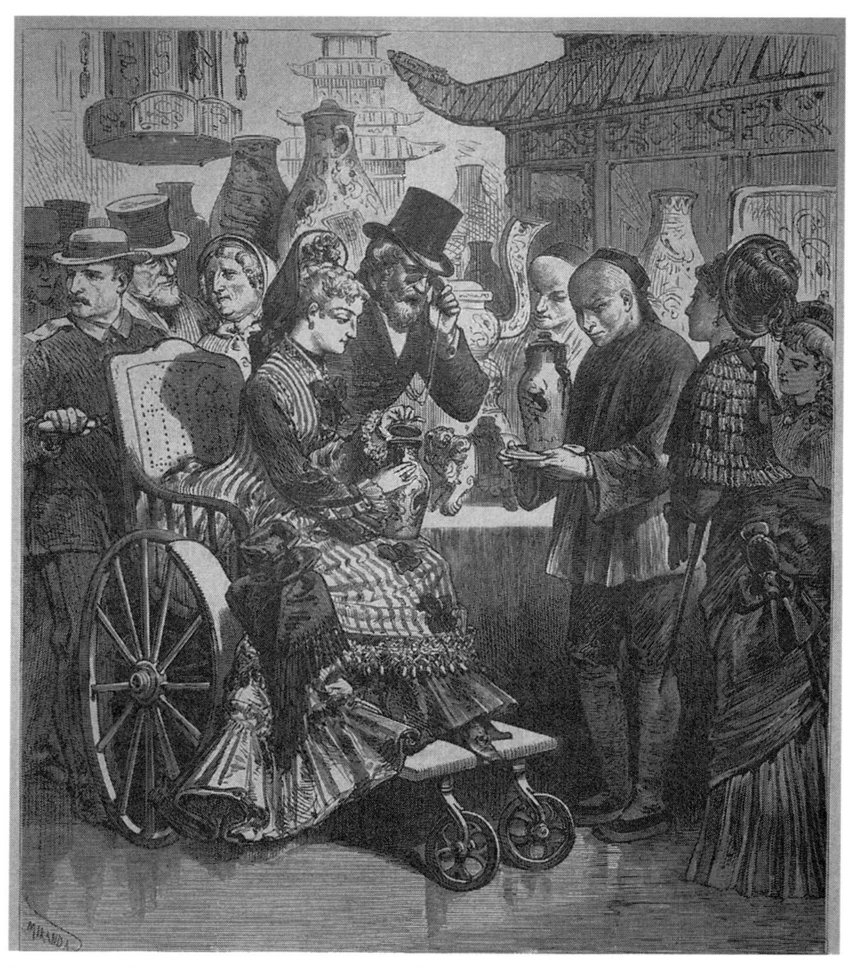

Fig. 1.20. *"Celestial Exhibitors Explaining Their Wares," The Illustrated Historical Register of the United States Centennial Exposition 1876.*

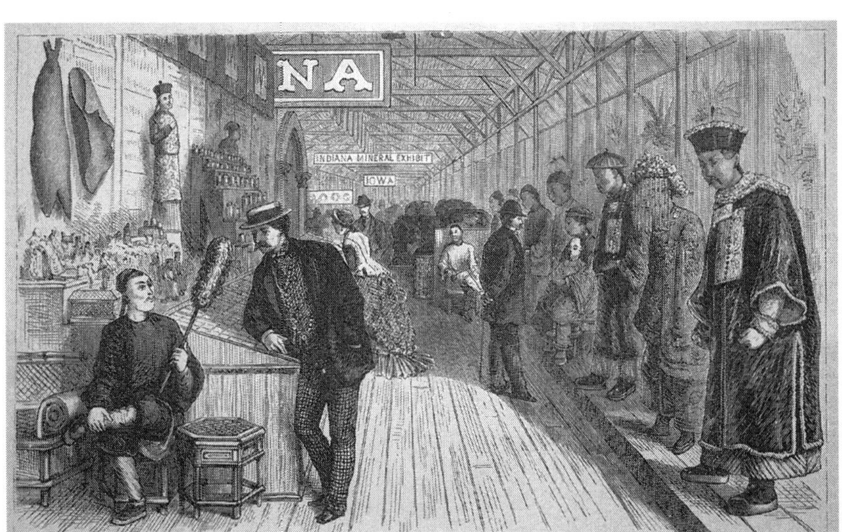

Fig. 1.21. The Mineral Annex, Chinese Mannequins, *The Illustrated Historical Register of the United States Centennial Exposition 1876*.

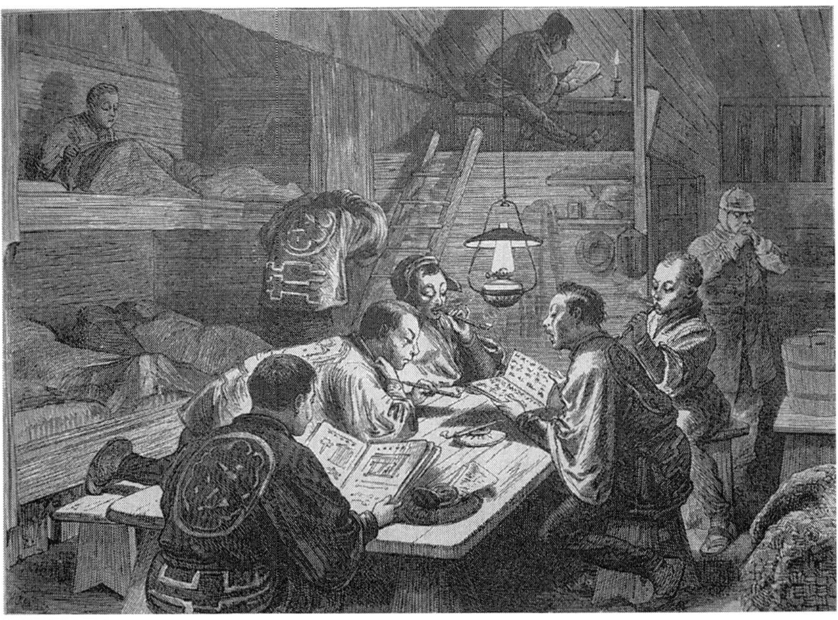

Fig. 1.22. Interior of the Japanese Workmen's Temporary Quarters, *The Illustrated Historical Register of the United States Centennial Exposition 1876*.

continue in his description of the objects, exemplified in his discussion of Chinese screens:

> The collection of screens is very interesting, some of them being inlaid with porcelain tablets, others having carved black-wood frames; many of these screens being made of silk. The furniture also includes bamboo sleeping-chairs and armchairs of different shapes, armchairs in black-wood, enamel and marble; small tables or tea-poys [sic] in camphor-wood, red-wood and black-wood; lacquer writing-desks and couch for opium-smoking, inlaid with pearl; silk panel screens painted by hand with black-wood frames; one of these representing the growth and use of silk. Some of the screens present historical scenes or Chinese romances, while others have birds or flowers painted upon them.[165]

Norton continues in this vein, primarily a list of the materials used, interrupted only by an occasional bit of praise for a particular Chinese thing. Turning then to the Japanese exhibition, he summarizes the Japanese government, providing a brief synopsis of its history and then, as for the Chinese exhibit, in his detached tone he begins to enumerate the materials and variety of the objects. But in contrast with his monotone on Chinese objects, in speaking of Japanese objects his attitude changes: becoming animated, he uses comparatives and even superlatives. Compare Norton's review of Japanese screens:

> The Japanese screens are among the most wonderful articles in their exhibition. In these the most astonishing effects are produced by combining embroidery with painting, the faces of the photographs being painted on a silk background, and the costumes, etc., brought out into relief. . . . The best decorative art in Japan appears to be devoted to the screens. . . . In embroidery, the Japanese equal the world. . . . The delineation of small birds is exquisite.[166]

Out of context, his aesthetic excitement could appear to be predicated completely on the objects' appearance. However, reading further, a subtext emerges in his abrupt departure from descriptions to commentary, expounding on the moral differences between Japanese and Chinese people. In the middle of praising the technical deftness in Japanese lacquered work ("Here are cups and saucers of wood as light as cork and protected by varnish to a degree that they will withstand the hottest water"), Norton interjected a polemic against Chinese and additionally against the West for its "taste for the nude." Pleased in his (erroneous) perception that the Japanese were more chaste, he observed:

It has been remarked, and it is only fair to mention the fact, that in all the designs exhibited in Japanese art work, there appears no prevalence of the taste for the nude which obtains in Western, and as is assumed, more civilized nations. Whether this be a general fact in the history of all Japanese art is not stated. If it be, it is certainly creditable both to the morals and honor of this remarkable people, and especially when we take into consideration the immediate contiguity of China, where the reverse is the case.[167]

The Centennial documentation suggests a departure from the idea prevailing even today that the art of a people can be received and appreciated objectively, with no other influence but the object itself: that art "speaks for itself." Instead it appears that, not infrequently, critics' interpretations of art support their ideologies, and often incorporate ideology into aesthetic interpretation. These critiques demonstrate that antipathy toward the Chinese, coupled with approval of Japan, was an unseen quality, a factor in interpreting the respective objects, suggesting why Americans categorically, and often zealously, advocated "Japanese" objects, while at the same time seldom being capable of distinguishing between Japanese and Chinese goods.

Writing in 1875, Jarves succinctly formulated the position that an art object as a thing in itself reveals the society from which it derives: "An inquiry into the art of any people is not unlike feeling the pulse of a man to ascertain the state of his blood. . . . what it reveals of the character of the race that creates it, and its psychological meaning as a distinctive idiom of the universal language of our species."[168]

Such arguments presuppose that art is a kind of litmus test of the people who make it, and that it is decoded accurately by any other people: that it arrives to another nation pre-understood. In this scenario, those receiving the art, then, are not a consideration in the equation of art and meaning. But, we have seen that, on the contrary, art reveals as much about those who receive it—what associations they project onto the art, and how they interpret all these factors—as about its makers. Even the elementary classification of an object as a work of art within a culture is a product of those receiving it, and not of its prior status in its place of origin. Craig Clunas articulated this point in his essay "China in Britain":

Indeed 'art' is not a category in the sense of a pre-existent container filled with different contents as history progresses. Rather it is a way of categorizing, a manner of making knowledge. . . . It remains a site of conflicting interpretations, fissured on class and gender lines, among others, and the right to define something as 'art' is typically seen as an important attribute of those dominant in society at a given moment.[169]

The American reception of Chinese and Japanese art and people, perceptions and even expectations projected onto a people spilled over into aesthetic evaluation and influenced judgments on art. Americans' contrasting attitudes toward the Japanese and the Chinese people contributed, albeit unwittingly, to its resounding preference for Japanese things and to the commensurate silence about Chinese objects. Objects take on associations, they are a metonym for their culture. Paul Crowther hints at this when he discusses the limits of visual knowledge:

> Knowledge—visual or otherwise—logically presupposes reference to factors which are not given in immediate experience. We can only recognize things insofar as they are embedded in a context of expectations concerning how things of that kind behave and are amenable to perception and bodily manipulation. The given is intelligible only in the context of a field of possibilities and relations that are not themselves immediately given.[170]

He goes on to explain:

> Given any three-dimensional item or state of affairs in our visual field, what enables its recognition in the fullest sense is a contextual space of expectations based on its unnoticed or hidden aspects, or its possible transformations or relocations, and indeed its relation to things not given immediately in the visual field, including those arising from association on the viewer's part.[171]

For the viewer, the value of an object is determined by its dialogue between its physical attributes and the ideas, thoughts, and perceptions that the viewer brings to it. Although items from Japan and China looked indistinguishable to many Americans, the horizon of expectations emanating from the Chinese objects linked the American consumer to China, to Chinese people, and to the uneasy emotions surrounding Chinese immigration. Japanese objects had a horizon of expectations that opened onto a charming country, a delightful people, bringing the American consumer into that world. Given the political relationship between America and China and the tensions toward Chinese immigration, it should not be a surprise that for almost two decades surrounding the Chinese Exclusion Act, Chinese art, or rather reference to Chinese art, dropped out of existence.

Objects clarify fundamental cultural perceptions and thoughts: they are the sites for manifesting what would otherwise be more abstract imaginings. If, as Michael Sprinker states, ideology is a part of the material of an object's construction, this chapter has also shown that ideology is also a component of the object's reception.[172] Chinese objects absorbed the ideology of the American consumers. Their initial popularity presented claims about Chinese culture that conflicted with the prevailing American political thought. Chinese objects were not as much critically rejected from the emerging American definition of art and art discourse as they were disregarded: conveniently renamed "Japanese." In a cultural counterpart to the political exclusion, Chinese objects have been denied their part in an American art historical discourse.

TWO

THE POWER OF INACTION

Chinese Objects and the Transformation of the American Definition of Art

If politics and aesthetics, virtue and beauty [in previous centuries] are deeply at one, it is because pleasurable conduct is the true index of successful hegemony. . . . The maladroit or aesthetically disproportioned thus signals in its modest way a certain crisis of political power.

—Terry Eagleton, The Ideology of the Aesthetic

To Americans in the Victorian era, fine art conveyed—or rather, they hoped it would convey—a seemingly transparent message of morality. The English art critic John Ruskin advocated this thesis authoritative declarations to that point, stating: "the greatest thing a human soul ever does in this world is to see something and tell what it saw in a plain way."[1] And the Victorian values of honesty, simplicity, and economy, which they applied to art, further fused morals and aesthetics. Even today, we often discount the difficulty in separating aesthetic categories from value judgments: although we assert a definitive split between them, the names themselves—"fine arts," "romanticism," "modernism,"—carry an imbedded appraisal.[2]

In the middle of the century, alongside the comforting Ruskin paradigm positing art as a moral enterprise, a representation of moral harmony between nature and culture, an opposing paradigm of Aestheticism arose, asserting that art inhabited a distinct domain, separate from moral or natural systems. In the last quarter of the 1800s, for a brief period, these two opposing paradigms of art vied for supremacy, an artistic battle that mirrored strife arising between classes as the money and political power was being

73

wrested from traditional elites. As Terry Eagleton points out in the above quote, doubts concerning the easy equation between virtue and art, as well as politics and aesthetics suggest a change or unease in the upper echelon of cultural power.

Chinese art was understood differently in these two competing visual systems. Within the museums, Chinese objects reinforced the new aesthetic, codified as "art for art's sake," and assisted in the transformation from one system to the other. This chapter discusses Chinese objects as the vehicle allowing us to encounter this period diachronically rather than synchronically, analyzing a system in flux.

This chapter explores the effect that the inclusion of Chinese objects in art museum had on the American understanding of art. The initial Chinese collections seen by Americans—at world's fairs, at import stores, and interspersed in loan collections in the newly established art museums—were eclectic mixtures of traditional Chinese art, cultural artifacts, and fantastic polyglot objects created in China specifically for Western taste. None of these objects fit comfortably into the predominant Ruskinian paradigm, and their initial role in museums was less as examples of fine art; rather, when they were mentioned in the early museum bulletins, they were used as examples for industrial education or described as bric-a-brac. But their presence in art museums, problematic and unresolved in the Ruskinian rubric, became comprehensible through the new aesthetic, and thereby helped to validate that more formal system of art understanding. Circumventing the intentions of the collectors and curators, Chinese objects gradually surmounted their uncomfortable lack of coincidence with the Ruskinian alliance of art and morality, and reconfigured within the new aesthetic paradigm, gained the status of fine high art. At the end of the century, a new collection of rare Chinese objects, not newly made for the export market but having cultural integrity, centuries old, was exhibited in the art museums and valued as exemplary artistic masterworks.

The chapter gives equal focus to the two primary protagonists in this history of the changing significance of Chinese things for American art— Chinese objects themselves and the museum founders. Section I centers on the Chinese objects in the art museums and will investigate (1) morality of objects; (2) the educational premise of museums; and (3) plaster casts—the original and the copy. Section II, primarily on the founders, will explore (1) class—museum founders and the public; (2) businessmen as art leaders; and (3) the merchandizing of art—alternatives of denial and exploitation. The ideas explored in the two sections will converge in the final section, examining the new art paradigm, in its relocations of morality and commodity. By investing the role ascribed to Chinese objects within each topic, the shift in the American ideas about art become clear.

SECTION I. CHINESE OBJECTS AND THE AESTHETICS OF MUSEUMS

1. Aesthetic Morality and Nationalism, America's Ruskin-Based Art

In the middle of the nineteenth century, Americans esteemed artworks and architectural decorations that incorporated easily understood symbols embodying idealized public virtues and other highly principled messages. Ruskin's books were multiply editioned in America, championing the moral significance of art, and advocating that it was "in some sort the embodiment of the Polity, Life, History, and Religious Faith of nations."[3] Ruskin's popularity was enhanced by the ease with which anyone could understand art's meaning as defined by his system: no specialized art knowledge was necessary. Instead, by the mid-nineteenth century, morality provided a definition of aesthetics and also linked aesthetics with popular concerns, specifically with nationalism. Linda Dowling captured the power of Ruskin's "quenchless eloquence" in her description of his ability to make "the aesthetic dimension of society and the social dimension of art cohere as never before into a single, vitally important sphere."[4] Historians have identified Americans' search for cultural autonomy (and a concomitant search for a uniquely American language of visual representation) as one of the primary concerns in U.S. culture in the last third of the century. Following Ruskin, most Americans interested in fine art believed unequivocally that a nation's aesthetic capability indicated its (political) morality.[5] Powerful men in the American art world—Harvard's first professor of Art History, Charles Eliot Norton, along with American art theorist James Jackson Jarves and art critic Russell Sturgis—were personal friends of Ruskin, and disseminated his aesthetic system throughout America.[6] Ruskin's particular eliding of aesthetics and nationalism was emulated, even surpassed, by Jarves and Norton, whose writings endorsed the moral reciprocity between America's nature, values, and its art. Jarves contended that "the rules of Art are absolute. They are moral laws implanted by God in the heart of Nature, and are independent of human frailty or invention."[7]

Taking this triad to a more political plane, Norton defined beauty as "the ultimate expression and warrant of goodness," and stated that the "highest achievements in the arts" were expressions of a nation's "faith," and its "loftiness of spirit"; indeed, a nation's art was the "embodiment of its ideals."[8] He outlined the importance of artistic morality to American nationalism even more explicitly in a letter to the president of Harvard:

> In a complete scheme of University Studies the history of the Fine Arts in relation to social progress, to general culture, and to literature,

should find a place, not only because architecture, sculpture, and painting have been, next to literature, the most important modes of expression of the sentiments, beliefs, and opinions of men, but also because they afford evidence, often in a more striking and direct manner than literature itself, of the moral temper and intellectual culture of the various races by whom they have been practiced, and thus become the most effective aids to the proper understanding of history.[9]

However, this belief in art as a barometer of a nation's moral temper and intellectual capacity brought with it unsettling complications. Most art in the United States derived from Europe: made either by European artists or by American artists born or educated in Europe, and it was judged as closely as possible in accordance with European standards. While some Americans asserted the uniqueness of their own national culture, Henry James, for one, was skeptical of its legitimacy. James stressed that "whereas the English, French, and Germans all found their intellectual and aesthetic ideals in their own countries, only the Americans felt obliged to go abroad for them."[10] While his statement is tongue-in-cheek, nevertheless adaptations of European classical art seemed most compatible with American ideals of art, which have been described as: "conservative, largely European oriented art . . . with tinges of exoticism that delighted in ornamental richness."[11] How could this derivative Europeanism proclaim the ideals of the American republic?

This question of national culture's self-identification presented an awkward problem for America. In Paul Greenhalgh's summation, "Questions of immense complexity had to be faced. At what point did the population, political institutions and culture cease to be European and become American? Was American culture wholly borrowed and if so, did this matter? Should there be new cultural forms to go with the new continent, if so what should they look like?"[12]

At stake, then, for those who refuted a borrowed culture, was finding an unequivocally American style to represent preeminently American virtues. And, while nature was the most apparent American symbol of its distinction (indeed, Asher Durand wrote in the *Crayon* about what he perceived as "transforming the love of nature into a national weapon"), morality was eventually discovered in another, unexpected source: the manufactured object.[13]

Prior to the industrial revolution, the intricacy associated with labor-intensive handwork had a concomitant correlation with a higher valuation. In part through its association to labor, this aesthetic hierarchy became linked to moral virtues. The early industrial age had often produced low-quality machined objects, lacking handwork and of little aesthetic interest, and these were often associated with debased morals. In fact, one of the goals behind Henry Cole's push for the Great Exhibition in London in 1850 was to compare handicraft objects to industrial ones, side by side, to see if Western industry could surpass works made by hand in the East. Through that comparison Cole demonstrated the sorry state of machine products and the inferiority of European ornamentation; according to Siegfried Giedion: "Spectators were shocked by the contrast."[14]

This led to reforms in industrial production as well as in taste, producing revisions in the moral assessment of manufactured goods.[15] With the improved quality of machine fabrication, by the end of the nineteenth century each consumer had to face the question that Giedion formulated as: "Did not the vases, statuettes, and rugs resemble handmade objects? Were they not as miraculous in their own way as the railroads then beginning to sweep the breadth of the land?"[16] Described by Leo Marx as the "technological sublime," manufactured objects began to assume moral content.[17]

In *Land of Desire*, William Leach discusses America's rapidly expanding consumerist culture at the turn of the nineteenth century and the subsequent redefinition of morality to accommodate industrial consumption. Leach describes American culture as "urbanized and commercialized, increasingly severed from its religious aims and focusing ever more on personal satisfaction."[18] Studying America's traditional characterization as a land of plenty he distinguishes the older interpretation of "plenty," which encompassed both spirituality and materiality, from its late-nineteenth-century metamorphosis, which magnified the material connotations of this vision.[19]

With the increased availability of objects at the end of the century, the spiritual component of "plenty" became subordinated to the material meaning. Market strategies, in the form of advertising via trade cards and, later, magazine ads, promoted purchased goods as a means to participate in progress, itself a virtue, and argued that morality was available through market commodities. Machined objects were promoted as containers of republican virtue; for instance, the president of Johns Hopkins University commended the products available through machine manufacture for providing comforts and adornments more democratically, luxury previously not known "outside of the palace."[20]

The marketing of manufactured products was successful. By the 1880s handmade items were less frequently recommended in articles on interior decorating, fewer women made accessories for their homes, machines made domestic items from butter to baskets and people more frequently purchased mass-produced objects.[21]

Through associative logic, a kind of telescoping of a domestic object's ever-widening range of influence, this aesthetic morality was seen as leading to political morality. American's were urged to trust that objects properly collected and assembled in the home would create a moral environment. The home surroundings would exert an enduring influence on the inhabitants, and the body politic of these moral individuals would ultimately give rise to a more righteous society. In *Moralism and the Model Home*, Gwendolyn Wright cited an extreme but prototypical example of the ubiquitous correlation of home and morality. She described a work of short fiction detailing a boy's descent into depravity, a sordid tale designed to illustrate the author's thesis: "The single explanation is all-sufficient: he never had a pleasant home."[22]

Turning to our subject of Chinese objects, then, given the prevalent jingoistic nationalism, how could any Asian object become included within this American moral canon of art and objects? Surely, Chinese objects bore the taint of a decadent society: the Chinese people were so effectively demonized across the country that the nation legislated their exclusion in 1882.

Japanese objects, however, were different. We have seen in the previous chapter how, in the surge of excitement and goodwill toward the Japanese after Commodore Perry's "opening" of Japan, Americans idealized Japanese people as virtuous and artistic, albeit naive. The Ruskin paradigm alleging a moral reciprocity between art, nature, and society, exalted the Middle Ages (or rather, the mythology of Gothic cooperative creations) as its ideal. For Ruskin, the Gothic style was the culminating manifestation of a society unified by religious faith in which each worker saw his or her contribution as part of the larger vision and thus worked willingly and creatively. As he wrote, "my endeavor has been to show that good architecture is essentially religious—the production of a faithful and virtuous, not of an infidel and corrupted people."[23] This provided a blueprint, easily transferable to a mythologized Japanese culture: the morality of the people demonstrated in their artisanship and art. Fueled by steady media endorsements, this expanded into a mania for collecting Japanese objects and incorporating Japanese style. We see this in the newspaper coverage of a loan exhibition at the Met in 1873. After stating that "The distinguishing feature of the Metropolitan Museum, among the loan collections, is undoubtedly the objects of Japanese Manufacture." "One cannot but be struck," he asserts, "with the marked resemblance of these carvings to early Saxon and Gothic efforts in which ignorance of the human form lead to the most ludicrous renderings of very sacred subjects. Like the Japanese, however, our early art redeems itself from evil by the thorough, hearty love for natural objects which it reveals."[24]

The tremendous positive response of the American press to Japanese things was meticulously tabulated and documented by Jane Converse Brown. In her dissertation, "The 'Japanese Taste,'" she analyzed 2,882 separate writings printed in America concerning Japanese influence or style between1876 and 1916, discovering 186 publications discussing Japonisme in 1889 alone.[25]

But, sheer numbers do not indicate that Americans understood the cultural integrity of Japanese objects. Americans understood the Japanese aesthetic only as far as it coincided with the prevailing presuppositions of Ruskinian ideology. Convinced of the morality of the Japanese people, Americans found Japanese objects, with their affectionate portrayal of animal and plant life, representative of virtue. The "Japanese" aesthetic, especially as it frequently depicted nature, coincided with the morals advocated for art and objects in the American home, and, as such, Japanese things were widely accepted and frequently recommended.[26] American art criticism overflowed with attributions of sentiments such as "nature's inner divine beauty" to Japanese images of flowers.[27]

Because of the lack of distinction between many Chinese and Japanese objects imported to America, occasionally Chinese things were included in the articles on domestic morality, but the focus was clearly on "Japanese." For example, the 1884 book, *How to Make Home Happy: A Housekeeper's Hand Book*,[28] conflated instructions on good manners with instruction in home furnishing. Its elaborate subtitle reads: "Eminently Useful and Practical Suggestions upon Home Furnishing; Cheerful Decorations; Economy in Necessities; Rules of Polite Deportment; What to Do in Emergencies; Taking Care of Children; General Hints upon Various Subjects; Social Games; Amusements, Entertainments, etc., etc."[29] After a description of Chinese and Japanese rooms, the book rarely refers to Chinese things again. But subsequent chapters, particularly "Portable Internal Decorations," continued the discussion of placing Japanese decorative objects throughout the home.[30]

Similarly, the number of Japanese objects exceeded Chinese ones in the 1883 book *Treasures of Use and Beauty: An Epitome of the Choicest Gems of Wisdom, History, Reference and Recreation*. The book specifically purported to instruct the reader in the creation not merely of an aesthetic but also a moral environment. The "Corps of Special Authors" rhapsodizes that "the grandest and noblest motives that can stir the human heart are those awakened within the pale of domestic life" and that "beautiful art can only be inspired by pure and beautiful thoughts."[31] Discussions about Japanese items crop up throughout the chapters. Small Japanese fans seem to have been especially versatile: recommended for the mantelpiece along with odd china and statuettes; tacked on the walls to create a frieze; placed in colorful arrangements with Japanese scrolls and Japanese vases (which, the authors state, cost twenty-five cents). Judging gas fixtures as unsightly, the authors find that "again Japan came to the rescue," and they suggest purchasing a rose-colored umbrella to place over the pipe.[32] Chinese objects, although comparable in cost, availability, and, especially, appearance, receive no mention.

In popular culture, then, although China and Japan exported similar objects and occasionally Chinese things were encompassed within the

"Japanese" aesthetic, the significance of Chinese things generally remained distinct. To Americans, Japanese objects characterized a people as delightful as they were virtuous. The Chinese objects, contrastingly, could not as easily occupy a moral paradigm, because that would have encouraged respect for China and the Chinese people: an idea which, during these years leading to and legitimating Chinese Exclusion, many Americans were not willing to entertain.

2. The Educational Premise: Inaugurating Two American Art Museums

But not all Chinese objects were thought to be Japanese.

Two of the earliest American museums founded exclusively to exhibit art were the Museum of Fine Arts, Boston (the MFAB) and the Metropolitan Museum of Art (the Met), both incorporated in 1870. From the start, along with a scattering of oil paintings, an extensive collection of plaster reproductions of European statues, and Greek and Egyptian artifacts, these two museums also exhibited Chinese and Japanese objects. A list of Asian items in American museum collections compiled in 1929 showed the Museum of Fine Arts, Boston owned 88,074 Japanese and 4,393 Chinese items, most collected before the turn of the century. While the amount of Chinese objects can seem dwarfed by the enormous number of Japanese things, nevertheless the quantity of Chinese items was considerable. When compared with the more equal number of objects at the Metropolitan Museum of Art—5,500 Chinese and 6,200 Japanese—the magnitude of Chinese objects in both collections appears more clearly.[33]

Of significance is that over the last decades of the century, the Chinese collections in art museums continually increased. During those twenty years, why did the appreciation of Chinese art shift from relative neglect—therefore *Japonisme*—to interest, and ultimately to adulation? This requires an inquiry into the founders of art museums: an examination of their expectations of art, their knowledge of it, and their methods of promotion. Selecting art for museums involves defining, even implicitly, what constitutes an art object. Paul Crowther discusses how, to use his term, *artifactual imaging* has a profound effect on those who view objects: an object displayed in the context of established art begins to acquire an intrinsic art significance. This "juxtapositioning" extends our horizon of possibilities as to what constitutes an art object and changes our expectations of art.[34]

Despite their simultaneous presence in American museums, Japanese and Chinese arts have had distinct roles in American art culture.[35]Comprehending the significance of the Chinese collections in art museums requires examining why Chinese objects appealed to these guardians of culture on museum boards. The double status of Chinese objects as art and commodity in Victorian America illuminates changing theories of merchandise and aesthetics and clarifies transformations in the museums' valuation of Chinese things.

Both the MFAB and the Met deliberately included Chinese things in their earliest art collections and loan exhibitions. To some extent this resulted from practical considerations. The origins of American art museums differed greatly from that of their counterparts in Europe. European museums generally were reclaimed palaces; the transfer of the property from individual to state ownership preserved both the building and its treasures intact. With their aesthetic based on European art, American museums were at a disadvantage because a similar glut of ancestral treasures—and the place to put them—simply did not exist. And with little funding and many practical needs in their first decades the newly built American museums could afford very few original works of European art.

That is not to say that the American museums lacked objects. Before the creation of art museums, the overflow of artifacts, seldom regarded as great works of art, in both public and private collections had begun to present a problem; actually, there were too many objects and no place to exhibit or even to house them. Around Boston, for example, Harvard had a surplus of prints that needed careful storage and possible exhibition space; MIT had casts of architectural remnants. In fact, an excess of armor provided the impetus for the seed money that galvanized the building of the MFAB; Timothy Bigelow Lawrence had left his collection of antique armor to the Boston Athenaeum, which had no room for it, prompting his widow to donate $25,000 to create a place to house the collection.[36] But these collections did not amount to great art, indications of a wide cosmopolitan worldview.

As late as 1895, the museum held only about four hundred paintings and owned fewer than one hundred of these outright.[38] The majority of original objects in the MFAB's collection during its first decade came from nations across Asia and the Middle East. At the time of its first exhibition in 1872, 349 of the total 539 items given or loaned to the MFAB had been in the collection of antiquities, both Asian and European, owned by General Emanuele Pietro Paolo Maria Luigi Palma, Conte di Cesnola (1832–1904).[38] John Lowell donated his collection of Egyptian artifacts, and Denman Ross a collection of Japanese pottery.

On the close of the 1876 Centennial Exposition, the MFAB spent two thousand dollars purchasing exhibitions of bronzes, leathers, pottery, textile, and tiles from exhibitions from several Asian nations.[39] (Because of their prohibitive cost, items from the European exhibitions were not even considered.) And by 1879, the Metropolitan Museum had greatly increased its collection through its purchase of Samuel P. Avery's Chinese and Japanese porcelain collection (figs. 2.1 and 2.2).

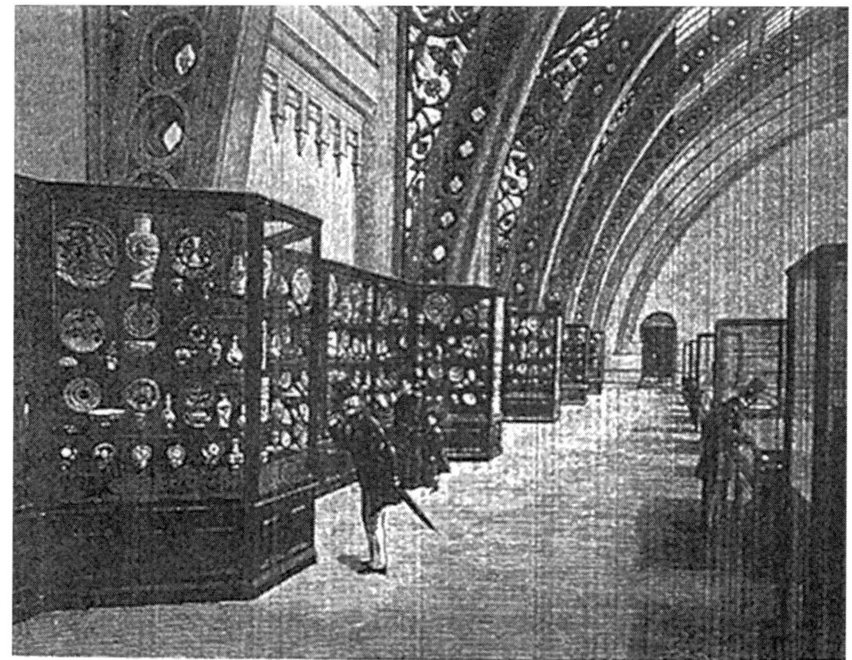

Fig. 2.1. Avery Collection of Chinese Porcelains, Metropolitan Museum, *Harper's New Monthly Magazine*, May 1880.

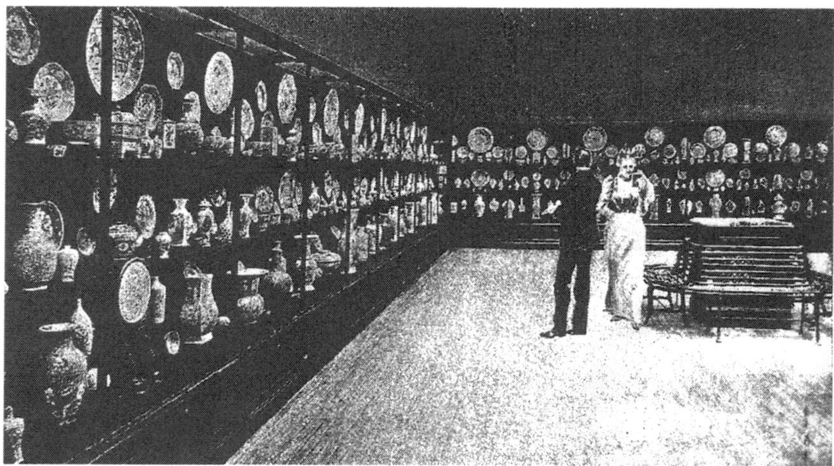

Fig. 2.2. Avery Collection of Chinese Porcelains, Metropolitan Museum, *Harper's Weekly Magazine*, November 10, 1894.

Due in part to relatively low costs, in part to gifts, and in part to the lack of other items to fill the available space, Chinese ware became a substantial collection in the fledgling American art museums. Before going any further in this investigation, it would be helpful to ask: What were these objects? And how were they viewed?

Very few of the original Chinese objects collected by the MFAB are still in its holdings. But photographs from 1903 give some idea of what was first purchased as Chinese art (fig. 2.3). In the image, in the typical "more is more" aesthetic standard of the time, numerous vitrines are packed with object on object. Most were created during the Qing, and only a few from the earlier part of that dynasty: in other words, most were newly made and probably for export. Rather than the formal restraint and calmness found in traditional Chinese pieces, these are highly decorated, more about surface than form, designed for their appeal to the Western trade. Japanese objects are mixed in with Chinese objects, and some vitrines collage in works from other Eastern nations. You can also see a European great master style work

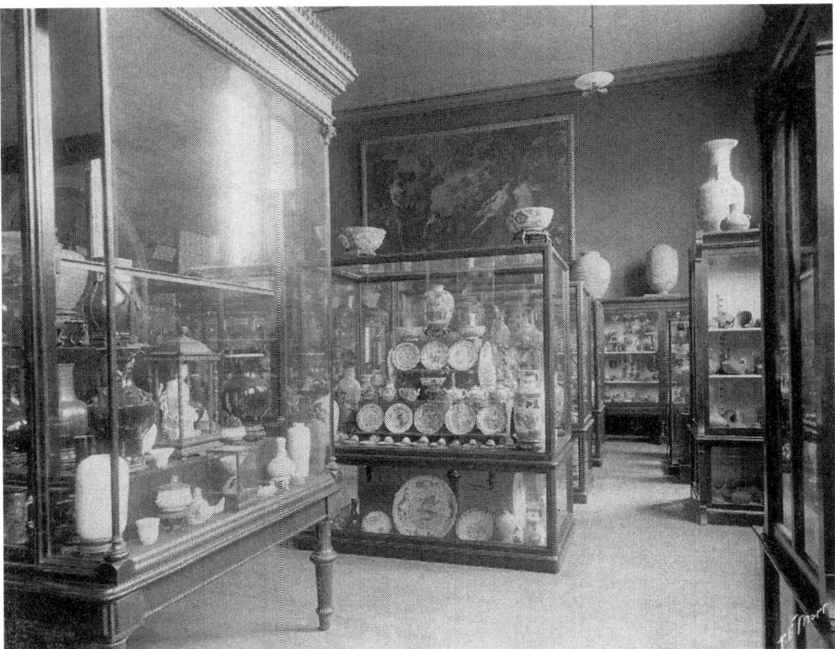

Fig. 2.3. Vitrines filled with Asian objects, Museum of Fine Arts, Boston. Note the European painting on the back wall. Photograph © 2011 Museum of Fine Arts, Boston.

on the gallery wall. Chinese art expert Jeffrey Moy examined several of these 1904 photographs and, with all the objects they depict, he singled out very few that could achieve today's museum standards. Even the Chinese-made stands are not of high quality. Only the case that holds hard mineral objects (found to the case labeled "Wm. Sturgis Bigelow") houses several unadorned jade bowls with the elegance of form characteristic to imperial Chinese art[40] (fig. 2.4).

The Met's Avery collection of porcelains dates from the same period and taste. While of high quality and exquisite workmanship, the aesthetic coincides with that of the MFAB: an abundance of surface decoration in a great show of gaudiness.

The objects collected by the museums were understood, and given meaning, in an art hierarchy based on the Ruskin paradigm. This becomes apparent in one of the first MFAB publications, *Boston Museum of Fine Arts: A Companion to the Catalogue*, written in 1877. Although the work

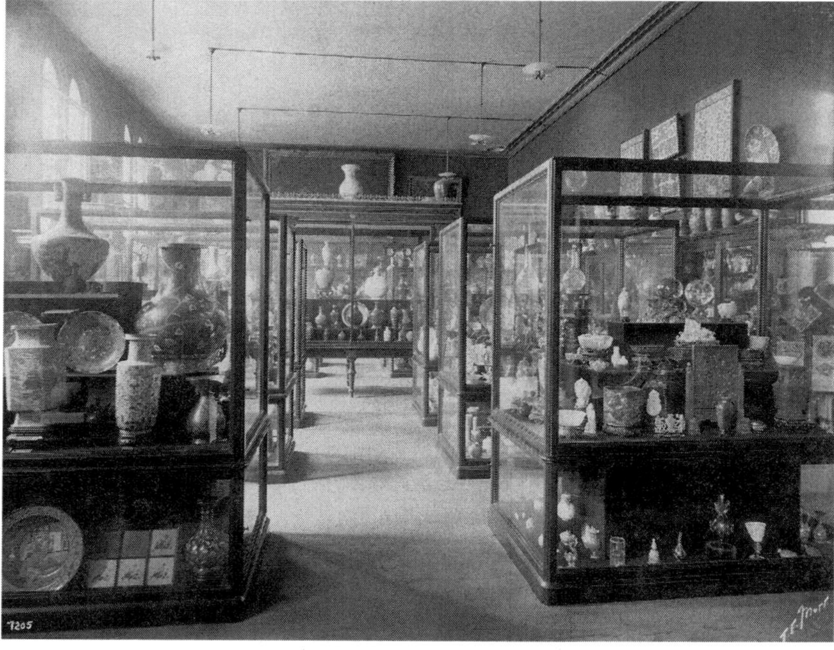

Fig. 2.4. A view of vitrines filled with Asian objects, Museum of Fine Arts, Boston. Only a few objects, such as a jade bowl in the vitrine at the right, are of high quality. Copley Square, Asian Galleries. Photo: T. E. Marr. Photograph © 2011 Museum of Fine Arts, Boston.

is unsigned and the narrative voice a persona, we now know that the author was Thomas Gold Appleton.[41] The narrator praises the paintings and
antiquities he encounters in the museum, unhesitatingly evaluating their
artistry and the integrity of the artists. Toward the end of the catalog he
discusses the Chinese and Japanese objects, grouping them with Majolica
under the heading "Art in Lesser Things" and referring to them all as "bric-
a-brac." The author describes Japanese pieces with a certain éclat. Looking
directly at the works he speaks admiring of their contemporaneity, from
the "subtlety of their craft," which appears "not only in this lacquer work,
it is everywhere," to their tinted bronze, "a marvel of finish and audacity."
And in Ruskinian fashion, he correlates art to nature and to the virtues
of the people: "Completeness of statement, careful outline, a notice of the
action and flight of birds, the lift and drooping of flowers, they contrive to
make suggestive of a nature which we feel to be true without having seen
it. . . . The Japanese are a little race with small hands and feet, a delicate
nervous system, which gives them a sensibility to grace and beauty."[42]

But because the Chinese objects could not easily be brought into the
rubric about morality, they resisted the art discourse. Unlike his previous
judgments on painters and paintings ("and now you come to America's
greatest painter—one who fed on the past, and recovered for us something
of the nobleness and beauty of the old masters,—Washington Allston"),
or his amusingly nation-centric appraisals of American art ("It is Greek,
but filtered through a Yankee mind"), the author relegates his discussion
of Chinese art to a few brief historical comments. Focusing solely on the
antiquity of Chinese technique, he laments that its origins have been lost
in obscurity. There is no great praise of the work, no equating objects with
moral values. Rather, musing on Chinese pottery produces a reflection on
the beginnings of the tradition:

> Must we go back farther than Spain . . . to find that hidden spring in
> the glazes whose beginning China herself does not know, and which
> she, the oldest of nations, may well have surrendered to her younger
> sisters? Some think that even the mariner's compass was the sacred
> mystery of each Phoenician ship. . . . if so, we may well believe that
> in the beauty of these glazes China led the way. She claims for all
> her arts a fabulous antiquity. Indeed, the power of invention seems
> to have perished there before it was known to Europe.[43]

Chinese objects could not be legitimated under this rubric as fine art; therefore
they were collected with a different justification: rather than being perceived
of as art with a didactic narrative, they served a somewhat different moral
purpose—that of education.

The MFAB stated its goal to obtain representative examples from "countries comparatively little known," presenting them for the "advancement of artistic design in the industries of Massachusetts."[44] The 1876 trustees' report from the MFAB presented their exotic acquisitions exclusively in this light: "Among the many desirable acquisitions brought within our reach by the Great Exhibition, will be enamels, porcelain, and pottery from China and Japan, whose influence has been so marked upon modern industrial arts."[45] With the collecting cabinet as a model, art museums pursued objects, even bric-a-brac, encyclopedically under the claim of education. In the same vein, the Met trustees stipulated that the museum's collection should be "illustrative of the History of Art from the earliest beginnings to the present time."[46]

Chinese things, then, coincided with the Ruskin rubric not in its emphasis on the morality of fine art objects (it was difficult to see morality in a Chinese object), but on the equally moral emphasis of a pragmatic, public visual education. While this educative characteristic assisted artists and art students, it was primarily directed toward serving industrial design and manufacture.

Technical education became the key factor legitimating the art museum, emphasized in almost every document; in fact, other motivations were seldom aired. Both the MFAB and the Met downplayed their low finances and collecting limitations by asserting ambitious roles in public education. At its first foundational meeting on March 17, 1870, the MFAB board members underscored the museum's educational function, stressing their desire that the museum be popular "in the widest sense of the term."[47] Education was the buzzword, repeatedly used as a validation and smokescreen for other motives.[48]

To look at just a few examples that stand for many: on the opening of the new Museum building in 1880, Joseph Choate (1832–1917), one of the trustees at the Met, and the founder and president of the New York Bar Association, extolled art's service for public good, perhaps a bit prematurely asserting that art "has become their best resource and most efficient educator . . . the vital and practical interest of the working millions."[49] A lengthy government report seemed to confirm "the people's" interest in the application of art to industry: "The great awakening of the people to the value of taste as an element of manufactures and to a knowledge of the many possible applications of art to industrial products, which came from a sight of the displays made of foreign wares and tissues at the Centennial Exposition, has led to general interest in all forms of art training which promise practical results in similar productions in our own country."[50]

Both art museums initially modeled their rhetoric if not their practice on England's South Kensington Museum, which had been established in the 1850s (since 1899, the Victoria and Albert). Museums such as the South

Kensington provided the opportunity to compare machine-fabricated products to handmade ware from other countries, thereby, so the premise went, setting an institutional goal of higher skill and better taste for industrial workers. In *Frank Leslie's Illustrated Newspaper*, August 26, 1876, the reporter discusses the Kensington Museum, describing its function as "a perpetual reminder of the defects and the triumphs of science and art, it is always open for study, and every facility is extended to those who wish to learn," and the subjects of this learning are the "manufactures, intelligence and commerce of the country."[51] The popularity of the museum seemed to confirm the interest of both working and middle classes in learning new methods of manufacture and good craftsmanship.[52] In American art museums, then, the majority of Chinese art was admitted through the back door: not initially regarded as fine art but considered to be decorative objects, useful for aesthetic and industrial instruction.

3. Expanding the Canon of Art; Plaster Casts as an Art Form

But, unlike a cabinet of curiosities, museum art collectively creates a public symbolic statement: each object contributes to the nation's definition of art. In speaking about cultural heritage, Barbara discusses how "all heritage interventions"—and the museum is a particularly persuasive intervention—"change how people understand their culture and themselves. They change the fundamental conditions for cultural production and reproduction."[53] Collections that were not comprised of European treasures, yet were placed in art museums, created a new public visual culture and contributed to transformations in the American definition of art.

Meaning is created through sequencing objects much like using words in a sentence. As Steven Conn describes:

> As visitors moved (horizontally) through the galleries, they saw objects which had meaning inherent in themselves. combined together from case to case and exhibit to exhibit, the objects formed coherent visual "sentences" that coherence, however, was achieved only after those objects had been deliberately selected, quite literally from the basement storehouse, and ordered properly within the galleries. Meaning was thus constructed visually, with objects, like words in a text, as the fundamental building blocks of the museum language.[54]

Although selected for museum collections under the auspices of education, once within the art museums, Chinese objects straddled their classification as object lessons and curiosities. The museum visitors saw them with a different understanding than that of the museum curators—under the auspices of an art museum, all exhibited objects gained the status of art. Paul Crowther clearly articulates this rather subtle point:

> If an artefact's purpose, however, is just to serve a particular function then its identity as this individual artefact is of no concern. In the case of painting [art], however, the work's stylistic individuality makes us attentive to the particular character of how this is manifest in the work.[55]

The Chinese pieces were collected more as artifacts, not as individually significant works but once within the art context, another aspect of their making, their unique stylistic qualities, hidden until now, became foregrounded. These qualities were always present, but they were not always seen or understood. As Crowther continues:

> We can only recognize things insofar as they are embedded in a context of expectations concerning how things of that kind behave and are amenable to perception and bodily manipulation. The given is intelligible only in the context of a field of possibilities and relations that are not themselves immediately given.[56]

Their differences from previous art objects contributed to an emerging new definition of art.

Throughout the1870s and 1880s, while the museums presented their Chinese things as less than fine art, numerous articles indicate that the popular press fully accepted Chinese and Japanese objects as art and held them in high regard. An early example is found in the *New York Times* review of an 1873 exhibition held in Paris. Speaking about ancient Chinese ceramics, the reporter states: "Vases such as these, says the enthusiastic critic of the *Siecle*, which are 3,000 years old, and which, for elegance of contour, are not surpassed by the accurate workmen of Etraria, or by the genius of the Greeks, are not to be met with every day."[57] And a year later, a full-page article on the loan collection at the Met takes the reader quickly through Cypriot art, directly into the Chinese and Japanese collection, where the reviewer comments and exclaims about the features of the objects. His descriptions, moving between one object and another and his gaze, lingering on specific details, display his unquestioning regard of these objects as art.[58]

Alongside the Asian art collections, a second collection also created a visual display that deviated from European fine arts. Museums collected plaster casts to replicate European statuary, but once installed, the casts emanated a different sensibility. Understanding this shift in visual culture necessitates returning to the museum boards' motivation in their formation of plaster cast collections.

Undoubtedly, casts were not purchased to deviate from the European canon but quite the opposite, as objects that would strengthen the presence of the European objects that defined fine art in the America's piecemeal collections. The rubric of education that admitted Chinese objects also became part of the driving force for collecting plaster casts. For example, an 1886 Boston Museum of Fine Arts report stated:

> Original works will generally be beyond our reach, or else of doubtful or inferior value; but, through casts, we can acquaint ourselves with the best, the standard examples, *in their most essential qualities*. A collection of casts will have, at a very moderate cost, and without any danger of wasting our money through mistakes of judgment, *would be in some respects of more value for study* than any existing collection of originals, since there is none that affords the means of comparison which the student needs (emphasis added).[59]

By January 1883, the Museum's trustees had spent $18,005 for reproductions of art, while in that same period spending only $7,756 for original artworks. $1,912 of the sum for original works went for painting and sculpture; the bulk of the money was spent on decorative works.[60]

Turning the disadvantages of being relegated to collecting copies into an ideological advantage, the board members validated their enterprise by contrasting it to the hedonism they perceived or imagined characterizing the opulence of European museums. A democratic nation, conversely, would use objects to instruct and edify. Contrary to the perception of European art accumulation as an indulgence, American art museums would maintain moral values by amassing collections not as a desire to possess unique and lavish goods but as a means to instruct the masses in good fabrication and good taste, ultimately leading to national refinement. While art museums relied on casts to fill their halls, by framing the collection of plaster copies in this way, museums clearly made a virtue out of a necessity. Members of the board of the MFAB had no difficulty agreeing about the Museum's mission to become "a comprehensive gallery of reproductions, through plaster casts of the many treasures of Antique and Medieval Art, or photographs of original drawings by the most renowned artists of all periods."[61] True, the founders claimed they did not want to create a treasure house, but then, neither could they have one.

Initially, by collecting plaster casts of European art as well as forming collections of Chinese and Japanese objects, American museums may seem to have had a double, perhaps even a schizophrenic definition of art. The two collections appear at first glance completely antithetical, the vivid colors and uniqueness of the Asian ceramics signaling an alternative aesthetic, markedly contrasting the white plaster scrupulously replicating the figures of famous European statues and fragments of architecture.[62] Certainly the casts' monotony in color and material created a contrast to the diversity of textures and materials in the Asian pieces displayed in other galleries: the bronzes, porcelains, jades, and lacquers, not to mention colors and unconventional forms (fig. 2.5).

But despite these essential differences, the plaster casts and the Asian objects formed a fundamental alliance. They both posed alternatives to the traditional European objects of art and reinforced an aesthetic that contributed to the change from the European-centric definition.[63] Although each cast piece duplicated a particular European sculpture, it diverged from its model in three essential ways: through a lack of uniqueness (original vs. reproduction), material (marble or stone vs. plaster), and time (classic or renaissance vs. modern). Directly in front of the museum founders, yet unnoticed by them, these three elements subverted the desired classic aesthetic. While representing classic art, they simultaneously presented it as remote and in a sense unattainable, appearing only in a ghostlike afterimage. And many Americans had no idea of the originals to which the casts alluded. Writing

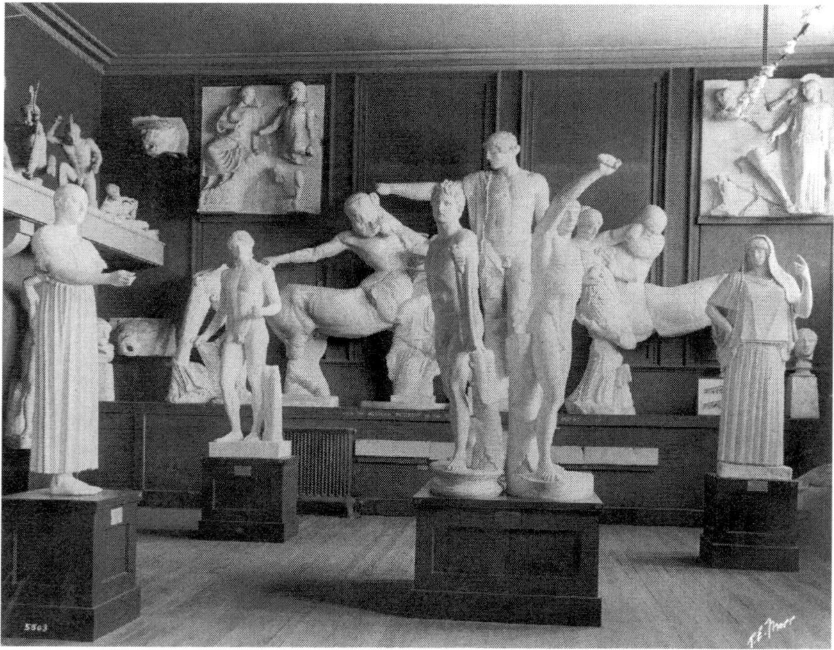

Fig. 2.5. Plaster Cast Statues in the Copley Square Classical Galleries at the MFA Boston, c. 1895. Photo: T. E. Marr. Photograph © 2011 Museum of Fine Arts, Boston.

for *The Nation* in 1883, Russell Sturgis, lamented: "And yet, *so* many persons form their conceptions of Greek sculpture from casts, often inaccurate, generally soiled and injured, and always cold and hard in the surface and color, which but poorly represent the living marble, that it is right to call attention to the wonderful beauty of the originals."[64] But through deviating from the original, casts helped advance a radically new aesthetic.

The cast collection occupied the large ground-floor galleries and was extremely popular, and not just as education; it was featured in the Museum's own sparsely illustrated catalog[65] (fig. 2.6). In the 1880s, with significantly more funding available, museums purchased original antiquities. Yet they not only continued purchasing plaster casts, they bought them in greater numbers amounts and purchased more expensive ones. An 1883 bequest to the Met from the wealthy businessman Levi Hale Willard of over $100,000 stipulated that the money be used exclusively for the purchase of architectural casts. Some members of the museum board so preferred casts that they refused to collect originals when they were available: when several experts in Classical antiquities offered to purchase superlative original pieces for the museum,

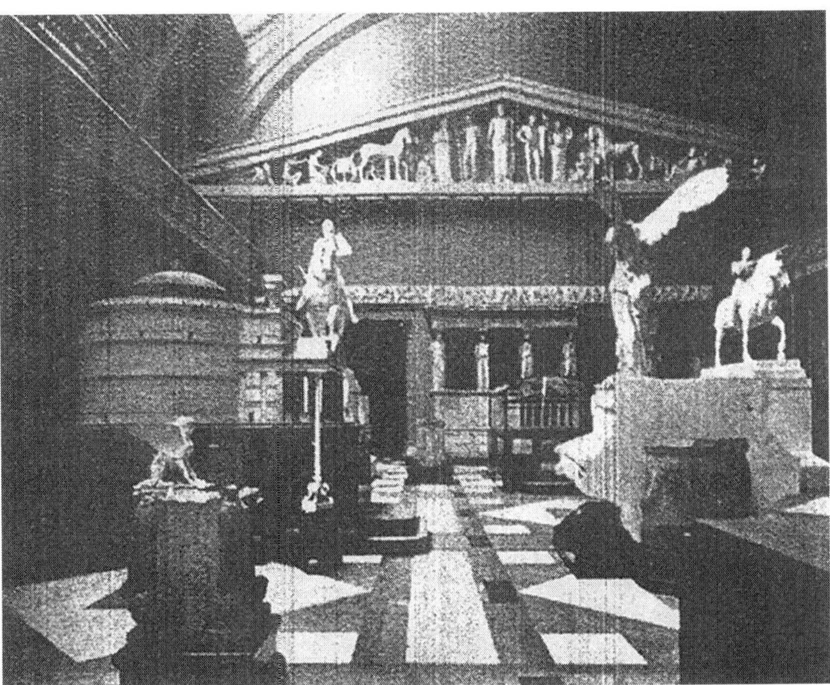

Fig. 2.6. Hall of Casts, Metropolitan Museum of Art, New York, Bulletin 1908, p. 232.

they met with considerable resistance. The president of the MFAB, Martin Brimmer, rejected the purchase of a collection with the fifth-century relief of the Birth of Aphrodite, stating almost contemptuously: "We cannot be wholly collectors, i.e. we cannot be governed in our purchases by artistic merit alone, even with archaeological interest and rarity as subordinate considerations. We must also be controlled by the needs of those who use the museum."[66]

He turned down a collection of rare coins and extraordinary gems saying that the coins were "interesting historically rather than artistically and can be represented by reproduction, while gems are difficult to exhibit."[67] One BMFA committee member allegedly provided the collector with a list of the most reproduced statues at the Louvre as an indication of his most desired selections; another dismissively rejected an original terracotta figure contending "no healthy woman could be formed at the hips like that."[68]

With the display of casts, we see the definition of art swerving away from that based on readings of Ruskin and European art. Rather, as Walter Benjamin would discuss decades later, for the first time no regard was paid to the "aura," or the authenticity and uniqueness of the original work. Instead the copy became an artwork in its own right. In accepting the cast copy, American art embraced the idea of multiples, rather than singular objects, as art; creating an overlap with industry and raising the possibility of mass-produced objects eventually considered to be art. (Although this avenue was avoided in the nineteenth century, it became revived as a major theme in the twentieth century.)

Unabashedly, MFAB personnel insisted that plaster casts and other copies of European art fulfilled the ambitions of the museum collections. An article in the Boston Advertiser, October 10, 1879, praised the Museum's investment in plaster casts: "Naturally enough we can never expect to rival the older museums of Italy in the possession of original works by the masters of the great periods of art. Our aim must be to bring these within the reach of our people by means of the best available copies and this is exactly what the directors of the museum . . . have done."[69]

But even as this statement denied the ability to "rival the older museums of Italy," it raised another agenda: a sense of competition with Europe. Reproductions of European objects would not satisfy a nation as ambitious as the United States for long.

Nevertheless, the preference for originals over reproductions in American art museums, especially in the Met, occurred only after arduous battles. While generous endowments at the end of the century made possible any sort of acquisition, many board members and patrons of art museums had an inclination toward casts, not as a matter of finances but of taste, linked to a particular ideology. Increased capital alone does not explain the eventual preeminence of the singular and original work of art over the copy. This change occurred only with the assertion of a new art paradigm, preferring aesthetics over claims of education.[70] The museum's original objective of displaying items that provided objects lessons of technique or aesthetics became subordinate to a new paradigm favoring originality, singularity, and integrity of materials.

After helping unhinge the hegemony of European objects as fine art and support a new rubric, the differences in the two collections, Chinese art and casts, became amplified and they parted ways. With the new emphasis on uniqueness and personal artistic expression, plaster casts became untenable as art. Copies were no longer suitable as substitutes for the original art piece. On the other hand, the Chinese objects, always individual, at times eccentrically so, reinforced the emerging paradigm.[71] And, as moral legibility diminished as a criterion for art, the non-narrative qualities of Chinese objects became increasingly appreciated. By 1890 the MFAB hired a Japanese art expert, Ernest Fenollosa, as the first curator of Oriental Arts, and by 1894 he had organized the museum's first exhibition of Chinese painting.

A change occurred in the museum exhibition of Asian pieces. Appreciated now more for their formal qualities and less as object lessons, the new pieces selected by Fenollosa were installed with substantial space and ample lighting on the main floor. Rather than ceramics, Chinese painting took center stage as the quintessential Chinese art. The extravagant hybrid objects that once had been the darling of the Centennial Exhibition and the newer art pieces now became seen as embarrassingly eccentric, and were quietly de-accessioned along with the plaster casts, or relegated to museum basements or dining halls.[72]

SECTION II. CHINESE OBJECTS AND THE BUSINESS OF MUSEUMS

1. Art Museums Founders and the Issue of the Public

A question asked by one member of the museum committee at the Met to another reveals the fundamental ambiguity and the lack of confidence in the American definition of art at this transitional time: "I want to ask you for my own information—and I'll take your word for it—whether an original sculpture is in any way more valuable than a cast."[73] A series of articles in the *New York Times* during this same time shows a similar insecurity in the area of Chinese art, detailing the mistaken provenance, inflated prices, and frank fraud in objects previously unquestionably accepted as Chinese antiquities. Terry Eagleton has discerningly analyzed such periods of artistic reassessing and reframing, finding that when the social structure is integrated into an individual citizen's sense of order, the forms of its symbolical representation also appear as if natural, inevitable.[74] Hesitancies and revisions concerning aesthetic evaluation and art accompany anxiety over the threat of change in political power. And, in the United States, this hesitancy was magnified by the persistent artistic uncertainty deriving from its simultaneous dependence on and rejection of European art standards.

The art museums' inadvertent dislocation of Ruskin ideology contributed to a shift in the definition of art. The changes occurring in the perception of art in general and Chinese art in particular were noted as they were happening, and the discussion of art indirectly denoted and even participated in class conflicts. We see this class tension documented just a few months after the Met's opening in 1873, in a *New York Times* article titled "The Art Museum." From its first sentences, the lengthy article focuses almost exclusively on the Asian objects exhibited in the museum, praising them highly.[75] Writing a kind of pan-Asian history, a composite based on both Chinese and Japanese objects, the reporter provides us with a glimpse into public perception of Asian objects and of art museums, especially revealing divergences between his viewpoint from that of the museum's founders. His article allows us to see fissures between the museum's rhetoric and its practice, thereby disclosing the more elusive reasons motivating museum founders to collect Chinese art. Because the article unites several segments of our inquiry, it warrants detailed consideration.

Chronicling changes in the Western perception of Chinese art over the last century, the reporter provided a brief history of its reception before examining its current status:

> Those readers who are well acquainted with English classical literature cannot fail to remember the scorn and contempt which the standard writers of the last century and the early part of this felt for Chinese art. . . . The fact that the women of those remote times discovered what was hidden from the eyes of even artists, namely, the intrinsic value of Chinese and Japanese art, should ever be remembered by those who are inclined to pooh pooh the claims made in favor of female intellect. . . . It is true that men were taught in those days to accept classic art, and the old masters of Italy as gospel truths which were not to be even questioned. Men got by heart any lists of old masters. The moderns were in everything humble imitators of their predecessors, and looked only through the glasses of Italian art. Hence both to the educated and the uneducated, the truly artistic, and the pseudo-critics, Chinese and Japanese art was a monstrosity which gave them cold shudders. This lesson of the weakness of judgment is one that ought to be

carefully treasured up, since we may be guilty of similar errors now by reason of the vast mass of prejudices with which we cloud our understanding, and to which we proudly give the name of learning. The minority, who find ideas for the majority, have, in the matter of Asiatic art, accepted the truth which women, uneducated, had found out long ago.[76]

Unlike Ruskin, the reporter did not demand, or even consider, the necessity for moral qualities as a prerequisite for instilling the status of art. He ascribed the idea of judging Chinese art as grotesques as a sign of mass prejudice acquired through learning. We can see in this a judgment with class basis—the women and the minority who saw as they did versus the more educated patriarchs who vilify all art but old European masters. The reporter sides with the minority and saw the Asian objects as art, despite their non-narrative characteristics, indeed despite their very notable non-communication:

> It is unfortunately one of the drawbacks of the Museum that there are few people competent to catalogue its treasures. The writer could not obtain any information whatsoever concerning Japanese art. . . . Two things may be done at the Metropolitan with great advantage to the public. One is the establishment of an art journal in connection with the Cooper Institute Female School of Engraving, whereby good illustrations of these rare things might be spread abroad over America. At the same time, explanations of their nature and value might be given by Mr. Scott Stuart, one of the few men who possess knowledge on the subject. The other thing would be to designate free days, when those persons might come who love the beautiful, but who have not a great supply of fifty-cent pieces. And if the motives of the institutors of this Museum have not changed from the time of its inauguration, they will throw it open every night for the benefit of the working classes and the mechanics, who, if they have less knowledge of the beautiful than some of us, have quite as much appreciation as any. This ought to be looked to.

This "ought" expresses the critical distinction between the Museum and its audience. While the reporter agreed with the call for education, his assumption of what should be taught significantly differed from that of the museum's founders. The founders conceived of education as the Museum's gift to the laboring class, providing an education that would be entirely technological: "all forms of art training which promise practical results in similar productions."[77] In contrast, the reporter urged museum education to illuminate the art's significance; he seemed indifferent to their technical manufacture. The class issues inherent in the museum's endorsement of technical education become more distinct when we recall Fredric Jameson's description of such intellectual hierarchy. He described these patterns of thought as transferring "the notion of the division of labor, of economic specialization, from the social classes to the inner functioning of the mind."[78] Just as the ruling class regarded employment as the manifestation of the work proper to each class, so the intellect became a site of class division, allotting a more ideated education for the upper class only, and restricting the lower class only to practical instruction. The art content of the objects was not something the lower classes were thought to concern themselves with specifically; the mere sense of them as having a high quality would instill the proper respect and disseminate the desired ideology.

This discloses the inherent classism in the educational intentions of the museum authorities. They assumed that the working class needed, and could only apprehend, technical aspects of art. The Ruskin-based theory relied on such a hierarchy, persuaded that "high art demanded high capacities," as Ruskin wrote, "met and understood by persons having some sort of sympathy with the high and solitary minds which produced it—sympathy only to be felt by minds in some degree high and solitary themselves."[79] While Ruskin's writings and interests always had a decidedly social reform and he desired art to reach the laboring class, indeed he designed a museum—the St. George's Museum—expressly for the working class; nevertheless, a class bias was seen in his words, and, fairly or not, he was often labeled "elitist." A sarcastic article in the *New York Times* typifies this sentiment, mockingly stating: "His [Ruskin's] grand idea is that the common people do not know enough to go alone, and should be kept in leading-strings by an elevated, pure, unselfish aristocracy."[80]

The implicit hierarchy of art museums is further revealed in the reporter's call for the Met to be open when the laboring class could actually attend. Leaders of the museum movement repeatedly stated their objective for art collections to benefit the people through improving the aesthetic sensibility of American craftsmen, thereby advancing industry. Indeed, the Met trustees boasted of "mechanics and artisans" as "our most steady and studious visitors"—proof that the Museum succeeded in educational outreach.[81] The Met's unavailability to the working class, its alleged audience, brings its commitment to this group into question.[82]

Initially only the MFAB provided adequate access to this public. The MFAB's documents of incorporation stipulated that the museum would be free at least four times a month and these free days—Saturday—were immediately popular. According to Neil Harris, in 1877, its first full year, the MFAB had "more than seventeen thousand paid visitors and more than one hundred and forty thousand free visitors." By March 1877, Saturdays had become so popular that the Museum also opened free of charge on Sunday afternoon[83] (fig. 2.7). Harris observed that the weekend attendance was extremely high: "this represented as many as four or five thousand people a weekend; before long there began to be complaints of crowding in the galleries."[84] The public reciprocated through their support of the Museum, manifested in the readiness with which people participated with financial contributions. During years of financial hardship, the Boston fire of 1872 and the Panic of 1873, a subscription fund for the Museum still resulted in $260,000 contributed by one thousand individuals, and an additional $125,000 over the following two years.

Contrastingly, when the Met opened in a temporary site in 1872, it considered it "unadvisable to throw it at once open to the general public." But even the wealthy and fashionable were reluctant to attend on days requiring an entrance fee. As Calvin Tomkins described: "Barely a dozen people a week were willing to pay for the privilege of having their tastes refined." Months later, as an experiment, the Met opened on Saturdays without payment. Saturday, however, was still a workday for many laborers. As the *New York Times* reported, the museum expected working-class people to "joyfully profit by the privilege and attend, unfortunately this result was not

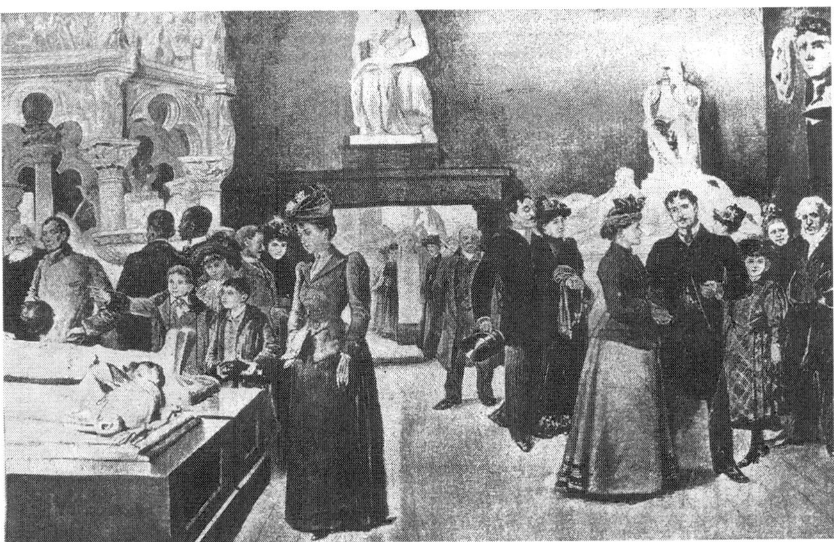

Fig. 2.7. "A Sunday Afternoon at the Boston Museum of Fine Arts," *Harper's Weekly*, February 27, 1892.

arrived at." Although many people did make use of the free day, "they were all people of leisure, who could have come on other days," while "those for whom the gallery was specially thrown open did not choose to profit by it."[85]

Over the decades the gap between the Met and its professed audience had still not been bridged as, from 1871 until 1891, the Met repeatedly refused to open on Sunday, insisting that it would not defile "God's day" by opening "a place of amusement."[86] Certainly, for all the moral emphasis on the educative purpose of the art museum, the Met's problematic irresolution in distinguishing its educational mission from entertainment hints at something more sanctimonious than educational in its relationship to the working class.[87]

The MFAB and the Met served as sites for display and performance of class hierarchy. Although the museum founders had reconfigured the goal of art collecting from one of sensual delight and privilege to the more munificent purpose of mass education, nevertheless social status and class advantages still informed the accumulation of rare and desirable objects. Assembling these large collections clearly required great expenditure and signaled the power and wealth of those most closely involved.[88] Remy Saisselin discussed the investment of the wealthy class in the formation of the American art world, describing it as the "ultimate bourgeois aesthetic, social and artistic phenomenon, the cosmopolis, complement of the international art market and aesthetic phenomenon of the beautiful rich people in the beautiful places looking at beautiful works of art available for the right price."[89] The museums' collections were the product of the centralization of wealth in the control of a few families: by 1892 an estimated 9 percent of the nation owned 71 percent of the wealth. In the 1880s, many workers were near or below poverty level: "About 45 percent of the industrial laborers barely held on above the $500-per-year poverty line; about 40 percent lived below the line of tolerable existence. . . . about a fourth of those below the poverty line lived in actual destitution."[90] Despite reassurances from notables as William Lawrence, Episcopal Bishop of Massachusetts, that "Godliness is in league with riches," anger over such overt inequity irrupted in the violence of the Haymarket Riot in the 1880s, the Homestead Strike and the Pullman Strike in the 1890s, and the Panic of 1893, to name only four.[91] Against this backdrop of financial and social disparity, the wealthy class looked to public institutions, among them art museums, to provide constancy and a way to stabilize and buffer the changes threatening their authority.

In describing the small group that instigated the Metropolitan Museum, Tomkins emphasizes their membership in "that extraordinary group of liberal-minded reformers who came to prominence in New York during and soon after the Civil War—leading abolitionists like Frederick Law Olmsted and Henry Tilden Blodgett, moral idealists like William Cullen Bryant, enlightened clergymen like the Reverend Henry Bellows, the popular pastor of All Souls Unitarian Church." Their liberal and ministerial background are the demographic addressed by Ruskin's teachings, most influenced by his assertion of art as a pathway for reaching God.

Kenneth Hudson, however, underscores the latter group's monetary strength more than its liberal qualities. In his book *Museums of Influence*, he writes:

> In the 1860s, more than a few people were making a great deal of money out of the Civil War. New York was, to use Leo Lerman's graphic phrase, 'bustling rich." There was money to spend and among the newly rich the interest in art was rising fast. The time was clearly ripe for the establishment of new art galleries, and New York was the obvious first choice. The moving spirit behind a museum . . . would do credit to the nation's most important city.[92]

The hegemony of the upper class becomes immediately apparent in looking at the composition of founding groups at the two museums. In both New York and in Boston, the impetus for an art museum, and the means to achieve it, came from very narrow circles. The MFAB board was comprised of a small group of men from the upper society, since mid-nineteenth century referred to as the Boston Brahmins. Neil Harris enumerates the primary families: "Eliots, Perkinses and Bigelows took their places; almost all of the twenty-three elected trustees were descended from old Yankee families and were men of wealth. All but one were Proprietors of the Athenaeum, eleven were members of the Saturday Club, five served (or would serve) on the Harvard Board of Overseers, half were members of the Somerset or St. Botolph clubs and quite a number were blood relations."[93]

And, while they acquired their wealth more through individual efforts than inheritance, nevertheless, like the MFAB founders, the Met board members were exclusively upper class. An initial meeting of the committee to investigate the practicality of an art museum in New York was held at the Union League Club and open to interested individuals; more than three hundred people attended. But all the members of the foundational committee were wealthy and powerful in their respective fields; even the most artistic among them, the poet William Cullen Bryant, also was the high-profile editor-in-chief of the *New York Evening Post*.[94] Alan Trachtenberg underscored this relationship, writing that "Organized by the urban elite . . . art donated by wealthy private collectors, the museums subliminally associated art with wealth."[95]

A hint of other, less philanthropic, factors in the relationship between the museum board and the laboring class had emerged as early as the Met's dedication ceremony in 1880. In the opening statements, Choate, who was a self-made millionaire, defined the educational mission of disseminating art to the working class:

> the diffusion of a knowledge of art in its higher forms of beauty would tend directly to humanize, to educate and refine a practical and laborious people; that though the great masterpieces of painting and sculpture . . . could never be within their reach, yet it might be possible in the progress of time to gather together a collection of works of merit, which should impart some knowledge of art and its history to a people who were yet to take almost their first steps in that department of knowledge.[96]

The altruism expressed in Choate's mission statement is mitigated by his appeal to art to humanize the laborers, along with educating them. This presents a whiff of elitism along with benevolence in the founders' ideology, sectarianism mixed into their philanthropy. More was implied in "education" than merely instruction in technology and aesthetics. Education also meant becoming governable. Answering their own needs, the founders wanted to remove the very present threat of "unindoctrinated" masses, and their apparent tendency toward socialism and unions.

Perhaps the most revealing indictment exposing the class bias in the museum's establishment is found in a letter written in 1885 by William Cowper Prine, a founding trustee and an active board member of the Met. In the letter, Prine explicitly declares his disdain for the public and its mistaken identification of the class allegiance of the museum: "*Now* they think the museum is a public institution, in the management of which the public has a voice. They must be *forced* to think of it as a private institution. . . . they must stop thinking they support the Museum, and be compelled to see that *we* own and support the Museum and give it in pure charity for public education."[97]

Museum founders were not alone in their aspiration for art to serve as a method of indoctrination. The gap between the living standards of workers and their employers was becoming enormous. The prominent nineteenth-century economist Samuel Patten thought a solution lay in habits of consumption. Poorer people had cheaper taste and spent less money, while upper-class people's refined taste led them to more expensive purchases. He and other reformers advanced the existence of a "pleasure seeking" impulse, and advocated making cultural activities more available to the lower classes as a means to pacify their appetites. Art was viewed as an activity that would provide an "attractive entertainment of an innocent and improving character."[98] Patten endorsed this strategy, noting that "Drinking, smoking, and other amusements which tend in the wrong direction are much cheapened; while music, art, and education have become in their higher forms more costly."[99] Patten then advised, "Let us then reverse the priorities, making culture cheaper and mere amusements and vices more expensive."[100] Art would provide a means for the wealthy class to educate the poorer in the correct democratic ideology and generate a sense of participation by allowing the masses access to high-class culture. This would raise their standards of taste, encouraging the lower class to aspire to and ultimately to purchase more expensive goods, thus stimulating the economy while unifying society. This use of art as a site for enacting class antagonism will be explored more fully in chapter 4.

Not only did the museum impetus derive from the wealthy class; once built (and persisting in museums today), the museum courted and catered to that class by holding private parties for the upper-class audience, never for the working class. Although partially camouflaged by the gloss of industrial education, this orientation did not go unnoticed. In fact, in the same year that Choate spoke of beauty's ability to humanize, educate, and refine a "practical and laborious people" the *Tribune* accused the museum of pandering to the wealthy, and it disparaged the Met as "an exclusive social toy."[101]

Kenneth Hudson reminds us that although education and other reasons have been used to validate collecting objects, it is probably wise to remember the powerful motivating force of social prestige.[102] Therefore, we need to be a circumspect in believing the assertion of a predominantly educative role to Asian collections in art museums. Certainly, the premise of industrial education allowed Asian objects to enter into the museums. But the rhetoric of this premise has overshadowed almost all other motivations explaining the museums' readiness to collect these particular non-European art objects. For instance, native American objects were equally abundant to American collectors, and could have been similarly educative in demonstrating alternative methods of manufacture and use of materials, yet they found no place in the art museums. To understand the basis on which Chinese things appealed to the museum founders, we must take a closer look at the men who sat on the museum boards, especially examining their relationship to merchandise and how that mediated their understanding of objects, particularly Chinese objects, as art.

2. Museums, Art, and Commodities

On what basis, with what criteria and guidance, did the museums form their collections of art? Immediately, we can rule out art knowledge. From the museums' inception, this lapse was conspicuous: in 1869 when New York's John Jay, President of the Union League Club (and Minister to Germany), appointed the Club's Art Committee to investigate the viability of creating an art institution, the critical difficulty, apparent immediately in their preliminary meeting, was the virtually complete absence of art professionals.[103]

Most founding members of the museums had very little art knowledge. Indeed, writing about the founders Tomkins states bluntly: "These men believed in art without knowing very much about it." Possibly the only exception was the Boston Museum's Honorary Director for Life, Charles Perkins, who had lived ten years in Italy and had written about Italian sculpture. But, apart from this anomaly, the remainder of the board were businessmen and politicians: presidents and ex officios from Harvard, MIT, the Athenaeum, the Lowell Institute, Superintendent of Schools, and included the mayor of Boston.[1044] Not one was conversant in the arts. As a group, their money and business acumen far outweighed any art knowledge.

Predictably, this deficit was a liability: in 1880 Cornelius Vanderbilt became a Met trustee and presented the museum with nearly seven hundred Italian drawings collected by James Jackson Jarves. The works were falsely attributed as nine Michelangelos, two Raphaels, eleven Titians, nine Rembrandts, two Leonardos, and on and on. Had there been even one art scholar on the Met's board, stated the contemporary art critic Clarence Cook, these works would never have been accepted, but without a critical eye, they were not only accepted, but even worse, camouflaged with incorrect attributions, they were displayed prominently for many years.[105]

The lack of critical scholarship was part of a circular problem. Art enthusiasts needed professional institutions such as museums to provide the exposure to art to gain sufficient knowledge to gain professional expertise. And the institutions needed art experts to guide their purchases and direct them. Devoid of competent people in the arts, the art founders were forced into a choice that they imagined as a temporary solution. Weighing the merits and detriments of the three groups available from which to select a director for the Met, Bellows mused that "men of affairs and enterprise and executive ability are seldom interested in art, or marked with a taste and appreciation of the delicate interests of the Beautiful." Artists, however, tended to be diffident: "a brooding, dreamy, meditative class, closed to the world by their intensity of passion for their coy mistress, are seldom men of practical wisdom, push, and enterprise."[106] And reflecting on the public, Bellows concluded that it also could not be depended on as a source of support for art: given a choice, it would never vote to fund aesthetic enterprises. After appraising the three groups, then, he concluded that only the business class could develop and advance an art museum.

In order to circumvent the circularity, this looping problem of no one with art expertise capable of running an institution, Bellows's task, then, was to find a group of businessmen who, with little or no art knowledge, could be motivated nevertheless to care about art and to assist the museum "long enough to allow the few who know their wants to perfect the plan, against the protest of their poorer taste and judgement."[107] His committee appointed businessmen as heads of the Met, thereby making the existence of an art institution possible despite the lack of art professionals. Proposed as an interim condition, once in the hands of businessmen, the continued appointment of businessmen became instituted and perpetuated, remaining the common situation today.[108]

The business affiliations of the founders significantly influenced the direction and policies of art museums. Although art collections in America as in Europe were generated by the upper classes, American museums deliberately avoided following a European precedent of art serving the aristocracy as a symbol of privilege. Rather, art served the businessmen in the name of market and industry. In reality, the premise of education actually served the needs of business. Justifying the creation of an art museum in American, one Metropolitan Museum founder optimistically reassured skeptics: "Every nation that has tried it has found that every wise investment in the development of art pays more than compound interest."[109]

In fact, all previously discussed premises for the founders' interest in art can be seen as collaborating with business concerns on two crucial and distinct levels. On one hand, improving the nation's industrial output by instructing the lower classes in higher-quality production would also increase profits for the business owners. Equally important, the businessmen's interest in art controverted a common reproach they faced as ambitious Americans: the accusation of having "little or no soul."[110] The critique resounded from foreign critics as well as from fellow citizens. As early as 1870s, Walt Whitman condemned the entrepreneurial class for its complete lack of scruples: "The depravity of the business classes of our country is not less than has been supposed, but infinitely greater"; and he continued: "The official services of America, national, state and municipal, in all their branches and departments, except the judiciary, are saturated in corruption, bribery, falsehood, maladministration; and the judiciary is tainted. The great cities reek with respectable as much as non-respectable robbery and scoundrelism."[111]

Whitman's exhorting was echoed in a gentler form in 1882 from Oscar Wilde on his American tour. The *Herald* reported his challenge to Americans: "You in America don't want that we should look upon you as a mere collection of money-making merchants. . . . the only way you can influence us [Europeans] is by producing noble art and a noble civilization. Believe me that we value your American poets much more than your American millionaires; and that we estimate you by the amount of great men you have produced not by your hoarded wealth. Can you seriously compare your art with ours?"[112]

These condemnations were not unique nor did they go unheeded. Corruption in the newly moneyed class had been one subject in William Cullen Bryant's previously mentioned remarks at the critical meeting leading to the Met's foundation. Bryant emphasized three key factors he felt would encourage and persuade Americans to invest in such a cultural pursuit. He appealed to nationalism, stating that nearly all European countries had national art museums, even Spain, "a third rate power of Europe and poor besides."[113] And he appealed to education: when collections, either European or American, became available for purchase, there was no institution to house them, and no place for American artists to study great artworks. But besides these forward-looking appeals, Bryant also described the current environment of unparalleled corruption: men "most dexterous in villainy" and "most foul in guilt," infecting the urban environment.[114] Bryant championed art as an antidote to the rampant vice occasioned by the rapid acquisition of money.

At a subsequent meeting, Bellows united the concerns about vice within the business class to the desire to increase profits, denouncing "the redundant wealth with which our property threatens to possess us" and advocating using the surplus wealth to build an art museum.[115]

The emphasis on good business sense and on ideological motivation does not negate the genuine humanitarian interest in creating art museums. But it demonstrates that the founding of art museums was neither occasioned exclusively by the founders' love of knowledge, nor by their desire to educate the masses. The awareness of their elite status led to both the noblesse oblige of the education mission, and also to their attempt for their art interest to buffer the corruption within their own class. Along with their altruistic public declarations, museum founders had a more private motivation of self-protection and self-interest. At its root, the museum movement coincided with the ideology of progress, an expression of social and financial gain. Kenneth Hudson noted this self-interest, bluntly commenting: "The Metropolitan was, in fact, running a business."[116]

It is this business acumen that oriented the relationship to the objects collected and underlay the museums' collecting and exhibition of Chinese art.

3. Merchandising Art

Now we arrive at the heart of the matter. The museum founders and art collectors were not art experts, nor were they inquisitive, and they bought art conservatively, choosing what was familiar. Invited to choose ten pictures from William H. Vanderbilt's extensive art collection, Met trustees selections included Van Marcke's *Cows in a Field* and Erskine Nicol's oil painting *Looking for a Safe Investment*, works that depicted the familiar scenes of commerce[117] (figs. 2.8 and 2.9). The trustees had a similar commercial relationship with Asian objects, especially through world's fairs or through their own investments with China and Japan. They understood that visual delight in objects was the stock in trade of contemporary market culture. Originally attracted to these objects as desirable commodities, they collected them for the museums.

Many members of the wealthy class had inherited fortunes through mercantile enterprise, especially the China trade, and objects proliferated. In the growing urban centers, newly rich businessmen and merchants, especially proprietors of huge department stores, selected the merchandise to sell and shaped the public's relationship to consumerism. Deluxe stores did not exist before 1880; by 1890 they dominated the retail market.[118] Through their displays and sales they shaped and whetted and gratified the public's material taste. The owners of these businesses not only controlled the available merchandise, they also influenced urban spaces and the access to them, transforming the very environment to promote consumption. Their buildings introduced innovations in architecture, while through negotiations with the legislature they directed movement within the city, establishing

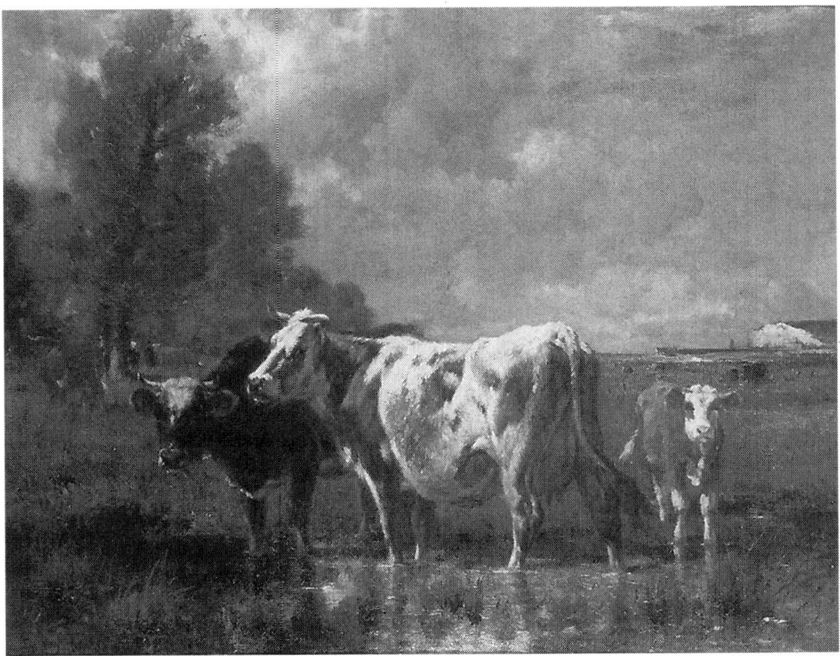

Fig. 2.8. Emile Van Marcke de Lummen, *Cows in a Field* (1827–1890).

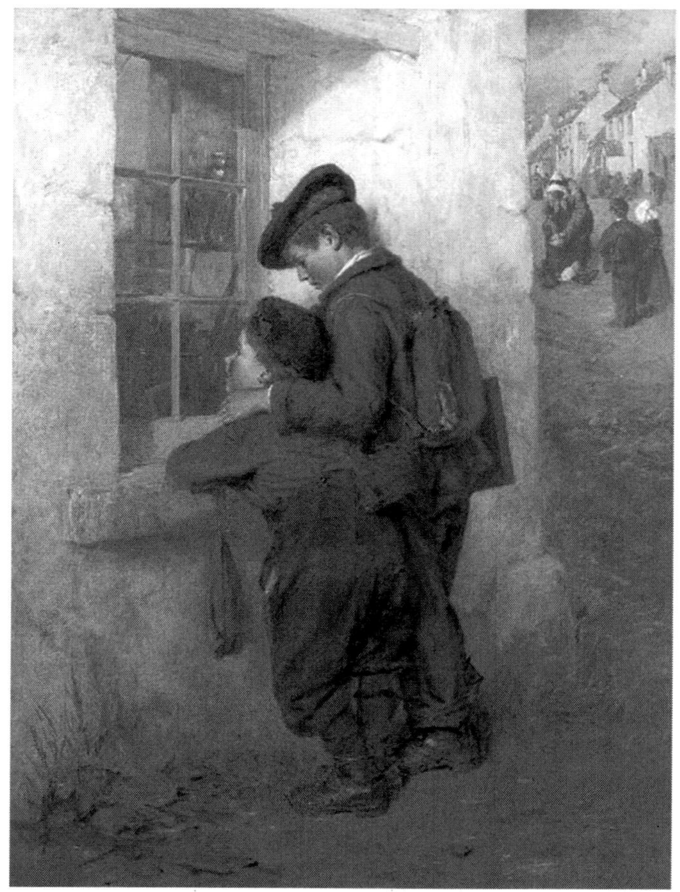

Fig. 2.9. Erskine Nicol, *"Looking for a Safe Investment,"* oil on canvas, n.d.

pedestrian and vehicular traffic patterns. For example, Abraham Abraham, owner of one of the largest stores in Brooklyn, New York, became a member of Brooklyn's Traffic Committee in 1907, resulting in the convergence of subway lines downtown by his shop.[119] Through such manipulation of traffic patterns, large stores seemed natural destinations, encouraging already eager consumers to use their leisure time to shop.

By the 1890s, so many things were available in the United States that merchants feared a glut, and, in an effort to increase sales, they intensified display techniques and began to study strategies for advertising and decorating.[120]

Acquisition was not without its critics. The *Crockery and Glass Journal* from June 20, 1878, documented the case of a man who "developed a failure of mental powers by enormous purchases of old china.[121] And there were many in the art world who deplored the overt expansion of capitalism into art. An article in *The Arena* indicted commercialism as a deadly power: "It sapped 'manly' instincts and 'dipped its hands into the warm blood of the common people.' Would it now 'seek to make art its plaything, its tool, something for ignorance to toy with and cast aside because it has not the wisdom to know its worth?'"[122]

But such dour responses to production and consumption were rare. Indeed, not only businessmen and capitalists, but reformers and visionaries became fierce proponents of a moral universe based on material consumption. Shopping and consuming became part of Americans' idealized worldview, exemplified in Bellamay's celebrated *Looking Backward*, and found in both the title and the subject of Bradford Peck's utopian novel, *The World a Department Store*.[123]

Such habits of consumption effected the art world as well. Art collectors became known for buying quantitatively and categorically rather than discriminatingly and particularly. On his return to the United States, Henry James visited the Met and wrote:

> Acquisition—acquisition if need be on the highest terms—may, during the years to come, bask here as in a climate it has never before enjoyed. There was money in the air, ever so much money—that was, grossly expressed, the sense of the whole intimation. And the money was to be for all the more exquisite things—for *all* the most exquisite except creation, which has to be off the scene altogether; for art, selection, criticism, for knowledge, piety, taste.[124]

Remy Saisselin described this tendency in *The Bourgeois and the Bibelot*, examining Americans' equal rapaciousness and superficiality in collecting portraits of European aristocrats, citing Paul Bourget's quip: "Yes, they have the portrait of the grand emperor, but where is the portrait of the grandfather?" Saisselin continued, stating that this witticism pointed "to society in which art . . . has been reduced to the status of a bibelot, bought by someone who probably knew nothing of what it once had meant."[125]

Perhaps not surprisingly, the strategies toward objects in shops became extended into museums. Some museum directors urged redesigning museum installations based on the department store displays, transforming the relationship between audience and artwork from one based on edification (with an implicit hierarchy), to one based on consumption.

Innovators in museum displays, such as Stewart Culin of the Brooklyn Museum and John Cotton Dana of the Newark Museum, vehemently rejected museums' traditional emulation of palaces and temples and championed a new image modeled on department stores. Admiring their clarity and directness of display, Culin asserted that stores, not churches, are the "greatest influences for culture and taste that exist today. They make it possible for us all to participate in the creative thought of a new and revolutionary era."[126]

Naturally, not all museum workers advocated these changes. G. Brown Goode, an ichthyologist and administrator at the Smithsonian Institute, chastised museums for being a "cemetery of bric-a-brac."[127] In a series of articles appearing in the New York magazine *Forum* in 1893, the English philosopher Frederic Harrison criticized the commercialization of art: "We buy works of imagination, like plate or jewelry, at so much the ounce or the carat; and we expect the creator of such works to make his fortune like the 'creator' of ball costumes, or of a dinner service. . . . [art has become] as much a matter of professional dealing as a corner in pork, or a Bear operation in Erie bonds."[128]

These comments reflect the first manifestation of one of the defining issues of the emerging paradigm of modernism: the predicament of how to distinguish art from (other) objects: if, indeed, this was possible. While this issue has become quite polemical in the twentieth and twenty-first centuries, when it first arose in the nineteenth century, the perplexity its caused seemed to lead to an impasse. On the one hand, both the handcrafted objects that were associated with (an imagined) less complex time began to seem anachronistic and the accompanying moral platitudes obsolete. Entrenchment in a Ruskinian worldview of art, refusal to acknowledge the overlap of the art market with business concerns became increasingly untenable. But, on the other hand, the wholesale celebration of fabricated goods and industrial objects as art seemed to lead to ludicrous consequences—a democratization of art to an excess—not resulting in a nation of artists but a nation of philistines, buying art indistinguishably from products.

Chinese and Japanese objects provided a way out of this dilemma. Although they were merchandise, they were absolved of their taint of commercialism by their perfume of exoticism. They were at once hand-made—the fine-crafted quality looked for in art—yet also novel, not antiquated; and these two characteristics worked in tandem. They seemed to bridge the virtues demanded by the older art paradigm while at the same time providing a glimpse of the formal qualities of a more cosmopolitan modernism.

William Hosley elaborated one aspect of this appeal, observing the attraction of Japanese art to those longing to uphold Ruskin's idea of art:

Western reformers attributed declining standards of art to the dehumanizing conditions of labor. From the small, single-proprietor craft shops of the preindustrial era had emerged the modern factory with its time cards, mind-numbing repetition, and division of labor. Small wonder that the old ways, now splendidly reaffirmed in the discovery of Japanese art, would be invoked as a new standard. . . . Western critics believed Japanese art was the product of a moral economy characterized by small family shops and labor practices that validated the dignity of the individual worker. It was an ethic that opposed specialization and the division of labor. The unity of art and artisanry, variation in ornament, and the use of traditional tools and technologies became positively charged. The Japan idea developed into a kind of shorthand for the affirmation of tradition.[129]

Yet, Japanese and also Chinese art fit a less traditional perception of art, an aesthetic moving away from the alleged morality of art, reflecting the emergent American ideology. Roger Stein's characterization of the Aesthetic movement provides an alternative description, which could equally serve as a description of Asian art:

Although the 1876 Philadelphia Centennial Exposition stimulated a certain nostalgia and even a Colonial revival—a belief that Americans could reinstate some of the forms and the supposed work habits of craftsmanship as well as the local and national loyalties associated with the founding fathers—the majority of Americans sought to come to terms with the new urbanized and industrialized society. The Aesthetic movement as a cultural phenomenon played an active role in the transformation of American life in the 1870s, 1880s, and early 1890s. It was a critique of previous modes of life and thought and both a response to and an expression of contemporary American culture, that is, the material conditions of late nineteenth-century America and the ideology—the system of values and beliefs—that supported, reinforced, and gave direction to certain patterns of life and work.[130]

The Chinese objects that, in contradistinction from the Japanese, had not been able to speak in the language of morality and the romanticized artistic enterprise occurring in mythic locations now began to assert, with the collaboration of the American aesthete, the composite reality of the emerging cosmopolis: the internationally interlaced economy and the contradictions as well as the delights of a more polyglot culture.

From their initial admittance into art museums as decorative and affordable commodities available for purchase after the Centennial Exposition, to their esteem in providing object lessons in material fabrication, Chinese objects now provided a step into the aesthetic sensibility of modernist culture.

4. The Change of Paradigm

Public acclaim of Chinese art in the last decade of the nineteenth century was a result of the excitement surrounding the purchase and exhibitions of Chinese and Japanese art by the newly hired curator/scholars of Asian art, more than increased cultural understanding of Asian art. Walter Muir Whitehall writes that "as the West had . . . acquired a taste for Japanese bric-a-brac, second-rate craftsmen were busy grinding out cheap products for export, while first-rate artists were neglected."[131] But, spurred by the increased visibility of Chinese things in museums, the public's taste and enthusiasm for Chinese art grew, although their cultural understanding of the artworks remained negligible. Like the general public, newspaper reporters also had no specific knowledge of Asian objects. On the receipt of the loan of Charles G. Weld's collection of Japanese swords, the reporter resorted to describing them as "superb" and the loan collection of ninety-nine pieces of Chinese porcelain as "very fine and rare specimens."[132]

Art expert Edward S. Morse was one of the first Americans to study Japanese aesthetics, and his immense knowledge, originating with his excitement over a mediocre Japanese porcelain bowl shaped like a shell, came only after years of study with Japanese artists and art experts. But years of studying Japanese art did not translate into a comprehension of Chinese aesthetics: while Morse revered Japanese art, even he had no corresponding appreciation of Chinese art.

The influx of Japanese and Chinese objects into the museums throughout the last few decades of the century continued at an increasing rate. In 1892 the MFAB purchased Morse's personal collection of Japanese ceramics (spurred by rumors that he would otherwise sell to the Met), and several years later it acquired 4,733 paintings from two major American collections of Japanese art: the William Sturgis Bigelow's collection and the Fenollosa-Weld collection. With the MFAB's hire of Ernest Fenollosa as Curator of Asian Arts in 1890s, followed by equally knowledgeable curators in the years since then, education about Asian culture and arts became available through the museum exhibitions and the public lectures. When Fenollosa curated an exhibition of Chinese Buddhist Paintings in 1894, the reporter now had more easy access to cultural information and could write more informatively: "The paintings are about 800 years old and represent . . . the glory of the Sung dynasty (1100–1300). . . . Two great schools of lofty esoteric religion have existed in China and Japan; one relied principally on works and sacraments, the other upon contemplation."[133]

The transition from an undifferentiated reception of Chinese things prior to 1880 to a more developed critical assessment occurred fairly rapidly over the 1880s. We see this change documented in newspaper articles that increasingly question the age of Chinese objects, wondering about fraudulent provenance, reaching its most public discourse with the fascination in what would have seemed to be of exoteric interest at best: the famous "Peachblow" vase. A bidding war for a rare color of porcelain led to reports that a single vase had sold for $18,000. The buyer denied purchasing the piece, other experts rejected the existence of the "peachblow" color, claiming it to be an ordinary strawberry red, and mystery and controversy surrounded all Chinese objects with this particular coloration. For a period of months the topic of the vase's authenticity became so popular that the newspapers published a lengthy doggerel verse composed about it![134]

Despite this type of media popularity, only a handful of people in the United States appreciated traditional Japanese arts. Art experts were rare and few understood traditional Chinese art.

But as discussed above, the greater presence of Asian objects in museums began to change what people saw as art: both what they actually viewed and what they imagined art could be. The increasing presence of non-Western objects, admired without narrative understanding or cultural context, helped precipitate a transformation to a new paradigm of art based on formal art qualities.[135] An article on both Western and Asian arts captures this transition, in fact, enacts it. After describing the Western oil paintings anecdotally, admiring one for having "much expression in the very pretty face," and another for "a noteworthy degree of sentiment" and "genuine sympathy for the subject," the article turns its attention to Asian objects. Immediately, and consciously, it changes tacks: "The difference between the Oriental and the Occidental temperament could not be impressed upon one more forcibly than by going from the sculpture hall of the Art Museum to the Noyes Art Gallery. In the one we see the grandeur and nobility of art, in the other its beauty and delicacy."[136] Despite attempts to describe the Asian art, especially the Japanese things, anecdotally, more frequently descriptions remain grounded in observations of line and form.

The articles' commentary typifies reviews of Chinese art in the later part of the century. Rather than through an understanding of traditional Chinese aesthetics, or its history, Chinese art became re-evaluated and appreciated in America primarily through its reinforcement of a new approach to art, contributing to the formulation of a new theory of aesthetics.

We have seen that, in Ruskin's paradigm, the analogy between art, nature, and morality viewed art creation as occurring in a semi-sacred space, with no taint of industry or the commercial. However, even by the late 1870s, adherents to this tradition were finding it increasing difficult to maintain the idea that art inhabited a rarified moral world excluded from incursions of industry or mercantile struggles. Nor had it been convincingly demonstrated that art objects embodied the moral and ethical circumstances of their fabrication or their culture. Nature itself was morally messy. Ruskin himself, discovering "the inadequacy of his own earlier complacent equations between good painting and good men," found art far more complex than he had initially presumed. He was left frustrated, his art convictions disabled, his assuredness of a direct correlation between nature and art vanishing into his awareness instead of a "calamitous mystery."[137]

But as Ruskin's ideas of art became increasingly disputed, another theory began to be advanced. Rather than denying the penetration of commodity culture into the sanctified world of art, instead a few artists audaciously aggrandized the merchandizing aspect of art. The very tone used in writing or speaking about art changed. Ruskin's voice was evangelical and his ideas persuasive like a sermon. Whereas this familiar tone resonated popularly in mid-century America, by the end of the century it sounded archaic, anti-quated. A new voice and attitude, a component of the Aesthetic Movement, is often considered the beginning of Modernism in art. This new tenor, epitomized by the sensationalized marketing strategies of James McNeill Whistler's during the 1860s to the 1890s, at first sounded strident, but with acclimation resonated as fresh, and a welcome frankness.[138]

Contrary to the Victorian taboo against perceiving art as a commodity, Whistler defiantly exploited the commercial market, utilizing marketing strategies that created a new hierarchical pricing. For instance, previously, all prints in an edition would have received the same price. Whistler inflated his prices based on whether or not his signature was on the particular print.[139] He refused to cater to the limits of taste of either the parvenu or of tradition, instead creating an aesthetic that demanded the audience accommodate to his vision. Rather than strive toward morality and modesty, he flagrantly courted publicity through his art, his dress, and his wit, arguing with critics and disparaging public opinions with relish. In 1887 the majority of millionaires still preferred "the sentimental and sugary Salon paintings."[140] Whistler made his contrary position about this aesthetic absolutely clear: "Mediocrity flattered at acknowledging mediocrity, and mistaking mystification for mastery, enters the fog of dilettantism, and, graduating connoisseur ends its days in a bewilderment of bric-a-brac and Brummegem!"[141]

His ostentatious display of his monetary transactions created an uneasy atmosphere for many art patrons, revealing the unresolved tensions revolving around the significance of art objects in a consumer society. The status quo immediately condemned his actions as vulgar but couldn't disguise its implications, and despite the predisposition to the contrary, an awareness began of the ambiguity, even caprice, in separating art from material goods and from national morality. With characteristic brashness Whistler scoffed: "Listen! There never was an artistic period. There never was an Art-loving nation."[142]

Changing the marketing of art turned the aesthetic status quo on its head. Rather than hypothesize the art world as akin to religion, a revelation of the moral sphere far from the vulgar marketplace, instead the emerging aesthetic theory acknowledged that mercantile currents penetrated into the art world. This radically changed the understanding of an artwork.

In fact, Whistler's main contribution to the changing paradigm of art was through his paintings: in their movement toward abstraction and their refusal to be reduced to a narrative description or depict moral sentiment. He explained his orientation, describing art through its negations:

> Art should be independent of all clap-trap—should stand alone, and appeal to the artistic sense of eye or ear, without confounding this with emotions entirely foreign to it, as devotion, pity, love, patriotism, and the like. All these have no kind of concern with it; and that is why I insist on calling my works "arrangements" and "harmonies."[143] In the new paradigm, the art object was regarded as inviolable, in itself, a separate reality. Unconditionally denying any moral or educative impulse in aesthetics, the modern art movement did not see works of art as speaking a narrative language. Rather, it asserted that subject matter was (relatively) insignificant, that anecdotal and moral content was superfluous, and that only intrinsic qualities of an artwork—line, color, form—mattered. The shift of emphasis from Ruskin to Whistler is a shift in location of the art within an object. Ruskin saw the entire art piece as separate from a commodity market; Whistler saw the artwork as part of the commodity market. Ruskin understood artistic communication as participating in other concerns, specifically moral and ethical, even religious; Whistler saw the artwork's communication to be nothing but its own aesthetic relationships. In the old paradigm, the artwork was inviolable, but its message participated in the discourse of the moral system; the new paradigm saw the artwork as a commodity, but its message was inviolable, setting up a discourse of form purely its own. Whistler resisted the popular commercialization of art, but not its commodification, while art that fit the Ruskinian rubric was becoming increasingly commercialized, used on advertisements and candy boxes, but maintained horror at the idea of the art image itself as a commodity.

The modernism ushered in with the Aesthetic Movement trumpeted the declaration: "l'art pour l'art"; the assertion that an artwork never expresses anything besides itself. Robert Rosenblum describes the new paradigm as a belief that art "represented a highly personal order" containing "new systems of decorative coherence as those found in Japanese art" distinct from, and, in fact, in opposition to "the shared, inherited order of the Western past that was still preached by the academies."[144]

Whistler also spoke of the qualities he desired and expected from an artwork. And in his synopsis of Aesthetic theory, the new art paradigm seems equally applicable to Chinese objects as to modernist paintings: The masterpiece should appear as the flower to the painter—perfect in its bud as in its bloom—with no reason to explain its presence—no mission to fulfil [sic]—a joy to the artist—a delusion to the philanthropist—a puzzle to the botanist—an accident of sentiment and alliteration to the literary man"[145] (figs. 2.10 and 2.11).

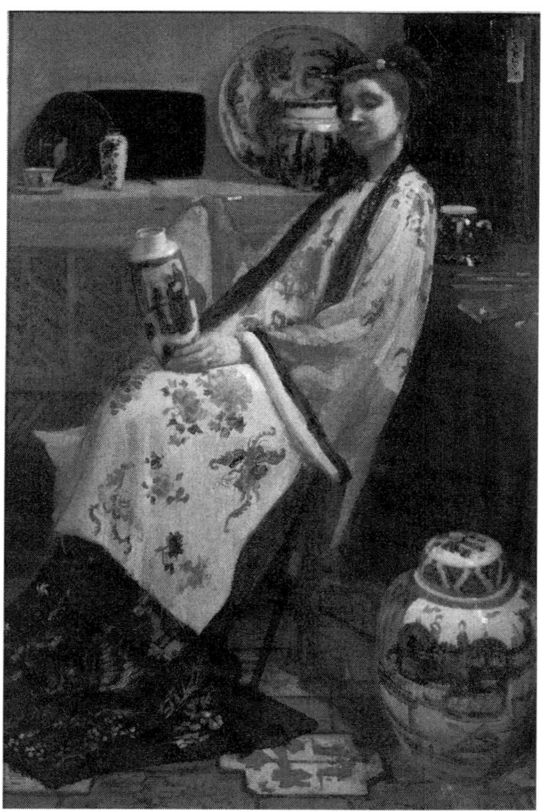

Fig. 2.10. James Whistler, *Purple Rose, the Lange Laizen of the Sixmarks*, 1864. Photo: Erich Lessing/Art Resource, New York.

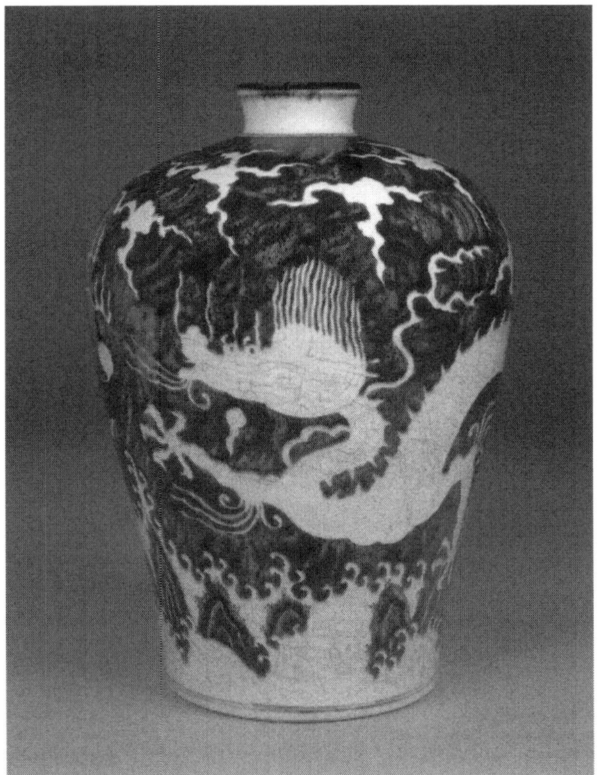

Fig. 2.11. Meiping-shaped vase with dragon. Chinese, Qing dynasty, early eighteenth century. Jingdezhen porcelain with blue underglaze and reserve white decoration. 37 cm (14 9/16"). Museum of Fine Arts Boston, Denman Waldo Ross Collection. 07.31. Photograph © 2011 Museum of Fine Arts, Boston.

Alfred Werner describes Whistler's artistic insights:

He slowly succeeded in educating the more sensitive that art should be an evocation rather than a statement; that a picture was not nature but an artifact, and must not compete with, or try to be mistaken for, reality; and that a person looking at a picture should be moved to exclaim, "How beautiful!" rather than "How true!"[146]

We can immediately correlate this to qualities found in Chinese art. But, on reflection, the overlap between Chinese objects and the new language of Aesthetics should not be surprising; Chinese objects were studied and admired by many of the innovative artists. Whistler designed the Peacock Room to house Frederick R. Leyland's collection of rare Chinese porcelain, and it is well known that modernists such as Manet studied Chinese porcelain and Japanese prints, incorporating their non-anecdotal eloquence through balance and rhythm of color and line. And, significantly, Whistler's passion for Chinese blue-and-white ware was frequently expressed in his art, depicting the porcelain and the female figure through the aesthetic remove, expressing the female form as if it were an Asian object.[147] Indeed, the Aesthetic's love of Chinese ceramics was so well known that George de Maurier lampooned it in a series of cartoons in Punch (fig. 2.12).[148]

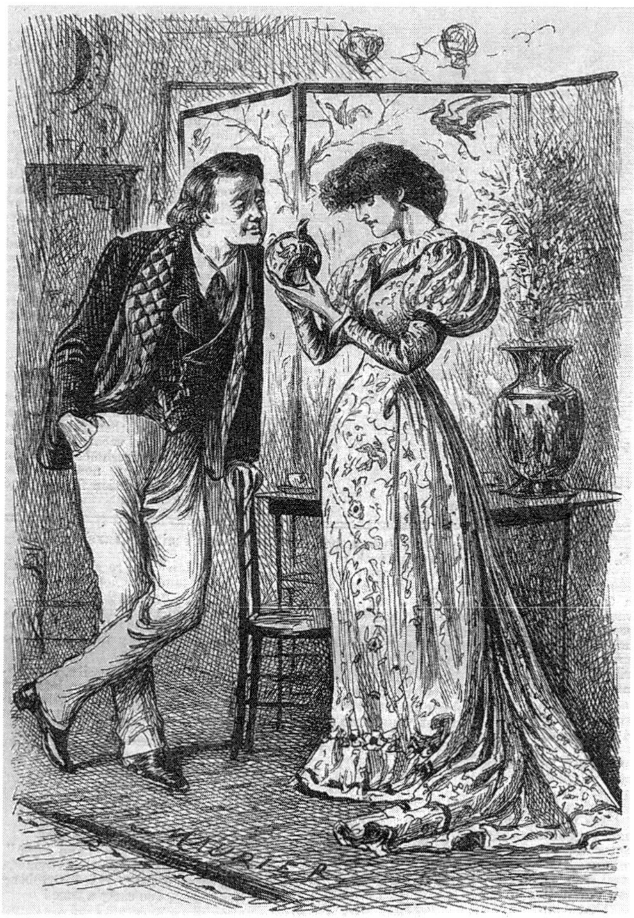

Fig. 2.12. "The Six-Mark Tea-Pot," in *Punch*, October 30, 1880.

In fact, an affiliation between Chinese objects and a proto-Aestheticist approach to art had preceded Whistler and his theories by almost half a century. Its earliest statement appeared in 1835, when Theophile Gautier wrote: "The useless alone is truly beautiful; everything useful is ugly, since it is the expression of a need . . . To a particular pot of which I make nightly use, I prefer a Chinese vase, covered with mandarins and dragons, which is of no use whatsoever."[149]

The initial repudiation of Aestheticism is well known: exemplified in the well-publicized ridicule of Whistler's paintings as unfinished sketches and Ruskin's infamous description of Whistler, after seeing his painting at the Grosvenor Gallery in 1877, as a "coxcomb ask[ing] two hundred guineas for flinging a pot of paint in the public's face."[150] In the subsequent law suit between Ruskin and Whistler, the American public remained equivocal regarding who emerged the winner. Nevertheless, despite the protestations by people as influential as Harvard art history professor Charles Eliot Norton, throughout the 1890s the taste for academic Salon works continually diminished, giving way before the presence of more formally astute art.[151]

The contribution of the Aesthetic theory of art to a new regard for Chinese art can be seen in the MFAB's Asian art expert Ernest Fenollosa's explanation of his ideology of aesthetics.[152] Fenollosa's discussion of Chinese aesthetics expresses the same orientation as modernist theory:

> I do not like the word 'decoration.' It seems to imply too much artificiality, a superficial prettiness. The word we ought to use is 'structural.' The lines, the spaces, the proportions lie in the structure of the thing itself.[153]

He also made the distinctly modernist separation between the image in the work and the subject of the work:

> Representation is not art, it is literature. That a picture represents a man does not interest us . . . It is a question of spacing, of how the pattern is worked out, that interest us . . . not the representational element but the structural element . . . not the realistic motive but the desire to find finer and finer space relations and line relations.[154]

By the 1890s, the type of Chinese and Japanese objects collected for American art museums had changed significantly from that collected in preceding decades. William Hosley describes the changes in museum collections of Japanese art:

Only one of the three major Japanese collections assembled by Victorian art museums (Metropolitan Museum of Art, New York) is still intact, and even there the early accessions are rarely shown. The two other great collections (Museum of Fine Arts, Boston and the Philadelphia Museum of Art) have been pillaged, their contents neglected and dispersed, and their memory nearly expunged from the record. Since collecting Japanese art was one of the major goals of American art museums during the nineteenth century, it is small wonder that the best treasures—the material that epitomized the Japan idea—found its way early into public collections. It is hard to believe that it is now almost impossible to find any of the tens of thousands of Japanese art objects that remained in the United States after the Centennial.[155]

Like Aesthetic paintings, Chinese objects crossed the thin line separating fine art from merchandise. Their function unknown or rendered insignificant in the museum context, they were viewed as esoteric and silent objects. Aesthetic theory provided access to a deeper appreciation of Chinese objects, especially to the works of greater antiquity and cultural integrity that had remained impenetrable under Ruskin's conception. Through Aestheticism, the metamorphosis of Chinaware from an educative decorative object to one of masterwork became complete.

But why did this change occur? Change of aesthetic taste is not merely a factor of abstract art appreciation but results from materiality, from the access to objects. Increased familiarity with a foreign art is often due to political 'change—frequently violent in nature. Looking at transitions in China—its increasingly weakened state after the wars of 1842 and 1860, and its inability to resist Europe's military backing of a forced opium market—we see its resulting instability, leading to civil wars, and war with Japan in 1895. The West took China's debilitation as an invitation to partition China for its own commercial interest and a justification for appropriating rare objects as spoils of war. Alexis Krausse's *China in Decay*, written in 1900, betrays the attitude predominating in the West, rationalizing the seizing of Peking and confiscation of its treasures as a necessity to prove the superiority of the West to China:

> The air of superiority which the Chinese had always been encouraged to cultivate made it impossible for them to realise that a nation of mere traders, such as the English, would dare actually to attack China. . . . The repetition in 1860 of the lesson which had been wasted in 1842, proved efficacious, and the capture of Peking caused the idea to dawn upon the Celestial intelligence that the "barbarians" were after all more than a match for the natives.[156]

The capture and looting of the Imperial Palace in Beijing, first in 1860 and then in 1900, allowed Westerners access to the most treasured Chinese artworks, a quality of Chinese art seldom seen in the West. This art was quickly removed from China and, within the decade after Chinese Exclusion in 1882, large collections were placed in both the Met and the MFAB.

The timing coincided with the increasingly stringent litigations expanding the original Chinese Exclusion Law of 1882: the Scott Act of 1888 and the Geary Act of 1892. American excitement over Chinese antiquities occurred only after the Chinese people no longer presented a remotely conceivable intimidating or polemical presence in the United States. New American art museum installations, influenced by Aestheticism, celebrated the Chinese art as they dehistoricized and neutralized Chinese history, reframing the objects within associations of American imperialism.

Indeed, the dehistoricizing of these objects became their membership card into modernism. The knowledge of their great age didn't translate into a sense of history, rather it reinforced the sense that they were suspended from "constraints of time."[157] Just as China was imagined as an unchanging culture, its ceramic art was seen as embodying a non-narrative timelessness. This non-narrative quality had made little sense in the early nineteenth=century world, seeking some form of story in visual art, but became appreciated in the later part of the century. In the new paradigm of Aestheticism, Chinese art also seemed in harmony with, indeed appeared to encapsulate, the Western experience of Chinese culture.

The MFAB is known as a historically conservative institution. Especially in the early decades, it did not collect modernist artworks. This lack of enthusiasm is generally understood to indicate its general resistance to modernism. Yet quite early, the museum distinctively altered its presentation of objects from a Victorian arrangement to an innovative display based on the modernist aesthetic. This became especially noticeable in its architecture: the expansion of the museum building on Copley Square in the 1890s to include a Japanese Corridor to house its collections of Asian objects formed under the guidance of Asian art experts such as Morse and Fenollosa in the 1880s and 1890s.[158] The sensitive response to the art's formal qualities required installations that emphasized this reading. The curator and scholar of Asian arts, Benjamin March, commended the MFAB as a "pioneer" in providing special settings for the Far East artworks.[159] In other words, although the Museum did not exhibit modernist tendencies in its selection of paintings, nevertheless modernist sensibilities permeated the aesthetics of display.[160]

While not embraced in the selection of paintings at the MFAB museum, the theory of "Art for Art's Sake," conditioned the changes in installations and display of Asian art. This enhanced their comprehensibility, as well as domestication. It allowed the American audiences to interact with and admire the more esoteric and traditional Chinese things now being acquisitioned by American art museums.

Chinese objects not only helped initiate a change in their own status, but they correspondingly altered the way Americans perceived and categorized the art world. By 1895, this change was institutionalized: the Met published a slim volume called *Garland Collection of Chinese Porcelain*, with an impressive bibliography of scholarly research from several European nations as well as China, illustrated with full-page photographic images of selected extraordinary chinaware.[161] And in the MFAB bulletin from the turn of the century, the museum celebrated its ownership of exemplary Chinese objects, simultaneously, and adroitly, refashioning its history of collecting Chinese things: "The importance of the collection of Japanese and Chinese paintings in the Museum has been recognized for many years by students of Oriental arts."[162]

THREE

FROM CLASS TO RACE

The New York Times *Reconstructs* *"Chinese"*

As anthropologist David Napier explains in his book *Foreign Bodies*: "Strangers within our midst are indeed the strangest of all—not because they are so alien, but because they are so close to us."[1]

—bell hooks

SECTION I. A BRIEF HISTORICAL CONTEXTUALIZATION

1. Introduction

In 1870, the idea of excluding Chinese from the United States seemed an absurd goal, not to mention an impossible undertaking. The minority agitating to exclude an entire nation's people was initially viewed by most people on the East Coast as disreputable, and their opinion patently wrong. Protest against Chinese immigration arose in the West Coast states, yet even there the population of Chinese people was barely statistically significant: the greatest immigration was in California, where Chinese comprised only a scant 11 percent of the population, while in New York State there were only 200 Chinese people in total. Most Americans outside of California had never actually seen a Chinese person, and in fact often imagined them as extraordinary and curious, basing their images on the seventeenth-century's lingering legacy of an exotic Orient. The vote in favor of exclusion occurred with a statistically insignificant population of Chinese throughout the entire East Coast.

The President has signed the new bill to suspend the immigration of Chinese laborers for a period of ten years. It is to be hoped that this will settle the much-vexed Chinese question for a time at least. The bill was drawn with special reference to the objections raised by the President in his Message disapproving the first bill passed by Congress. As it now stands, the law suspends the immigration of Chinese laborers, whether skilled or unskilled or employed in mining. It provides for a system of certificates, to be issued on the identification of Chinese persons now living in this country or who may hereafter arrive here under provisions of the law authorizing them to come. The naturalization of all Chinese is expressly forbidden. Various fines and penalties are imposed upon the masters of vessels who shall bring unauthorized Chinese persons into this country, and upon any person who shall forge, alter, or make fraudulent use of the certificates to be issued to Chinese who are allowed residence in the United States. The bill as it has become a law does not infringe upon any of the rights of China as defined in existing treaties. The people of California will probably be satisfied with all its features, unless they may object to the shortness of the term during which immigration is to be suspended.

Fig. 3.1. "Exclusion Law Signed," *New York Times*, May 9, 1882.

And yet by 1882, the Chinese Exclusion Act was voted into federal law (fig. 3.1). Although most often portrayed as an agenda solely of the western states, the federal Chinese exclusion law required a congressional majority, necessitating legislators from eastern as well as western states to vote in its favor. For this anti-Chinese mind-set to gain ascendancy in the eastern states, the *image* of Chinese people circulating through the East Coast had to change radically. The consensus to exclude the Chinese people from the United States was achieved by demeaning and demonizing the Chinese people, largely through verbal images disseminated through the newspapers.

This chapter concentrates on the newspaper medium and its ability to create powerful images. At stake is the question raised by James Clifford: "Who has the authority to speak for a group's identity or authenticity?"[2] And dovetailing with that inquiry: "What is the process by which one image gains that authority?"

The decisions concerning Chinese immigration were not tangential in US policy but a definitive element in the reformulation of the underlying matrix of national cohesion, a critical issue after the Civil War. While not obvious at the time, the Exclusion Act signaled a landmark change in American thought: it was the first American policy excluding people on the basis of race or national origin. Through the outcome of this debate, thought at the time to concern only Chinese people, Congress also delineated and effected all subsequent definitions of who and what was "American."

However, the relation between Chinese and American was not the dichotomy constituted as "self" and "other" (as if they existed in fixed and clearly delineated opposition). The boundaries between identity and difference, "us" and "them," are always transforming. More than merely depicting the American ideas of Chinese people, the Chinese image became a marker in American culture, a way for other Americans to visualize themselves.

Society is unified, coded, disseminated, and debated through media. It sends ideas and images zigzagging in unique patterns across the culture. In the absence of direct encounters with Chinese people, the idea of "Chinese," strong enough to mandate exclusion, was created largely by the images disseminated through media flowing through America.

Throughout the 1870s, two opposing narratives about Chinese people dovetailed in the eastern states, colliding finally in the 1882 congressional debates on Chinese exclusion.[3] How did a nation striving to create laws that would be reasonable, justify, and then reconcile itself to the idea of Chinese exclusion laws? How did the negative Chinese image, created by a minority of Americans, eventually, albeit uneasily, overtake a neutral and even a positive attitude, and become the national standard? By a close reading of the *New York Times* between 1870 and 1882, this chapter examines the construction of a dominant Chinese image.

This chapter is divided into three sections. Section I, "A Brief Historical Contextualization" has two subsections. The first, "Newspaper History and the *New York Times*," establishes the applicability of using the *Times* for this chapter's investigation by comparing the most widely distributed New York newspapers of the 1870s. This comparison clarifies the appropriateness of the *New York Times* for the questions addressed by this chapter.

The second section provides a brief historical context to sections II and III, both of which are textual exegeses of the *New York Times* from 1870–1882.

Section II, "Creating a 'Them,'" documents the transformation in the image of Chinese from a relatively affirmative description in the earlier years, to an increasingly antagonistic portrayal. This section explores ten traits, based on the main adjectives disseminated by the newspaper, that assisted in constructing the racial image of "Chineseness."

The traits examined in this section include descriptors of Chinese as coolies, hordes, heathens, barbarians; as people who carried contaminants, were sexual deviants and drug abusers; and who were ignorant and effeminate. The final trait explored is the increasing correlation of "coolie" with slavery. Through repetition and dissemination of these alleged characteristics, Americans became acclimated to the demonized rhetoric about the Chinese. And the investigation reveals that the decade began with equating all Chinese with a coolie class, but ended by considering them as a coolie race.

The theory of polygenesis appears as a subtext throughout this section. Originating in the sixteenth century, polygenesis hypothesized that mankind arose from multiple origins, only one of which had divine significance. Although the original versions of the theory were not racist per se, in fact, for the time they were quite universalist, with the Europe's global exploration and imperialism, by the nineteenth century the theory had been modified to assert the superiority of the white "race." White scientists created hierarchies of race in which nonwhite people were classified as inferior in intelligence and morality and frequently were disparaged as submissive and as carriers of diseases.[4] Even the most cursory reading of Louis Agassiz's theory of polygenesis will show a close relationship between his criteria and the categories I derived from reading the *New York Times*.[5]

With the ideology of Chinese as a race now firmly entrenched, section III, "Creating an 'Us,'" differentiates four voices struggling to create the dominant image of Chineseness in the United States. Again, my source for all four voices are articles in the *New York Times* that show the complexity of the Chinese persona circulating throughout the eastern states. The first voice is that of the *New York Times* itself: an ambivalent voice on the ethics of Chinese exclusion. Two voices come from the Congress: one asserting the pro-exclusion position and the other the anti-exclusion position. The final voice is that of the Chinese people living in the United States. Underlying each is the conviction that its view truly speaks for the meaning of America. The racialized coolie, the predominant caricature of a Chinese person, was used to advantage by the pro-exclusion voice, and became the image against which the other voices struggled.

Through its two separate sections "Defining the 'Them'" and "Defining the 'Us,'" this chapter demonstrates that there is a complicity in representing a group and presenting oneself. It is impossible to create one without modifying the other: the battle for defining Chineseness was, in essence, also a battle over American self-definition.

2. *Newspaper History and* The New York Times

This chapter is not an overview of images of Chinese disseminated through a panorama of late-nineteenth-century newspapers. Rather, it investigates the creation of Chinese characteristics from 1870 to 1882, leading to the construction of a dominant Chinese image that contributed to, and in a sense even sanctioned, passing the Chinese Exclusion Act in 1882.

To discuss this as a diachronic process rather than as an array of disparate images of Chinese people, rather than gathering images from a wide range of newspapers, I look at one newspaper, documenting the changes in its descriptions of Chinese people over that twelve-year period. After comparing East Coast newspapers available in the 1870s, I selected the *New York Times*.

Newspapers in the first decades of the century had been created for a male, affluent readership, and sold for six cents each. Referred to as "blanket sheets," they required a solid table to adequately read them: historian Elmer Davis describes them as "massive, expensive, and dull."[6] They persisted through mid-century.

In contrast to these older-style newspaper read by the old elites, later papers articulated their region's way of thinking about ideas and issues as well as presenting newsworthy occurrences: and they sold for only a penny. The penny paper created a revolution in the newspaper industry. In 1830 there were only sixty-five daily papers in the nation, increasing ten years later to 138, and from 489 in 1870 to 1,967 in 1900.[7] By 1850 New York City had fourteen dailies and a circulation of over 150 thousand; stated another way, one newspaper per four people. If its own figures are to be believed, a single newspaper claimed that at times its circulation rose over one million.[8]

From the end of the Civil War, newspapers became increasingly important participants in a national dialogue. For many readers, newspapers helped create a sense of community and belonging, helping solidify their identity as Americans. Priscilla Wald refers to this in her examination of nation-rebuilding after the Civil War, discussing how: "with the emergence of the nation as a world power and the arrival of immigrants in unprecedented numbers, came the need for new (and renewed) stories of American identity."[9] But one route to American identity came through the Chinese body; newspaper's commentaries about Chinese immigrants created a sense of distinction, and addressed the audience across this difference. Their dissemination of Chinese caricatures helped them become commonplaces, a part of a narrative of communion, a new component of the "cultural glue" unifying other groups in the United States.

By 1870, newspapers had undergone tremendous change from the days of exclusive upper-class readership. New York's newspapers served a readership that was 80 percent foreign-born or of foreign-parentage.[10]

The *Sun*, for instance, targeted a working-class demographic. Established in 1833, its founder, Benjamin Day, wrote about the change he saw in the laboring classes, that "they understand their own interest, and feel that they have numbers and strength to pursue it with success."[11] Its detractors, however, claimed it was read chiefly by "domestics in quest of employment, and cart-men dozing at street corners in waiting for a job."[12]

At the other extreme, many of the other penny newspapers often exhibited fanatic partisanship for one political party or another. *The Herald*, created in 1835, reveled in sensationalism; in fact, it is said to have invented "yellow" journalism. Catering to the popular taste for stories on vice and crime, the paper simultaneously whetted and capitalized on this appetite: and became extremely wealthy in the process. However, like *The Sun*, *The Herald* was also an admittedly democratic paper.

Responding to the sensationalist *Herald*, the more socially proper and conservative *Tribune* was established in 1841. The *Tribune* was the voice of the Whigs. Its owner, Horace Greeley, stated his intention for the newspaper to be "a welcome visitor at the family fireside." For its first decades, in its efforts to avoid all sensationalism and "immorality," it wouldn't publish any articles or even any notices about theatrical shows.

Arriving a decade or more later than these major New York papers, the *New York Times* was created by Henry J. Raymond and George Jones to fill a niche for a newspaper that strove for reflection, balance, and tolerance. Raymond had been a journalist as well as a politician, and in both roles had been noted for his ability to see both sides of a question clearly. Similar to the *Tribune*, the *Times* aspired to be a family newspaper, but wanted to achieve this not through moral purity, but through temperance and balance, stating that it was "not established for the advancement of any party, sect or person."[13]

This might at first seem antithetical to the advertising slogan in 1872 as "the only Republican morning paper in New York." But the *Times* always maintained its independence from Republican control. Their relationship has been described rather colorfully as a marriage of unequals, one that "suggested the simile of a loyal wife doing her best to get along with a scandalously dissipated husband. The *Times* had not exactly married the Republican party to reform it, but it did what it could to bring the party back to the strait [*sic*] and narrow path."[14] While the *Times* was Republican, it supported non-partisanship, and criticized the party, even at times supporting Democrats.

Of all East Coast newspapers, the *New York Times* seems the most appropriate choice for the purposes of this chapter, because of its wide readership and its reputation for presenting balanced news rather than spouting extremism.

Newspapers are not univocal. The *New York Times* provides access to several at times competing images of Chinese people circulating in American culture, and sometimes it even describes its deliberate attempts to distinguish its stance from the rabid anti-Chinese sentiment ascribed to California labor politics.[15] In this way, the *Times* functioned as a site in which different voices were located and broadcast publically.

Through its articles, as well as through its own rhetoric, the *Times* documented the intensification of negative characterizations of Chinese people circulating in the eastern states during the twelve years prior to the Chinese Exclusion Act. Equally, the articles confirm that the Chinese image in America was not a static one: the *Times* articles document the changes in the characterizations over time. Read consecutively, the articles establish how the positive imagery, at first dominant in these states, gradually became subsumed by negative portrayals. In the course of exploring the Chinese image, the chapter confronts the nature of the news media: the conundrum between reporting views and forwarding them.

3. A Glance at History of Labor, Politicians, and Anti-Chinese Agitation

In the middle of the nineteenth century, although some East Coast newspapers published articles with derogatory content, most articles spoke about these newcomers to America as hardworking: perhaps they portrayed them as quaint, but not as undesirable. The *New York Times* found that its audience was interested in the Chinese, and their activities made good copy.[16] But as more Chinese immigrants entered the country—as many as thirteen thousand recruited as laborers for the transcontinental railroad alone—they ceased to be merely an exotic abstraction.

Over the period of sixty years, 105,465 Chinese people entered the United States—some for the gold rush of 1848, most recruited in subsequent decades to work on railroads and in the mines. Because of the influx of Chinese laborers, the call for Chinese exclusion was represented primarily as a labor issue. And in California, although only one-tenth of the population, Chinese made up a quarter of the labor force. However, the extent of Chinese immigration is mitigated when placed in context with the general increase in all immigrant groups: between 1870 and 1879, the United States's immigration total was approximately 2.7 million, but 71,800 Chinese people lived in the United States in 1870, increasing to only 108,200 by 1880.[17]

While the representation of Chinese exclusion as a labor issue had a kernel of truth, it was largely a cover. Early in its inception, the anti-Chinese movement had transitioned from a working-class protest to one led by the politicians invested in wealthy-class interests.[18] Andrew Gyory makes this distinction clear:

> contrary to the claims of numerous scholars, most workers evinced little interest in Chinese exclusion. Organized labor nationwide played virtually no role in securing the legislation. The motive force behind the Chinese Exclusion Act was national politicians who seized and manipulated the issue in an effort to gain votes, while arguing that workers had long demanded Chinese exclusion and would benefit from it.[19]

As political interests in Chinese exclusion moved from professing concerns over labor issues to being used by politicians to serve their own agendas, the tenor of pro-exclusion arguments changed. Articles in the *Times* demonstrate that in early pro-exclusion arguments, the objection to Chinese immigrants on the basis of race would occasionally emerge, but only surreptitiously. But when politicians for exclusion found that labor arguments were ineffective, their race bias became overt.[20] By the mid-seventies, labor issues lingered only as a smokescreen, inadequately concealing the underlying racialized animosity.[21] Through the *Times* we can witness the demonization of the Chinese image as the issue justifying exclusion changed from labor and class to race.

SECTION II. CREATING A "THEM":
THE STRATEGIES OF DEMONIZATION

1. Part Becomes the Whole: Turning Chinese into Coolies

Coolieism is not a Chinese classification but a Western social and political category that was applied to Chinese people. The term *coolie* derived from India, referring to specific Indian servants for the British.[22] From designating a low-income servant or laborer, it gradually became identified with more slavish characteristics, gaining popularity in the United States through its frequent use by anti-Chinese groups desiring to generate anxiety about Chinese people. The image of a debased laborer—a *coolie* was first applied only to a specific group of Chinese workers; then construed to constitute a class; and then expanded to encompass all Chinese.

In the early 1870s some *Times* articles attempted to find rational and definitive criteria for distinguishing the idea of the *coolies* from *regular* Chinese workers. But the distinction proved so evasive that eventually most articles settled on using *coolie* interchangeably with *Chinese*. This synechdochial transformation took less than a decade.

Times articles indicate that, initially, opposition to Chinese immigration was circumscribed within an intensifying dispute between labor and capital. The objection to Chinese workers began as a weapon of the labor movement, but could not get very far, as employers found much to praise in the Chinese immigrants. The first Chinese workers came to the East Coast in 1870, when Mr. Sampson, a shoe manufacturer in Massachusetts, thwarted the organized labor group, the Crispins, by hiring seventy-five Chinese workers, bringing them from California to the small town of North Adams (see figs. 1.17 and 1.18). They were described as capable and diligent workers, especially commendable because of their willingness to work steadily and cheaply. The Chinese were also praised for not forming trade unions. This perception, although it remained entrenched for decades, actually was as specious as the negative images: in 1873, the Chinese shoemakers went on strike.[23] But the contention that Chinese workers created substandard expectations was picked up by savvy politicians in their bids for reelection. By manipulating the Chinese image, they aspired to gain popular favor by inciting working-class people, most of whom had no previous animosity toward the Chinese.[24]

Times articles in the early 1870s reveal their own uneasy negotiation between the contradictory representations of Chinese immigrants arising alternatively from labor and from capital. Some articles would occasionally interweave both viewpoints: one appearing overtly as the subject, and the other embedded within the subtext. On the first page of the *Times* on July 1, 1870, the article "The Coming Coolie . . ." ostensibly reported a rally in Tomkins Square in which laborers, trade unions, and politicians unrestrainedly championed exclusion as a solution to the labor problem.[25] But throughout the article the reporter's narrative strategy subtly undermined the viewpoint expressed and endorsed in the mass meeting. Despite the presence of New York Mayor A. Oakey Hall as a keynote speaker, the reporter downplayed the event's significance.[26] He pointedly described the paltry attendance at the two English Language podiums, emphasizing that the audience never exceeded 300 persons, and that one podium consisted "almost entirely of foreign-born citizens," and the other "mainly of small children who had assembled to witness the initiatory proceedings attendant upon the letting off of the fire-works." Only the third podium, with speeches in German, attracted about 2,000 listeners.

The rally's emotive speeches construed Chinese laborers as enemies of the worker, and repeatedly expressed the belief that "coolie importation" bitterly threatened the welfare of American laboring families. The Mayor's sensationalized speech maligned the entire state of Massachusetts because one shoe manufacturer, Mr. Sampson, had employed Chinese workers.[27] Another spokesperson condemned the employment of Chinese workers as an endeavor to "demoralize and ultimately suppress all classes of working men by an arbitrary and forced importation of the lowest and most degraded of the Chinese barbaric race."

In reporting these speeches the reporter stressed the brutish nature of the audience applauding these invectives: reporting a key speaker's declaration that "Sampson has bragged in the streets of Boston that he would break up the Crispins," the reporter also noted someone in the crowd responding "Shoot him."

Times articles favorably disposed to Chinese workers occasionally revealed an anti-union subtext. In an article on July 9 titled "The Celestial Shoe-Makers. The Chinaman at Work in North Adams, Mass,—Progress of the Apprentices—Characteristics and Appearance—Their Reception by the 'Natives'—Crispins Giving Up the Contest," the reporter praised the Chinese workers, pointing out how "speedily and thoroughly they have mastered the technicalities of the business" and that "their memories are alike quick and retentive and their facility of execution good." His remarks against the former workers, organized as the Crispins, express a less inclusive tendency: using arguments often directed at Chinese people, he summarily dismissed the Crispins with the statement that nearly all of them "were foreigners."

Chinese workers inadvertently became pawns in this political class struggle. A letter to the editor on July 11, 1870, unequivocally connected a positive attitude toward Chinese with hostility to labor unions.[28] The letter writer defended the Chinese as "a well-conducted, sober, saving, cleanly and expert people," suggesting that a look at the prison population would speak poorly not of the Chinese but of other immigrant groups. He continued:

> The wealthier classes in this country, both male and female, have become thoroughly tired of the encroachments of the laboring men and women. They are tired of their constantly-increasing demands for more remuneration their decreasing efficiency, and their growing disposition to be more mistress than maid, and more master than man, are generating a feeling in regard to them which will soon make any change desirable.

These, and many other favorable reports of Chinese workers added to the polarity of public opinion of the Chinese. Yet, exclusionists found that the labor argument had limited efficacy; it appealed primarily to certain members of the laboring class, as well as to inflammatory politicians, while leaving the rest of the country indifferent. Many *Times* articles concurred with the descriptions voiced in *Our Chinese Immigrants* on July 14, 1870, finding the Chinese to be sober and hardworking, "a docile and peaceable resident," and calling their condemnation "wholly unnecessary."[29] These articles echoed the conclusion that "To oppose free immigration would be as futile as ungenerous."

For an American majority to accept the exclusion of an entire nation of people, the opposition to the Chinese needed to be restructured: the locus of the dissatisfaction shifted away from labor and toward the Chinese persona itself, which became entirely reimaged. How this was done can be seen in the newspapers portrayal of Chinese, representing them with the following traits.

2. Hordes

The recently industrialized United States anxiously gathered and analyzed immigration statistics, desiring to find assurance of increasing immigration. But *Times* articles from the 1870s reveal one inconsistency: the movement desired for Chinese immigrants was a swift departure. Frequently misrepresented and misinterpreted, statistics often alleged exorbitantly high figures of Chinese immigration.[30] Some *Times* articles printed these inflated findings, forecasting the imminent invasion of Chinese hordes into the United States. While other articles reported actual immigration and departure statistics, they never dispelled the impending fear of hordes of invading Chinese. Similar to the lack of rhetorical structures countering the image of coolie, here too the reporter devised no alternative to counter the image of a horde. Saying "not a horde" still leaves the idea of horde as the dominant image.

In *A Grammar of Motives*, Kenneth Burke discussed the power in the concept of a "primal horde," arguing that its significance is not within the society allegedly giving rise to the horde but in the accusing culture.[31] Burke's conclusions are pertinent to understanding the effective political use of the fear of Asian hordes in the United States during the 1870s and 1880s.

The premise of hordes dehumanized Chinese immigrants, characterizing them as a singular violent and mindless entity, and persuaded many who might be reluctant to discriminate against individuals to join in protest against the terrifying group. Hordes helped recast pro-exclusion ideology as self-protection, rather than as racism.

Although the imputation of a Chinese invasion originated in the western states, as early as 1870 the East Coast participated in the horde imagery. In that year the *Times* printed a tirade against Chinese immigration written by the ex-governor of New York, Horatio Seymour, describing the threatening Asian invasion.[32] Seymour's "Letter to the Working Men at Rochester," reprinted in full by the *Times*, displayed a degree of hostility against the Chinese often ascribed exclusively to Californians.[33] Beginning his address by commending the American virtue of welcoming immigrants, Seymour subverted this magnanimity by slyly substituting European peoples for the welcomed immigrants.[34] His lack of facts added force to his fantasy of a mythic Asian monstrosity against whom the Crispins and other brave souls must battle. Seymour's letter insinuated an unnamed conspiracy bringing in untold a numbers of Chinese, portrayed as an undifferentiated mass of destruction:

> Strong influences are at work to open the flood-gates and pour in upon us the worst classes of over-crowded China. They can get to our shores at less cost, and in greater numbers than the people of Europe. If they continue to crowd in, they will overthrow the customs, civilization and religion of the whole Pacific coast, and they will also crush down the position of laboring classes throughout the country.

He clarified, "I am against this."

Seymour exhorted against the Chinese not only in regard to their present employment as laborers but for their potential role as voters, insinuating even their votes to be anti-American, thereby compelling their unqualified exclusion. He condoned violent measures to achieve exclusion, endorsing the ill-treatment of Native American people as a prototype. His viewpoint bears repeating, because it presents a justification for excluding Chinese that has largely been repressed:

> Today we are dividing the lands of the native Indians into States, counties and townships. We are driving off from their property the game upon which they live, by railroads. We tell them plainly they must give up their homes and property and live upon corners of their own territories, because they are in the way of our civilization. If we can do this, then we can keep away another form of barbarism which has no right here.

The *Times* reprinted Seymour's diatribes without editorial comment.

The power that resulted from shifting the animosity toward an individual to an entire group can be seen in a lengthy letter to the editor titled "The Chinese Labor Question," appearing in the *Times* on July 11, 1870.[35] In the course of his letter, the letter writer's initial advocacy of equal rights for Chinese immigrants became transformed because of an imagined Chinese horde and ultimately self-destructed, ending by supporting exclusion. The letter began favorably with "I am of the opinion that the Chinese are as much entitled to work in this country, by contract or otherwise, as any other class of people upon the globe"—and then, suddenly capitulating, hypothesized—"If Congress, however, after deliberation, should determine that a large influx of Chinese would seriously damage the interests of the country." Once the argument allowed the conditional tense, and with it the horde, its reversal to a position supporting exclusion resulted almost automatically.

Nevertheless, the specter of an invading horde did not go unchallenged. Throughout the decade, various arguments ranging from fact to flights of fancy disputed the threat of invasion, attempting to bolster and reaffirm the white majority's conviction of its own unfaltering dominance. Brief statistical articles in the *Times* cited the startlingly low numbers of Chinese traveling both to and from the United States.[36] For instance, an article from the *San Francisco Bulletin* reprinted in the *Times* on the first of January 1871, reported that only sixty-nine Chinese had arrived on the last boat. The same article also addressed the seldom mentioned topic of Chinese departures: "For some time past the departures of these people from this port have been more than the arrivals.' Two days later the *Times* printed an article, Statistics of Immigration. Comparisons with 1869 and Other Years—the Decline During the Last Year and the Causes," which cited even lower figures for Chinese immigration.[37] The accompanying immigration chart determined China's immigration at 20, Japan at 1, compared to Ireland at 64,168, Germany at 72,368, and Australia at 9.

Several articles marshaled other stereotypes to counter the stereotype of an imminent arrival of Chinese hordes. One, titled "John Chinaman," reassured the reader that "the fears then entertained of an immense influx of Mongolians, who were to fill all branches of labor to the complete exclusion of their white rivals have been found to be wholly groundless.'[38] To substantiate his claim, the reporter referred to the "national traits of character of the Chinese,' stating: "Never was there a race of men to whom the attractions of home are so strong." Reflecting that the circumstances bringing so many Chinese to America were unprecedented, the reporter recalled: "Few seem to consider that at the time the Chinese immigration began, California, and the entire Pacific coast as well, offered inducements to men from all over the world, such as in all probability will never again be held out in any part of this country."

Having encountered the term *John Chinaman*, it merits comment. Rather than being a name proper, a signifier of an individual, it signifies the antithesis: a generic designation. It is in fact a metonym, a way of turning Chinese individuals into an undifferentiated whole, an absolute and indivisible entity. Thus, even as he spoke against the concept of Chinese hordes invading the United States, the reporter presented an image of a faceless single Chinese man that sustained the image of a faceless, multiple body of Chinese.

And in a composite of humanism and prejudice possible only in the nineteenth century, one reporter advanced this reassuring argument against the imminent threat of an overtaking horde: "If we can manage to live with three or four millions of people with black skins, who once were believers in Mumbo Jumbo, we might, perhaps, contrive to get on with as many people with yellow skins who are believers in Confucius."[39]

Despite these several reassurances, the topic of hordes remained a powerful rhetorical tool in many pro-exclusion arguments. It gained momentum over the decade, emerging even in the congressional debates; in fact exclusionists used the image of hordes to great advantage there, proselytizing against the threatening Chinese deposition of the United States' white hegemony. The *Times* printed a letter titled "The Anti-Chinese Agitation. The Hon. Montgomery Blair Approves of Senator Miller's Recent Speech . . ."[40] Referring to the Senate debates on Exclusion, Blair capitalized on the image of hordes of Chinese, stating: "I do not see how any thoughtful lover of his country can countenance this Mongolian invasion, involving as it does primarily the subversion of our civilization. Mr. Hoar[41] seems intent on submerging us with Asiatics in the mistaken notion that our declaration for equality and the rights of man compelled us to open the country to all comers." In response, Senator Brown's argument against exclusion put a rare realistic spin on the chestnut of the imminent invasion of the United State by hordes of Chinese by observing that in actuality China was already more overwhelmed by the West, through telegraph, railroad, and so on, than the United States ever would be by China.[42]

3. Heathen

Religious epithets were common denunciations of the Chinese, but religion itself was rarely used as an argument against the Chinese immigrant. And, while the *Times* occasionally printed articles such as one written by Rev. W. H. Boole, castigating the Chinese not only as a problem to the American nation but also to the entire Christian Church, it more frequently reported the speeches of Rev. Beecher who defended the Chinese against such accusations.[43] Other articles found reassurance in the idea that the Chinese were steadily, if only gradually, converting to Christianity.[44]

Religious defamation mainly resorted to name-calling. "Heathen," the most frequent epithet applied to the Chinese, had been popularized in 1870 by Bret Harte's poem "Plain Language from Truthful James" (later shortened to "The Heathen Chinee") and immediately became a permanent fixture in *Times* rhetoric.[45] The poem opens with these lines:

> Which I wish to remark,
> And my language is plain,
> That for ways that are dark
> And for tricks that are vain,
> The heathen Chinee is peculiar,
> Which the same I would rise to explain.[46]

The *Times* followed suit, titling articles "Converted Heathens," and "The Woes of a Heathen Chinee," and describing incidents surrounding a "heathen Chinee poker game"[47] (see fig. 3.2).

CONVERTED HEATHENS.

Much of·the opposition manifested to Chinese immigration on the Pacific slope has been owing to the expressed apprehension that these new-comers were importing to our shores a life and habits utterly alien and repugnant to our own. It was colonizing heathenism, we were told, in the midst of Christianity. Their ways were not as our ways, nor their God our God, and would never become so. As long as they remained here they would be an insoluble element in our population, adding nothing to our wealth or our prosperity, "bearing" our domestic labor market, and preying upon our industries like some strange swarm of locusts from over sea. Visions of a pig-tailed and almond-eyed invasion, which should cover the land with joss-houses and chop-sticks, haunted the uneasy dreams of the statesman, and poisoned the whisky of his constituents; and the San Francisco "hoodlum," as he joined in the daily hunt of the yelling Celestial, felt himself urged on to his destruction by the holiest impulses of patriotism and religion.

These fears have fortunately proved at least partially unfounded. The Chinese are a wonderfully adaptive people, and here they have not belied their reputation. The rapidity and zest with which they are adopting some of our finest and most characteristic national traits is really surprising.

Fig. 3.2. "Converted Heathens," *New York Times*, June 16, 1874.

However, for all the instances of the newspaper's "Heathen Chinee," and its references to the Chinese as pagans (often meant humorously), few *Times* articles expressed alarm about heathenism.[48] *Heathen* became an almost automatic modifier of *Chinese*. While its very ubiquity possibly offset some of the venom maligning an individual Chinese person, its greater perniciousness lies in its accentuation of the separation between "real Americans" and Chinese immigrants as an entire group.

4. Barbarity and Contamination

Quite the opposite of the, relatively speaking, benign "heathen," tales of Chinese savagery emerged early in the decade, in vivid and salacious detail. An article published on February 23, 1873, titled "A Chinese Murder" gave a lurid account of Chinese barbarity[49] (fig. 3.3). Beginning with the indictment that "A murder of the most horrible nature was perpetrated at Soochow," the writer described a cannibalistic scene: "They now all set upon the unfortunate person bound to the pillar, biting him over his whole body till dead. When the magistrates arrived, these savages had just finished their devilish work, not having yet had time to wash the blood off their mouths." The entire populace of Soochow became condemned as equally diabolical:

> Horrible as this affair is, the account of it is told in Soochow from one to another, with a gusto and grin over the whole face, as if it had been a capital joke that had been played. There seems to be no feeling in them; they are hardened, having got used to such scenes, thanks to their paternal Government.[50]

The reporter appended a warning to his article, providing his readers with an "insight into some of the customs prevalent among this strange people," and cautioning them about "what Chinese guides are capable of doing when they think their rights and time-honored customs have been outraged." Using the pronoun "us," he includes himself in the group, furthering the separation of Chinese people from Americans.

In 1873, sensationalized allegations associating Chinese with small pox and leprosy appeared in the *Times*, most often in articles reprinted from California newspapers. Claiming obscure links between Chinese and contamination, the government in California more brazenly discriminated against the Chinese immigrants. Almost immediately, however, other *Times* articles reacted against such defamation, connecting the slanderous reports about Chinese with small pox to the Californian opposition to Chinese immigration.[51] One article harshly indicted the Californian press for resurrecting old cases of the disease as if they were new. Several months later,

A Chinese Murder.

A murder of the most horrible nature was perpetrated at Soochow, a few days ago, says a Shanghai paper. The whole affair gives us an insight into some of the customs prevalent among this strange people, and shows us what Chinese guides are capable of doing when they think their rights and time-honored customs have been outraged. It appears that the gold-beaters of Soochow have it, among other old-established customs, that a master gold-beater can only engage one apprentice at a time. and this is even limited to large shops only. An apprentice of this craft is bound for three years, and only after the expiration of this time can the master employ another one. The object is to keep the number of craftsmen within certain bounds, and so to guard against a decrease of their present high wages, about 7,300 cash per diem. A master gold-beater and head of the guild lately ventured to break this established custom by employing an apprentice before the time of the old apprentice had expired. This roused the members of the craft, and they opposed. The master gold-beater carried his case before the magistrate, who decided that, notwithstanding the old custom, more than one apprentice could be employed ; but advised, for the sake of peace, and in consideration of the prejudice of the workmen against it, that this should not be done too often. The workmen of the craft were not satisfied with this decision, and tried by all means in their power to make the head of the guild desist from taking a second apprentice. He, however, on the strength of the magistrate's decision, would have his own way, and, as he was threatened by the workmen, asked assistance from the Yamen to protect him. The workmen at last invited him to come to their public hall to talk matters over. He went, accompanied by some Yamen runners to protect him. Having arrived at the guild-hall, some 120 men were found assembled there who, after having pushed the Yamen runners out, closed the doors. All efforts on the part of the Yamen people to gain an entrance were useless ; they were told by the workmen inside that no one but the magistrate himself would be admitted. The Yamen runners, hearing the cry

Fig. 3.3. "A Chinese Murder," *New York Times*, February 23, 1873.

a similarly discerning article reported that rumors of Chinese leprosy were: "totally groundless and mischievous."[52] Direct accusations of Chinese disease apparently had only limited credibility on the East Coast.

Nevertheless, the effect of these abusive images contributed to a general shift in the *Times* toward a more negative portrayal of Chinese people. Notwithstanding the eastern states' patent rejection of a direct relationship between Chinese people and disease, they responded more tolerantly to intimations of a connection between the two. For instance, the *Times* reprinted a California article with an analogy between Chinese immigration and contamination:

> If my neighbor carries all the dirt and garbage from around his house and placed it at my door, must I be compelled by the spirit of the golden rule to sit quietly by? I say not. In like manner, I say that the golden rule does not require us, as Christian men, to sit quietly in our homes and see this great business of international scavengeing [*sic*] going on.[53]

Besides referring to the articles as "moderate," the *Times* made no comment.

The newspaper's dissemination of these articles without verifying the allegations helped nationalize images connecting Chinese with a particularly virulent pollution. A letter presented by a Pennsylvanian legislator to the House of Representatives, reprinted in the *Times* on February 12, 1873, indicated the escalation of negative images to national prominence. The legislator brazenly declared Chinese habits to be "so debasing as to insure the demoralization and degradation of all Christian communities brought in contact with them."[54]

5. *Sex and Drugs*

Certainly since the "Opium Wars" (1839–1842), China and opium were firmly connected in Western minds, though this relationship had never been exploited in the press. By the date of the Senate's exclusion vote, however, various *Times* articles showed that the perception of opium use had altered, becoming a crime, an immoral addiction associated with the Chinese.

In the early 1870s the *Times* printed only one or two articles on opium per year, portraying opium as an exotic curiosity. Two articles with diametrically opposed attitudes toward the Chinese both show no moral indignation when discussing opium use. In an article (humorously) deriding Chinese things written in the format of a travelogue, the reporter described his visit to China and his mandatory visit to an opium den, encountering the predictably "wretched-looking lot" with "repulsive, vicious expression of countenance." But his low image of Chinese people was not restricted to opium habitués, it was echoed in his visit to a nunnery, where he found "young Chinese girls, repulsive in features and form, their dresses in tatters, and their persons filthy." And, similarly, in his descriptions of people at a Chinese temple. (He did, however, manage to encounter two places to his liking. Not incidentally, they were places of commerce, more than of culture. The first, a tea shop, a gathering place that he compared favorably to New York saloons, finding it cheerful and polite, leading him to endorse Eastern culture over Western at this point. And he also rhapsodized over the shop wares, claiming they exceeded their counterparts in Europe.)[55]

In the second article, "The Chinese New Year. Idolatry in Baxter Street—Feasting and Smoking Opium," despite the promise of the headline the article barely mentioned opium at all.[56] In this investigation of the living conditions of the New York Chinese, the reporter commented on "the trials of the Chinese life in the United States . . . [t]he wretched life, the poverty, and misery to which the unhappy Chinaman is doomed in this country," but he portrayed the Chinese people favorably. He described his Chinese guides as young, with a friendly intelligence. When he asked about the food the Chinese were preparing, "his guide, smiling, said: 'Oh, ho! you think we Chinamen eat nothing but rice. We have chicken! Put that down in the paper.'" The only reference to opium arose in the non-judgmental last line: "the festival will close to-morrow with a grand opium-smoke."

But the middle of the decade saw a tension arise between the earlier, more indulgent image of opium and the modern criminalized attitude. The older tolerance toward opium appeared in an article in which the reporter affably narrated his own experience of opium smoking.[57] He described his pleasure in attending the cigar makers banquet in San Francisco, an occupation dominated by Chinese workers, especially in discovering the elaborate preparation and high quality of the food. After the banquet, the reporter was invited to try opium, which he sampled but pronounced his experience "a nauseating novelty."

Yet just a month earlier a presumably different reporter railed against opium and the Chinese, stating that an elusive Chinese black market "in some mysteriously manner smuggled [opium] into the country." In 1875, a lengthy article tried to assess the validity of these opposing images, surveying factual information provided by experts about the consequences of opium use.[58] The reporter described the range of arguments among medical professionals, from Dr. Eatwell's affirmation that opium had no evident negative physical effects, to Dr. Little's dire conviction that opium was so harmful that, without immigration, the native population of Singapore would be extinct from its use. The reporter concluded that more facts were needed before the question of opium's effect could be resolved.

But, when marshaling criteria against the Chinese, facts did not always matter. Reconstructing history, a *Times* article defended the Anglo-Indian government against the "constant attacks" that it introduced opium into China.[59] Claiming access to a "more careful study of the facts," the writer contended that the Chinese willingly participated in the all aspects of opium commerce, scoffing that "The question of forcing opium on the Chinese is then only a commercial question."

An occasional counter-opinion would be heard, such as that of E. B. Drew, the commissioner of the Imperial Customs to China, who had lived in China since 1865.[60] But his measured viewpoint had to compete with antagonistic views of opium that were broadcast ever more frequently and became a way to vilify the entire Chinese people. For instance, on July 6, 1875, the *Times* reprinted a long article titled "CHINESE CUSTOMS. Their Life and Education. The Craving for Opium and Its Effects—Superstition Among Them—A Trick That Prevailed." With a kind of gusto, the article the article equated thievery, stupidity, and opium addiction with all Chinese:

> The thieving proclivities of the Chinese are generally ascribed to the moral and religious principles of the race and their low mental calibre . . . , which is a great mistake. Investigation will show that nine-tenths of the Chinese criminals in this city are inveterate opium consumers and that it is solely to supply themselves with this drug that they plunder. To be sure, there are many consumers of the drug among the race who are not criminals, but a negative proves nothing.[61]

Additional shock value was provided by graphic newspaper reports of opium use infiltrating into the white population:[62]

> Even those of our own proud Caucasian race, however respectable they may formerly have been whenever they have acquired this terrible habit and have impoverished themselves seem to lose all moral restraint and will commit any crime, and run any risk in order to procure opium.

By 1882, the newspaper referred to white American's opium habits as "common knowledge," sensationalizing it through allegations that children, "boys and girls," also used opium. Articles warned that if opium was not banned, its use would infiltrate further among the white population.[63] This dire prophecy was repeated in articles describing visits to the sordid New York Chinatown, encountering opium dens, evil Chinese men and young, white, female, prostitute addicts.

The accusation of prostitution became another effective weapon against all Chinese immigrants: Chinese men were maligned as lascivious and imagined in the role of pimps and procurers, but the consequences were even more extreme for Chinese women.

All nineteenth-century immigrant populations initially had fairly high male to female ratios. Eventually, over several decades, women would join the men and the balance gradually became equalized. But as early as 1874, California politicians recognized that defamation of Chinese women provided an effective weapon for deterring immigration, and they began the outrageous and unilateral accusation, defaming all Chinese women as prostitutes. This image was extremely suggestive and quickly influenced the law: seven years before the 1882 exclusion of all Chinese people, Chinese women had already been excluded through the 1875 Page Law. While the law prohibited "immoral" women only—those coming to the United States for "lewd" purposes—the equation between Chinese women and prostitution had become naturalized to the extent that the burden of proof of morality was on the female immigrant.[64] Consequently, unlike other immigrant populations, the Chinese American population remained extremely skewed for over a century, a result of legislation preventing immigration of Chinese women that promptly followed the slanderous accusations.[65]

The *Times* brief described the 1874 proposal hearing:

> Representative Page, of California, was heard by the House Committee on Foreign Relations to-day in an argument to show the necessity of action by the Federal Government to prevent the importation of coolies under servile labor contracts, and Chinese women for immoral purposes. Mr. Page proved the unanimity of public sentiment in California on this subject by reading from the platforms of both political parties. . . . Mr. Page also showed that . . . no steps whatever had been taken by Congress to prevent the importation of Chinese women as slaves for prostitution. . . . The members of the committee expressed themselves fully impressed with the magnitude of the evils described, and gave the California Representatives assurances that action on the subject should be promptly taken.[66]

Although as late as 1880 only two Chinese women lived in New York, this link of Chinese women with prostitution and enslavement rallied white people on the East Coast. Under the auspices of participating in a moral cause, many joined in, calling for prohibition of immigration of all Chinese women.[67] The *Times* added to this condemnation by disseminating narratives of sexual depravity among the Chinese: lascivious men and women as sexual slaves. On June 14, 1873, under the category "Minor Topics," the *Times* printed an article describing Chinese girls, decoyed with candy, kidnapped to become slaves in Chinese homes in San Francisco.[68] Following a report of a Chinese girl's story of abduction from China, and her plea for rescue, the *Times* reporter declared support of California's attempt to block Chinese emigration, ostensibly as a stand against the enslavement of Chinese girls, commenting that "Such cases are said to be not uncommon."

In the following month, on July 30, 1873, the newspaper cursorily described an auction of Chinese women in San Francisco's Chinese sector, listing the general prices fetched.[69] Continuing this scandalous journalism, the next day, under the headline "The Chinese in California. Alleged Discovery of an Immoral Secret Society—Disclosures Made by the Police," the *Times* reprinted a San Francisco article reporting evidence of a secret Chinese society formed for "traffic in Chinese women to be sold into lives of prostitution." After alleging that "it is thought that other similar societies exist," the article provided statistics attesting to the very small number of Chinese arriving on the latest steamer, and concluded by remarking that the "falling off in the number is significant as showing the effect of the dispatches sent by the six companies to China, warning their countrymen not to come."[70] Evidently, demonizing Chinese women as prostitutes, and men as pimps and slavers, effectively curtailed immigration.

6. Ignorance

Articles in the *New York Times* testify to Americans' equivocal relationship with the idea of Chinese intelligence. While certainly exclusionists would have liked simply to disparage the Chinese immigrants as ignorant, and some articles did just that, many others recognized that the Chinese reputation for mental quickness and philosophical aptitude contradicted that imputation. Chinese tradition emphasized learning, and the immigrants' current desire for education created a strong positive image, particularly resistant to any attempts to debase their intelligence. However, this was deftly circumvented by accusing the Chinese not of ignorance but of being too smart, too clever, crossing a line into a devious shrewdness. Especially after 1875, articles in the *Times* alternated between presenting either polemic to undermine Chinese intelligence, willy-nilly contradicting previous accusations in the process.

Repeatedly, Chinese intellectual efforts were belittled and their achievements undermined. One common devise for undercutting Chinese intelligence was the press's mimicry of a stereotyped Chinese idiomatic English. Previously parroted relatively amicably, it was now (mis)quoted in a more hostile tone, turning educational aspirations into greed, inverting virtues into vice:

> the Chinaman in the United States desires to learn everything that the American knows. He says he must "sabbie all same Melican

man." The "Melican man" (or American) is his social and commercial superior. For politics he cares nothing; but it irks him to
be worsted in a trade or pushed off the sidewalk. This explains the
avidity with which the Chinese absorb instruction in the mission
schools in California. Whether the text-book be the Bible or the
First Reader, the Chinaman dives into it with wonderful greediness.

After distorting the Chinese interest in education as lasciviousness, the
reporter then dabbled with the always volatile arena of interracial amalgamation, here with the embellishment of child exploitation:

Another, who had the natural man's eye for female beauty, remon-
strated with his missionary teacher, who was no longer young: "Me
no likee you; you too old. Me likee pinkee littee girl."[71]

In April 1875, one century before the renowned bravery of Ruby
Bridges, Chinese parents petitioned the Sacramento School board to admit
their eight-year-old American-born daughter to public school.[72] She was
eventually admitted in a vote of five to two. But even this victory received
a negative spin in the press:

The San Francisco *Bulletin* says that there are hundreds of Chinese
children born in California, and this question of their admission
to the public schools was certain to arise sooner or later. The
Sacramento case is the first time that a Chinese parent has made
application for the admission of a child to the public schools, but it
may be expected that others will soon follow, for John Chinaman is
not slow in taking advantage of American institutions where they
can be made of service to him.[73]

The use of the hackneyed phrase "John Chinaman" in the last sentence
transformed this individual and courageous accomplishment into one that
was both rapacious and anonymous.

Pursuing a traditional Chinese education also became construed nega-
tively. A *Times* article reprinted from the *San Francisco Bulletin*, "How the
Young Heathen Are Taught Their Written Language," conceded the "well-
known fact that nearly all the Chinese in San Francisco are to a certain
degree educated," yet still managed to disparage their education as ignorance,
ancient information learned purely by cant.[74] The same article also found
a way to denigrate the rapidity with which many Chinese learned English,
and ridiculed Chinese scholars for working menial jobs.

Exclusionists worked both sides of the intelligence issue and by 1882
Congressional debates damned the Chinese equally for intelligence and for

idiocy. Compounding several of the negative images they had spun over the decade into one, they negated the virtues usually associated with intelligence by linking Chinese intelligence to contamination, now maliciously contending that Chinese used their intelligence to infect others. In "Dire Evils Predicted If Immigration Is Not Stopped." the *Times* reported the Senatorial speeches:

> Mr. Farley expressed his belief that should the Mongolian population increase and the Chinese come in contact with the Africans, the contact would result in demoralization and bloodshed which the laws could not prevent. . . . Mr. Maxey opposed the Chinese because they do not come here to be citizens, because the lower classes of Chinese alone are immigrants, and because by contact they poison the minds of the less intelligent.[75]

How that poisoning was accomplished was never explained.

7. Effeminizing the Chinese Man

In *Orientals: Asian Americans in Popular Culture*, Robert G. Lee discussed the challenge that Chinese men posed to the white male hegemony through accepting work traditionally relegated to women: "This entry into the domestic sphere not only displaced female labor . . . but, by opening up possibilities for relations of intimacy and desire across race and class, also threatened to disrupt the patriarchal hierarchy of the family."[76] This androgynous role gave the Chinese male a subversive sexuality, doubly threatening to white men through its deviation from traditional gendered behavior as well as through allowing a perceived intimacy with white women. The androgyny of Chinese employment appeared to give license to effeminize the Chinese male. Lee described such mocking caricatures as a way of displacing the sexuality of Chinese men in the attempt to defuse anxiety and reaffirm the white social order. Melding characteristics of women with Chinese men mitigated the white fear of the power of the Chinese male, immediately subordinating him within the pre-existent gender and social hierarchies.

Through its scoffing response to the rival *New York Tribune*, a *Times* editorial allows us a glimpse into the *Tribune*'s initial argument against the Chinese male as well as the *Times*'s reply to that fear. The *Times* mocked the *Tribune*'s innuendo in coupling what it referred to as two "suggestive facts": the first, that "the first organized bodies of industrial Chinamen have been taken to the State of Massachusetts"; and the second, that in Massachusetts there was a "vast preponderance of the 'female element.'" Ridiculing the *Tribune*'s consternation concerning the "wholesale admixture of races," the

Times dryly stated: "We think they [Massachusetts women] may be trusted in the same village or State with the Chinese shoe-makers."[77]

However, from a very early date, the *Times* articles also showed an anxiety regarding the Chinese male, although not expressed as directly. As James Clifford observes, this anxiety occurs when "a troubling outsider turns up *inside* bourgeois domestic space. [S]he cannot be held at a distance."[78] The Chinese man entered Caucasian domestic space, entered right into the heart of the home. For some, this provoked fear of the instability resulting from changes in gendered roles and also from the reconfiguration of interior space to include a male presence working along with women. The mere thought of such changes threatened the domain of individual male dominion.

One strategy to diffuse this threat was to revise the challenging image of the Asian man by melding him physically into part women, thereby making him the butt of amusement. For example, the awkward humor in the July 6, 1870 article "A New Solution of the 'Servant Girl' Question," farcically lamenting the willfulness of servant girls, served as a pretext for reframing the image of the Chinese male. The article complained that: "The servant girls here have it all their own way. Our American mistresses are at the beck and call of these most fastidious 'helps.'" Having identified the topsy-turvy problem in the social order, the reporter proposed a solution, meant to be comical, by blurring boundaries of race and of gender:

> But now, with the dawn of the "Chinese question," a new light breaks upon us. John Chinaman is to rid us of the old plagues of domestic life. As all who know the East well understand, he is an incomparable servant. Quiet, docile, clean, imitative, accustomed to continuous labor, and not desirous of changing situations often, he is the very person for a model house-servant.

This gender bending of assertive female students and passive, domesticated Chinese males was meant to belittle both groups. It damned the woman for their lack of decorum; for the Chinese male it was tantamount to semantic emasculation.[79]

Several years later another article in the *Times* made this conflation even more explicit, identifying Chinese men with women, and crazy women at that.[80] Three articles appearing on consecutive days argued back and forth the level of civilization evidenced by the Chinese celebrating their holiday, Monki. In one of the two defamatory articles, the reporter exploited the homonymous relationship between "Monki" and the animal "monkey." His description represented the Chinese celebrators appallingly as monkeys, alleging that they "danced and grinned and gesticulated to the wheezy, squeaking sounds of an odd-looking fiddle." But his final image correlated

Chinese men with women: through the skirtlike image of their clothes, the effeminate environment of the "ironing apartment," and finally, bluntly in direct analogy, likening them to "a room full of insane women."

Also in the early 1870s, two *Times* articles narrated the failed romantic aspirations of two Chinese men. In both "The Fate of Ah Gim" on September 7th, and its near twin "Wong Chin Foo" on October 4th, the reporter(s) adopted a wry tone in descriptions of Chinese men's struggles, and eventual suicide, over relationships with white women.[81]   The intention in these tales of unrequited love was not romanticizing the unsuccessful Chinese lovers but emasculating them, through humorously despairing over their ineptitude in the traditional male role.

In 1882 Chinese male sexuality remained unsettling. A *Times* article about a Chinese victim of a crime's appearance in court shows the maligning of the two Chinese men, both the defendant and the victim, with contrasting disparaging images. Referring to the accused, the article's title: "A Murderous Chinaman," played on the already circulating barbaric image of Chinese people.[82] And the victim who appeared in court with his head was swathed in bandages, due to the assault, had his masculinity challenged. Despite the reporter's description of the victim as "a pretty muscular looking Chinaman," this did not prevent the officials of the court from questioning: "Is this a man or a woman?"

8. *Chinese into Coolies into Demonized Race*

Although Chinese people were largely an unknown entity, or perhaps because of this, debasing the entire immigrant body was accomplished without untoward difficulty. At first the *Times* reporters attempted to find a suitable template on which to model the unfamiliar Chinese immigrants. Not unexpectedly, the Chinese were placed into categories correlating them with other disenfranchised groups. By 1873, the Chinese had already been compared to "Red Indians,"[83] wayward children needing a thrashing,[84] women,[85] and African slaves.[86]

The African American template proved most effective, providing exclusionists with the strongest weapon. Through it they found a way to (mis)label these barely known people. Indeed, according to Ronald T. Takaki, "What whites did to one racial group had direct consequences for others, and whites did not artificially view each group in a vacuum: rather, in their minds, they lumped the different groups together or counterpointed them against each other"; and he describes that the "Chinese were subjected to what historian Dan Caldwell has described as a process of 'Negroization'" in which they were equated with (stereotypical views of) African Americans." By comparing Chinese with Africans, the parallels strongly fostered a view of the Chinese as a race.

In an article in 1870, "A New Solution of the 'Servant Girl' Question," the reporter tried various tactics to neutralize the unsettled and unsettling definition of the Chinese male, among them associating images of the Chinese servant with those of the mythic happy Southern Negro:[87]

> When "John" is fairly in the field he will carry everything before him; and Chinese men as waiters, chamber-maids, and cooks, will be as much a part of a well-regulated household as blacks were once at the South. Then will begin a happy day for our long-oppressed mistresses. . . . The "leading race," having its domestic affairs arranged by competent persons, will then have brains and vitality to devote to the most important interests, and the world move all the faster and better.

The reporter also drew on the bromide of the servant "coveting . . . his neighbor's chickens." This strategy was meant to heighten the "humorous" correlations between Chinese and African American servants and accentuate classification of Chinese along racial lines.

Besides using adjectival descriptions, the reporters made frequent use of nouns placed in quotation marks. M. M. Bakhtin described the function of this type of quotation: "The word used in quotation marks, that is, felt and used as something alien . . . The infinite gradations in the degree of foreignness (or assimilation) of words, their various distances from the speaker. Words are distributed on various planes and at various distances from the plane of the authorial word."[88] This is an example of the *Times's* ambivalence: a kind of "having your cake and eating it too," its rhetorical manipulation of contradictory attitudes, which we shall examine more closely in section II. By using negative descriptions, while at the same time placing them in quotes, the reporter implies a certain ironic intention in his use, thereby simultaneously both stating and disclaiming the remark, separating himself from those who actually think that way.

From the template of African Americans, only a short step was needed to arrive at slavery as a model for describing Chinese laborers. Early in 1870, when rival newspapers were using this imagery, the *Times* had argued against it. In *Theories and Facts About the Chinese*, the *Times* presented arguments that were archetypical of pro-Chinese arguments for the next twelve years:

> The *Tribune*, yesterday, published a long statement designed to prove that it is the duty of Congress to relegate or prohibit the importation of Chinese coolies, "just as it first regulated and then prohibited the importation of African slaves." In these few words the whole question is misrepresented and confused. The Chinese shoe-makers now at North Adams are not slaves. The *Tribune's* own

correspondence from the village proves that. The following passage appeared, yesterday, almost side by side with the statement about "slaves" in the article referred to: "These cheerful faces, these eager learners, these faithful workers, these lavish purchasers of shirts and stockings carefully charged to them by their own book-keepers, have no suggestion of slavery. . . . The only slaves in North Adams are the men who have sworn fealty and sacrificed their independence to an arbitrary Union. . . . and the freest men in the village are the immigrants who have come from crowded China to a land which offers opportunities for all." Congress may doubtless prohibit the introduction of slaves into this county, but has it any right to in-terpose unnecessary or vexatious obstacles to the importation of free labor? This question the *Star* disposes of by asserting that the coolies are slaves. . . . "Immigrants are welcome," says the *Star*, "slaves are not." Exactly—but we cannot legislate against the Chinese as slaves until we have some positive proof before us that they *are* slaves.[89]

This article was one of the few that constructed a positive portrayal of Chinese—"cheerful faces," "eager learners," and so forth, to counteract the negative.[90] But at the same time his statements opened the door for some "positive proof" of Chinese slavery.

Pierre Bourdieu describes this as a paradox of culture—that under-standing an opposing position requires a form of abandonment of one's own structured position, both in language and in society, which can result in a crossing over of viewpoints.[91]

Throughout the decade, additional articles augmented the parallel of coolie and slave. The title of a report on January 16, 1871, "The Slave Trade Revived," offered no solution to the sordid conditions of passage on the ships conveying impoverished Chinese, but merely compared them to the still volatile subject of the African slave trade. Merging of these terms created an image of all Chinese workers as enslaved coolies, and eventually penetrated even the pro-Chinese viewpoint and undermined it. This was not so subtle as to pass unnoticed and in 1874, a *Times* reporter protested that the exclusionist argument effectively redefined all Chinese workers as coolies, and he took umbrage at the anti-Chinese connotations in the term. In "A New Raid on the Chinese," he insisted that Chinese workers and not coolies were arriving in America, bluntly asserting that the new attempt to prevent Chinese immigration "looks suspiciously like a new form of an old and violent protest against all Chinese."[92] His article enumerated the old and the new tactics of the exclusionists and ended with a rational objection to referring to Chinese immigration as slave trade:

It is not certain that the partisan aspect of this question is so marked as it once was. Indeed, while thoughtful men of both parties admit that the problem of the introduction of a considerable pagan element into our social fabric is a difficult one, they also protest against any form of legislation that shall discriminate against the Chinese as a race; and among the leaders of both parties there are also men who consider the Chinese an unmixed evil, to be legislated out of the country. . . . But the matter is pressed beyond the special issue, and it is once more alleged that a large proportion of the Chinese arriving in this country are really held in bondage. This is mere assertion, and, unless some proof of the statement is forthcoming, a law forbidding the importation of coolies, or bondmen, would not effect anything under existing statutes. . . . If there is any [bond-age], it is of such a mysterious force that not one Chinaman ever attempts to evade it.

Yet other reporters were not as astute, and were taken in by the rhetorically sleight of hand, or perhaps they simply were not so staunch in their convictions. In a few articles an initially pro-Chinese argument un-raveled, ending in an anti-Chinese stance. The 1870 article, "What Shall Be Done with John Chinaman?" evidenced the reporter's overt desire to be fair-minded toward Chinese immigrants, but his credulity or some other trait allows him to be taken in by the slavery chimera. His initial remarks exhibit goodwill to Chinese people:

If Chinese labor could be brought hither by legitimate emigra-tion, no trouble would be involved any more than in the case of emigration from European countries. We are thorough believers in the broad American doctrine of extending a welcome to all com-ers, demanding only in return that they shall as speedily, and as completely as possible, cast off their natural allegiance, and merge their nationalities in American citizenship.

But, for the reporter, the facts unfortunately seemed to confirm that Chinese emigration was not free but bordered on slavery:

Taking advantage of their necessities, cruel and unscrupulous men have organized what is known as the coolie trade, and in many in-stances kidnapping, and the grossest oppression and fraud have been practices. The ostensible emigrant very often becomes marketable property, and is publicly bought and sold precisely as slaves were.

The lack of definition in the demarcation of the term *coolie*, allowed him to gravitate toward the exclusionist's argument. And eventually the reporter revealed that his anxiety was not based on labor issues after all, but on something less benevolent. This becomes revealed in his puzzling over how the "Mongolian element shall be blended with the Caucasian."[93] Still, despite his reservations, he stopped short of advocating exclusion, waffling over what to do: "We can hardly say to John that he shall not come to our shores unless he comes on his own account, for we know that he could not come without assistance." Nevertheless, albeit inadvertently, the erstwhile pro-Chinese argument became party to a pro-exclusion attitude.[94]

The reporter's propensity to tacitly adopt anti-Chinese assumptions, as well as his worries concerning racial blending, exposes a subtle form of bias, which Teun van Dijk characterizes in *Elite Discourse and Racism*, as "the continuous conclusion . . . that We are somehow superior to Them."[95]

Labor issues had not successful created a widespread aversion to the idea of Chinese as American citizens, but this was finally accomplished by exploiting uneasy attitudes toward race and racial mixing still lurking in America after the Civil War. A letter to the *Times* shows the depth of the prejudice existing in the East by 1882, describing Chinese as: "mere machine men, utterly destitute of all sense of honor, patriotism, or religion, and absolutely incapable of being impressed with such feelings."[96] We see the triumph of term *coolie*; that, while the category "Chinese" remained, all positive traits were effectively removed from it, leaving only the mythic, slavish coolies.

SECTION III. DEFINING THE "US"

1. The Exclusion Debate: Four Voices Struggle Over Imaging Chinese

The second part of this chapter articulates the four different voices vying to construct the definitive image of "Chineseness" in the United States. Two voices derived from alternative sides of the congressional debates on exclusion, held between 1879 and 1892; one voice was of the *New York Times* itself; and the forth voice was a Chinese one. Each expressed what was at stake for its group and viewed itself as a guardian of American values. Yet how could the idea of "America" be reconstrued so it could redefine itself as a nation that would no longer have open immigration and still perceive this as not shifting the original ideals of America's founding?

Three sections correspond to the four different voices, all reported in the *Times*. While Congress debated the issue of Chinese immigration for several years, the later part of the debate in 1882 was reported in great detail in the *Times*. The two conflicting sides passionately vied for the last word in determining what was meant by Chinese and who was American. A newly racialized image of the Chinese people was accepted almost without exception throughout the Exclusion debates. Race underlay all the arguments, both pro- and anti-exclusion; in a sense, it became the common ground for their viewpoints.

The second section investigates the construction of *Times* own voice as it reported the debates. Especially through its use of California's anti-exclusion vehemence as a foil, the newspaper created its persona. And, because the *Times* was a major mouthpiece for New York and other eastern states, its persona extended to include much of the East Coast. Eagerly adapted, the eastern statesmen and populace could portray themselves as not anti-Chinese per se, but rather as reluctantly accommodating the pro-exclusion position of California; a subtle distinction that has resulted in the persistent impression that the east was more tolerant, less racist, than the west. But how accurate was this portrayal? True, the *Times* opposed Californian policy, but was that equivalent to being pro-Chinese? How did the East Coast vote for legalized exclusion, and yet manage to maintain a liberal self-image?

The final section examines the voice created by Chinese immigrants. It emerged, isolated but clear, in the *Times's* infrequent publications of letters expressing opinions from Chinese individuals and groups. With measured rationality in word and in reports of actions, the Chinese voice countered all the calumny ascribed to the people, and the allegations of neither wanting citizenship, nor being able to assimilate.

2. The Opposing Race Arguments from the Congressional Debates

As we have seen, through a gradual process of associating Chinese with caustic descriptions, the press aided in creating and disseminating the idea of Chinese as a racial entity, equating a slavish coolie with all Chinese people. The debate arguments, both pro- and anti-exclusion, demonstrate that race was the motivating force underlying the call for exclusion. By the year of the congressional exclusion debates, this image was solidly instilled in the American imagination and affected (infected) the arguments of exclusion for proponents as well as for opponents.

Beginning with Senator Willis's proposal of an anti-Chinese immigration bill on January 24, 1882, the *Times* reported the congressional debates on exclusion in detail, continuing until the passage of the Exclusion Law in early May. In these debates about Chinese people two discordant voices emerge with radically divergent ideas of what constituted an American.[97] In one, Chinese were imaged as the antithesis of American, as an irredeemably alien race, and incapable of ever being naturalized.[98] Americans, in this view, were Caucasian, preferably with ancestors from west European countries. Admitted only reluctantly and on a lower level, were people of African descent. In the other opinion, slowly being dislodged, Americans constituted a diverse group, without racial restriction, united in shared humanity. Chinese people were included in this image of those who could be American.

On the heels of a civil war fought with such passion for racial equality, it would certainly seem misguided for Exclusionists to imagine that by racializing the Chinese they could achieve an advantage. But because of the rhetorical shift magnifying the image of the coolie as a new slave, proponents of exclusion were able to play off the antislavery victory of the recent Civil War. No one could argue with the desire to protect the United States from a new slave, the coolie.

The nearly seamless change from coolie as a signifier of class to its signifying race is demonstrated neatly in a report to the House Committee on Education and Labor in late January. It began by calling for Chinese exclusion based on arguments about class, but midway through shifted to racial criteria.[99] The rationale, such as it was, mobilized the horde fear in its sweeping allegation of a massive coolie class in the United States. It cited as an "undisputed fact" that most of the 100,000 Chinese in California were coolies. From there the report concluded by indicting all Chinese immigrants with no attempt at any distinction, and with no verification, stating: "The Chinese have no desire to assimilate with our people, and have been and always will be a separate and distinct race."

Several congressmen rose to this challenge and vehemently resisted a unilateral amalgamation of coolie with Chinese immigrant, and the *Times* reported their ardent speeches.[100] On March 2nd Senator Hoar explicitly correlated the exclusionist's vehemence with the depth of their bigotry, bluntly asserting that the heart of all objections to Chinese immigration was "the old race prejudice." Comparing the current ill-treatment and indictments of Chinese immigrants to that previously directed against African Americans, Hoar defied the allegation that either group was incapable of development, repudiating it "absurd."[101] Further, he quoted the Declaration of Independence, asserting freedom and equality as the premise of the American government, the defining image of Americans.

But a week later, defending exclusion, Senator Edmunds countered Hoar with an alternative interpretation of the Declaration of Independence, stating that it "was made by a people for themselves, and not for anybody else. It did not contemplate that all races should indiscriminately swarm into this country, but rather the exercise of criticism as to the fitness of all immigrants to share its privilege."[102]

Exclusion debates seesawed back and forth in Congress for the next eight weeks, each propounding their vision of America and whether or not Chinese were able to be included. The proponents' arguments became increasingly preposterous: racial slander ran rampant as the entire gamut of demonization techniques were drawn on. Capitalizing on previous demonization of Chinese individuals as diseased and ignorant, exclusionists now portrayed all Chinese as a barbaric and mentally deficient race. One session culminated with Senator Maxey's declaration of American values, insisting that the founding fathers never would have wanted the rights of United States citizenship extended to other races. Chinese, he declared, "poison the mind of the less intelligent," and he claimed that, while Anglo-Saxons had withstood the corruptive influence of the Africans, the Africans would not be able to withstand the Chinese.

Protecting Africans was a frequently heard exclusionist claim. But looking at their arguments one sees a view of race based on paternalism and hierarchy. For instance, on April 27, an article titled "The Foes of the Chinese," recounted a barbed exchange in which Senator Farley simultaneously defamed African Americans and figuratively emasculated Chinese men in his description of the "peculiarities of the Chinese which make them offensive to Californians":[103]

> Mr. Farley expressed his belief that should the Mongolian population increase and the Chinese come in contact with the Africans, the contact would result in demoralization and bloodshed which the laws could not prevent. Pig-tailed Chinamen would take the place everywhere of the working girl.

Farley's accusations were contested by Senator Ingalls:

> "Why do you hire them?" asked Mr. Ingalls, and then he went on to say that the people of Kansas do not employ leprous, diseased, or immoral persons to do their work. . . . the Californians could refuse to employ them and the remedy against Chinese cheap labor was in their own hands and no legislation would be necessary.

But such measured rationality passed almost unnoticed.

Of course, racism was at the heart of this inability to accept Chinese as American citizens, but it was always presented as altruism. When it suited the exclusionist's purpose, they claimed that they were helping the poor Chinese from being turned into slaves. Yet at other occasions, they claimed that they were helping the poor African Americans from being influenced by the insidious Chinese. Consistency never entered into their arguments, which ultimately prevailed.

As the congressional hearings became a free-for-all, exclusionists wielded all the previously mentioned aspersions against Chinese people in extravagant combinations. The very irrationality of an argument became its greatest defense. Exclusionists bypassed reason altogether in their appeal to an emotional reconstruction of American identity. Senator Jones fabricated a new version of Chinese history; contending that the Chinese had never had the capability for invention, even alleging that the Chinese had stolen the ideas of the printing press and gunpowder from "Aryans or Caucasians." Rather than engage in logically debate, they deflected rational arguments nonsensically: Senator Maxey proclaimed his refusal to consider exclusion from the view of "ecstatic sentimentality and sublimated humanitarianism."[104] Senator Edmunds dismissed one argument as a "highly too utterly utter idea"; his use of Oscar Wilde's frequently lampooned "too utterly, utterly" phrase betrays the suggestive merger of Chinese and aestheticism that will be addressed more closely in chapter 4.[105]

In *A Grammar of Motives*, Kenneth Burke discussed the success of such emotional rhetoric in championing national supremacy: "the more insistently one presses upon such a view . . . the more it tends to become pure mysticism. The 'American way' is offered purely and simply as a purpose, our business pragmatism having thus been transformed into a mystical nationalism."[106]

Mystical nationalism is perhaps the best definition to describe the exclusionist's pronouncement that "The Constitution was ordained and established by white men," and their contention that the white people of California needed protection "against a degrading and destructive association with the inferior race now threatening to overrun them."[107] Through playing on the dread of white-and-black "amalgamation," Senator Edmunds joined into the hyperbole. By using racial allusions to associate Chinese immigrants with Asian hordes, Edmunds capitalized on the fear over "colored" people immigrating en masse into the commonwealth. He asserted that "no republic can succeed that has not a homogeneous people," but he never clarified what qualified as American homogeneity.[108]

In response to this rhetorical chaos, Senator Hoar quoted Abraham Lincoln's famous repudiation of slavery; speaking directly about the Chinese exclusion bill, he declared: "If this is not wrong, nothing is wrong."[109] But by this time anti-exclusionist words had little effect and were thwarted even as they were reported. With frank hostility, the *Times* itself rebuffed Hoar's assertions of equal rights. Its editorial, candidly titled "Negro and Chinaman," argued the anti-Chinese opinion (fig. 3.4). The reporter's interpretation of the differences between Africans and Chinese led him to write a disquisition on American values:

the negro is here, was brought here against his will, and has been domesticated during many years of residence. The Chinaman, on the other hand, is not here to stay; he never has and never will come as a permanent resident, and Chinamen have not yet come in such numbers as to warrant us in elevating into a serious question the consideration of their relations to American citizenship. . . . The defending of a negro from injustice does not involve on the part of the defender a desire to embrace him. Even New-England, jealous of the rights of the black man, would not welcome an immigration of a million black men. The question now is not as to the relative merits of the Chinese race, but whether that race will assimilate with our own. The black man is already a citizen of the United States. Whatever may be the attrition evident in the relations which he bears to American citizenship and American institutions, those relations cannot be changed by any revision of his acquired rights and privileges. The sooner we get this idea firmly rooted in the minds of men, the sooner we shall have passed the line where even debate of this question will be possible. There is no rational connection between the settled problem of negro citizenship and the unsettled problem of Chinese immigration. The restrictive bill now under consideration in the Senate does not take away any right from the Chinaman. In the language of Senator Edmunds, it undertakes to assert the right of the United States to decide who shall and who shall not come here.[110]

Thus, the article concluded that the most significant difference between the African and Chinese was that, while the African presence in the United States was now unavoidable, the Chinese could still be excluded. Yet the assertion that "the chinaman . . . is not here to stay" begs the question why an exclusion law should then be necessary.

The irrationality of this claim suggests something else underlying it. James Clifford gives us a hint of what this might be when he discusses what happens "whenever marginal peoples come into a historical or ethnographic space that has been defined by the Western imagination. 'Entering the modern world,' their distinct histories quickly vanish."[111] The Exclusionists' difficulty in accepting Chinese as Americans was, in part, that because of the distinct appearance of many Chinese immigrants, these white observers could not visualize them as disassociated from their traditional culture and therefore could not naturalize their appearance as Americans. Rather, they imagined every Chinese person as attached irrevocably to China, no matter how many years or generations had passed.

On March 10, the day of the senatorial vote on exclusion, the debate turned on the two radically opposed interpretations of fundamental American

that he should be understood, Mr. GEORGE
added that as the Constitution was ordained
and established " by white men," to secure
the blessings of liberty for their posterity,
this great pledge should be fully " redeemed
in favor of the white people of the South."

If this meant anything at all, it meant that
Mr. GEORGE believes that negro citizenship
in the South may fail, and that, when it does,
the whole question of negro suffrage and its
cognate branches must be readjusted. Now,
if anything is settled, it is that the American citizen of African descent is for-
ever a citizen. He is entitled to all
the rights and privileges of citizenship,
and there can be no legal method of taking
from him the powers and duties with which
he has been clothed. Furthermore, the fal-
lacy of Mr. GEORGE's attempt to connect
the two questions is apparent when we consider that the negro is here, was brought
here against his will, and has been domesticated during many years of residence. The
Chinaman, on the other hand, is not here to
stay; he never has and never will come as a
permanent resident, and Chinamen have not
yet come in such numbers as to warrant us
in elevating into a serious question the consideration of their relations to American citizenship. Mr. HOAR, in his speech on the
Chinese restriction bill, was equally unfortunate in his attempt to make the negro
and the Chinaman stand as exemplars of

Fig. 3.4. "Negro and Chinaman," *New York Times*, March 9, 1882.

values, each side carefully underscoring its position.[112] Senator Hawley described the intrinsic prejudice within any Exclusion law, which he saw as a direct violation of the Fifteenth Amendment that "no person should be deprived of the right of suffrage by reason of race, color, or previous condition of servitude." Further, Hawley distinguished right from power: "While Congress had the right in a shallow and technical sense to do many things, it had in that sense the right to do many things that were wrong to do." Nevertheless, Senator Jones contended that he had waited in vain to hear why the exclusion bill should not be passed.[113] Jones challenged the Senate to show where it said that a nation cannot exclude whomsoever it wishes. Pressing racial segregation beyond rational limits, he professed that Benjamin Franklin had founded the country specifically and solely for the white race.

At the end of the debates, identifying who and what constituted a coolie still remained unsettled. This was a problem that Congress never answered—or even directly addressed. At no time did either side dispute the legitimacy of racial categories or question what constituted coolies. Through exploiting this lacuna, exclusionists gained control over the definition of "Chinese laborer"; it became a weapon against all Chinese immigrants. To a great extent, the Exclusionists had been allowed to insert their opinions into the definitions of Chinese. Their construction became the controlling norms, and with that, the debates were weighted from the start. The *Times* reported the passage of the Exclusion bill in the Senate by a vote of 29 to 15, nearly two to one.

The language and ordinances of the bill reveal the complete abandonment of assertions that exclusion was a protection for low-wage laborers in California. Rather, it changed the definition of "Chinese laborers": many forms of employment, previous shielded (mainly by common definition) became eclipsed into coolieism. Within the enlarging field circumscribed by *coolie*, the term no longer denoted only unskilled workers but was extended to include "both skilled and unskilled laborers," as well as the Chinese working in mining. And now laborers were defined as "teachers, students, merchants and curiosity seekers, and personal servants," although they would be "allowed unrestricted mobility in and out of the country."[114] Additionally, the bill imposed a fine against the master of a ship carrying any Chinese person to the United States. It called for identification cards for all Chinese people currently in the United States. And finally, it prohibited any U.S. Court from admitting a Chinese person to citizenship.

Although this Exclusion bill was vetoed by President Arthur on April 5th, Congressman Page immediately submitted a revised Exclusion bill—revised only by lessening the exclusion period from twenty-five to ten years.[115] This, too, immediately was debated in Congress. The emotional pitch about race became more overt and the *Times* became pulled in: One reporter referred to an exclusionist speech by Senator Vest as "the most interesting speech of the day," and continued, "It was a Caucasian speech, an out and out demand that this Government should be regarded as a white man's Government." He also referred to the anti-Exclusionists as "the aesthetic Senators from Massachusetts," and claimed they defended the Chinese "who care so little for this country that when they die their polygamous bones are returned to the home of their polygamous ancestors." Besides the blatant bias belying the impartiality of the press, we again see the undercurrent of aligning Aestheticism to pro-Chinese attitudes; they were unified in their alterity to the dominant patriarchal roles.[116]

On April 29, 1882, the Exclusion bill was passed. The article announcing it was inconspicuously relegated to the fourth page of the *Times*. It reported the passage of the Anti-Chinese bill in the Senate by a larger majority than the previous bill, 32 to 15, compared to 29 to 15. Besides the consummation of a demonized image of Chinese people, it was also the triumph of the articulation of America as a white hegemony: the victory of ideas thought defeated in the Civil War.

After the fact, the *Times* finally acknowledged this explicit racial agenda: "The courts have ruled that only white foreigners and Africans can be admitted to citizenship under existing laws; and it has been argued that the prohibitory clause was . . . a sinister discrimination against the Chinese. The Senate refused to strike out the section, however."[117]

On May 9, also relegated to the fourth page, an equally brief article reported that, despite his previous veto, President Arthur signed the exclusion bill into law (see previous fig. 3.1). And so Chinese were added to paupers, criminals, and idiots—the short list of people legally excluded from the United States.[118]

3. The Times Doublespeak: Blame California, Profess Fatigue

And what was the *New York Times*'s stand throughout these speeches? How did it define Chinese amid these oscillating Chinese images? And how did it define itself, its role in representing both sides, its choices of the news it found fit to report or reprint? We have looked, in Section I, at the *Times*'s construction of a negative dialectic regarding Chinese persons, isolating ten characteristics used in demonizing the Chinese, and we have seen an instance where the *Times* chimed in, mocking the anti-exclusionist argument. But it would be inaccurate to present the idea that the newspaper was *intentionally* anti-Chinese, at least not the majority of the time. Throughout the 1870s, it would periodically publish positive and sympathetic reports about the Chinese immigrants. Indeed, we have seen articles that appeared empathetic toward Chinese people, and read anti-Exclusionist editorials, even as the demonization process occurred. The *Times*'s attitude remained polemical and unresolved, perhaps the result of several different writers and editors with contradictory opinions.

While the *Times* did not overtly endorse a position either for or against excluding the Chinese, it published several articles showing that powerful business groups in the eastern cities voiced support for the Chinese immigrants. On April 13, 1882, the *Times* wrote about the positive reception of a petition circulated via the Chamber of Commerce. The petition asserted that any legislation restricting or obstructing Chinese immigration to the United States would be an affront to China, a friendly nation, and would destroy the growing commerce between the two countries. Almost unanimously, the Clearing House banks signed the petition, as did 90 percent of the dry goods trade, all of the tea, sugar, and iron trades, and over 70 percent of the insurance companies. Big business had in fact became a leading force in America for advocating more liberal policies and thinking across national boundaries.

It also let the readers know that among the religious and political leaders, some stood out as being anti-Exclusionist. An article reported on Rev. Henry Ward Beecher's[119] sermon characterizing the Chinese as model immigrants, distinct from other groups who drank and brawled and filled the jails.[120] And a week after President Arthur's veto of the initial Exclusion Bill, a brief article in the *Times* mentioned the unanimous support of the veto by the Union League Club, a powerful social organization whose members included Thomas Nast, Chester Arthur (prior to his presidency) and several of the founding board members of the Metropolitan Museum of Art.[121]

But the intermittent supportive articles neither evolved into a definitive position of support, nor an endorsement of a pro-Chinese contingent. In fact, as the Exclusion debates escalated in Congress, with the exception of several ironic statements, the *Times* dropped all its assertions of indignation and incredulity that such a thing should be taken seriously.

Articles attest to the newspaper's decreasing resistance to the exclusionist argument, especially through its choice of articles reprinted from other newspapers. Californian newspapers provided the most frequent, in fact almost the single, source cited for opinions on Chinese immigration, and these opinions, of course, were unashamedly anti-Chinese. The determinedly ambivalent position of the *Times* is seen in how it retitled some of the reprints. Through a new, ironic title, the *Times* would appear to be offering an anti-exclusion viewpoint, not expressed by the content of the article. For instance, a headline, apparently retitled by the *Times*, suggested an ironic distance from the animosity emanating from California: "The Terrible Chinee. An Entirely New Wail from California—He Is Smarter and Shrewder Than the American Capitalists and Is Going to Drive Them All

Out of the Country." The title seemed to indicate the newspaper's opposition to such blatant racism. But beyond revising the title, the *Times* made no comments on the flagrantly virulent article, which called out: "Merchants of San Francisco, you have a great and pressing duty to perform. Your self-preservation demands Chinese exclusion. See to it that you exclude them in time."[122] The reprints, then, allowed the *Times* a double voice: alleging sympathy with the Chinese and reprimanding California for a lack of moderation, while, simultaneously, disseminating the anti-Chinese viewpoint.

In an article titled "The Anti-Chinese Feeling," the *Times* reported a massive holiday demonstration in San Francisco specifically against the Chinese.[123] 30,000 people assembled in a hall decorated in red, white, and blue, applauding while children were carted around in a wagon carrying the slogan "Shall our boys and girls, or Chinamen, have California?" Yet the reporter wrote favorably about the rally, praising its "dignity of tone and calm argument," and never addressed the antagonism in its very premise, or the volatile content of the speeches incorporating "Californian" exclusion sentiments into their own tone and message.

The *Times*' choice to emphasize deprecatory articles became most transparent in reprinting the San Francisco *Call*'s sympathetic review of Dennis Kearney's inflammatory anti-Chinese speech.[124] The *Call* reporter conferred an air of self-possession and gravity on the rally and quoted Kearney's description of exclusionists as previously misunderstood but rising leaders with a righteous commitment. With rhetorical sleight of hand, Kearney turned the aggressors into martyrs, the victims into an evil force: "we have done everything that a free people could do to rid ourselves of this curse lawfully. We have submitted to indignities, slurs, vilification and persecution. We have been called hoodlums cutthroats, villains, Communists, Socialists, Nihilists, Kearneyites and everything that a rising snobbery could invent, so as to make us odious before the world.' To this, as to other inflammatory remarks, the *Times* gave no commentary.[125]

Linguistic scholar Teun van Dijk explains this by pointing out that "even controversial white speakers, such as notorious racists . . . are not only widely quoted, but sometimes also given ample space to openly voice their racist opinions, even when most journalists will define them as being beyond the consensus."[126]

Times subscribers read such opinions as: "The veto appalls every Republican in the State, and proves that the President is the slave," and "the Chinese blight comes home to the heart of every man." One article direly predicted the degradation of civilization through Chinese immigration: Americans would be forced to live as the Chinese, here defined as without real homes, marriage or children, eating only rice, sleeping in a room on shelves, and wearing Nankin cloth.[127] After the President's veto, the *Times* reprinted only the acerbic articles from California papers, publishing them verbatim. The careful selection of reprints, with no counteropinion, familiarized and naturalized the anti-Chinese position.

The *Times* seemed of two minds about the issue of exclusion. Indeed, at times the two contrary viewpoints occurred within the same article, making it appear slightly schizophrenic. Referring to Exclusion, the *Times* spoke of being much "vexed" by the "Chinese question," and fretfully awaited the verdict as though lives and liberty were not at stake. Rather than counter demonizing imagery with positive imagery, the negative assertions with positive ones, the reporters mockingly repeated the negatives, saying them again but distancing themselves from their own words.

Passage of the Exclusion Act required a majority of East Coast congressmen voting in favor of it. But repeatedly, the *Times* advocated exclusion under the guise of claiming it as an exclusively Californian desire. Through reprints of articles from Californian newspapers, the *Times* allowed the extreme anti-Chinese persona to typify the West Coast, against which the *Times*'s own pro-exclusion articles could appear reasoned and moderate:

> As those who have long fought against all proposed restrictive legislation as applied to the Chinese have been finally forced to admit, the people of California, who have faced this "invasion" for twenty-five or thirty years, are best qualified to judge of its effects. With great reluctance, probably, many of us have been obliged to concede that those who have so long demanded restrictive legislation are entitled to what they ask for, because, after a long experience in which we have not shared, they are constant to their conviction of the need of a remedy for the ills they endure.[128]

That the reporter was not entirely candid in his justification of exclusion, as a concession to California was betrayed by his remarks later in the article, describing Chinese people as unassimilable and making a show of deference to California racism, claiming that the people of a region know best the ills that most oppress them. And through the device of the vaguely defined coolie, the reporter found the Chinese to be the antithesis to the American, and as such, impossible to endorse.

> The European laborer conforms to American ideas, becomes Americanized, and surrounds himself with the comforts and luxuries of civilized life. The Chinaman is a Chinaman wherever he goes. He does not become assimilated. He lives in a sty and subsists upon the refuse of the land. He cannot become an American citizen, being debarred by provisions of the older treaties, and having, apparently,

no concern whatever in that direction. . . . Mr. Ingalls took the sensible view that the people of the Pacific States best know the magnitude of the ills that oppress them, and that they were entitled to the only remedy now apparent. This is the deliberate judgment, probably, of a majority of our fellow-citizens.

When the congressional debates began, the *Times* position was to assume the inevitability of legalized exclusion; witness an article as early as February 27, 1882: "Notwithstanding the evident fact that Congress will pass one of the two anti-Chinese bills now pending . . ." The predominant tone of the *Times* during the congressional debates is characterized by an article in March 1882, which rationalized exclusion on the basis of the new treaty with China, while simultaneously acknowledging that the treaty had been wrongly acquired. With circular logic the article stated, "It is true that the new treaty was only obtained by pressure; but, since it is now a part of the fundamental law of the land, we may as well make one more effort to lay the Chinese question by an exercise of the rights secured by it."[129] Such circularity begs our questioning the extent to which this attitude of acceptance fostered an inertia to injustice, creating an atmosphere complicit with exclusion, rather than merely denoting a foreknowledge of the impossibility of effective critical opposition.

The pro-exclusion inclination of the *Times* editorialist appeared in brief comments as well as editorials throughout the debates. This bias can be seen, for instance, in a *Times* editorial on March 24, the day that the House passed the Exclusion bill by a vote of 167 to 65. Congressman Pacheco's ludicrous argument claimed that, in order to compete with the Chinese laborer, "the American laborer would have to renounce home, wife, child, religion, and the institutions of his country." This passed without comment. But the editorialist did comment on the pro-Chinese argument, insinuating that it was based in false sentiment, and desire for profit, not morality, facetiously questioning, "How much of the sweet prattle about 'the land of the free and the home of the brave' was really inspired by selfish traffickers in Asiatic bone and sinew the world can never fully know."[130]

A voice eventually emerged from all this equivocation, and gained sway, becoming a resolution of sorts. It was one of accommodation, an important voice in a democracy, but one that has a tendency to denounce taking a stand as radical and condemn it as being inappropriately partisan. Capitulation to California's extremism became the *Times*'s main explanation for the East Coast's support of exclusion. Through its premise that exclusion was inescapable, the *Times* affected an air of detached exhaustion, implying its own lack of culpability.[131] And though its showcase of neutrality, the *Times* gained an advantage: like California, it disseminated a portrayal of the Chinese as an alien "them," but it created an "us" that not only distinguished "white" Americans from the Chinese, it also characterized the white people on the East Coast as distinctly more fair-minded than those on the West.

Even after Chinese Exclusion had become law, the *Times* played up its attitude of exasperation and continued placing the onus of the law on Californians. It bolstered the facade of East Coast guiltlessness through a profusion of articles expressing fatigue with the entire Chinese exclusion issue and assigning blame to California. This disclaimer continued throughout the year, always with the same emphasis: "It is to be hoped that this will settle the much-vexed Chinese question for a time at least. . . . The people of California will probably be satisfied with all its features, unless they may object to the shortness of the term during which immigration is to be suspended."

Ultimately, an attitude of democratically justified but superior resignation best defines the *New York Times* persona. Indeed, this evasion of culpability for Exclusion extended to the nation as a whole and persisted for almost a century.[132]

4. The Chinese View through Word and Action

The least disseminated of the four voices was that of the Chinese immigrants who chose to represent themselves to the newspapers and managed to get their letters published. Chinese people did not wait idly by during this decade of physical, legal, and verbal violence. In the face of legislated prejudice, they continued to pursue the available routes for education and assimilation, while challenging the threat of Exclusion both in word and deed; and occasionally their actions and protests appeared in the *Times*.

The most direct and eloquent statement from Chinese people in the *Times* was a very early response to indications of the mounting momentum for exclusion, protesting the increasing racial violence. On June 16, 1873, the *Times* printed a letter which it titled "The Chinese Question. A Calm Statement of the Case from the Chinese Stand-Point."[133] The letter, signed by leading Chinese merchants and introduced and translated by Chinese missionary Rev. O. Gibson, asked, "Will you listen to a calm statement of the Chinese question from a Chinese stand-point?"[134] The letter proceeded to enumerate the anti-Chinese actions encountered daily by Chinese immigrants:

> Public sentiment is strongly against us. Many rise up to curse us. Few there are who seem willing, or who dare to utter a word in our defense, or in defense of our treaty rights in this country. The daily papers teem with bitter invectives against us. All the evils and miseries of our people are constantly pictured in an exaggerated

form to the public, and our presence in this country is held up as an evil, and only evil, and that continually.

The writers did not portray themselves as victims; instead, they presented a perspective on America not frequently represented, especially in the press: "If these enactments are the legitimate offspring of the American civilization and of the Jesus religion, you can hardly wonder if the Chinese people are somewhat slow to embrace the one or adopt the other."

The letter also called attention to the structure of power, particularly in relationship to accessibility and command of the media: "Unfortunately for us, our civilization has not attained the use of the daily Press—that mighty engine for molding public sentiment in these lands—and we must even now appeal to the generosity of those who perhaps bear us no goodwill, to give us a place in their columns to present our cause." This observation regarding the constitutive power of the media is quite precocious. Media influence was not often discussed in the nineteenth century; its significance became a subject of academic writings only in the mid-twentieth century or later. But the Chinese knew the powers of the press from direct experience as it maneuvered against them, and they understood the critical importance of learning English if only in order to counter the allegation of non-assimilation. As Braj B. Kachru states in "The Alchemy of English," "whatever the limitations of English, it has been perceived as the language of power and opportunity."[135]

The writers described the reasons for the large numbers of unemployed Chinese immigrating to the United States: the history of aggression on the part of the United States and acquiescence by China to achieve the present treaty, facts unfamiliar to most Americans. But beyond clarifying facts and history, the letter also indirectly challenged biased assumptions about the Chinese:

> This country ought to know, what is well known to every intelligent Chinaman, that the introduction of American and English steamers upon the rivers and coast of China has thrown out of business a vast fleet of junks.

This statement alone addressed three separate aspects of prejudice. It presented evidence that Chinese poverty resulted in part from Western intervention in China, it attempted to offer these unfamiliar facts in a congenial manner, and it asserted the discernment of the Chinese. The letter included a wryly pointed proposal to abrogate the treaty between the two countries and to withdraw all the Chinese from the United States if, reciprocally, America would withdraw all Americans and American trade from China. But until such time, the writers asked only that they be treated in the friendly manner stipulated by the treaty. The letter ended with five signatures: "Lai Yong, portrait painter. Yang Kay, 74 Commercial street. A Yup. Lai Foon. Chung Leong" (fig. 3.5).

THE CHINESE QUESTION.

A Calm Statement of the Case from the Chinese Stand-Point.

At a late meeting of the San Francisco Board of Supervisors, Rev. O. Gibson, Chinese Missionary, appeared with the following petition, signed by many leading Chinese merchants, which he had translated :

To the Honorable Board of Supervisors of San Francisco :

GENTLEMEN: Will you listen to a calm statement of the Chinese question from a Chinese stand-point? Public sentiment is strongly against us. Many rise up to curse us. Few there are who seem willing, or who dare to utter a word in our defense, or in defense of our treaty rights in this country. The daily papers teem with bitter invectives against us. All the evils and miseries of our people are constantly pictured in an exaggerated form to the public, and our presence in this country is held up as an evil, and only evil, and that continually. Laws, designed not to punish guilt and crime, nor yet to protect the lives and property of the innocent, have been enacted and executed, discriminating against the Chinese, and now the Honorable Board of Supervisors of this city proposes still further to afflict us by what seems to us most unjust, most oppressive, and more barbarous enactments. If these enactments are the legitimate offspring of the American civilization and of the Jesus religion, you can hardly wonder if the Chinese people are somewhat slow to embrace the one or adopt the other. Unfortunately for us, our civilization has not attained the use of the daily Press—that mighty engine for molding public sentiment in these lands— and we must even now appeal to the generosity of those who perhaps bear us no good will, to give us a place in their columns to present our cause.

THE POLICY OF CHINA.

1. We wish the American people to remember that the policy of the Chinese Government was strictly exclusive. She desired no treaty stipulations, no commercial relations, no interchange whatever with Europe or America. She

Fig. 3.5. "The Chinese Question. A Calm Statement of the Case from the Chinese Stand-Point." *New York Times*, June 16, 1873.

This letter was followed up the next day by a *Times* article, clearly by a reporter, that advocated for the Chinese people and quoted from the letter in an attempt to emphasize the rationality, as well as the integrity, of its argument (fig. 3.6).

Occasionally throughout the 1870s, the *Times* published short articles on the Chinese in New York who converted to Christianity or pursued a course of Western education. Through such measures, some Chinese immi-

Of course Americans will refuse to entertain this proposition, but will continue to insist upon their right to live and do business in China. How, then, can they refuse to permit Chinamen to live and do business here, as, by treaty, they have the express right to do ? With what possible pretext of justice can we say to the Chinese: "Open your country to the Americans or we will batter down your cities; but beware of coming to America, or we will mob and oppress you ?" Is there a Christian man in the United States who will not echo the words of the heathen Chinaman, LAI YONG—"In the name of our country, in the name of justice and humanity, in the name of Christianity as we understand it, we protest against such severe and discriminating enactments against our people while living in this country under existing circumstances ?"

Fig. 3.6. "Lai Yong's Letter." *New York Times*, June 17, 1873.

grants embraced and sought assimilation into the dominant culture. But for nearly a decade, no other letter from Chinese immigrants appeared, until 1882 when the newspaper printed a letter from fifty-one Chinese Christians in Chicago, particularizing their objections to the Exclusion bill and petitioning the president for a veto.[136] They listed their reasons:

> First, the fact that the Chinese make quiet, industrious, and law-abiding citizens, not filling our jails and Poor-houses as do some other nationalities. Second, that they spend as much money in proportion to what they make as any other foreigners, and give an equivalent for every dollar earned. Third, that so far as they are reached by Christian influences they readily accept our Christian faith. Fourth, that to discriminate between them and other nations is not in accord with the free institutions of our country. The section of the bill which we consider most obnoxious, and least in accord with our uniform policy hitherto, is the prohibition of naturalization, regardless of qualifications or earnest desire on their part to become citizens. We pray most earnestly that you may be led to withhold your approval of a bill which seems to us so unjust in all its bearings.[137]

The letter contradicted the increasingly accepted portrayal of Chinese as neither able nor willing to assimilate into American culture. And it also belied the image of Chinese as passive or incapable of participating in the democratic process, demonstrating that Chinese groups had organized in an attempt to have their voices heard in the debate over the bill. The US Chinese understood the repercussions of a permanent non-naturalized status, and they singled out the denial of the right to naturalize as particularly invidious.[138] Their letter questions: If the Chinese were being excluded from the country in part on the assumption that they had no desire to naturalize and wished to remain sojourners, why should such a mandate be necessary? Indeed, if the Chinese did not want to naturalize, why were they now uniting to express this as their desire?[139] The *Times* published their letter with no response, leaving their questions unaddressed.

An indication of China's condemnation of exclusion is found in the November 20th article on "The Anti-Chinese Bill in China."[140] A Chinese diplomat raised the possibility that the Chinese might withdraw diplomatic contact as well as market availability to Americans. But, although the *Times* printed the letter, it subverted its impact through its own editorializing. Teun Van Dijk has described this phenomenon, remarking that "if minorities are quoted at all, then their opinions are nearly always balanced by those of white speakers."[141] The *Times* presented the letter with a preface: a reporter expressed indignation over Chinese violations of American rights, particularly mentioning the protests of an American Minister against (alleged) Chinese violations of American shipping and merchant rights.

Immediately after the passage of the Exclusion Law, Chinese immigrants' voice was heard in their actions as they began to test and challenge its legality. On March 10, 1882, the very day the law was passed, the *Times* reported a successful application for citizenship from Hop Sing, a Chinese immigrant in New York.[142] He had immigrated to the United States in 1863, converted to Christianity, and declared that he intended "to remain in this country and contribute to its prosperity as a loyal citizen."

The next day, however, the *Times* corrected its report in a short, untitled article stating that Hop Sing's application had been refused.[143] The Exclusion bill was firmly in place.

But an enigmatic little article appeared several month later. On June 27, 1882, without explanation or elaboration, a brief report stated that two Chinese men became naturalized: "Chinamen Reported Naturalized. Philadelphia, June 26.—Mark Tuck and Harry Lum, Chinamen, were naturalized by Judge Fell to-day."[144] Apparently there must have been a judge willing to legislate an alternative interpretation of the law.

The *Times* articles, which directly allowed the voice of the Chinese to be disseminated in their own words or manifested through reports of their actions, offered a striking contrast to the demonized image of barbaric hordes of slave-like, opium addicts disseminated through the reports from California, and the emotional debates based on conjecture and hearsay. The sober circumspection and determined actions of the Chinese immigrants contravenes the image circulating in the congressional hearings. Despite the *Times*'s ambiguous position, these glimpses allowed its audience to perceive a different image of Chinese, one that to the greatest extent possible challenged racism in America and negotiated paths through it to create options in their lives.

What is arresting in studying the various voices is that, through the course of the Exclusion debates, the American voice that ultimately dominated most resembled America's negative description of China: a country that didn't want to change, a country that resented foreigners. And the voice that perpetuated the American dream of welcome and tolerance belonged to the Chinese immigrants.

In "The Congress," a short story by Jorge Luis Borges, a character remarks that "newspapermen wrote for oblivion."[145] Most newspaper articles are written to communicate topical events in a vernacular language that can immediately reach the broadest audience. The *New York Times* articles reviewed in this chapter held fugitive ideas of brief duration that, nevertheless, had enduring effects, helping to shape public opinion and national policy. Their transient quality admits our entry into past moments of a still continuing conversation.

FOUR

THE CHINESE OF THE AMERICAN IMAGINATION

Nineteenth-Century Trade Card Images

SECTION I. TRADE CARD IMAGES

Art and politics met again in the images of Chinese people on American nineteenth-century advertising trade cards. In the last third of the nineteenth century, these vernacular images became so plentiful they contributed to the culture's expanding fluency in visual language. Innovations in color lithography transformed print media from monochrome inkings into a riot of colorful images that historian J. Jackson Lears so vividly described as the "carnivalesque commercial vernacular."[1] Among the abundance of chromatic images these small, hand-held chromolithographed advertisements announced every new product and innovation, from medications to farm implements.

Between 1870 and 1900, tens of thousands of trade cards were designed, hundreds with Chinese images that illustrated a far broader range of ideas of Chinese people than their counterpart in written media. In the same decades that saw the demonization and exclusion of Chinese immigrants, what motivated the creation of such extraordinary and varied pictures of Chinese people? What significances did the idea of "Chinese" hold for Americans? Trade cards provide a window into the conversation about Chinese circulating through the general population at the time of exclusion. They reveal that the Chinese image became a marker in American culture, used fluidly in a variety of circumstances: a way for other Americans to observe themselves.

Few people in the eastern states had direct knowledge of Chinese people: the census of 1870 showed that among New York's population of

169

63,254, only 200 were Chinese.[2] By 1888, only 2,000 Chinese resided in New York and in 1900 the number remained low, barely reaching 7,000, with even fewer in other East Coast cities. This comprised such a minute fraction of the population that most Americans had never actually seen a Chinese person. From the 1870s to 1890s, white contact with Chinese people east of the Mississippi was generally limited to occasional visits by the curious to one of the urban Chinatowns, or to seeking out the seventy-five Chinese shoemakers employed in North Adams, Massachusetts, or perhaps to attending Barnum's Circus.[3]

Yet not just California and a few other western states, where Chinese constituted a small proportion of the inhabitants, but also the majority of eastern states without any statistically significant population of Chinese people, sanctioned and voted for an exclusion law.[4] With the lack of direct knowledge of Chinese people in the eastern states, most Americans' concept of Chinese depended on disseminated descriptions, both written and visual. These images were crucial not just for circulating but also for creating ideas of the Chinese people.

The trade cards' effectiveness as a vehicle for disseminating precepts of modernity cannot be overemphasized. They were part of the informal mass instruction in the new language of modernism emerging in America.[5] Each card helped America advance by providing individualized, personal access to two-dimensional representations, shaping a public capable of engaging with and manipulating images and representations, a primary vehicle for modernization.[6] Through their ubiquity, the general population became familiar with the emerging new language of paper culture and fluid exchange.[7]

Advertising manufactured goods of all sorts, trade cards not only promoted knowledge of ready-made commodities but simultaneously fostered an atmosphere of receptivity to novel products—including the trade cards themselves. In effect, the cards created a tautology: they promoted commodities by providing desirable images that ensured their own acceptance as a commodity.[8] Some trade cards even advised, "put this in your scrapbook," "ready to add to a collection" and "suitable for framing." At least one trade card series imaged trade card collectors.

Not merely a means for advertising merchandise, trade cards were themselves objects of desire, intimate and seductive microcosms of the world of merchandise they promoted.[9] Available for free and in multiples, they provided a means for everyone to feel ownership in the new technology and participate in the sense of abundance. These hand-held cards appeared as gifts, personal pieces of modern America inviting the possessor into the ever-greater world of things.[10]

And the power they wielded was considerable: miniature full-color pictures given away for free at a time when even the most popular magazines such as *Harper's Monthly* "politely refused" to carry color ads.[11] During their primacy, these cards had an almost universal appeal. In a statement part boast, part wishful prophecy, a print-trade journal in 1885 claimed: "No one is either so refined or so vulgar that he will not admire a pretty advertising card and save it. The ultimate destination of all cards is to swell some collection or to adorn some home, and they may be found in even the remotest parts of the land."[12] All ages collected trade cards, placing them, artistic side up, in special albums analogous to albums housing family photographs. Everyone essentially could curate their own art museum. And no one seemed to mind if the images had advertising or not.

Trade cards testified to a wide range of ideas about Chinese people, as well as to the penetration of Asian design and objects into American culture at the end of the century; a much more diversified reception than the contemporary written texts gave voice to. Some cards, such as the 1879 card designed by L. Prang and Co., for the R. & J. Gilchrist Importers and Drygoods dealer in Boston, made use of vivid combinations of reds and yellows and design asymmetry originating from Asian art. Other cards replicated Eastern objects and motifs and even lettering. Many Chinese household objects became domesticated within proper Victorian interiors, and trade card images of these domestic interiors fulfilled a double agenda: familiarizing the viewer with the object and furthering its naturalization in the American home. In a trade card for Hires Root Beer, a pretty young girl in a white frock and bonnet, holding a quintessentially American root beer carton, pauses at the doorway of her prosperous home (fig. 4.1). She gazes lovingly at her elegant mother who is seated at a table. And behind the mother's chair, occupying the entire background of this paradigmatic American scene, stands a sky blue oriental screen, painted with stylized Asian birds and trees.[13]

But beyond these benign fusions of Asian and Western styles and objects, Chinese people themselves also became props within American scenes. In one of the few books discussing trade card images, Robert Jay analyzes and condemns the ethnic portrayal, stating that, although the Chinese are not imaged frequently on these popular cards, when they do appear "they are almost invariably treated in a most insulting manner."[14] Certainly many images are blatantly racist, meant to characterize Chinese people as debased and alien, reinforcing the viewpoint in a period that excluded Chinese people from the nation and demonized them in the press. Especially the depictions of Chinese people eating: with lunatic expressions they greedily lust for dogs, devour rats.

Yet there are cards in which the Chinese people appear ethereal and gentle or scholarly, and others portray Chinese people as decorative designs. One such card pictures a Chinese boy in beautiful silk clothes within a

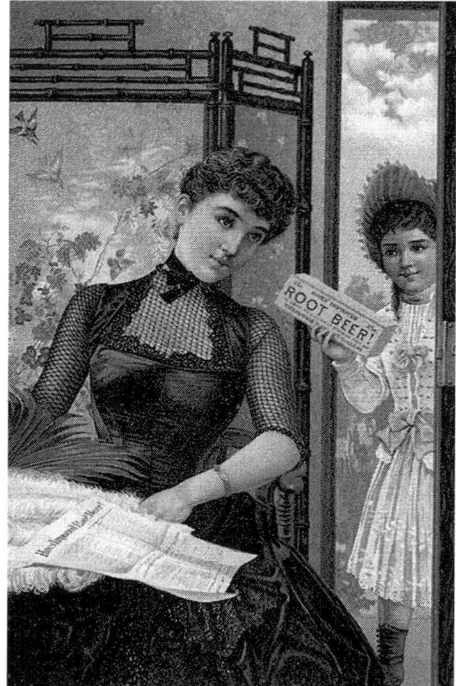

Fig. 4.1. Hires Root Beer, nineteenth-century trade card.

trompe l'oeil frame; in another a willowy Chinese figure gracefully holds an equally graceful long-feathered fan (fig. 4.2).

Indeed, a more comprehensive look at trade card pictures of Chinese people discovers a complex iconography with a broader range of images from demonic to (relatively) benign. Illustrators turned to the Chinese figures again and again with images that defy expectations.[15] The cumulative effect is a complex and rather enigmatic presentation of Chinese people and characteristics, compounded by the lack of any discernible logic connecting the Chinese motif to the product it advertises. This, to modern eyes, is remarkable.

The majority of trade cards utterly lack concern about relating image to product. Any correlation between the image, on the one hand, and the advertised commodity, on the other hand, is, to current sensibilities, ambiguous, problematic; at the very least, strange. The significance of these Chinese motifs on trade cards can be baffling, if they don't elude us completely; whereas on rare occasions, and then perhaps only mistakenly,

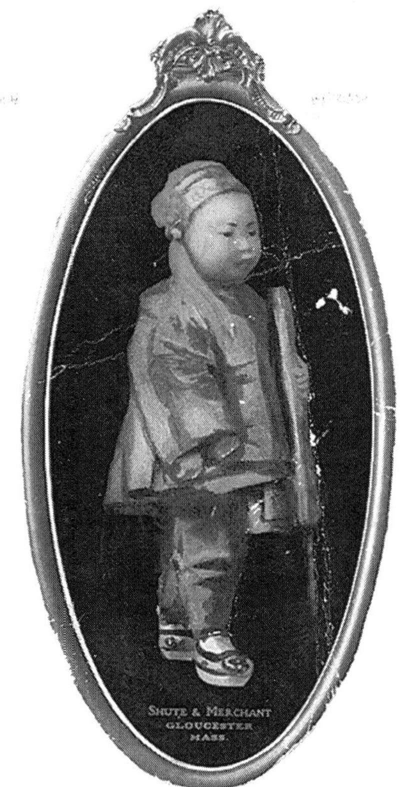

Fig. 4.2. Shute & Merchant, fish company, nineteenth-century trade card.

they seem perfectly clear. The assumption of a necessary correspondence between a Chinese image and a product is quickly thwarted. With the significant exceptions of laundry products and tea importers, the majority of the goods coupled with Chinese images has no connection with any aspect of a Chinese trade. One odd association, for example, is a card portraying an exquisite and delicate line drawing of a Chinese fisherman seated serenely on a riverbank as a dragon boat floats by. The text advertises Edwin C. Burt's fine shoes. In another odd coupling, on a die-cut card advertising enamel paint, in brilliant oranges and yellows, a Chinese man emerges as a butterfly[16] (fig. 4.3). And on a fan-shaped trade card selling newspapers, a Chinese magician sporting a tall pointed hat and wand hovers in the air, confounding any direct understanding (fig. 4.4).

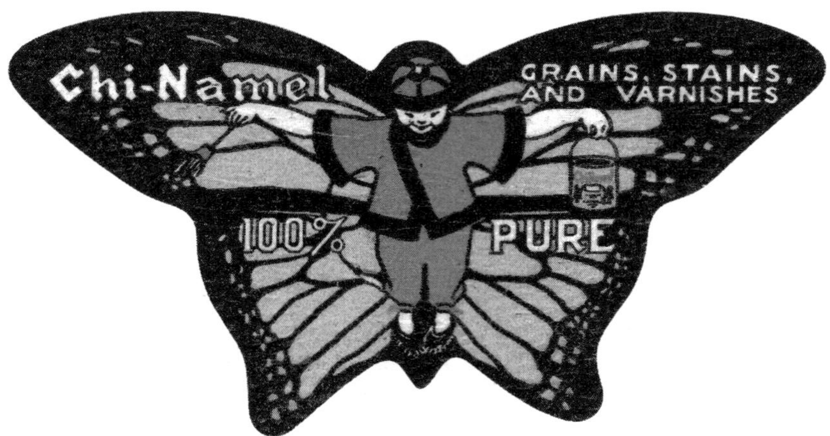

Fig. 4.3. Chi-Namel Grains, Stains and Varnishes, nineteenth-century trade card.

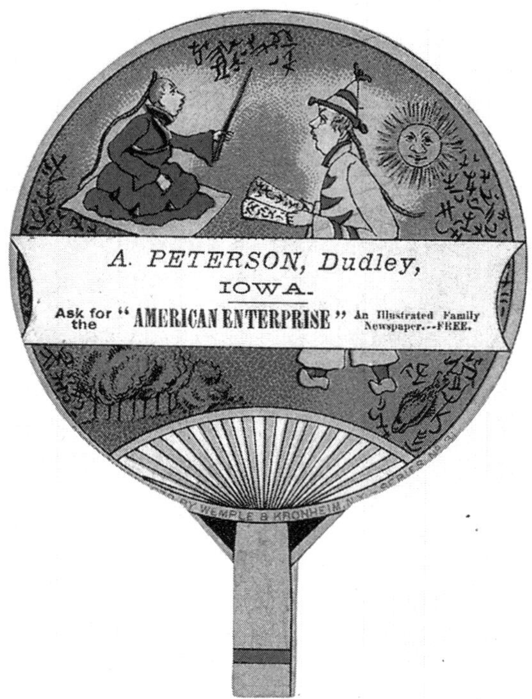

Fig. 4.4. "American Enterprise," A. Peterson, Dudley, Iowa, nineteenth-century trade card.

Lest we imagine a psychological explanation for these choices, we must consider that many cards were not commissioned for specific merchandise. Rather, lithographic companies would hire illustrators to design stock cards as prototypes available for any product.[17] The images were part of a system of consensus; drawn by an individual, selected by a manufacturer, and approved, even cherished, by viewers. A salesman for the company would bring the enormous book of sample cards to the potential client, encouraging their selection from hundreds of already-available images. The specific advertiser's name and product information would be stamped or overprinted onto the card later. Often several manufacturers would select the same card: popular cards such as one depicting a Chinese acrobat jumping over a large ball are found advertising widely disparate products. Perhaps a correspondence between product and image was seen or intuited by the company, but this connection is rather tenuous. More likely, something about the image itself, unrelated to the product, appealed to the person responsible for selecting the card.

It requires a step back to remember that the congruity between an imagistic portrayal of a product and the product itself—so familiar now it seems inherent—is not natural, or indeed essential, but is created.[18] Prior to the twentieth century the congruity we now expect was viewed as only one among many equally acceptable choices.[19] In fact nineteenth-century trade card images have more in common with earlier centuries' visual language: their extravagant encounters have a precedent in the bestiaries of certain medieval churches as well as in the outdoor visual disarray of the current century. In the colonial period, bold and colorful signs began to proliferate in urban areas such as Philadelphia and Baltimore. Advertising The Bull and the Mouth, The Seven Stars, The Golden Hare, and The Maypole the signs' images only idiosyncratically announced these as taverns; they have little in common with current notions of product-image identity.[20]

Rather than attempting the almost certainly unfeasible task of trying to decode the trade card images' relationships to products, it is more valuable to explore the significance of the images in terms of visual language and cultural meanings.

Visual language is constructed of formal qualities, the internal elements used to create the image, and of iconography, the forms and images as signifiers pointing outside into the culture. Trade card images utilized both parts of this language to involve the Chinese images within a wide range of issues in nineteenth-century American cultural.

Scholars have discussed advertising iconography during the nineteenth century as "an effort to impose civilized values on 'inferior' native populations."[21] But within the United State this situation was different: the audience receiving the trade card messages was the same population as those creating the advertising messages. Jan Pieterse reminds us that:

Images of otherness relate not merely to control over others but also to self-control. Thus, representations of others relate to power, not merely in the sense of imperial power but also of the disciplinary power exercised by the bourgeoisie within metropolitan society, or power as it permeates the 'society of normalization,' Images of otherness as the furthest boundary of normality exert a disciplinary influence, as reverse reflections, warning signals. The savage is indispensable in establishing the place of civilization in the universe. The cannibal represents a counter-image to bourgeois morality.[22]

As ideas of America and exclusion were debated and transformed, Chinese figures became floating signifiers, identifying liminality in some trade cards, functioning as symbols of inclusion in others. The Chinese figure in the trade card became a devise by which white Americans visualized their own social boundaries and reminded themselves about constraints and control.

An advertisement for Keystone agriculture implements illustrates the role of Chinese motifs as a vehicle for expressing cultural ideas through visual language. At the end of the century, two different visual systems were vying for hegemony. The older system used the play of color and fanciful imagery, similar to the old shop signs. The newer system was moving toward a rationalization of imagery, emphasizing linearity and gravitating toward the photographic style of realism. The Keystone card's strategic use of formal qualities from both these systems helped it deliver the product's message.

To heighten the difference between the two visual language systems, the Keystone card used two distinct printing processes. In full chromo-lithographic color, which is was associated with the sensual or the exotic, on the lower left of the card a small caricatured head of a Chinese man floats among a group of other abstracted and disembodied male heads of various ethnic groups and nations. Facing them on the right, a large and colorful three-quarter length Uncle Sam appears as a kind of a schoolmaster, gesturing magnanimously toward a display case. The trade card has a mechanical devise—a rotary wheel—attached to its back. A window has been cut out on the card's front, created to correspond to the window of the display case, behind which a turn of the wheel consecutively exposes one of five pictures of modern agricultural machines. These machine images are not chromolithographs but finely drawn woodcuts emulating the specificity of photography.

Through these formal qualities, the images lead into issues found within contemporary culture. Linear realism bestowed a sense of authority on the new implements, conferring an appearance of factuality and "giveness." On the other hand, the colored lithography, referring to the more ribald world of sensation rather than fact, presented the world in which non-Western peoples existed as multicolored and rather fantastical, as they now learned the modernism taught by the more rational Western world.[23]

Similarly, a series of trade cards selling baking soda accentuated these intricate connections between trade card imagery and contemporary concerns. Quite a contrast to the business of the previous card, in this series formal aspects have been reduced to emphasize the solemnity of the ritualized scene. On cream-colored paper, two black ink silhouettes of Chinese men with hair in long queues and dressed in traditional garb bow deeply, one on each side of an enormous can of baking soda, which is taller than they are (fig. 4.5). As an American comment on Chinese culture, the replacement of a traditional Chinese religious icon with an American household commodity trivializes Chinese religion and custom, rendering it ludicrous. But images function in multiple directions. The card not only projected a mocking attitude toward Chinese culture and religion: it simultaneously served as a screen allowing white Americans to project unspoken thoughts about their own culture. Through the depiction of Chinese figures, the card explored a new relationship emerging with manufactured products, questioning its effects on the American system of values. As the image makes clear, surrounded by bowing Chinese men, the baking soda became a deity by proxy—an American-made deity. It begs the query: How do we value our own products? We find that same relationship between commodity and worshipers expressed in Henry Adams's memoir of the same period. Lavishing praise on a beautiful Japanese lacquer object, Adams declared it to be "too pure for man. We pray to it."[24]

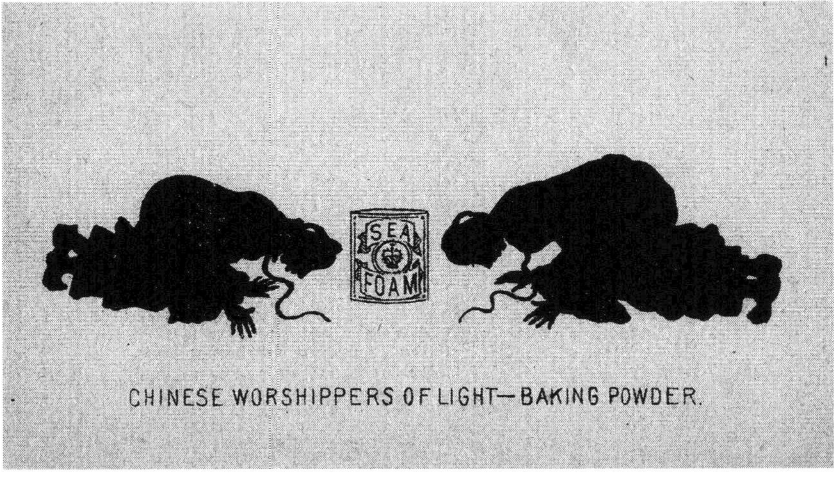

Fig. 4.5. Sea Foam Baking Powder, nineteenth-century trade card.

Adams's description is perhaps more candid than the trade card image as the nationalities are not interpolated. However, the Chinese imagery provided white American culture with a means to guardedly, indirectly, explore their relation to changes in their culture: the increasing materialism, the emerging capitalism and their resulting changes on all relationships and values. As Francois Jullien observed: "China presents a case study through which to contemplate Western thought from the outside. . . . A theoretical distancing is desirable—and this is exactly what China offers."[25]

To explore these connections between Chinese iconography and American culture further this chapter is divided into three sections. The first section discusses the role and language of trade cards as a medium: "The Politics of Chromolithography" is an overview, a brief history of trade cards and the power struggles over visual representation within the changing American culture. In "Between Two Worlds," the materiality of the trade card becomes identified as an integral component of its success. "An Addition to Visual Language: Floating Signifiers" explores the introduction of the "floating signifier," an iconographic shell or mold, a familiar sheath packaging and conveying a variety of separate and nonfixed meanings.

The second section, "The Chinese Figure as Outsider," investigates the iconography of trade cards in which a Chinese figure functions as a *foreign* element in American culture. "Dislodged Objects as a New Art" begins the section by describing a new art paradigm: art created by dislodging functional objects and removing them from their context, into a new one. "Paper Nations" continues this exploration of dislodged pieces of other cultures, now focusing on their reappearance as motifs on ephemeral bits of paper. And "The Safety of Exotic Distance" shows the visual parallels to the *New York Times* categories of sexual impropriety and decadence.

The third section, "The Chinese Figure and American Self-Definition," also focuses on the Chinese image, but unlike the previous section, it examines the Chinese figure as a personage *within* America. Here the iconography of Chinese figures discloses its intrinsic significations for American self-definition. Three themes become prominent: "Disjunctions, and Collisions: The Iconography of Displacement," analyzes the motif of a Chinese figure to express displacement or surprise, showing the use of the Chinese to signify the attempted domestication of something new into American culture; in "American, Un-American" the trade cards' iconography locates the Chinese figures within American scenes and imagines the displacement; "Hybrid Incorporation and Cultural Margins" visualizes amalgamations of Caucasian and Chinese as vehicles for exploring the cultural boundaries of such things as gender or aesthetics.

SECTION II. THE POLITICS OF CHROMOLITHOGRAPHY

1. Power Struggles Over Definitions of Art

Americans' attraction to mass-produced colorful pictures began in the 1840s, when Louis Prang perfected chromolithographic technology and began marketing the prints as an affordable alternative to fine-art painting.[26] Prior to the arrival of chromolithography, full color had been assumed to be a quality only attainable in a hand-painted, unique artwork. In the initial enchantment with chromolithography the prints' appeal cut across divisions of race and class: everyone marveled at the technical wonder in the painterliness of the works, their convincing replication of the look of oil painting, and their affordability. Images became prolific: Prang's chromolithograph based on Arthur F. Tait's painting *Group of Chickens* was so popular it was reproduced in 30,000 prints.[27]

The sudden profusion of images created a visual play contributing to the freewheeling spirit intrinsic to the constantly shifting culture of the late nineteenth century.[28] Chromolithography set images loose to wander randomly at will. Like wild animals released from zoo cages, allegorical symbols from the previous century collided with newly appreciated motifs from Asia; comforting and familiar images of precious little children and lovely demure women rubbed shoulders with caricatures of ethnic minorities, disembodied body parts, and personified fruit, all overflowing in full color.

The initial site of this image revolution was not in its subject matter. The majority of the chromolithographic audience preferred sentimental subjects, either copies of famous paintings or original print works: along with the chromolithograph of several chickens, another beloved print was a barefoot boy on a dirt road. It was the medium itself that was groundbreaking.

In the early years of chromolithography, Americans sang the praises of an art that arose from the commercial culture and existed in multiples. The availability of chromolithographs and their mimetic abilities—their ability to reproduce any painting—were seen as testimonies to the nation's amazing technological innovations in mechanical replication. Allowing equal art ownership for all, they were hailed as the art form for a democracy. A painter declared: "Innovation became a sign of liberty, as it was really the fruit of liberty; it is now as natural for us to experiment as it is to breathe. Our mechanical superiority is therefore, it seems to me, the outgrowth of a moral principle for which we may take credit to ourselves."[29] And although nationalism must certainly have been a factor, nevertheless, while studying in Europe the American artist Paul Durand proclaimed his preference for American advertising images, not American fine art, above European arts:

"yet when all this looking and studying and admiring shall have an end I am free to confess that I shall enjoy a sight of the signboards in the streets of New York more than all the pictures in Europe."[30]

For centuries art images had been unique and stationary, serving the powerful elites—traditionally the Church and the aristocracy. The emerging world of democracy, and with it market capitalism, overturned this order and images were released from exclusive service to the rich and powerful. Now they became available for all, and in multiples. Artworks moved through society in various sizes and costs; and with advertisements they were free.

With or without advertisements, chromolithographs were found in large numbers in almost every home. Mark Twain's *A Connecticut Yankee in King Arthur's Court* comments on the phenomenon with both irony and wonderment when his main protagonist reflects on what he misses most from the nineteenth century. After merely enumerating the lack of soap, matches, and mirrors, he pauses to describe his longing for a "chromo."

> I had been used to chromos for years, and I saw now that without my suspecting it a passion for art had got worked into the fabric of my being, and was become a part of me. It made me homesick to look around over this proud and gaudy but heartless barrenness and remember that in our house in East Hartford, all unpretending as it was, you couldn't go into a room but you would find an insurance chromo, or at least a three-color God-Bless-Our-Home over the door; and in the parlor we had nine.[31]

But the introduction of a new visual language is never neutral. The acceptance of a new process of imagery ultimately concerns not only taste and aesthetics but also power and control.[32] Within this unregulated democracy produced by the flood of chromos, a far less democratic world still existed, containing inequalities and hierarchies between ethnicities and class. Indeed, Walter Benjamin provided an accurate characterization in describing modernity's surfeit of objects, not as a democracy but as a "phantasmagoria of equality."[33]

These leveling efforts met with a belated but fierce resistance by the upper class, traditional masters of images and their dissemination. For those already in power, the readily available colored lithographs were not perceived as benignly democratic images but indeed as radicals, highly promiscuous in their nature, agitating against the established boundaries of artworks inhabiting a separate and rarified sphere.[34] An editorial by Oscar Lovell Triggs, in an 1897 edition of *Brush and Pencil*, condemned the chromolithograph for "destroying individuality":

If beauty did not require the expression of the human soul, if beauty were simply a matter of the material . . . then the machine might populate the earth with objects of beauty. But the fact remains, that to have beauty in an object the human hand must touch the materials into shape. . . . Do we prefer infinite productivity . . . universal cheapness . . . or can we afford to deny ourselves the luxury of infinite cheap things . . . and live according to human ideals. We cannot have both production and creation.[35]

A tug-of-war ensued, largely demarcated by class, with chromolithography at the epicenter of the struggle. The wealthy class contended that chromolithographs did not have the quality of fine art, that they were missing something ineffable but nevertheless discernible. They condemned chromolithographs as "cheap," a lesser replication. The rising middle class, with little financial ability to purchase original oil paintings, had welcomed the new form of image-making, which allowed it ownership of art. In its aspiration toward cultural power and prestige, the middle class sought only to share the image world with the upper class, and chromolithographs seemed to them the way to enter into it. Despite the contentions of the elite class, chromolithography looked very much like oil painting, adroitly replicating not only the picture but in some of the finer works, also the texture. In *The Real Thing*, Miles Orvell describes a contest at a mechanics exhibition that baffled and amazed the viewer, challenging "the observer to tell how they [chromolithographs] differed from the original paintings at their side." But this very ability to baffle the viewer proved to be chromolithography's undoing.

And this is the heart of the struggle. The upper class feared chromolithographs not for their cheap or shoddy *replication*, but for the opposite—for their virtuosity. In fact, "the better the quality" of the chromolithographs, "the more they challenged the elite classes."[36]

Poor aesthetic quality, then, was only a straw man. The real struggle was much more elemental involving class relationships and hegemony: a power struggle over ownership of culture, starting with the very definition of art and its purpose within culture. Disagreement over what constituted a work of art became an area exposing the friction between the classes.

The empowered class fought hard against accepting chromolithographs as legitimate art, not only to keep the other classes separate but for their own needs. Aware that the nation's most notable reputation was its lamentable quest for money, they wanted their art to showcase a different aspect of American life, its more spiritual side. Art was thought to be (and often still is seen as) an indication of the intrinsic qualities of a nation, its crowning ability to showcase its values. Hegel defined art as the way in which a society represents itself to itself and so constructs its identity.[37] Having culture became equated with being cultured. Harvard art history professor Charles Eliot Norton echoed Hegel's ideas in his statement that the "highest achievements in the arts" exhibited the nation's "faith" and its "loftiness of spirit."[38] For this correspondence between art and nation to be possible, art had to be seen as sublimely residing above the daily lusts of consumption. Art was imagined as pure, not serving any master, certainly not that of commerce. The uniqueness of traditional art objects insured that art would remain remote from the mass market.

As mass-produced objects, chromolithography, on the other hand, unabashedly bared its commodity nature, openly participating in commercial activity and as historian Peter Marzio states, "rating itself in dollars and cents."[39] Chromolithographs played to the market while asserting themselves as art. For the moneyed class, accepting chromolithographs as art threatened to expose artworks' hidden, suppressed characteristic—that it too was merchandise.[40]

To defend the paradigm of art as spiritual and pure, not part of the world of business, the elite fought against this too-democratic medium, and by implication, this too-democratic culture, by raising the suspicion that multiples with no single original generate a sham democracy. In *Hints on Household Taste*, written in 1868, reprinted by Dover Publications, New York, 1969, Charles Eastlake cautioned against chromolithographs: despite their popularity and supposed encouragement of good taste "with a few rare exceptions, they do more harm than good in this respect. . . . it accustoms the eye to easily-rendered and therefore *tricky* effects of colour which falsify rather than illustrate nature."[41]

Chromolithography became labeled as "sham art" and indicted for contributing to the emergence of a "faux" culture. E. L. Godkin, editor of the *Nation*, provided the seminal strategy to preserve the status quo, notoriously coining the term *chromo-culture* to signify what he saw as the lack of moral and mental rigor in American culture.[42] But what did "sham art" and "faux culture" signify, except, in other words, a culture that the power elite did not own?

Godkin's tactic, however was particularly insidious. Nineteenth-century culture, in counterpoint to its celebration of innovation, also turned on a suspicion of appearances, of style without substance. Themes of inauthenticity and the duplicitous characters of "confidence men" were strewn throughout the literature of the day.[43] Hesitant about the new art form, in the face of diatribes against it from cultural leaders, even those people who admired chromolithographs became unsure of the artistic legitimacy of mechanically reproduced images. Still partial to the images, nevertheless, they settled into an uneasy acquiescence with the empowered class and gave up the idea that this medium was really an art. The democratic spirit would be acknowledged with the upper class's creation of museums to showcase original art works for the masses to view; noblesse oblige substituted for ownership.[44]

In reality, the upper class actually always held the advantage in the struggle against chromolithography because both sides actually shared much of the same traditional criteria for art: moralizing narrative images, or images that showed beauties of the natural world. The middle class saw in chromo-lithography a desired replication of the upper-class relationship between art and owner for a greater number of persons and was unaware that chromoli-thography was asserting a new paradigm. The fear of the wealthy class, that in its very allowance of a wider population of art owners, chromolithography was a radical and divergent art form, was more astute.

But, although the upper class won the battle over chromolithography, the new image technology proved doggedly indifferent to its lowered status, and persisted in profoundly transforming culture, although not in the way expected. While it was prevented from having the authority to allow the middle-class entry into elite circles, as it originally seemed to propose (fright-ening enough to the wealthy class), unintentionally, the process of mechani-cal reproduction instead created a transgressive alternative to the dominant cultural hegemony. Art remained defined as singular objects, something for the elite to own and the working class to visit in a museum; nevertheless the upper class lost their sovereignty over image culture. Chromolithographs themselves lost their distinction as art objects, but they remained ubiquitous in modern culture, fluidly moving between commercial and fine arts and confounding the two.[45]

This intense debate over chromolithographs recalls Marx's observation that "capital is not a thing, but a social relation between persons."[46]

2. Between Two Worlds: The Dual Role of Trade Cards

In the 1860s, whetted by his successful marketing of chromolithographs and capitalizing on the public's appetite, Louis Prang masterminded the printing of full-color small and "handable" advertising trade cards. Like all other chromolithographs, the cards received an exuberant reception, celebrated as a new image media participating in the project of democratization.

Trade cards appeared at a liminal moment embodying the intersec-tion of two worlds—the transition from rural to urban, from agrarian to industrial. They arose while America's worldview lingering from premodern origins still centered on the tangible thing-in-itself, which prioritized the sense of touch. Through both their fluidity and their imagery, they helped create the more abstract and fluid contemporary world of appearances that privileges the sense of sight. The phenomenon of the nineteenth-century rise of spectacle and the associated demise in privileging the sense of touch has frequently been commented on. Guy Debord, especially, clarifies reasons for this transformation: "Since the spectacle's job is to cause a world that is no longer directly perceptible to be *seen* via different specialized mediations, it is inevitable that it should elevate the human sense of sight to the special place once occupied by touch: the most abstract of the senses, and the most easily deceived, sight is naturally the most readily adaptable to present-day society's generalized abstraction."[47]

Poised between these two worlds, the departing world valuing touch, and the emerging one giving primacy to sight, the trade cards' seductive appeal to their nineteenth-century audience derived from their combined visual and tactile legacies. Their visual legacy came from chromolithographic pictures. The other half of their inheritance, their physicality, derived from the widely circulated photographs called "cartes de visite," or "CDV." Invented in the mid-1850s, by 1859, these photographs had become "the rage," largely superseding the preceding form of photo portraiture, the daguerreotype. Both daguerreotype and CDV provided an intimate visual experience: a close look at a cherished portrait or, more rarely, a picturesque scene, held by hand while being viewed. But each daguerreotype was a unique image on a fragile surface, easily scratched, protected by glass housed in a leather case.[48] Unlike daguerreotypes, CDVs were made in multiples and backed inexpensively on cardstock. With their economy, their durability, and their easy replication, they became part of the culture as a fluid medium of exchange, often used as a personal memento in place of written calling cards.

Although both CDVs and trade cards offered the consumer images, while the former were photographic, the latter more often offered invented images, a crucial difference. But, trade cards were modeled on the CDVs' physical traits: using the same material and dimensions. With their "handable" size replicating CDVs' tactile qualities, trade cards exploited the emotional intimacy pioneered by the photos. The tangibility of the trade card counterbalanced its more abstract nature as image and spectacle, giving it the means to domesticate the plethora of visual images entering into American culture. The effectiveness of this strategy can be gauged by their esteem: enormous numbers of people collected trade cards as they collected portraits of friends, placing them, artistic side up, in special albums analogous to the albums housing family photographs.

3. An Addition to Visual Language: Floating Signifiers

Although initially chromolithographs merely repeated the conventions of traditional and sentimental oil paintings, within a short time the demands for new images, especially in advertising, gave unprecedented freedom and opportunity to create more images and quickly. The images became as ingenious as the process itself. And when chromolithographic artists veered away from the rote fine art conventions and their constraining moral agendas, they created visual innovations. A new genre with imagery consisting of separable and recombined interchangeable parts emerged from the new culture, and only later was designated as "montage" and "collage." This was not only a sign of modernism, it was the language of modernism itself: new visual imagery taken directly from the language of technology—think of the assembly line.

Trade cards created new ways of imaging for all sorts of images: they invented new contexts for older allegorical images and simultaneously they explored new concepts of representation.[49] A cacophony of enticing, desirable images overflowed in the advertising cards: historian J. Jackson Lears described their surreal merging of humans and animals, punning word play, and ironic raiding of high culture for sales slogans.[50]

Their sheer inventiveness is staggering. Trade cards intermixed words and images in strange new ways: bottles become top-hatted men, water pumps sprout legs and stride in formation across the land (fig. 4.6), In an

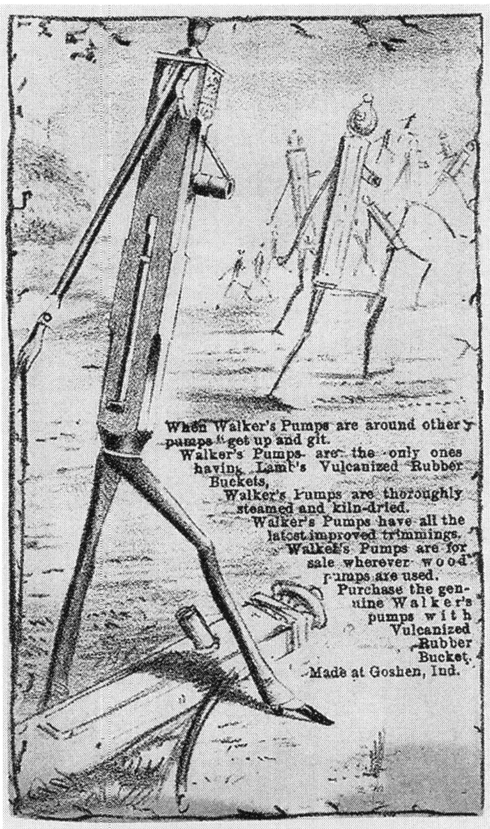

Fig. 4.6. Walker's Pumps, nineteenth-century trade card.

ad for Soapine soap, objects on a mantel twist and contort into bizarre but intelligible letters fig. 4.7. Such work defined a new genre, mixing "humor, insanity and drama."[51]

Because they were employed to produce multitudes of images and quickly, trade cards artists were at the forefront of inventing a new visual syntax, one that captured this sense of haste: one type of representation interrupts another, iconic symbols abruptly appear in modern contexts, and words elide into images. For instance, in a trade card advertising Ebersole Pianos, sixteen pictures or letters are placed in six rows, forming an anagram (fig. 4.8). A small image in the lower left depicts a tiny Chinese man kneeling under a trellis with a banner saying "Cin-Cin." Unlike captions in traditional allegories, these words do not clarify the meaning of the image. Together the word and icons are evocative but any certain meaning is elusive, hieroglyphic. Similar experiments in the (dis)association of word and image in the fine arts occurred only decades later in works by Rene Magritte such as his *The Key of Dreams* (1930) or Man Ray's *Indestructible Objects* (1924) (fig. 4.9).

It wasn't until the 1930s that discerning critics understood the paradigm shift brought about by chromolithography and other forms of mass-produced images. Walter Benjamin identified a new form of allegory in the innovative techniques of collage and montage, describing it as an "art of interruption."

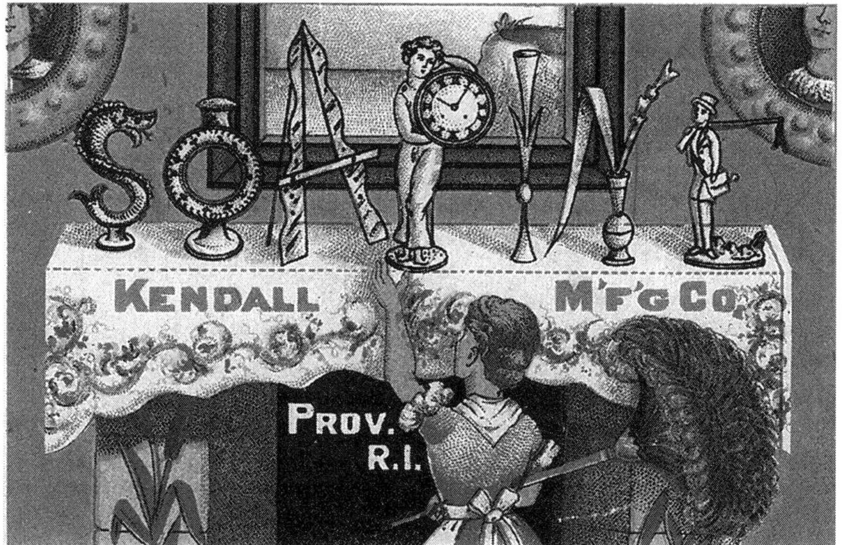

Fig. 4.7. Soapine soap, nineteenth-century trade card.

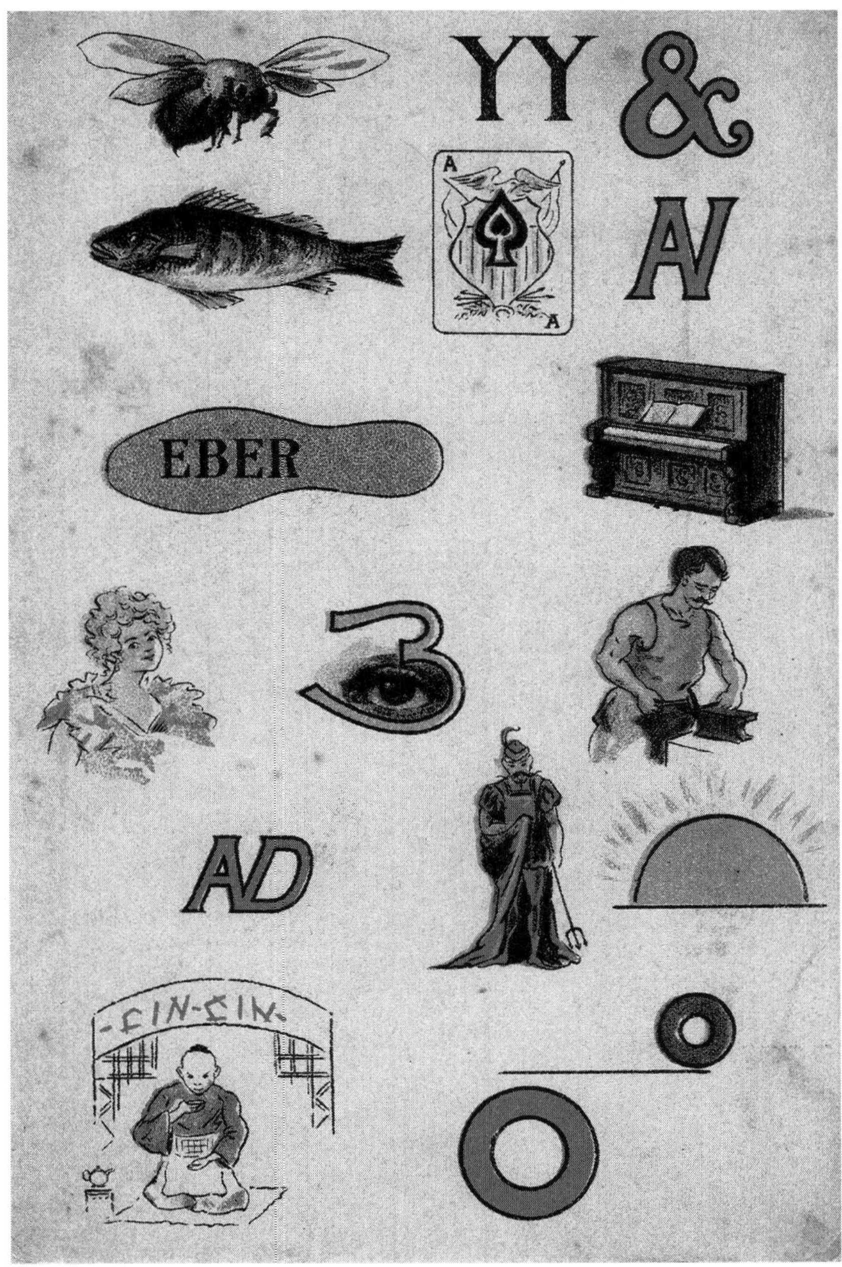

Fig. 4.8. Ebersole Pianos, nineteenth-century trade card.

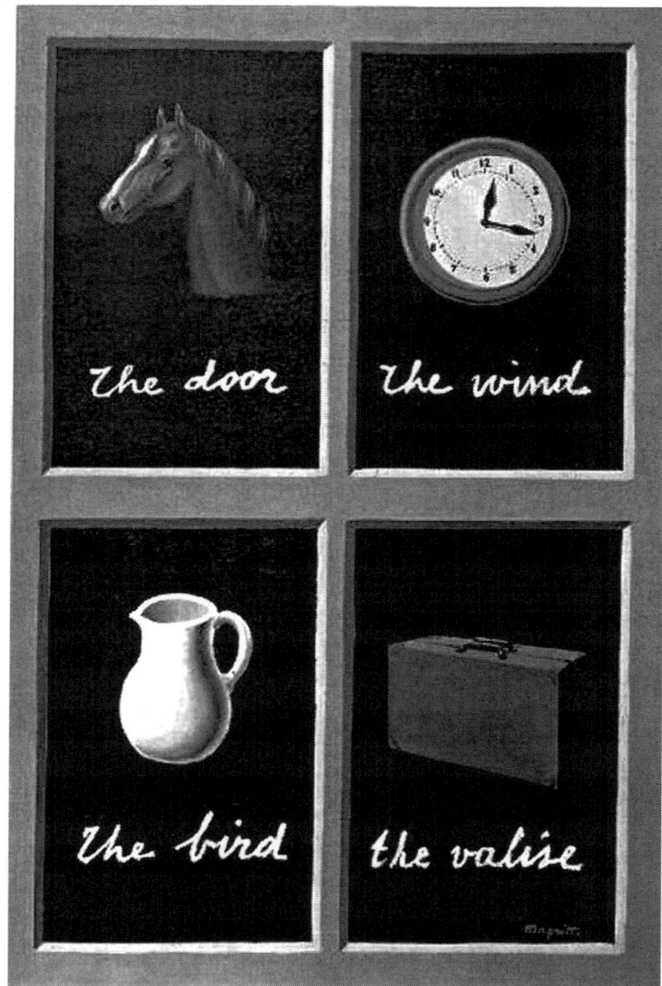

Fig. 4.9. Rene Magritte, *Key of Dreams*, 1930. Photo: © 2011 C. Herscovici, London/ Artists Rights Society (ARS), New York.

The revolutionary filmmaker Sergei Eisenstein contemporaneously character-ized montage as "a dialectic leap from quantity to quantity."[52] Both describe new techniques analogous to the break-up and disintegration of inherited convention in the modern world. In his now famous essay, Walter Benjamin eloquently described the fundamental transformation in art due to mechani-cal reproduction and its ease in creating multiples:

> When the age of mechanical reproduction separated art from its basis in cult, the semblance of its autonomy disappeared forever. The resulting change in the function of art transcended the perspective of the century; for a long time it even escaped that of the twentieth century. . . . The primary question—whether the very invention of photography had not transformed the entire nature of art—was not raised.[53]

The changes Benjamin identifies as occurring because of the invention of photography, were also brought about by photography's partner in mechanical reproduction: chromolithography. The transformation he notices in the 1930s was unnoticed in the late nineteenth century, occurring under the radar of the fine arts, and within the vernacular visual culture.

These innovations—dialectical leaps—described by Eisenstein and Benjamin in allegorical representations, provide a key to understanding the role multiples played in American culture, and the broader societal issues that these multiples raised. Trade cards share in the qualities Peter Marzio perceptively attributed to chromolithographic images, describing them as "an eclectic and uneasy union between classical forms and nineteenth century inventions."[54] One way a nation asserts its historical legitimacy is through its self-representation through images. This "eclectic and uneasy union" is a typical visual trope used by newly emerging nations attempting to establish their legitimacy. In *Inventing Tradition*, Eric Hobsbawm articulates this strategy, stating that "we should not be misled by a curious, but understandable paradox: modern nations and all their impedimenta generally claim to be the opposite of novel, namely rooted in the remotest antiquity, and the opposite of constructed, namely human communities so 'natural' as to require no definition other than self-assertion."[55]

Nineteenth-century America is noted for its use of allegorical imagery. It was a nation that saw a phenomenal rise in wealth and world status as it became a major contender on the world market. But it was defensive about its newness and worried about its self-image. Allegory became the way that the ideology of an idealized American nation, firmly established and successful, could be projected and made manifest. Such allegorical representations appeared frequently in images that would be encountered every day, especially through prints found as book illustrations, almanacs, chromolithography art, and trade cards.[56] The allegories naturalized the new nation by invoking past symbology to serve the present.

Vernacular culture appropriated the discarded classical images used in European art during the preceding centuries. But American artists dehistoricized history as they raided it, subordinating Greek and Roman gods, and French and English icons to American republican virtues. To fabricate a sense of historical continuity and culture in the United States, many American artists relied on allegorical handbooks, referring to readily available guides, such as George Richardson's 1778 English edition of Cesare Ripa's *Iconologia*.[57] In previous centuries allegorical pictures included specific explanations of their symbolic components. But for those created in the late nineteenth century, and recycled for American allegories, specific knowledge of their prior meanings was no longer necessary. The American allegories often fused vastly disparate archetypes into one entity that had no specific decoding. In fact, nineteenth-century representation has been aptly described as the persistence of the classical models of vision coupled with the collapse of their classical meanings.[58] With more mutable meanings, nineteenth-century allegories communicate more impressionistically.[59]

In light of this, for instance, Marvin Trachtenberg has referred to Bertholdi's Statue of Liberty as a "synthomorphosis" of forms (fig. 4.10). The

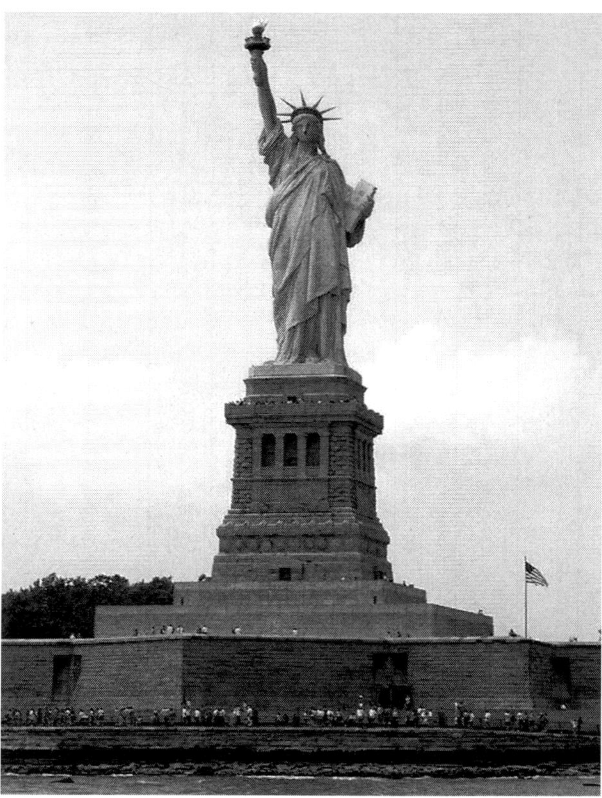

Fig. 4.10. Statue of Liberty, Frederic-Auguste Bertholdi.

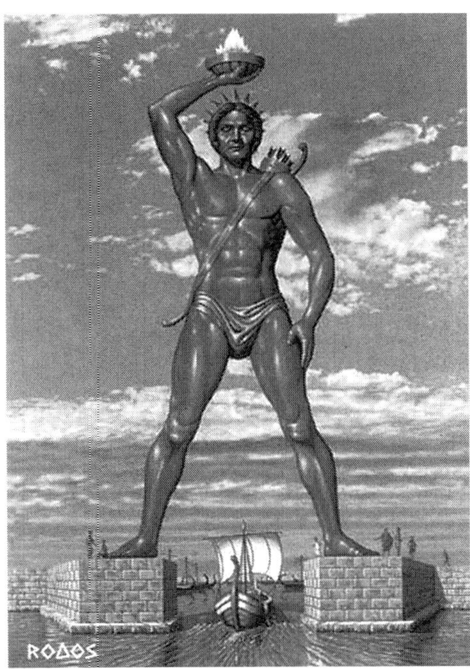

Fig. 4.11. Imagined Illustration of the Colossus of Rhodes.

statue idiosyncratically combines a helmet, whose sun rays derive from the Colossus of Rhodes; an arm gesture adapted from colonial iconography of an American Indian princess; and a Greek toga[60] (fig. 4.11 and 4.12). Yet most viewers never differentiate specific allegorical meanings of each component of the statue. The precise meaning of each part was subsumed as the Statue of Liberty in itself became the signifier: the grand title of "liberty," along with the idealized antique form, however vague, becomes its identity, legitimating its authority. Each iconographical element becomes displaced from its original meaning in accommodation to the adjacent iconographic elements, creating one overarching new meaning. And that meaning in turn gets placed into the larger American world of commodities. In the domain of trade cards, we see the icon of the Statue of Liberty used frequently as a form of celebrity product-endorsement, its iconography of patriotism put to work selling products ranging from thread to pig medicine (fig 4.13).

In reference to such iconic forms with variable meanings, the term *floating signifier*, applies, signifying fluid signs connecting social power, image, and commodity.[61] Floating signifiers indicate the cultural transformations

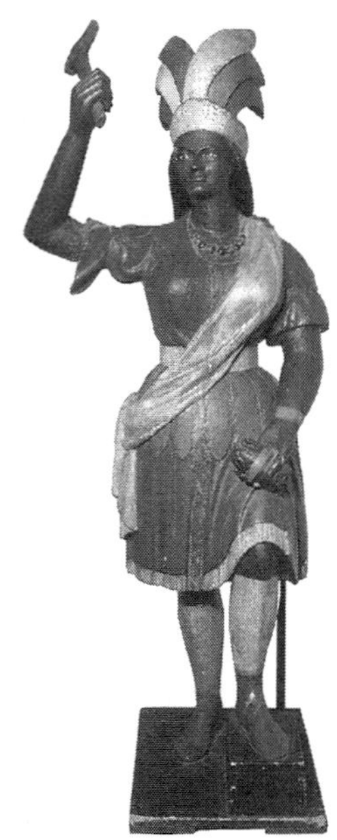

Fig. 4.12. Nineteenth-century, wooden cigar store Indian princess.

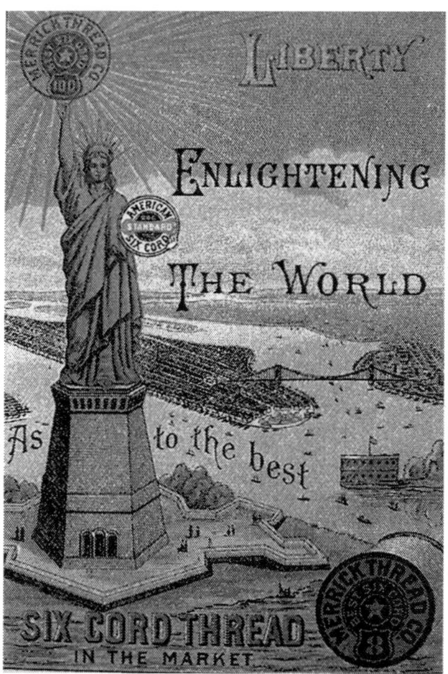

Fig. 4.13. Merrick Thread, nineteenth-century trade card.

that defined the nineteenth century, especially in contrast to the previous belief in fixed cultural markers and an eternal value system. Using traditional forms to house modern techniques and relationships, floating signifiers thereby normalize the new.

As the emerging world of market capitalism overturned a worldview based on fixed values and eternal hierarchies, both politics and technology demanded the creation of a new kind of sign, with the capability to circulate and the capacity to be readily replicable.[62] The floating signifier appeared prominently within the world of economics: paper money and banknotes defined as disembodied monetary signifiers, discrete and replicable units that move through the culture, promoted for their elastic qualities and not their inherent value. J. Jackson Lears captured the importance of paper ephemera in this unfamiliar world of flux and change: "This destabilizing tendency was reinforced by the emergence of new, more ephemeral modes of representing reality and value. In a developing money economy, paper became a vehicle for fantasy."[63]

Floating signifiers and decontextualized images were part of the nineteenth century's (re)construction of knowledge. In that time period, floating signifiers became ubiquitous, found not only as paper money and trade card images but as old names for new commodities (e.g., "horseless carriage"), as new building types based on ancient architecture (i.e., the entire Greek revival movement), and even as new religious practices in older denominations.

Trade card images are also such floating signifiers: a nexus of variable value or meaning within an iconic or familiar form. Their denotation is not fixed, formed within a closed system, but arises from a broader context. Stated concisely: There is no longer a definitive meaning associated with a single image or text.

As Jean Baudrillard discussed in *Symbolic Exchange and Death*, a principal qualitative difference distinguishing modern from traditional societies is modernity's arbitrary signs, proliferating on demand, and available to all classes.[64] Prior to the nineteenth century, Western power operated under the rubric of an ultimate legitimizing authority, distinguished by signs that were assumed to have eternal valuation. Although aware of human agency in creating culture, traditional cultures held signs, such as the scepter carried by the king, and even the very body of the king, to be everlasting and binding, inseparably fused to the meaning ascribed to them.[65] The modern sign, however, made no secret that its value was arbitrary, thereby appearing even to its own culture, in Baudrillard's words, "as counterfeit."[66]

The blatant artificiality—the fabrication—in the relationship between signs and power contributed to American's disquieting sensation that their entire culture was neither natural nor eternal but manufactured. These perceptions contributed to a transformed worldview in which all categories and hierarchies were no longer seen as immutable but were now perceived to be in constant flux and change. Floating signifiers helped dislodge the conviction that any aspect of the human world can hold permanent value. Maintaining the traditional forms, they now housed modern values and meanings that could always shift and be replaced. By the end of the century, most beliefs in fixed standards had been demolished, or, at the very least, called into question. Insecurity reigned as the connection between new sources of power and their associated markers left their arbitrary nature conspicuous.

The concept of floating signifiers is fundamental in the analysis of the Chinese trade card figures, helping identify the significance of a wide range of Chinese iconographic motifs used in exploring American identity and cultural transformations.

SECTION III. THE CHINESE FIGURE AS OUTSIDER

1. Dislodged Objects as a New Art

In *The Rare Art Tradition* Joseph Alsop argues that the appreciation of objects as "rare art" has occurred in only five cultures.[67] He claims that all other cultures have had no category of art, per se; they valued an object for its materials and for its skillful fabrication, and for its use in a particular event, rather than its imagistic significance or its provenance.[68]

Whether or not this viewpoint is accurate, in the nineteenth-century many non-Western objects became thought of and, even more, coveted as artworks by Western viewers. Napoleon set this in motion when he expropriated unprecedented amounts of treasure, taking it back to Paris. Unlike other conquerors though, he viewed the spoils from his enemies as a form of movable art and he placed it in the first international art museum, the Louvre. Along with material wealth it bestowed instant prestige.[69] We can say that Napoleon initiated the nineteenth-century enthusiasm for the souvenir on a grand scale.

American culture entered into the Napoleonic spirit. Functioning within the same cultural paradigm as Napoleon, wealthy Americans traveled throughout Europe and Asia, buying art, displacing objects from their indigenous culture.[70] The Western idea of art fixated only on the objects, not on their surroundings, catalyzing the destructive craze of dislodging desired objects from their history and environment and bringing it back to the Western nations: transportable art. Museums of art were created in which to sequester them for viewing. Art aficionados no longer had to travel to view the art in situ, but could take the art home, the spoils of the tourist.[71]

It is no surprise that American raids on the objects of other nations coincided with the proliferation of trade card images: the physical dislodging of objects from their original site was paralleled by the more abstract dislodging of their designs and images and their re-emergence in Western images. Both were aspects of the same cultural system of consumption. In 1869, Owen Jones greatly facilitated the abstract imaging of this ideology with his book affirming a "grammar" of "ornament": he dislocated and de-historicized non-Western art through his proposal of an evolution of design that placed the non-Western motifs and color combinations, such as the Chinese key scroll, within an encyclopedic catalog of stylistic elements available to the West.[72]

Trade cards also embody this paradigm of images without place, and place as image, freely circulating and available to anyone. Trade card imagery fragmented and dislocated previously fixed places from their space and time. Every major historic monument and event, every known country from the past or present, took its place on one advertisement or another: on one side the pyramids of the Pharaohs, on the other side an advertisement for Clark's "ONT" Thread—both seemingly equally at hand. In the world of images, all visualizations were contemporaneous and equally available for recontextualizing, for either entertainment or profit, or both.[73] Through their widely diverse images, trade cards asserted equality between all sorts of representations.

2. Paper Nations

Trade cards not only reflected what was already known, they helped to construct and familiarize Americans with a new system of visualizing the world. William M. Ivins Jr. reminds us that modern information systems rely on the relatively new ability to quickly and conveniently reproduce images. He contrasts this with the system of knowledge construction available to the ancient Greeks, demonstrating that, due to the lack of mechanical replicable pictures, Greece's major advances occurred in the areas of greatest visual accessibility without dependence on mechanical duplication. Consequently, in geometry and astronomy: "for the first of which words amply suffice, and for the second of which every clear night provides the necessary invariant image to all the world."[74] Contrastingly, from weapons and warfare to our profession of art history, so many nineteenth-century innovations and investigations depended on the ability to mechanically reproduce multiples of an image or an object. A similarly constructed conception of an entire continent must have had equal authority and, consequently, plausibility. Victorians structured their ideas of entire countries on the dissemination of the relatively flimsy paper evidence authored by the few Western visitors. It is no wonder, then, that distant nations such as China seemed strangely without depth, with a singular lack of history.

In part, through advances in ocean transportation China was no longer perceived by the West as geographically remote.[75] Increased world travel and trade brought the distant close. By mid-century not only had Westerners traveled East, Chinese people had arrived in America, as merchants and as living displays in World's Fairs as well as immigrants. In *Imperial Leather* Anne McClintock proposes a new spatialized concept of time, connecting the contemporary theory of evolution to the nineteenth-century understanding of geography.[76] Separations once imagined as geographically remote were reconstrued as temporally distant.[77] And nineteenth-century theorist Victor Segalen described how colonizing nations imaged the colonized territories as fixed and static in time, "unchanging landscapes that existed in temporalities outside of modernity: vast, ethnographic museums of alien cultures and peoples."[78] Indeed, Western nations began to characterize colonized and non-Western peoples as the living archaic or primitive cultures. The Chinese distance from the West became imagined temporally, as if occupying a prior chronological time.

Trade cards reflected this way of exoticizing China, creating images that illustrated American's lack of experiential knowledge of China. The cards primarily presented China as an anachronistic space, out of phase with the Western, modern world.[79] A trio of unrelated trade cards representing China depicts the various strategies used to present China as antique, distinct from modern America (fig. 4.14–4.16),

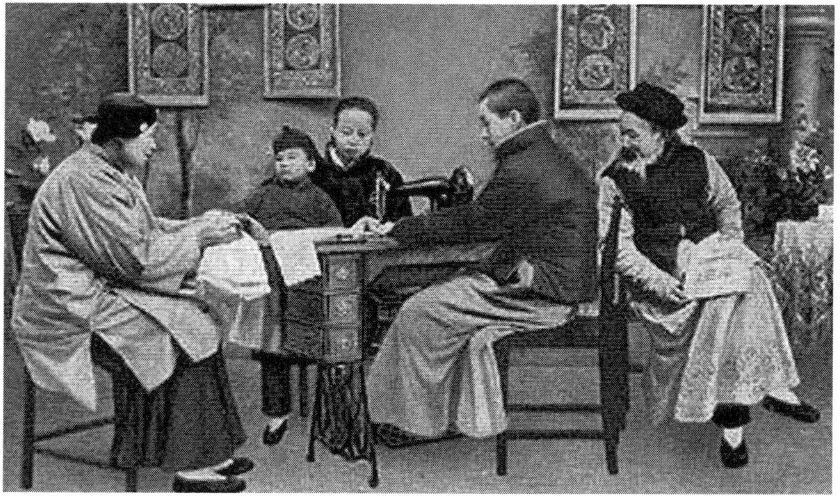

Fig. 4.14. Singer Sewing Machine, nineteenth-century trade card.

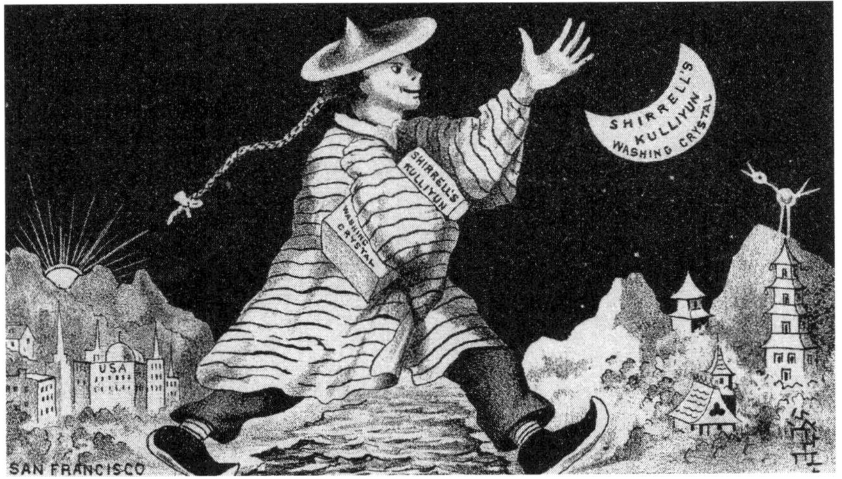

Fig. 4.15. Shirrell's Kulliyun Washing Crystals, nineteenth-century trade card.

The Singer Sewing Machine Company produced a trade card series portraying their machines in use in numerous exotic countries. The scenes do not reveal insights into foreign domestic life as much as invite comparisons to their American equivalents. Playing on a resemblance to the intimate cartes de visite, the Chinese card in this series simulated the look of a

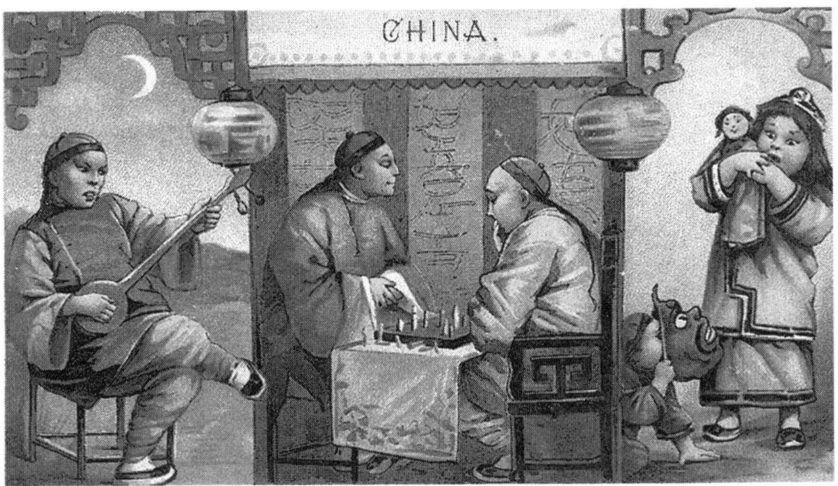

Fig. 4.16. Arbuckle Coffee, nineteenth-century trade card.

hand-tinted photograph and depicted a grouping of Chinese people, to be read as a family. At a glance, the interior space appears strangely illogical. This becomes clarified on closer inspection, with the realization that it is comprised by collaging several incongruous motifs: an Asian garden serves as an interior backdrop within an austere interior room; and a Romanesque column rather grandly dominates the oriental garden. It's hard to tell if it is supposed to be an actual garden or a painting of one. The "family" congregates around the sewing machine, giving their rapt attention to the one person that operates it. The card has no words, relying on the visual incongruity of the sophisticated machine in the anachronistically exotic setting to create a dissonance that demonstrates America's separateness as well as its material assistance to this backward Chinese nation.

And, under the guise of a mission to help China progress, Shirrell's Kulliyun Washing Crystals unified two of America's most prominent conceptions of China, combining their idea of China as a backward, primitive state with the theme of Chinese Exclusion. The upper two-thirds of the card is dramatically occupied by the black night sky. A large male Chinese figure strides left to right across the center. His back is to the city on the left labeled "San Francisco," where the sun peeps over the mountains, his legs straddle the ocean. One leg is already securely placed on the distant shore where pagoda-style buildings are scattered in the mountains, the other trails behind in the San Francisco setting. The crescent moon hanging over his head advertises "Shirrell's Kulliyun Washing Crystals," and he carries a box with the same label under his right arm; with his left he waves a greeting to China. Under the picture, the caption, stating "Going Abroad," reinforces the iconographic implication that the forced expulsion of the Chinese from America was actually an educational mission: Chinese voluntarily leave a nation in the rising sunlight to bring Western products—progress—to their country, which as yet remains in the dark.[80]

Arbuckle Coffee also issued a trade card series portraying foreign countries, relegating the product advertisement to one side and the delicately colored exotic image to the reverse side.[81] Their China card, dated 1893, shows a scene divided into three continuous sections. In the section on the left, a Chinese man sits in a doorway under an intricate grid arch and plays a stringed instrument. A crescent moon rises over his head. Pink lanterns accent a doorway to an interior room, which constitutes the middle scene: two Chinese men absorbed in a board game; three scrolls are on the wall behind them. And at the right, in a more interior room, a young boy puts on an ogreish mask and startles a girl playing with a doll. In case the visual message of the premodern leisure of the Chinese and their relative inertia passed unnoticed, the text written on the back of the card makes it definitive. The actual product advertising is concluded in several brief sentences extolling the benefits of grinding Arbuckle Coffee at home. The much larger paragraph, titled "China." furnishes purported "facts" about that nation, beginning with the sentences: "China has made less progress than any nation of the world. Yet she possesses a civilization peculiarly her own. Her people are a phlegmatic and meditative race, but not given to independent thought."

This hierarchical attitude constructing a flattened idea of a static China was pictured clearly in trade cards such as the three above, and disseminated on these widely circulating paper images. J. Jackson Lears coined the consummate term, defining such attitudes as *imperial primitivism*.[82]

3. The Safety of Exotic Distance

Early in the century, advertisements set in a lavish, exotic, and remote land, typically pictured Chinese men classically, as distinguished Mandarins, highly cultured and safely distant. Later trade cards, created during the highly politicized immigration of Chinese people, began depicting Chinese figures within an American setting. Yet a careful look shows that while the Chinese were situated in America, paradoxically they were almost exclusively pictured in the role of an outsider, a counterpoint to the American image on the card.

Comparing the almost parallel iconography in two nineteenth-century advertising images exposes the striking transformation from respect to ridicule created by a shift in location from China to America. The transformation illustrates the change in attitude toward the Chinese that occurred as they entered into the United States, no longer exotically remote but a challenge to American values, both personal and as a nation.

The older advertisement is not actually a trade card; more likely it was an advertising page in a book, with image and text on one side only (fig. 4.17). In block letters, the text both above and below, and even within the image, advertises a Philadelphia dealer: "Thompson Black's Son and Co. Dealer in Fine Teas and Coffees and Every Variety of Choice Family Groceries." The image is centered in the middle of the page, a window onto an elegant Chinese scene. A carved wooden scroll and vines drape across the upper border. In the distance we faintly see an arched bridge and odd egg-shaped pagodas. In the foreground, a Chinese Mandarin and his very Spanish-looking, albeit Chinese, bride, sit on elaborately carved benches placed on a balcony overlooking a garden, while a servant graciously serves tea. All three figures wear rich and colorful clothing, indicative of their grace and class. On the far left, almost outside the pictured scene, a wooden crate discretely advertises "Choice Black and Green Teas & every variety of fine groceries." The entire scene projects an atmosphere of dignified exoticism.

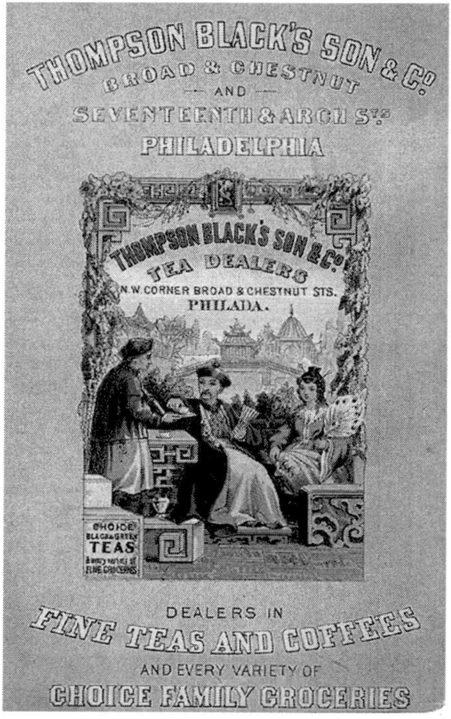

Fig. 4.17. Thompson Black's Son & Co, Teas and Coffee, advertising image, early nineteenth century.

The trade card created later in the century also depicts a Chinese man having tea with a companion (fig. 4.18). But unlike the brilliant colors of the previous card, here color has been limited to a dirty sepia wash. Burlesquing the majestic girth of the Mandarin in the first card, the Chinese figure has become quite loutish and frankly fat. Oblivious to his crudeness, he sprawls over the crate of tea with his legs stretched out in front of him—a far cry from the pomp and ceremony in the earlier advertisement. His clothing, too, has been demoted from regal status; in fact his garment resembles the rugged buckskin associated with Native Americans. In an additional faux pas, his broad backside dominates the picture plane as he faces away from the viewer, toward his companion. The caption has the Chinese man nonsensically stating: "Melican Man he mus dlink Tea an den he get so fat like me."

The second personage no longer is an elegant Chinese woman but an American man perching rigidly upright on his tea crate, identifiable at once as a very gaunt and uncomfortable Uncle Sam. His face is pinched as

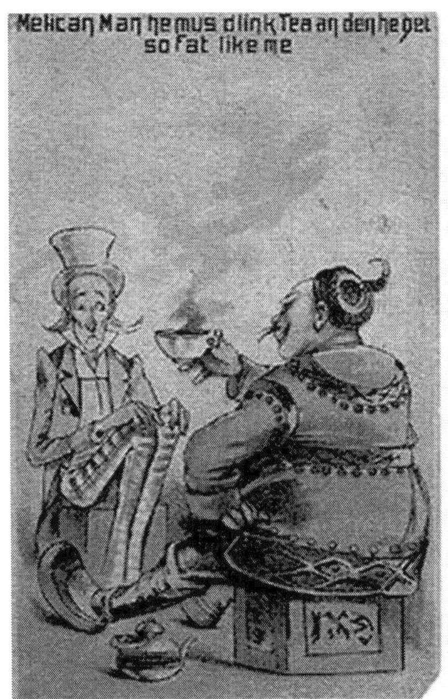

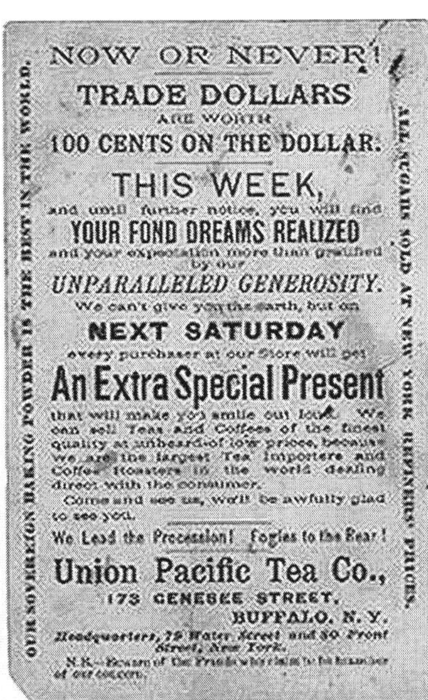

Fig. 4.18. Union Pacific Tea Co., front and back of nineteenth-century trade card.

he awkwardly shrinks from the boorish intrusion of the Chinese man. The proximity of the two men, symbolic of the nations they represent, results in an encroachment into American space.[83] China's presence in the United States is imaged as familiar—uncomfortably so—and most of the exotic distance has been degraded, appearing now mainly as an outlandish style and a ludicrous manner of speaking. In this, we see visual parallels with categories derived from the *New York Times*, specifically lack of intelligence, even to the written mimicry of speech.

Contrasts between images in a second pair of trade cards also demonstrate how meaning was transformed when iconography was recontextualized from there to here. In these cards, the sexual dynamic between a Chinese male and a woman is changed from polite to uncouth with a few shifts in depiction. The first card shows three Chinese figures. Its simple lines portray a polite, dignified encounter between a Chinese man and two Chinese women carrying parasols (fig. 4.19). Drawn with great precision, all three figures appear stately in their elegant, flowing clothing. The man stands to the right, pointed hat in hand (based on some concept of Chinese haberdashery), and bows slightly to the women as they gaze at him courteously. His hair is swept back and smoothly tied. The image sets up a sexual frisson between the man and women, but it simultaneously mitigates it by their postures and expressions. The two demure women stand together: each becomes the chaperone of the other, diffusing the sense of a tryst. The decorum of the exchange is accentuated by a witness in the form of a small dog standing calmly at attention between the women and the man.

The second card shows a Chinese man and two other figures in almost identical placement and posture to the first group, with one main exception (fig. 4.20). A white, upper-class Victorian woman has been substituted in place of one of the Chinese women. A young ruffian, perhaps a shoe-shine boy, stands in place of the other, slightly in the distance. The sexual drama between the Chinese man and the woman now is unmediated. Standing by herself, the sole woman is isolated in her encounter with the Chinese man; there is no chaperone to intercede. As in the first card, the man bows, but his bow is now imaged as exaggerated, obsequious, as he bends almost horizontally at the waist. Although otherwise dressed entirely in Chinese clothing, instead of holding a Chinese hat in hand, the man doffs a shiny top hat, allowing his long, raspy braid to snake freely out behind him. Rather than showing his ability to assimilate, his recklessly exposed queue signals his distance from those who have real propriety to such a hat. His words,

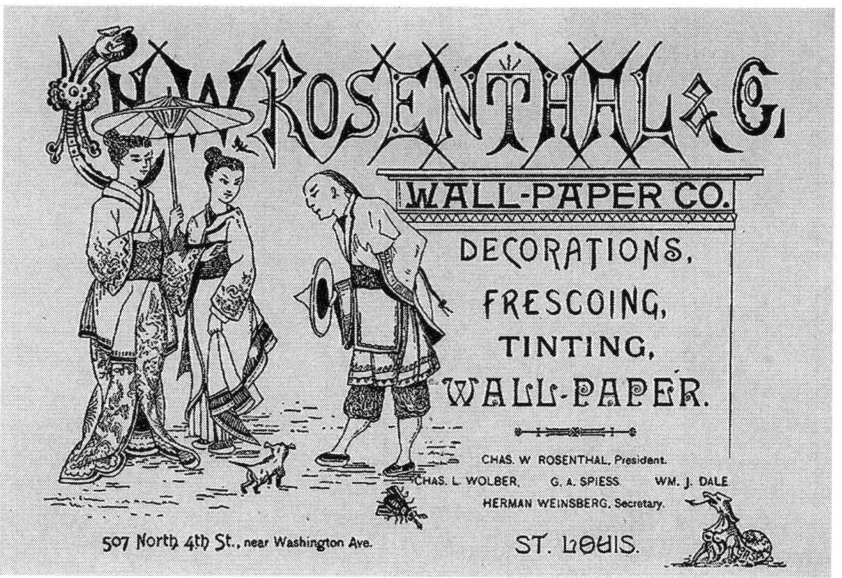

Fig. 4.19. N. W. Rosenthal & Co., wallpaper, nineteenth-century trade card.

given in a caption, reiterate this attempt at counterfeit: "Me masheee alle samee mellican man."

And the reaction of the white woman shows her disdain of the sham. Although she looks directly at the Chinese man, she turns her back to him. This places her large bustled derriere in closest proximity to him; in fact, it is at his eye level, on the same horizontal plane as his bowed head. Accentuating the ribald nature of the scene, the youth, in his patched pants with a small derby perched jauntily on his head and a saddlebag slung across his shoulder, stands at a distance and thumbs his nose at the Chinese man. Even in its rudeness, the youth's candid gesture confirms him as quintessentially American. And, as in the first card, the little dog provides commentary. No longer a patiently docile presence standing equidistant between the male and female figures, instead the dog, held on a leash by the woman, jumps rambunctiously and yaps at the Chinese man; its excitement augments the inappropriateness and tension of the encounter.

American society, at once anxious and intrigued about miscegenation, clarified the parameters between races through visualization. Trade card imagery, such as that described above, reconstrued male Chinese interactions with women when they were relocated into the United States. Almost all the shifts in meaning from the first card to the second stem from the change of the woman's race to white. With that as a catalyst, the iconography no longer depicted a decorous encounter of equals but a bawdy one, emphasiz-

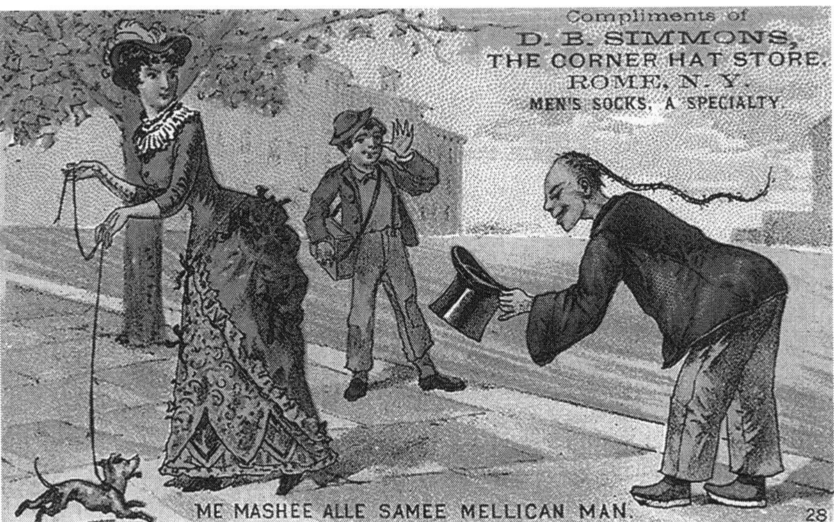

Fig. 4.20. D. B Simmons, Corner Hat Store, nineteenth-century trade card.

ing perceived differences between gender, race, and class. Within America, previously respectable Chinese behavior became a source of mockery: Chinese refinement became counterfeit, civility became parody—especially when a white woman was involved.

SECTION IV. THE CHINESE FIGURE AND
AMERICAN SELF-DEFINITION

1. American, Un-American

Chinese people living in America complicated the idea of who and what was an American. By mid-century Chinese had arrived in America as merchants, laborers, and later even as living displays in World's Fairs. They were certainly a part of the new American landscape. But how were the Chinese to be thought of? Could they be accepted as Americans?

Being American was perceived as a contract—an agreement to a value system rather than, as in other nations, exclusively a circumstance of birthplace. But there was no consensus about exactly what the criteria for that value system. Nevertheless, because "Americanness" was seen as an agreement, it gave rise to the idea of its opposing counterpart—the un-American.[84] No other nation has such a doppelgänger: while people are not French, or not English, or not Chinese, it is impossible to be similarly un-French, or un-Chinese.

While theoretically the un-American was defined as someone holding opposing values to the ones heralded in America, in reality it was more often applied to people who did not share the ethnic heritage or the affluence of the mainstream. Not coincidentally, the concept of "un-Americanism" first rose to prominence immediately after the massive influx of Eastern European working-class immigrants in the 1860s.

Trade cards illustrate the opposition of American and un-American often through the figure of Chinese males. The most reactionary cards distinguished Americans from Chinese by using the catchphrase "The Chinese must go," sometimes expressly written out, more often understood as the image's subtext. The phrase entered American culture as a political slogan in the 1870s, apparently remaining in vogue even after the first Exclusion Laws banning Chinese admittance into the United States had been passed in 1882. The advertisements that most avidly pigeonholed Chinese Americans as those who "must go" were designed for companies selling laundry products.[85] This is not surprising—they played on the fact that one of the few means for employment open to Chinese men was in laundries, a service job previously relegated primarily to illiterate females and housewives.

The ads advocated the departure of the Chinese through images showing that their specific role in the United States was now superfluous due to advances in laundry products and new technology. With their washing methods outdated, Chinese presence, barely tolerated, no longer had a justification. (This was meant to be seen as clever and humorous.)

Several laundry cards specifically portrayed Dennis Kearny, the zealous instigator behind Chinese Exclusion laws. His likeness attests to the complicity, even this early, between politics and marketing: celebrity endorsement, even notoriety, adding prestige to the product. One such card advertising "Waterproof Linen" shows a beach with two white men in the water incongruously sporting full dress shirts over their bathing trunks, demonstrating that their "celluloid collar and cuffs" are water- and perspiration-proof (fig. 4.21). A third figure, Kearny, appears in profile on the far left of the card immersed in the water up to his shoulders with only his tiny head protruding, critically observing the scene unfolding on the beach. Behind the three white men, stretching out across the ocean and toward the setting sun, are countless Chinese men with their washtubs, the tool of their trade, now obsolete and serving as crude boats to take them back to China.

The contrast between American and alien is accentuated through the degrees of specificity and uniformity. Unlike the individualized and rounded representations of the white men, the Chinese men are portrayed flattened and anonymous, a solemn procession of replicated figures, distinguished only by different colored clothing. The only individualized Chinese figure stands on the shore directly in Kearny's line of sight. With his washtub in tow, he rubs his eyes, weeping like a child, a diminutive, infantilized caricature. The caption at the bottom of the card reads ""o more washee washee, Melican

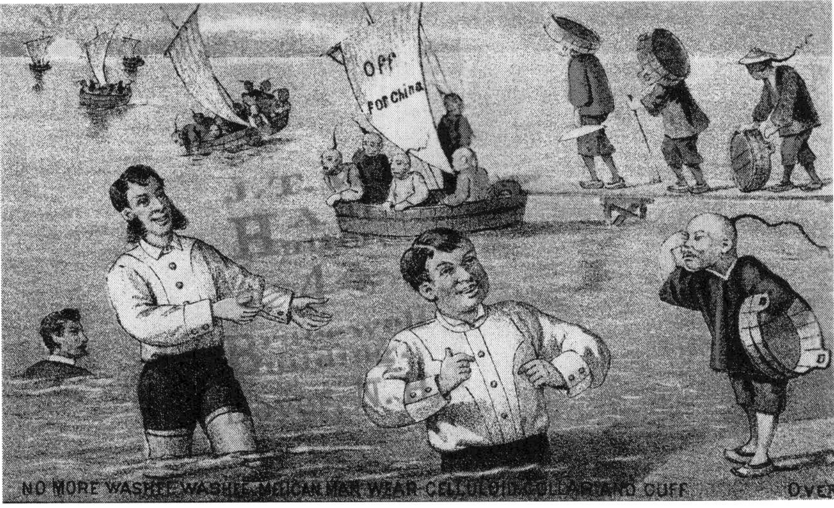

Fig. 4.21. Celluloid Collar and Cuff, Nineteenth-century trade card.

man wear celluloid collar and cuff." China itself is not depicted, only the vast ocean-scape and a distant horizon.

Some laundry trade cards went much further in their vehemence to contrast American and Chinese. The terms *non-American*, or even *alien*, are simply too neutral to describe these vicious renderings of Chinese people. Not content to reduce Chinese men to childishness, these cards portray them as lewd and demonic. In a card advertising "Celluloid Corset Clasps," three Chinese laundry men cavort in the shop as they wash women's corsets (fig. 4.22). Their indecent liberties exceed merely handling women's undergarments: all three leer lasciviously as they exhibit the undergarments for all to see. They seem to revel in the abject stains, the reddish color ostensibly rust but suggestive of more intimate body fluids, and they hold them high for scrutiny, making a spectacle of the private and feminine.

Not only is their behavior aberrant, their gender itself is warped because, although male, they engage in tasks previously delegated to female labor. Their proportions, too, suggest the female as much as the male body. The sexual ambiguity created by these mixings of gender furthers their deviancy. In fact, Richard Meyer states that in artworks coupling sexual deviance with ethnic minorities was typical: "that the most effete and decadent characters should be presented as foreigners."[86]

This category of sexual decadence appeared in the prior chapter on the *New York Times*, but the card pushes other extremes, other borders are

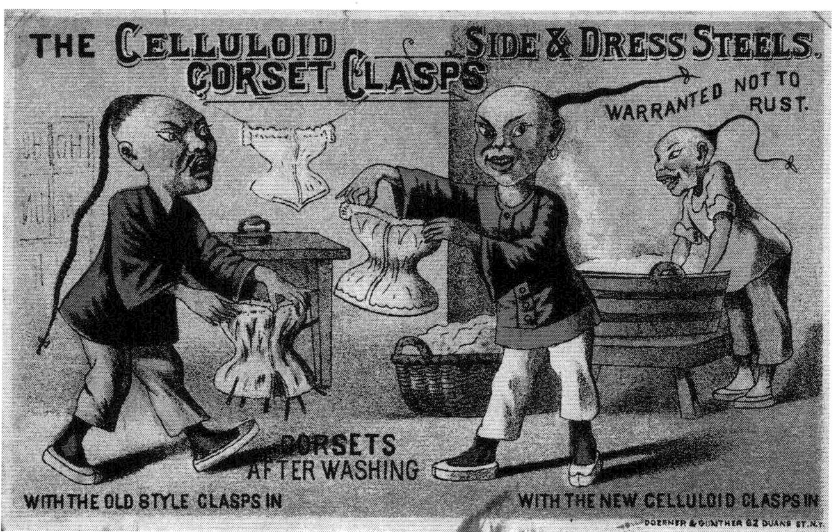

Fig. 4.22. Celluloid Corset Clasps, nineteenth-century trade card.

crossed. Adding to the uncertainty of their humanity, the bodies assume im-possible proportions. One has a queue that defies gravity, extending straight out behind him. Their angular and enlarged hands terminate in long clawlike fingers, equating them with rapacious birds of prey, further vilifying them as not quite human, and certainly not American. With such a depiction, no text is necessary to insinuate that, because of their own deviant, diabolic qualities, the Chinese really must go.

The strategy of dehumanizing the Chinese by insinuating an affinity between the Chinese man and animals ran rampant on ads showing Chi-nese eating. A continual source of humor apparently came from depicting alleged Chinese culinary preferences for dogs or rats. One card chosen by several merchants selling products ranging from cutlery to baking powder depicts a young Chinese man, shown as some strange hybrid creature with childlike proportions, his queue rising straight up and his fingers stretching out like talons. He clutches a dead rat in his hand while he fearfully tries to placate a large and intimidating dog that looms over him by promising that he does not eat "Bow Wow Pie" (fig. 4.23). Even more demonically, on a large ad created exclusively for a popular brand of rat poison, Rough on Rats (intended for use as a sign in the store display), a Chinese man holds rats in each hand and grins insanely, greedily dangling one rat in front of his mouth (fig. 4.24). His queue twists behind him, snake-like, visually symmetrical to the rat's tail dangling in front of him. At the top of the card red letters spell out "Rough on Rats." Under the letters, and almost equal in size to the Chinese man, is a giant rat, lying dead on its back with its four feet curled up helplessly. Beneath the rat is a facsimile of a banner saying "it clears out," and continuing down the left side of the card the banner, enumerates: "rats, mice, bedbugs" and on the right: "flies" and "roaches." And immediately over the man's head, in smaller block let-ters, placed in quotes and capitalized, is the phrase: "They Must Go." The double entendre of this caption, applying equally to the Chinese man and to the rat, reiterates the dehumanizing equation of the image.

Situated within an American location, the Chinese males are a part of the American cultural scene. In that sense, through the iconography of these trade cards we see that Chinese people did become admitted and incorporated into America, but confined to a narrow and racist place. Their persona invented through such cards became naturalized as their American identity—signifying a permanent alien.

2. Disjunctions, and Collisions: The Iconography of Displacement

The variety of peoples found in late nineteenth-century American culture, compared to those found in present-day America, have more in common

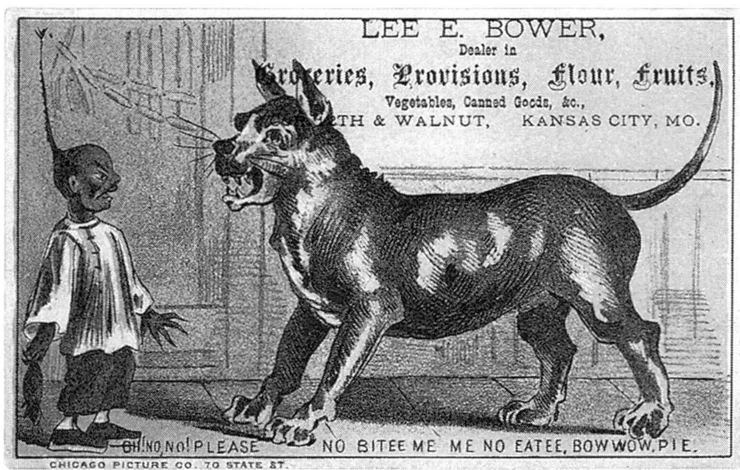

Fig. 4.23. Lee E Bower, Groceries, Provisions, Flour, Fruits, nineteenth-century trade card.

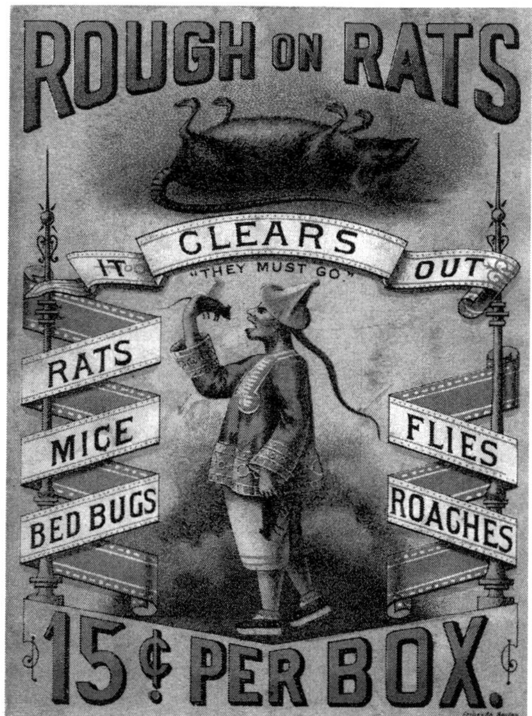

Fig. 4.24. Rough on Rats, large nineteenth-century trade card.

than does each period's distinctive response to them. In our postmodern culture, the collisions between disparate objects and peoples have become increasingly normalized; we call it globalization. Contrastingly, the twentieth century was more attentive to the occurrence of unusual juxtapositions, seen most notably in Surrealism. Late-nineteenth-century culture was extraordinarily sensitive to such displacements; in fact, it absolutely reveled in them. With great relish, late-nineteenth-century Americans confounded categories and upset hierarchies, visual and otherwise. Significantly, during this period the United States changed from a rural economy to a market economy; for the first time, the urban population became predominant, but it largely comprised previously rural and immigrant peoples. It is not surprising that many new urban dwellers had a sense of dislocation, or that this was visualized in trade card images. Chinese figures became one vehicle by which Americans registered incongruities and expressed something of their startling sensations.

As early as 1848, the process of capitalism in the Western world had been felt as a new and powerful force, and described as a "constant revolutionizing of production, uninterrupted disturbance of all social conditions, everlasting uncertainty and agitation." The description continued: "All fixed, fast-frozen relations, with their train of ancient and venerable prejudices and opinions, are swept away, all newly formed ones become antiquated before they can ossify. All that is solid melts into air."[87] In "The Painter of Modern Life," Charles Baudelaire responded to the same stimuli: "By *modernite* I mean the ephemeral, the fugitive, the contingent, the half of art whose other half is the eternal and the immutable."[88]

Elaborating on this theme, more recently, Jonathan Crary has described capitalism as a process that "uproots and makes mobile that which is grounded, clears away or obliterates that which impedes circulation, and makes exchangeable what is singular." He extended this dynamic to human relationships, that is, "images, languages, kinship relations, religious practices, and nationalities."[89] Crary emphasized that nineteenth-century modernization did not unfold in a linear continuum or effect only inanimate objects and processes, but occurred haphazardly, altering the very structure of relationships, personal as well as national. The new—appearing in the proximity of exotic peoples, novel products, immense new buildings—also became internalized through the "immense reorganization of knowledge, languages, networks of spaces and communications, and subjectivity itself."[90] During this liminal period, the experience of modernity became in part an experience of disruption, a feeling of movement between present and past, the prosaic and the extravagant.

Benjamin pinpoints a significant element in this sensation of surprise, describing "the close connection . . . between the figure of shock and contact with the metropolitan masses."[91] Exploring this theme further, he relates his own shock when thrown into unexpected proximity with Tibetan Buddhists sharing adjoining hotel rooms to his in Moscow.[92]

The Chinese image became a vehicle to express these dissonances. Trade cards imaged exotic Chinese people, in order to represent the sensation of an unusual encounter. Some cards went further to heighten this sensation, depicting not only a Chinese figure, but one at the extremes of (im)possible human dimensions: miniscule or giant. In these images the definition of humanity, both in ethnicity and in individual physicality, was strained to its limits. For instance, the text of a fold-out shoe trade card referred to a Chinese dwarf in a circus, not for a harmony between image and product but for quite the opposite effect: for the jarring sensation of the inappropriate—in this case correlated to the sensation of an ill-fitting pair of shoes (fig. 4.25). In the card a male character remarks to his female

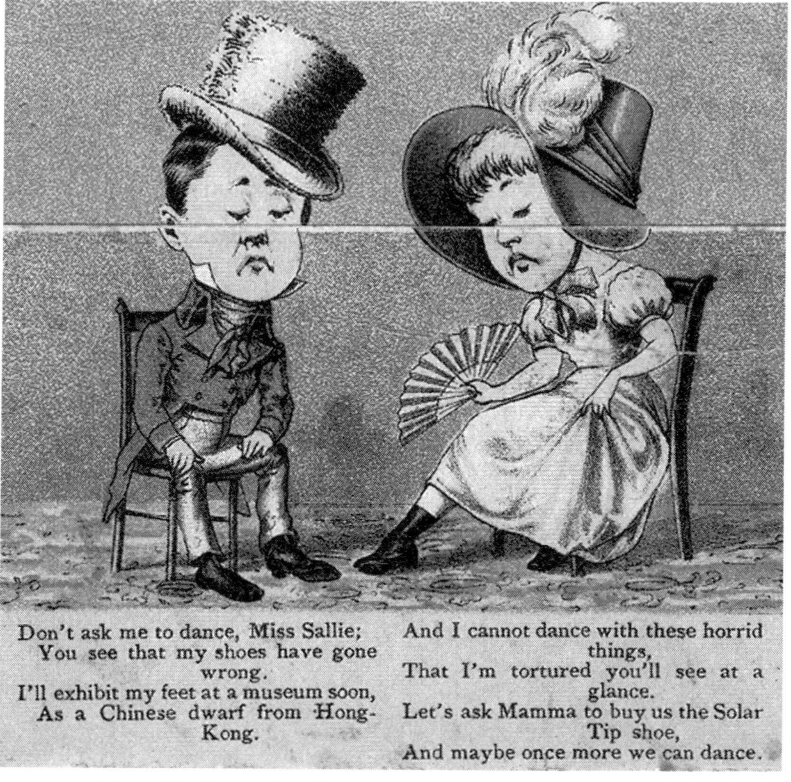

Fig. 4.25. Solar Tip Shoes, nineteenth-century trade card.

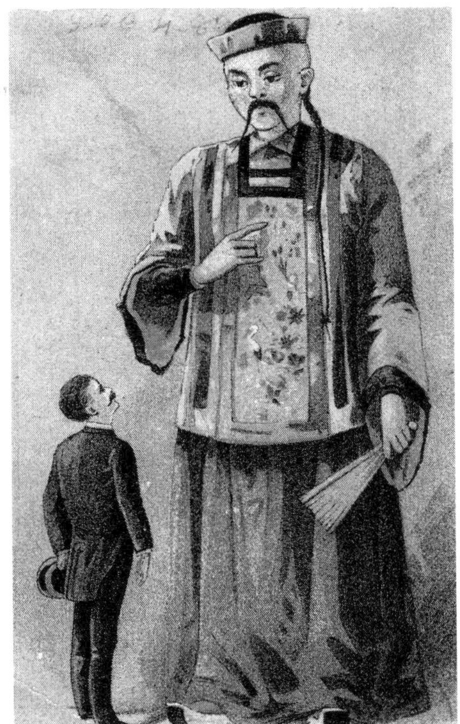

Fig. 4.26. Coffee Pot Sale, nineteenth-century trade card.

counterpart: "Don't ask me to dance, Miss Sallie; / You see that my shoes have gone wrong. / I'll exhibit my feet at a museum soon, / As a Chinese dwarf from Hong-Kong."[93] In addition to a Chinese dwarf, several trade cards also highlighted a Chinese giant: an ad for a coffeepot showed him dressed in a traditional colorful kimono, towering over a white man less than half his size[94] (fig. 4.26). Chinese in general conjured fantastic images, and Chinese dwarfs and giants even more so, made even more fantastical by the well-known fact that indeed both a Chinese dwarf and giant did reside in America and were featured as exhibitions in American circuses along with other Chinese anomalies: a woman with tiny bound feet and Chinese "Siamese" twins.[95]

This shock of the new and the incongruous prompted a peculiar but extremely popular trade card motif depicting strange, often unnaturally enlarged heads ripping through a paper scrim, much like those that animals leap through at a circus. Chinese heads frequently figured among such startling images. One trade cards series caricatured marginal types: Irish, Indian, Jewish—one ethnicity per card. On one card an enormous Chinese face looks directly at the viewer, grinning as it bursts through the paper circle (fig. 4.27).

The image of a permeable, breakable scrim is an evocative visualization of the sensation of displacement and discontinuity. The scrim, the thinnest of veneers, both separates and unifies two modalities of existence. These cards visualize the distinctly modern sensation of existing in two places simultaneously. They not only signify the sudden arrival of the new, but also capture something of the emotion, existing for the first time in history,

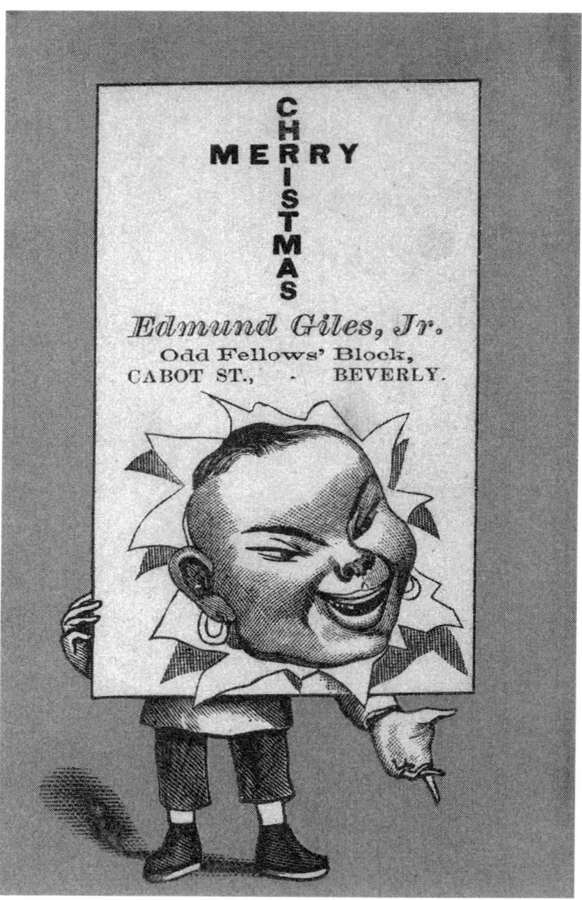

Fig. 4.27. Nineteenth-century trade card with Christmas greeting.

in the possibility of leaping from one modality to another, one class into another, one world to another. They allude to dislocations that arise both spatially and temporally: of the far suddenly being here and of the past or the future simultaneously existing in the present. One could pass between these worlds, entering with the slightest shift and leaving at will; overlapping realities continuous with each other but remaining discrete.

A trade card from 1885 marvelously depicted such a sensation (fig. 4.28). The image is a trompe l'oeil picture of an oil painting, a portrait of an elderly gentleman. But the canvas is represented as slashed, sliced both horizontally and vertically through the center. Because of the rip, the backside of the painting also becomes the front through the dangling flaps of ripped canvas, exposing the words advertising "Burdock Blood Bitters" printed on them. The tear has obliterated the portrait's mouth and nose and through the resulting gap in the old face, the face of a young boy demurely peers out. At the bottom edge of the trade card a caption explains: "At 3 years of age and at 80."[96] Paralleling the sensation of past, present, and

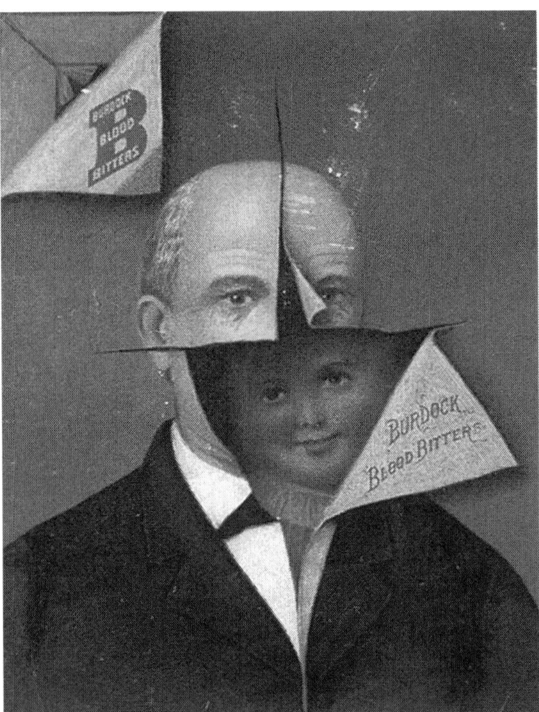

Fig. 4.28. Burdock Blood Bitters, nineteenth-century trade card.

future occurring simultaneously, the image shows them together spatially, collapsing temporal distance.

Shadows were also exploited for their simultaneous modality of appearance and obscurity. And again, the Chinese male figured in heightening the unusual sensations. Captioned "a queer shadow," a black-and-white trade card drawing depicts a dainty white woman, smartly dressed, with a fashionable bonnet and parasol (fig. 4.29). She looks toward the viewer, her hand open as if gesturing, halfway between demonstrating and entreating. Behind her, the shadow she casts against a rough picket fence takes the form of a Chinese man. The mirror-reality of the shadow reiterates her world but transforms it darkly: her ribbon becomes his pigtail; her hand gesture becomes an intimation of surreptitious approach. His shadow hand reaches out as if to touch her, grab her bonnet. The image embodies unease—specifically

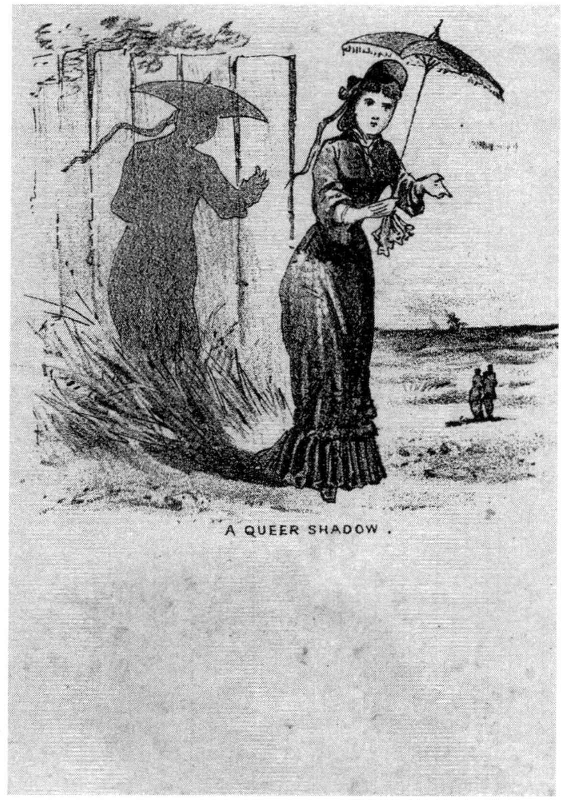

Fig. 4.29. Blank Message, nineteenth-century trade card.

white male unease, in regard not only to Chinese men but also to women. An equivalence is suggested between the two. Are they complicit? Are figure and shadow separate modalities or is the threat they elicit compounded in one shared shadowy nature? Is the Chinese shadow the woman's alter ego or is it a mirror opposite?

Both the scrim and the shadow register the culture's encounter with new modalities and paradigms: new sensations of time and space, of relationships, new entanglements of the commonplace and the unusual. The images helped to apprehend strangeness, perhaps to domesticate it. And Benjamin has the last word: "we penetrate the mystery only to the degree that we recognize it in the everyday world, by virtue of a dialectical optic that perceives the everyday as impenetrable, the impenetrable as everyday."[97]

3. Hybridity, Cultural Margins, and Incorporation

This last section brings together all the previously discussed themes for which the image of the Chinese man served as a floating signifier: product promotion, proximity, sexuality, demonization, Americanization, shock and transformation, and one area that we have not yet explored: art and aesthetics. Trade cards depicting art served as a metalanguage; art commenting on art. The cards allow us to see high art through a vernacular eye. They clearly reveal themselves as fantasy, projections derived from the white majority's anxieties, fascinations, and desires.

The final two cards couple the Chinese image with a fine arts theme. Both cards juxtapose these two subjects, causing them to reflect and comment on each other. However, the two cards exhibit almost entirely antithetical attitudes toward their subjects. The first, a card dated 1882, featuring Oscar Wilde, uses one marginal subject, Aestheticism, to mock the other, Chinese. Alternatively, the second card depicts a more tolerant attitude toward both fine art and Chinese, as well as denoting a subtle movement away from Eurocentricism. Together, they suggest the wide range in American attitudes toward the cultural transformations occurring in the late nineteenth century.

Chromolithography used the baldly commercial strategy of imaging sentimental moralizing to appeal to a newly developing mass-market. Many popular artworks, especially paintings with saccharine narrative content, had become appropriated by advertising, reproduced as chromolithographs and were now selling items from soap to chocolates. Artists such as Whistler and Manet rejected the commercialization, and turned away from subjects that lent themselves to commodification; in other words, they repudiated paintings that stylistically represented themselves as a window looking into the world, or thematically portrayed sentimental emotions. Rather, they embraced a style in which the artifice of the painting was part of the subject.[98] The viewer was not presented with an illusionistic image to wander in, but with the painting as an object.

Whistler, for instance, chose nocturnal ephemera and firework displays as a device to abstract his compositions, subjects that not only resist narrative but also could not become either iconic or moral. His paintings demanded to be looked at as surfaces enlivening the picture plane, and seemed resistant to advertisement and politics (fig. 4.30).

In the late eighteenth century, Aestheticism's precedents had also repudiated the popularized debasement—the "dumbing down"—of fine art. Enlightenment *philosophes* held similar convictions that art exists entirely in and of itself; in 1785, the German writer Karl Philipp Moritz described his engagement with the aesthetics of an object of fine art:

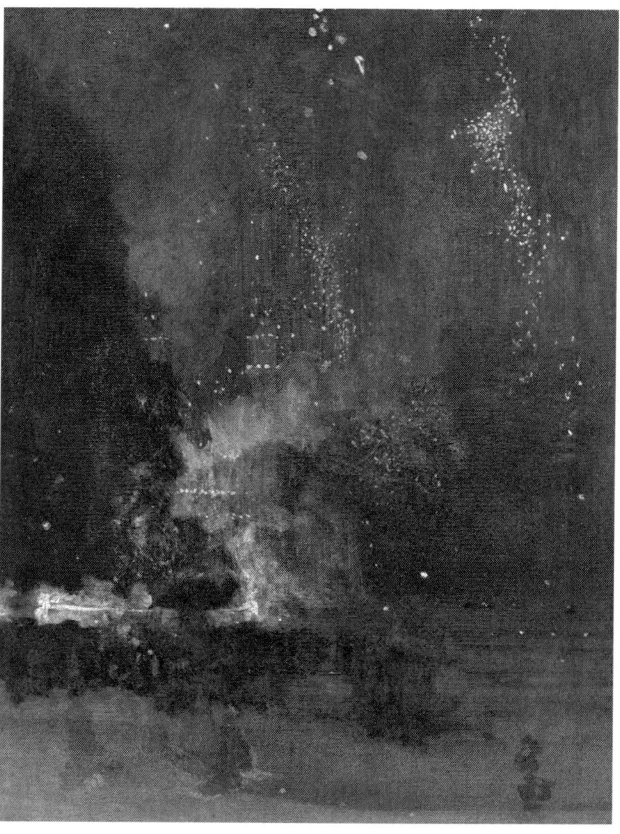

Fig. 4.30. James Abbott McNeill Whistler, *Nocturne in Black and Gold: The Falling Rocket*, 1874–77. Photo: Erich Lessing/Art Resource, New York.

> In contemplating a beautiful object . . . I roll the purpose back
> into the object itself: I regard it as something that finds *completion*
> not in me but *in itself* and thus constitutes a whole in itself and
> gives me pleasure *for its own sake*. . . . Thus the beautiful object
> yields a higher and more disinterested pleasure than the merely
> useful object.[99]

In this we recognize the seeds of the nineteenth-century concept of "art for art's sake," the beginning of ideas that came to fruition in the Aesthetic Movement, which valued art as a rarified sphere detached from other aspects of life: no politics, no moralizing, no sentimentalism—where art exists for itself and speaks only about itself, about its patterns and internal relationships.

The United States was both attracted to and derisive of the Aesthetic Movement. In 1882 Oscar Wilde arrived in the United States for a lecture series. Nicknamed the "Apostle of Aestheticism," he became an infamous figure as he preached his message with outrageous wit and elevated art to a status almost akin to a spiritual awakening. In poetic defiance of the close-cropped look of the professional gentleman, Wilde dressed unabashedly in velvet jackets and wore his hair long: he sought and received controversy at almost every stop. His variable reception across America thwarts most current understanding. Perhaps foreseeable, in an article titled "Unmanly Manhood," the civil war hero Colonel Higginson derided Wilde and his work, and an unsigned review in the *Daily Chronicle* peppered its critique with invectives such as "moral and spiritual putrefaction" and "effeminate frivolity."[100] Less predictable was Wilde's warm reception among Colorado miners, who welcomed him wholeheartedly as a "man's man." Whereas New York had whispers of feminine, effeminate crowds in the western states saw him in a different light. A reporter in Sacramento, California, wrote of Wilde as "the most misrepresented foreigner that ever visited our shores," indeed as "the poor man's friend." Wilde returned the compliment, stating that: "The further West one comes, the more there is to like. The Western people are much more genial than those of the East." His appearance, which had created such scandal in the eastern states, was accepted very differently in the west. When a newspaper in California described his appearance in a "black velvet coat," with his "long hair hanging below a sombrero," it saw nothing inconsistent with further remarking on his "strong square shoulders, manly waist and hips." As the authors of *Oscar Wilde Discovers America [1882]* reflect: "For almost a quarter of a century all Westerners had associated long hair with men of daring and adventure. On the plains, many cavalry officers, like General Custer, had preserved the shoulder-long locks which they had worn during the Civil War."[101]

Yet even with the congeniality in his reception across America, Wilde came to signify an outsider. But whether championed or reviled, his aesthetic ideas subversively infiltrated into all aspects of American culture: his distinctive idioms were echoed even by exclusionist congressmen in the 1882 debates on Chinese exclusion.[102] Aestheticism entered deeply into the American art world and the American vernacular.

However, despite its entry into the vernacular consciousness, as an art style, Aestheticism met with considerable resistance. The middle class had little desire to learn a new aesthetic language when they had barely acquired ownership of the old. The challenging avant-gardism offered few delights comparable to their newly attained proprietorship of images that spoke a more familiar language, illustrated morals and virtue, and traditionally had signified power and wealth. Aestheticism demanded a strange new way of approaching art, one that attended more to style than to morality. The new aesthetic involved understanding an art whose point of reference was as destabilizing as Wilde's paradoxical aphorisms. As he wrote in *Intentions*: "A little sincerity is a dangerous thing, and a great deal of it is absolutely fatal." And a bit later: "All bad poetry springs from genuine feeling."[103] In judging the new art movement by the old standard of perceived moral earnestness, most Americans viewed it with suspicion, then laughed at it and rejected it as a sham. They found more satisfaction in sentimental chromolithographs.[104]

The card of interest to this essay came from a series of cards devoted to caricatures of Oscar Wilde; each card depicting him as a member of a different ethnic minority. In this card he is imaged as a Chinese man (fig. 4.31). Through fashioning Wilde's body as Chinese, the drawing at once references two marginalized classes—aesthetes and Chinese immigrants—merging them into one singular individual: a Chinese Oscar Wilde. Reinforcing this amalgamation, the caption across the top of the image reads: "No me likee to callee me Johnnee. Callee me Oscar."[105] Bright yellows, reds, and blues saturate the image, further exoticizing it. Even more outrageous, animalization appears again as Wilde's fingers are stretched to the point of becoming talons and his trademark sunflower's petals are actually rats.

The Chinese Oscar Wilde stands in a cross-legged version of a contrapposto posture, an asymmetrical pose with one hip higher than the other, a stance that has signaled effeminacy for over two centuries, since at least 1753.[106] His pose seems intended to signify the idea of anomalous hybrid-sexuality that white Americans associated both with Aesthetes and with Chinese.

In writing about racialization, Jan Pieterse specifies that: "In the discourse of race, darker peoples were thought of as 'female.'"[107] During the nineteenth century most nonwhite people, as well as their nations, were coded as feminine, and only white society, viewed as a patriarchy, could create empire. We have seen this already in the laundry trade cards depicting Chinese men leering insinuatingly at woman's undergarments; a

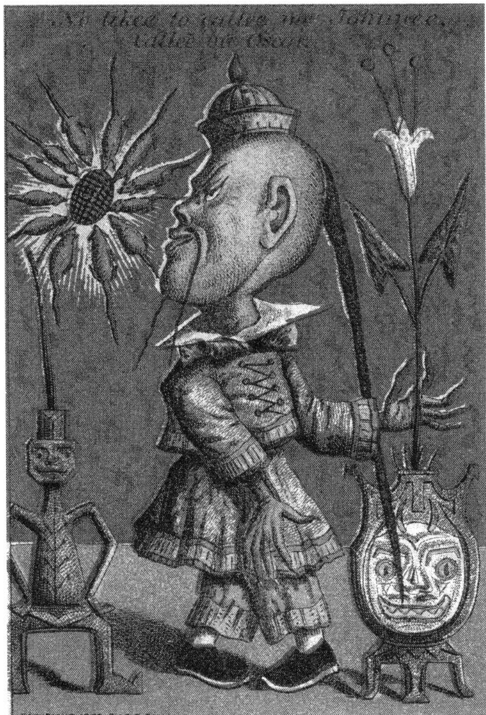

Fig. 4.31. Blank Message, nineteenth-century trade card.

representation of aberrant sexuality and deviancy, not only emasculating Chinese men but "feminizing" them. Both the Chinese male figure and Oscar Wilde simultaneously signaled sexual ambiguity and represented uncertain social standing within society. Eliding the Chinese with Wilde amplifies the cultural anxiety in the portrait. Recalling that it was, most probably, white male artists who chose to overlap the themes of Chinese men and male sexuality, the cards can be read as a manifestation of their fear of an unknown and challenging alternative paradigm of maleness, a threat to their prescription of behavior appropriate for a man.

The recurrent feminization of the male, however, is suggestive not only of anxiety but also of a fascination with fluid gender roles. While miscegenation created anxiety for Americans, they also were tantalized by it, drawn to the idea of mixes. Trade cards exhibit a wide range of possibilities, fanaticizing hybridizations of all sorts: peoples as fruits, women as fish, and so on.[108]

The change of Wilde's race from white to Chinese demonstrated the fluidity of categories and the ease of a possibly greater transgression.

Such markers can be understood to signify an exploration of alternative gender roles. The figure stands in his stage-like setting, neither defiant nor subservient, a self-contained challenge to standards. Pieterse sums up the relationship between the self and the other concisely: "*An ideology of* alter *involves an ideology of* ego. Representations of otherness are therefore also indirectly representations of self. . . . Images of 'others' do not circulate because of their truthfulness but because they reflect the concerns of the image-producers and -consumers."[109]

In the act of imaging a Chinese Wilde, the artist expanded the limits of behavior typically ascribed to his gender. Changing Wilde's race showed the need to distance this exploration—make it Chinese—while at the same time manifesting the maker's fascination in its expression. Chinese figures offered a means to investigate cultural alternatives, explored safely through illustrations of male alterity.

The second trade card about art offers a more graceful signification both to the male Chinese figure, and to high art, more discretely commenting on cultural permeability and intercultural exchange, moving away from Eurocentricism. This card, drawn with a simple fine line in black ink, echoed the visual vocabulary of rationalized, factual aesthetics. Its image acknowledged the transnational flow of both people and art between the United States and China[110] (fig. 4.32). The surprisingly sweet drawing shows

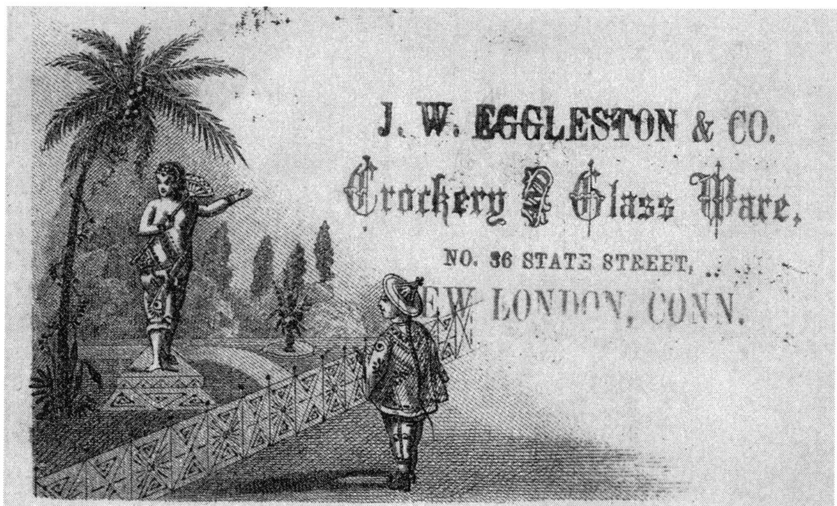

Fig. 4.32. J. W. Eggleston & Co., Crockery & Glass Ware, nineteenth-century trade card.

the back view of a Chinese man with a long queue dressed traditionally in a pointed hat and wide ornate pants as he walks alone through a park. On his left stands a statue of an exotic, even fantastical, Asian-style figure, a hybrid portrayal that could only result from a Western conception of an Eastern aesthetic. Placed on a triangular pedestal under a palm tree, the statue holds a long fan in one hand and extends the other hand as if in greeting. The Chinese man smiles and seems to cast a knowing glance in the direction of the figure as he walks by.

CONCLUSION

Throughout the nineteenth century, Americans used the Chinese figure as a means to explore contested areas of their culture. Unlike representations with a single established meaning, such as Uncle Sam representing the quintessential American, the Chinese figure had a wide range of possible meanings. A vast amount of cultural exploration, accommodation, and adaptation occurred outside the realm of words. Although trade cards also were publically disseminated, they were not perceived as the voice of authority, certainly not the voice of the dominant class. This allowed them to occupy a less mediated realm; their images were not policed. Their pictorial analogies had the freedom to express social explorations and anxieties.

The Chinese visual image, functioning as a marker of undercurrents and ideas, helped to negotiate changes occurring within American culture. As Francois Jullien (2000: 9) has observed, "China presents a case study through which to contemplate Western thought from the outside. . . . A theoretical distancing is desirable—and this is exactly what China offers."[1] Through the creation and use of an iconic Chinese figure, Americans found unexpected possibilities for probing boundaries and margins of gender, class, nationhood, and even representation itself.

Imagery affects the lives of the people it purportedly represents. Although we can legislate otherness, through the process of looking, we bring the alien into our vision. Looking at each other, we are not only aware of possibilities and alternatives, we become are altered, re-embodied. We are changed, extended, by our vision; as Merleau-Ponty states, "the same thing is both out there in the world and here at the heart of vision. . . ."[2] Defining difference is a way of describing oneself.

NOTES

INTRODUCTION

1. John M. MacKenzie, *Orientalism: History, Theory and the Art*, Manchester University Press, Manchester, UK, 1995, pp. 10, 14–16.

2. See James Clifford, especially *The Predicament of Culture: Twentieth-Century Ethnography, Literature, and Art*, Harvard University Press, Cambridge, 1988; Anne McClintock, *Imperial Leather: Race, Gender and Sexuality in the Colonial Conquest*, Routledge, London, 1995

3. Clifford, op. cit., pp. 5–6.

4. Bruce E. Hall, *Tea That Burns: A Family Memoir of Chinatown*, The Free Press, New York, 1998, p. 40.

5. N. Katherine Hayles, "The Condition of Virtuality," in J. Masten, P. Stallybrass, and N. Vickers, eds., *Language Machines: Technologies of Literary and Cultural Production*, Routledge, New York, 1997, p. 183.

6. Philip Fisher, *Making and Effacing Art: Modern American Art in a Culture of Museums*, Oxford University Press, New York, 1991, p. 6.

7. "In *l'art pour l'art*, the poet for the first time faces language the way the buyer faces the commodity on the market." Walter Benjamin, "The Paris of the Second Empire in Baudelaire," in *Walter Benjamin: Selected Writings, Volume 2: 1927–1934*, Belknap Press, Harvard, Cambridge, 1999, p. 65.

8. Quoted in Clifford, op. cit., p. 11.

9. Philip Fisher, op. cit., p. 18. James Clifford, op. cit., p. 8.

10. Elmer Davis, *History of the New York Times*, New York Times, New York, 1921, p. 118.

11. Carl Sandburg, *Storm Over the Land*, Harcourt, Brace and Company, New York, 1942, p. 87.

12. Jean Baudrillard, *Symbolic Exchange and Death*, Sage Publications, London, 1993, p. 92. T. J. Jackson Lears *Fables of Abundance: A Cultural History of Advertising in America*, Basic Books, New York, 1994, p. 54.

CHAPTER ONE. THE POLITICS OF CHINOISERIE: THE DISAPPEARANCE OF CHINESE OBJECTS

1. William Blake, "William Blake's Annotations to the Works of Sir Joshua Reynolds, 1798," in the *Complete Poetry and Prose of William Blake*, ed. by D. V. Erdman; quoted by Edward Said in *Culture and Imperialism*, Vintage Books, New York 1993, p. 13.

2. According to Ann Gibson in her essay "Avant-Garde," the two most renowned writers on avant-garde theory, Renato Piggioli and Peter Burger, both agreed that "the term 'avant-garde' was originally used to designate the conjunction of revolutionary sociopolitical tendencies and artistic goals," and "transgressions against anything established as a given." In *Critical Terms for Art History*, ed. by Robert S. Nelson and Richard Shiff, University of Chicago Press, Chicago, 1996, p. 205.

3. Richard Shiff, "Originality," ibid. p. 150.

4. Quoted in Catherine Lynn, "Decorating Surfaces: Aesthetic Delight, Theoretical Dilemma," in *In Pursuit of Beauty*, The Metropolitan Museum of Art, Rizzoli, New York, 1986, pp. 61–62.

5. Schlotterback, Thomas, "The Basis for Chinese Influence in American Art 1784–1850," unpublished dissertation, University of Iowa, 1972, p. 2. In *Chinoiserie*, Phaidon Press, 1993, Dawn Jacobson discusses the evidence that the Puritanism of the colonists did not prevent them from purchases of exotic luxuries from Asia. Boston was the center for the import trade as well as for the reproduction of Chinese techniques such as japanning furniture. The first exhibit of Chinese things occurred just twenty-three years after the founding of the country, in Salem, Massachusetts, when the East India Marine Society created a display of objects from overseas pp. 203–204.

6. Carl L. Crossman, *The Decorative Arts of the China Trade: Paintings, Furnishings and Exotic Curiosities*, Antique Collectors Club, 1991, p. 21.

7. Arjun Appadurai ed., *The Social Life of Things: Commodities in Cultural Perspective*, Cambridge University Press, Cambridge, 1986, p. 41.

8. Edward Said describes this situation of the ineffectiveness of the avant-garde among writers in the late nineteenth century: "Dissenting literature has always survived in the United States alongside the authorized public space; this literature can be described as oppositional to the overall national and official performance. . . . there has always been an opposition—one thinks of anti-imperialists like Mark Twain, William James, and Randolph Bourne—but the depressing truth is that its *deterrent* power has not been effective." *Culture and Imperialism*, Vintage Books, 1994, p. 287.

9. By 1843, the United States was, with the exception of Great Britain, the principal commercial country in the China trade and was granted the status of "most-favored-nation" treatment. However, Earl Swisher points out that this status was granted to the United States, along with all other Western countries trading with China, due to the consideration of Chinese Foreign Minister Ch'i-ying, an expert in foreign affairs, who based his policy on China's best interests in matters of security and practicable considerations, and not on trade of individual nation's. *Early Sino-American Relations, 1841–1912: The Collected Articles of Earl Swisher*, edited by Kenneth W. Rea, Westview Press, Boulder Co., 1977, pp. 53–55.

10. See, for instance, William Hosley, *The Japan Idea: Art and Life in Victorian America*, Wadsworth Atheneum, Hartford, 1990; Christine Wallace Laidlaw, "The American Reaction to Japanese Art, 1853–1876," unpublished dissertation 1996, Rutgers–New Brunswick, the State University of New Jersey; Jane Converse Brown, "The 'Japanese Taste,'" unpublished dissertation, University of Wisconsin, Madison, 1987.

11. Hosley, ibid., pp. 33, 36, 41.

12. Laidlaw, op. cit., pp. 334–335.

13. Hosley, op. cit., p. 39. While there was a substantial difference between the lack of print art from China, and the plethora of prints coming from Japan, which made such an impact on European arts of the time, if such prints were available at the Centennial the critics and writers did not mention them.

14. In *The Decorative Arts of the China Trade; Paintings, Furnishings and Exotic Curiosities*, Suffolk: Antique Collectors Club, 1991, Carl Crossman shows illustrations of wallpaper panels from the early 1800s, decorated with motifs of branches with blossoms, floral patterns, and various kinds of birds. Both the Peters Museum and the Dunn Museum catalogs list pictorial objects; Peters specifies: ". . . an immense number of Chinese views, paintings of birds, punishments, vessels, fishes, shells, insects, &c." in *Chinese Museum: Extensive Views of the Central Flowery Nation, Corrected for Philadelphia*, by John R. Peters, G. B. Zeiber & Co, Philadelphia, 1847, p. 193.

15. Jacobson, *Chinoiserie*, op. cit., p. 206. The *Empress of China*, although commended by the American government, was an entirely private commercial enterprise, underwritten not by the government but by entrepreneurs such as Robert Morris, who previously had helped finance the American Revolution. See A. Owen Aldridge, *The Eagle and the Dragon: The Presence of China in the American Enlightenment*, Wayne State University Press, Detroit, 1993, p. 100. Unlike the British, whose Opium War victory stipulated access to additional Chinese ports of Amoy, Foochow, Ningpo and Shanghai, the United States trade had been confined solely to Canton and Hong Kong. Ellen Paul Denker, *After the Chinese Taste: China's Influence in America, 1730–1930*, Peabody Museum of Salem, 1985, p. 22.

16. Aldridge, ibid., p. 63. He stated: "In the 1750s and 1760s, as I have already indicated, the China market for American ginseng became glutted in large measure because of unscrupulous merchandizing. . . . By the end of the century, however, the market revived, and ginseng constituted the chief cargo on the voyage in 1784 of the first American vessel to Canton, the *Empress of China*," p. 57.

17. Ibid., pp. 108, 111.

18. Edward D. Graham, *American Ideas of a Special Relationship with China, 1784–1900*, Garland Publishing, New York, 1988, p. 13.

19. *New York Times*, Friday, December 8, 1854, p. 1, col. 4.

20. Carl L. Crossman, op. cit., p. 323.

21. Schlotterback, op. cit., pp. 32, 34.

22. Dean Lahikainen, *World's Revealed: The Dawn of Japanese and American Exchange*, ed. by Edo-Tokyo Museum, Tokyo, Japan, 1999, p. 32.

23. The first Chinese were said to have arrived on this continent in 458 A.D., and three Chinese men are recorded living in Maryland by 1785. *Asian America: Chinese and Japanese in the United States Since 1850*, Roger Daniels, University of Washington Press, Seattle, 1988, p. 9; *An Illustrated History of the Chinese in America*, Ruthanne Lum McCunn, Design Enterprises of San Francisco, 1979, p. 10. Lum cites historian Ma Tuan-Lin, who wrote that a Buddhist priest named Hui Shen arrived in Canada in 458 A.D. In *1421: The Year China Discovered America*, Gavin Menzies hypothesizes that the Chinese traveled to what is now Rhode Island, building a round tower in the late 1500s, which stands today, pp. 284–290.

24. *New Haven Gazette*, June 21, 1787, cited in Aldridge, op. cit., p. 155.

25. Stuart Creighton Miller, "The Chinese Image in the Eastern United States, 1785–1882," unpublished dissertation Columbia University, New York, 1966, p. 202.

26. Aldridge, op. cit., p. 165.

27. Ibid., p. 229; Ronald Takaki, *Stranger from a Different Shore, A History of Asian Americans*, Penguin Books, New York, 1989, p. 81.

28. Miller, op. cit.

29. Miller, op. cit., pp. 92–93.

30. Aldridge, op. cit., p. 7. According to Aldridge, the Chinese had not always been so wary of foreigners. He writes "The Chinese had good reason for treating foreigners with cautious hostility, according to a Salem naval officer Amasa Delano, who several times touched at Canton. In connection with a visit in 1806, he remarked: 'When the Europeans first visited this country, they were received by the Chinese with great kindness and hospitality, granting them every indulgence in the pursuits of commerce, which was reasonable. They at first had full liberty to go where they pleased; but the strangers soon began to abuse this indulgence, and conduct themselves in such a manner, by taking liberties with their women, and other gross improprieties which a Chinese can never overlook, that the government were obliged to curtail their liberties and confine them to the port of Canton only, where they are permitted to reside for the express purpose of commerce,'" p. 105.

31. Quoted in ibid., p. 115.

32. Malte-Brun, *Universal Geography or a Description of all the Parts of the World on a New Plan . . .* , Anthony Finley, Philadelphia, 1827, p. 87. But Malte-Brun was not indiscriminately anti-Asian: contrast what he says of the Japanese. His initial opinions on both nations seem comparable, finding that "The civilization of the Japanese seems, like that of the Chinese, to be stationary," but he immediately adds that "Japan has germs of improvement that offer some possible prospect of a moral revolution. The brave and intelligent Japanese comes nearer to the European, by possessing a more masculine character, and a higher degree of civil liberty," p. 90.

33. Miller, op. cit., p. 58. Swisher states that "The opening of China to foreign trade [the treaty of Wang-hsia, 1844] appears to have been a great boon to the opium trade which had been steadily increasing since 1830. . . . Most of the opium came from India although Turkey opium was again coming into use. Most of the American firms undoubtedly dealt in it to some extent, and Russell and Company on a rather large scale, although entirely on commission from British firms. Olyphant and Company, the one firm that refused to trade in opium, earned the name of 'Zion's Corner.'" Swisher, op. cit., pp. 120–124

34. Edward D. Graham, *American Ideas of a Special Relationship with China, 1784–1900*, Garland Publishing, New York, 1988, p. 55.

35. Jonathan Goldstein, *Philadelphia and the China Trade 1682–1846: Commercial, Cultural and Attitudinal Effects* Pennsylvania State University Press, University Park, 1978, 54, 62; also see Graham, p. 65. In *Tea That Burns: A Family Memoir of Chinatown*, The Free Press, New York, 1998, Bruce E. Hall describes the aftermath of the opium trade in China, pointedly indicting the British: "The British bought up Chinese tea and silk, and built a city on their luxuriant stolen isle. They also made billions by flooding the country with opium produced in British India. China quickly became a nation of addicts, thus making Victoria the world's first international drug Queenpin," p. 11.

36. Graham, op. cit., pp. 52–74.

37. Ibid., pp. 58–60, 77.

38. Ibid., pp. 64–65.

39. Miller, op. cit., pp. 131–133.

40. Quoted in Graham, op. cit., p. 74.

41. Kevin Walsh, *The Representation of the Past: Museums and Heritage in the Post-Modern World*, Routledge, New York, 1992, p. 7.

42. Emanuel Weiss, "Hints as to the Development of our California-China Trade," *Hunt's* SLVII, 6 (December 1862), 523–524, quoted in Graham, op. cit., p. 117.

43. Miller, op. cit., pp. 150–151.

44. Miller, op. cit., pp. 138–144.

45. "England and China," *Democratic Review* VII: 516, cited in ibid., p. 72.

46. Ronald Takaki, *Iron Cages, Race and Culture in Nineteenth Century America*, Alfred A. Knopf, New York, 1979, p. 216.

47. Ibid, p. 20.

48. Ronald Takaki, *Stranger from a Different Shore*, op. cit., p. 11.

49. Hall, op. cit., pp. 14–15.

50. Robert G. Lee, *Orientals: Asian Americans in Popular Culture*, Temple University Press, Philadelphia, 1999, p. 21.

51. Stephen E. Ambrose, *"Nothing Like It in the World:" The Men Who Built the Transcontinental Railroad 1863–1869*, Simon & Schuster, New York, 2000, p. 150.

52. In *If They Don't Bring Their Women Here: Chinese Female Immigration Before Exclusion*, University of Illinois Press, Champaign, 1999, George Anthony Peffer points out that many European groups intended only to be sojourners, but "after perhaps ten to twenty years began shifting their focus to permanent settlement. Thus, among the Chinese, one would expect the strength of family structure and the sojourner mentality to have varied between individuals and to have eroded over time," p. 5.

53. Ruthanne Lum McCunn, op. cit., p. 70.

54. Lee, op. cit., p. 21.

55. Charles J. McClain, *In Search of Equality: The Chinese Struggle Against Discrimination in Nineteenth-Century America*, University of California Press, Berkeley and Los Angeles, 1994, p. 9.

56. Hall, op. cit., p. 23.

57. Compiled from various sources, especially Cheng-Tsu Wu, ed., *Chink!*, Meridian Book, New York, 1972.

58. P. B. Doestick, "Among the Chinamen," in *Frank Leslie's Illustrated Newspaper*, New York, Saturday, February 6, 1858.

59. Miller, op. cit., p. 58.

60. Jacobson, op. cit., pp. 178, 183.

61. Aldridge, op. cit., p. 115.

62. Ibid, p. 118.

63. Cited in Ibid., p. 216.

64. J. Emerson, J. Chen, M. G. Gates, *Porcelain Stories: From China to Europe*, Seattle Art Museum, 2000, p. 252. "Less than fifty years after the formation of the Dutch East India Company in 1602, the Dutch had already shipped more than 3 million porcelain pieces to Europe. They achieved this success largely by stimulating

the growing market with new Chinese products designed to cater to Europeans' lifestyles, instead of merely supplying whatever they could get from China."

65. Ibid., p. 256. "The English were especially fond of armorial porcelain; statistics have shown that armorial services destined for England accounted for almost half the total of such services sent to the European market."

66. Aldridge, op. cit., p. 118.

67. Quincy, 1847, quoted in Aldridge, op. cit., p. 117.

68. Ibid., p. 117.

69. Denker, op. cit., p. 21. The Dunn catalog begins with a description of the museum saying, "On passing through the vestibule, the visitor finds himself, as it were, transported to a new world. It is China in miniature," p. 3. *Ten Thousand Chinese Things; A Descriptive Catalogue of the Chinese Collection in Philadelphia . . .* , Philadelphia, 1839.

70. Warren I. Cohen, *East Asian Art and American Culture: A Study in International Relations*, Columbia University Press, New York, 1992, p. 10. Cohen compares this figure with the generous gifts of $8,000, each given by Thomas H. Perkins and his nephew to the Boston Athenaeum for their purchase of old master paintings.

71. Schlotterback, op. cit., p. 133.

72. Catherine Pagani, "Chinese Material Culture and British Perceptions of China," in *Colonialism and the Object*, ed. by Tim Barringer and Tom Flynn, p. 37.

73. Dunn, op. cit., p. 4.

74. Ibid. pp. 35–36. Dunn also tell an anecdote about the "fondness of the Chinese for lamps and lanterns." He relates that "when Captain Maxwell passed the Bogue in the Alceste frigate, as he came up with the battery of Annahoy, the fort appeared well lighted, and a brisk cannonade was commenced upon the ship. However, after the first broadside had been fired upon the fortress, . . . the Chinese were thoroughly frightened, and ran off with a most edifying precipitation. At the same time, instead of concealing their flight in the darkness of the night, each man seized his lantern, as he had done a hundred times before, and clambered with it up the steep side of the hill immediately behind the fort. The sight of so many bald-pated soldiers, with their long pig-tails dangling at their back, each with a great painted balloon in his hand, was extremely ludicrous, and took away any slight inclination the marines might have had to get a shot with their muskets at such excellent marks," p. 75.

75. Schlotterback, op. cit., p. 141; James S. Moy, *Marginal Sights: Staging the Chinese in America*, University of Iowa Press, 1993, pp. 12–15.

76. Hina Hirayama, unpublished dissertation, *A True Japanese Taste: Construction of Knowledge About Japan in Boston, 1880–1900*, Amherst College, 1989, pp. 59–60.

77. Peters, op. cit., p. 5. The catalog indicates that "to make the Museum still more attractive there are two Chinese attached to it, one of whom 'T'sow-Chaoong,' speaks English . . . ," p. 7.

78. Ibid., p. 5. This was also printed vertically down the front cover of the catalog.

79. Catherine Pagani, op. cit., p. 34. In *The Old China Trade*, AMS Press, New York, 1978, Foster Rhea Dulles alleged that almost all the American merchants

participated in trading opium, and he listed the Perkinses, the Peabodys, the Russells, the Lows and the Forbeses. Only Olyphant's company remained apart, p. 148.

80. Dunn, op. cit., pp. 118–119.

81. John R. Peters Jr., *Miscellaneous Remarks upon the Government, History, Religions, Literature, Agriculture, Arts, Trades, Manners and Customs of the Chinese, as Suggested by an Examination of the Articles Comprising the Chinese Museum in Marlboro' Chapel, Boston*, Eastburton's Press, Boston, 1845, pp. 180, 182.

82. The quote is found in a newspaper article cited in Cohen, op. cit., pp. 10–14.

83. *Gentleman's Magazine* IV (1839): 273, cited in Schlotterback, op. cit., p. 212.

84. Cohen, op. cit., pp. 10–12, 115.

85. Jacobson, op. cit., p. 178.

86. J. Emerson et al., op. cit., pp. 194, 209. "Chinoiseried themes reached their peak of popularity during the height of the rococo period, the second quarter of the eighteenth century." Laidlaw finds that the term *Chinoiseries* was not used in the seventeenth and eighteenth centuries and did not appear in any publication before 1840. Laidlaw, op. cit., p. 194.

87. Denker, op. cit., p. 23. Schlotterback, op. cit., p. 236. Initially, the visual correspondences that Schlotterback identifies in his meticulous examination suggest a profusion of correlations between Chinese and American painting. For instance, exploring the possibility of Chinese influence on American landscape painting, Schlotterback finds that artists such as Thomas Cole had many opportunities to see Chinese landscape art, and notes equivalences in the works: "Equally available to American painters were Chinese works depicting landscapes, and Chinese influences, especially Chinese traditional forms amalgamated with Western forms, could have had some affect on American landscape painting. There are interesting similarities between Chinese paintings and some works of the leading American landscape painter of the period, Thomas Cole."

88. Ibid., pp. 238–239, 243. Schlotterback enumerates: "Untrammeled nature, waterfalls with bridges, human figures subordinate to nature, rural domesticity and evidence of nature triumphant over man in the dilapidated mill, are all similar to traditional Chinese subjects. In additions "Landscape with Waterfall" also uses an ambiguous spatial structure resembling that used in Chinese landscape paintings. The foreground area . . . is seen from the level of the water, the cliff to the right is seen from the level of the pinnacle, and the central zone from above, while the cliff on the left and the far distance are seen form the level of the cliff on the right. This ambiguous spatial structuring was an important aspect in the tradition of Chinese landscape painting. The Chinese used multiple viewpoints in one painting to better present the reality of the vista. . . ." Similarly, noting stylistic affinities between Chinese depictions of animals and their handling by in American naturalist painters John James Audubon and Titian Ramsay Peale, Schlotterback argues that these American painters most certainly would have been familiar with Chinese iconography. Animal motifs were found on innumerable American household objects from China: furniture, wallpaper, and vases. Add to this the fact that, not only did the Peales know Nathan Dunn, their museum shared the same building with his Chinese

museum. But all this become moot as Schlotterback again concludes unequivocally that, despite American artists' familiarity with Chinese motifs, Chinese art apparently also had no impact on mid-nineteenth-century American depictions of animals.

89. Ibid., p. 236. Schlotterback writes that: ". . . with the exception of the visual similarities and circumstances cited here, there are no indications that any of the American naturalists derived any forms from Chinese influence. The contact between Titian Ramsay Peale and Dunn came after Peale's development of his style of illustration. Audubon's style, too, was developed well before the Dunn exhibition."

90. This has been seen previously in Waln's writings. It is made more complicated by the fact that despite American artist's devotion to European art, they also had a desire to break away from the comparison with European art, and the above artists seem to have had success in doing so through a route that looks like emulation of Chinese art.

91. Schlotterback, op. cit., p. 131. Schlotterback describes the relationship between Americans and Chinese things: ". . . many examples of actual Chinese objects were presented to Americans between 1784–1850. The exhibitions were not only plays about China and Chinese side show attractions . . . but also included works of art presented in major American art institutions. These exhibitions persisted until and proliferated between 1830–1850. Such a persistence and proliferation indicated a growing interest in America for exhibitions about China and of Chinese objects. The exhibitions evidence a growing interest in knowing about China itself. More to the point the presence of these exhibitions indicated an awareness by Americans at all levels of Chinese life, culture, and art."

92. Laidlaw, op. cit., pp. 185–186.

93. Denker, op. cit., pp. ix, x.

94. Marilynn Johnson, "Art Furniture: Wedding the Beautiful to the Useful," in *In Pursuit of Beauty*, op. cit., p. 149.

95. Jarves, *A Glimpse at the Art of Japan*, 1875, reprinted Albert Saifer, Philadelphia, 1970, p. 14. Jarves first saw Japanese art at the Paris Exposition Universelle in 1867. *In Pursuit of Beauty*, op. cit., p. 204.

96. "Harper's Journal of Civilization," New York, Saturday, August 6, 1870.

97. Ibid. "The intercourse with Europeans will, however, be sure to encourage the natural taste for ornamental objects and pictures, and we shall see this last development of a people's civilization arising as the railroad, the locomotive, and the electric telegraph make their appearance in the Celestial Empire."

98. Ibid.

99. Act of Incorporation and By-Laws of the Salem East India Marine Society Report, 1821, p. 40, found at the Peabody Library in Salem, MA; Peter Fetchko "Winds of Change," in *World's Revealed*, op. cit., p. 60.

100. Catherine Lynn, "Surface Ornament: Wallpapers, Carpets, Textiles, and Embroidery," in *In Pursuit of Beauty*, op. cit., p. 65.

101. Allen S. Joslyn, "R&E Japanese Design Hardware," in "The Doorknob Collector," July–August 2003, no. 120. Joslyn sites Henry E. Russell Jr. regarding his application for a patent in 1879 for "a new and useful Design for Door Knobs . . . It possesses the characteristic feature of being in the Japanese style of ornament . . . the design consists of the upper portion of the body of a Japanese and an open um-

brella. . . ." One set with this exclusive design was used in Joliet, Illinois, in the house of Hiram Scutt, the inventor of barbed wire. Despite the name, the set seems to emulate the Japanese design in figural devices and Chinese in scrollwork. The issue of aestheticizing Chinese will be taken up in the third chapter.

102. Hosley, op. cit., pp. 31–32. Essays by both Neil Harris and Warren Cohen agree with the Centennial as the date of American's initial excitement over Japanese art. In her dissertation, op. cit. p. 3, Hirayama states: "After the 1876 Centennial Exhibition in Philadelphia where many Americans had their first chance to see decorative arts of Japan, a greater and more diverse portion of Bostonians became fascinated with Japanese design principles and Japanese culture."

103. Julia Meech and Gabriel P. Weisberg, *Japonisme Comes to America: The Japanese Impact on the Graphic Arts 1876–1925*, Harry N. Abrams, New York, 1990, p. 25.

104. Ibid., p. 38.

105. Ibid. p. 17.

106. Laidlaw, op. cit., p. 3.

107. Jacobson, op. cit., p. 209.

108. Laidlaw, op. cit., pp. 97–98.

109. Jane Converse Brown, "The 'Japanese Taste,'" unpublished dissertation, University of Wisconsin, Madison, 1987, quoted by Hosley, op. cit., p. 45.

110. Laidlaw, op. cit., pp. 334–335; Denker, op. cit., p. 43.

111. Laidlaw, op. cit., pp. 334–335.

112. Ingram, op. cit., p. 559.

113. Cohen, op. cit., p. 22. For example, in *East Asian Art and American Culture*, Warren Cohen's analysis of the response to the Fair assumes a wide disparity in the reception of the two Asian exhibitions at the Centennial. As evidence he cites Neil Harris's conclusion that "while Japanese art appealed to Americans thirsty for exotica, fewer visitors were attracted to the Chinese exhibits," which leads Cohen to speculate on the reasons for this phenomenon, suggesting that the differences might have been occasioned by different methods in selecting the objects for each nation. Cohen stated:

Both China and Japan were invited to participate in the fair, but their offerings were placed in the main building, rather than in the art department or art gallery. Nonetheless, the Japanese government, which controlled the selection of Japanese goods to be displayed, chose to stress the aesthetic rather than the commonplace, high culture rather than everyday life. The Japanese exhibit was one of the largest and easily the most novel, but several reviewers insisted it was the quality of Japanese workmanship, its "delicacy and perfection," that attracted the crowds and the plaudits. . . . The Chinese exhibit had been chosen primarily by Robert Hart, inspector general of the Imperial Maritime Customs Service of China. Hart sent antique ceramics and watercolors. The ceramics were praised once more by the critics, but the watercolors, depicting a wide range of Chinese life, attracted larger crowds. The Chinese display, however, aroused considerably less excitement than did the Japanese. . . . Perhaps the relative spareness of line and decoration in Japanese art pleased Americans repelled by the ornateness of European *and* Chinese (export) art. The obvious explanation would stress the superior quality of the Japanese items, but it is at least possible that the aesthetic appearance of the display itself made the difference—that the Japanese had a better sense of how to display their treasures than Hart had of presenting Chinese materials.

114. J. S. Ingram, *The Centennial Exposition, Described and Illustrated, Being a Concise and Graphic Description of this Grand Enterprise . . .* , Hubbard Bros., Philadelphia, 1876, p. 571. Ingram also informs us that Hu Quang Yung "is worth $30,000,000 and his wealth increased $3,000,000 in one single year."

115. Ibid., p. 244.

116. Ibid., p. 562.

117. Ibid., p. 573.

118. Frank B. Norton, ed., *The Illustrated Historical Register of the United States Centennial Exposition,* American News Company, New York: Subscription Book Department, 1877, p. 244.

119. Ibid.

120. Ibid., pp. 335–336. Laidlaw also points out that prior to the Centennial Exhibition, most critics concentrated on Japanese prints and paintings, which presented more difficulty for them, while at the Centennial, they responded to decorative objects. This might account for some of the differences between the critique of Chinese things earlier in the century, which also concentrated on painting. Nevertheless, it does not account for the lack of a simultaneous encounter of the worth of Chinese decorative objects

121. Hirayama, op. cit., p. 66. Laidlaw also confirms this in her citations of comments on Chinese and even more, on Japanese bronzes. Apparently these were discussed more than any other type of object, receiving rave reviews about their variety, skill, and patience, one critic comparing them to "the fantasy of a dream." Indeed, the technology of the bronze astonished Americans at least as much as the artistry, confounding the assumption that any non-Western nation could be more advanced than Europe and America. But several more informed art critics found the work almost reprehensible; Raphael Pumpelly was almost grieved by the exhibit, and Charles Wyllys Elliott concluded that most of the work was "bad in form, and meaningless and unattractive in decoration." Laidlaw, op. cit., pp. 341, 342.

121. Laidlaw, op. cit., pp. 311–312.

122. Ibid., p. 344

123. Ingram, op. cit.

125. Crossman, op. cit.

126. Crossman, op. cit., p. 19. Compare this with Denker's assessment in *After the Chinese Taste,* op. cit., p. x, stating "Western exploration and military incursions into China between 1860 and 1911 brought to light treasures the Chinese had guarded jealously for millennia. In one way or another—by seizure as war booty or by ordinary means of acquisition—many of these objects fell into American hands. They have been cherished and admired and their designs imitated and adapted in this country ever since." We can say that Crossman and Denker examine different

parts of the Chinese trade with America; clearly, the type of objects obtained and the quality entered a complicated American market. Note, also, the tenure of writing suggestive of a "jealous" and therefore unjust, prior claim of these objects by China, and their "falling" suggestive of a passive, on their own accord into American hands, either by seizure or through ordinary means—implying equality of trade.

127. Crossman, op. cit., p. 19.

128. Ibid., pp. 287–288.

129. Laidlaw, op. cit., p. 182.

130. Denker, op. cit., p. 43.

131. Paul Greenhalgh, *Ephemeral Vistas: The Expositions Universelles, Great Exhibitions and World's Fairs, 1851–1939*, Manchester University Press, UK, 1988, pp. 142, 147.

132. Adams cited in Laidlaw, op. cit., pp. 108–109.

133. *Masterpieces of the Centennial International Exhibition*, cited in Laidlaw, op. cit., p. 337. She gives the place and date of publication as Philadelphia: 1875. Earl Shinn wrote the first volume, which was on the fine arts; Joseph W. Wilson wrote the third.

134. Neil Harris, "All the World a Melting Pot?" in *Cultural Excursions: Marketing Appetites and Cultural Tastes in Modern America*, University of Chicago Press, Chicago, 1990, p. 30.

135. Ibid., p. 22.

136. Of course, Japan had never been "sealed" and had steadily traded with other nations, including Europe, especially through the Dutch. Fetchko, op. cit., p. 60.

137. R. Van Bergen, *The Story of Japan*, American Book Company, New York, 1897, p. 5.

138. *Between Two Worlds*, pp. 119, 150.

139. *New York Times*, February 25, 1870, p. 1.

140. According to the census for 1870, in Hirayama, op. cit., p. 4. Hirayama states that by 1900, the number had only increased to twenty-nine, p. 4. And Ronald Takaki indicates that in 1890 the Japanese population in the entire United States was only 2039. *Strangers from a Different Shore*, op. cit., p. 180. But art stores abounded: "As we saw, there were three auctions of Japanese goods in New York before Perry's departure and one after his return. Also Japanese goods were exhibited at the New York Crystal Palace in 1853," Laidlaw, op. cit., p. 12. "By 1850 most of the American China trade had moved from Boston and was concentrated in the hands of a few New York merchants. One important firm was A. A. Low & Bros., founded by Abiel [?] Abbott Low in 1840, with offices in New York and Canton. [Many of these stores catered to the new taste in Japanese, rather than Chinese, merchandise and to the fact of the ready availability of Japanese objects.] Low started importing silk and tea from Japan around the middle of 1860 and in the early 1860s served as an agent for La Farge in buying Japanese prints." Laidlaw, op. cit., p. 12.

141. *New York Times*, January 10, 1870, p. 4.

142. "The Nineteenth Century in Japan," *New York Times*, January 10,, 1870.

143. "Modern Improvements in Japan," *New York Times*, January 25, 1870.

144. Louis Wertheimber, *Boston Herald*, November 25, 1883, p. 190.

145. *New York Times*, December 26, 1872, p. 2; December 21, 1872, p. 5.

146. Philip P. Choy, Lorraine Dong, and Marlon K. Hom, *The Coming Man: Nineteenth Century American Perceptions of the Chinese*, University of Washington Press, Seattle, 1994, p. 19.

147. Bernard P. Wong, *Chinatown: Economic Adaptation and Ethnic Identity of the Chinese*, Holt, Rinehart, and Winston, New York, 1982.

148. Ibid., pp. 39–41.

149. *New York Times*, August 25, 1872.

150. Looking at a few weeks in July alone: *The New York Times*, July 1, 1970, pp. 1, 4; July 6, p. 4; July 7, p. 4; July 9, p. 1; July 11, p. 2; July 14, p. 4, and so on.

151. Daniels, op. cit., p. 42.

152. Hall, op. cit., p. 25.

153. Ibid., p. 25.

154. Peffer, op. cit., p. 8.

155. Denker, op. cit., p. 43.

156. Cohen, op. cit., pp. 21–23.

157. McCabe, *The Illustrated History of the Centennial Exhibition*, p. 340.

158. Ibid., p. 341. Takaki states that the poem appeared in 1870, and on January 7, 1871, the *New York Globe* wrote that, due to the immense popularity of the poem, they had to print it twice, and that every newspaper in the country had printed it as well. Op. cit., p. 223.

159. McCabe, op. cit., p. 341.

160. Ibid., p. 417.

161. Ibid., p. 417.

162. Norton, op. cit., p. 42.

163. Ibid., p. 84.

164. Such portrayals of Chinese men appeared commonly in newspaper and magazine accounts of Chinese immigrants, see, for instance, the illustration in "Harper's Weekly," September 24, 1881, p. 645, or an illustrated article on March 20, 1880, p. 182. See also the discussion on opium and Chinese immigrants in the following chapter.

165. Norton, op. cit., p. 216.

166. Ibid., 216.

167. Ibid., p. 216. And, according to Aldridge, op. cit., the Chinese ateliers had many pornographic images along with the political and personal portraits desired by Westerners. He describes Waln's disapproval of Chinese art and his assertion that the state of Chinese morality could be determined by the "lascivious and indecent paintings hanging in the galleries of the most respectable artists." He would not accept the excuse that these provocative subjects emanated from the desires and purchases of other Westerners. Chinese moral fiber must have been weak indeed, he says, for the transitory residence of a few foreigners to be strong enough to permit the exhibition of "the most disgusting delineations," p. 216.

168. James Jackson Jarves, op. cit., pp. 13–14.

169. Craig Clunas, "China in Britain: The Imperial Collections," in *Colonialism and the Object: Empire, Material Culture and the Museum*, ed. by T. Barringer and T. Flynn, Routledge, London, 1998, p. 43.

170. P. 106.

171. Pp. 107–108.

172. Michael Sprinker remarked: "If it is the case, as Althusar says . . . that works of art do not simply replicate the ideological material of a given epoch, it is equally the case that they do take the ideologies as their material of construction." Michael Sprinker, *Imaginary Relations: Aesthetics and ideology in the Theory of Historical Materialism*, Verso, London, 1987, p. 270.

CHAPTER TWO. THE POWER OFINACTION: CHINESE OBJECTS
AND THE TRANSFORMATION OF THE
AMERICAN DEFINITION OF ART

1. Quoted in *Strangeness and Beauty: An Anthology of Aesthetic Criticism, Volume 1, Ruskin to Swinburne*, ed. by Eric Warner and Graham Hough, Cambridge University Press Cambridge, UK, 1983, pp. 3–4.

2. And today highly regarded scientists and philosophers such as Subrahmanyan Chandrasekhar and Elaine Scarry rhapsodically insist on speaking of beauty as if it is an "a priori" and not a construct, glossing it with scientific equations, justice, and truth, into one luminous but nebulous metaphysics. The more contemporary art styles: Minimalism and especially its Italian counterpart, Arte Povera, bring a connotation of dignified asceticism to the art style.

3. Cited in Gwendolyn Wright, *Moralism and the Model Home*, University of Chicago Press, Chicago, 1980, p. 13.

4. Linda Dowling, *The Vulgarization of Art: The Victorians and Aesthetic Democracy*, University Press of Virginia Press, Charlottesville, VA, 1996, p. 26.

5. James Clifford, "On Collecting Art and Culture," in *The Predicament of Culture: Twentieth Century Ethnography, Literature, and Art*, Harvard University Press, 1988, p. 220. Writing about the scholarly literature on collecting and culture, Clifford lists the major scholars who commented on the search for symbolic national identity: "Phillip Fisher . . . Krzystof Pomian . . . James Bunn . . . Daniel Defert . . . Johannes Fabian . . . and Remy Saisselin . . . among others, bring collecting and display sharply into view as crucial processes of Western identity formation."

6. Wilson, op. cit., pp. 11, 29.

7. Stein, p. 127.

8. T. J. Jackson Lears, *No Place of Grace: Antimodernism and the Transformation of American Culture, 1880–1920*, Pantheon Books, New York, 1981, p. 246; Richard Guy Wilson, *The American Renaissance*, 11, 29.

9. Lawrence Chisolm, *Fenollosa: The Far East and American Culture*, Yale University, New Haven, CT, 1963, p. 27.

10. Remy Saisselin, *The Bourgeois and the Bibelot*, Rutgers University Press, Piscataway, NJ, 1984, p. 78.

11. Wilson, et al., *American Renaissance, 1876–1917*, The Brooklyn Museum, 1979, p. 11; Greenhalgh, op. cit., pp. 128–129.

12. Greenhalgh, Paul. *Ephemeral Vistas: The Expositions Universelles, Great Exhibitions and World's Fairs, 1851–1939*, Manchester University Press, UK, 1988, p. 127.

13. Roger Stein, *John Ruskin and Aesthetic Thought in America, 1840–1900*, Harvard University Press, Cambridge, MA, 1967, pp. 14–15.

14. Siegfried Giedion, *Mechanization Takes Command: A Contribution to Anonymous History*, W. W. Norton & Co., New York, 1975, p. 351.

15. Ibid., pp. 350–357.

16. Ibid., p. 345.

17. Leo Marx, *The Machine in the Garden*, Oxford University Press, Oxford, England, 2000 (originally published 1964), p. 195.

18. William Leach, *Land of Desire: Merchants, Power, and the Rise of a New American Culture*, Vintage Books, New York, 1993, 4.

19. Ibid. Leach states: "Where the old ideas often conceived of America as a millennial land in which many different kinds of dreams might come true (spiritual, vocational, and political as well as material), this new era heralded the pursuit of goods as the means to all 'good' and to personal salvation," p. 4.

20. Cited in Wright, op. cit., p. 25.

21. Wright, ibid., p. 34. See also Lewis and Smith, *Oscar Wilde Discovers America, 1882*, Harcourt, Brace and Co., New York, p. 68.

22. Calvert Vaux, *Villas and Cottages*, cited in Gwendolyn Wright, op. cit., p. 2.

23. Cited in Henry Ladd's *The Victorian Morality: An Analysis of Ruskin's Esthetic*, Octagon Books, New York, 1968, p. 325.

24. "The Art Museum," *New York Times*, June 28, 1873, p. 3.

25. Jane Converse Brown, "The 'Japanese Taste,'" unpublished dissertation, University of Wisconsin, Madison, 1987, quoted by Hosley, op. cit., p. 45.

26. Ibid., pp. 15–16.

27. Ibid., pp. 155–158; 350–356; Clarence Cook cited in Laidlow pp. 89–91. Along with Norton, James Jackson Jarves and the art critic Clarence Cook especially were influenced by Ruskin.

28. *How to Make Home Happy: A Housekeeper's Hand Book*, ed. by a Skilled Corps of Authorities, Edgewood Publishing Company, Cinnaminson, NJ, 1884, pp. 150–151.

29. Ibid., title page.

30. One recommendation suggests that "a novelty in scrap-baskets" can be made by the correct selection of "a medium-sized Japanese umbrella with a plain ground and gilt figures." Another innovative idea proposes using a Japanese umbrella for a fire-screen after "adorning it with peacock's feathers."

31. Treasures of Use and Beauty: An Epitome of the Choicest Gems of Wisdom, History, Reference and Recreation, by a Corps of Special Authors, F. B. Dickerson & Co, 1883. The chapter "Home Decoration" begins with the statement that "It is almost impossible for the average female mind to confront unmoved the delightful possibilities now afforded by the many new and beautiful, yet inexpensive, articles of home adornment," p. 358.

32. Ibid., pp. 362–371.

33. Benjamin March, *China and Japan in Our Museums*, Rumford Press, Concord, NH, 1929, pp. 4, 6.

34. Paul Crowther, "Cultural Exclusion, Normativity, and the Definition of Art," *Journal of Aesthetics & Art Criticism* (March 1, 2003): 127.

35. When Chinese and Japanese objects function in tandem I will refer to them as Asian; in other instances I differentiate between them.

36. Nathaniel Burt, op. cit., p. 111. The Lawrence armor collection was destroyed in the great fire of 1872; the museum used the insurance money to purchase art.

37. Neil Harris, "The Gilded Age Revisited Boston," p. 553.

38. Cesnola was the American Consul to Cyprus and later Secretary and Director of the Metropolitan Museum. In fact, the Boston Museum's first exhibition, held for reasons now obscure in a jewelry shop, was of ancient Cypriote artifacts purchased in 1872 from Cesnola. Nathaniel Burt *Palaces for the People: A Social History of the American Art Museum*, Little, Brown and Company, New York, 1977, pp. 96, 111.

39. Neil Harris "The Gilded Age Revisited Boston," pp. 553–555.

40. Conversation with Jeffrey Moy, August 2010. Moy is an expert in Chinese art and furniture, a bibliophile, owner of Paragon Bookstore, and philanthropist.

41. R. Bowker, L. Pylodet, and C. Cutter, *Library Journal, Volume One*, Nabu Press, Charleston, SC, 2010 (volume one, number nine originally published 1877), p. 336.

42. Ibid., p. 68.

43. *Boston Museum of the Fine Arts: A Companion to the Catalogue*, Roberts Brothers, Boston, 1877, pp. 64–66.

44. From the *Trustees of the Museum of Fine Arts Annual Reports* (Boston, 1876). Quoted in Harris pp. 554–555

45. Report of the Committee on the Museum, from the Proceedings at the Opening of the Museum of Fine Arts, Boston, 1876, p. 12.

46. Quoted in Kenneth Hudson, *Museums of Influence*, Cambridge University Press, UK, 1988, p. 55.

47. Neil Harris, op. cit., p. 552

48. The 1873 report to the Museum trustees ended with a statement from the committee's chairman Charles C. Perkins, asserting that: "the growth of interest in art which has shown itself in so many ways during the past year, leads us to believe that the claims of an institution destined to play a most important part in the promotion of art education in America, will not be disregarded by the public. . . ." First Annual Report of the Committee on the Museum of Fine Arts, March 20, 1873, Alfred Mudge & Sons, Boston, p. 11.

49. Calvin Tomkins, *Merchants and Masterpieces: The Story of the Metropolitan Museum of Art*, Longman Group Ltd., 1970, pp. 16–17.

50. Michael Clapper, unpublished dissertation "Popularizing Art in Boston 1865–1910: L. Prang and Company and the Museum of Fine Arts." Northwestern University, Ph.D., 1997, pp. 78–79.

51. "Museums and Exhibitions," *Frank Leslie's Illustrated Newspaper*, August 26, 1876, p. 403.

52. Kenneth Hudson, op. cit., p. 49. The South Kensington Museum also innovated installing a restaurant within the museum.

53. Barbara Kirshenblatt-Gimblett, "Intangible Heritage as Metacultural Production," *Museum International*, May 1, 2004, p. 58.

54. Steven Conn, *Museums and American Intellectual Life, 1876–1926*, The University of Chicago Press, Chicago, 1998, p. 5.

55. Paul Crowther, *Phenomenology of the Visual Arts (Even the Frame)*, Stanford University Press, Palo Alto, CA, 2009, pp. 82–83.

56. Ibid., p. 106.

57. "Chinese Art," *New York Times*, September 21, 1873, p. 8.

58. *New York Times*, "The Loan Collection," November 29, 1874, p. 10.

59. Walter Muir Whitehill, *Museum of Fine Arts Boston: A Centennial History*, Harvard University Press, 1970, pp. 146–147.

60. Ibid., p. 63.

61. Neil Harris, op. cit., p. 549.

62. Ibid., pp. 558–559.

63. Clearly, other factors besides plaster casts and Asian art initiated and contributed to the propensities emerging in the new aesthetic theory. For instance, although not expressed in the United States, the demise of the democratic availability of the copy had begun in Europe as early as the 1840s. In 1848 a new bylaw of the Printer's Society declared that instead of an unlimited number of copies from any plate, the number allowed would now be limited. The resulting restriction of quantity would make each print a rarer, more singular commodity, and increase the acceptable asking price.

64. Russell Sturgis, *The Nation*, September 12, 1883, p. 246.

65. Calvin Tomkins, op. cit., pp. 70–71.

66. Whitehall, op. cit., p 70.

67. Ibid., p. 151.

68. Whitehill, op. cit., p. 156.

69. Neil Harris, "The Gilded Age Revisited Boston," *American Quarterly* 14, 4 (Winter, 1962): 553–555.

70. The Met's initial subscription fund of $250,000 in 1873 barely covered the purchase of one collection. See Calvin Tomkins, op. cit., p. 43. We also cannot overlook the impact of alternative methods of replication. Photography of art pieces became a viable alternative to the cast reproductions for teaching and reference.

71. Stephen A. Tyler stated "Something strange, exotic, different, problematic, alien, and exterior goads us into recognizing arbitrariness and opens the possibility. . . ." *The Unspeakable: Discourse, Dialogue, and Rhetoric in the Postmodern World*, University of Wisconsin Press, Madison, WI, 1987, p. 14.

72. Cornell University serving as an example of these changes.

73. Walter M. Whitehill, op. cit., p. 156.

74. See Terry Eagleton's discussion, op. cit., p. 42.

75. *New York Times*, "The Art Museum," June 28, 1873, p. 3.

76. The author of this prescient article maintained the language referring to Asian objects as "grotesques," but looked beyond the lack of photographic realism, and typical of Ruskin aesthetics, found connections with similar qualities found in Western "primitive" art: "The glory of the case rests mainly in the gold and silver lacquer-ware, the plain lac carved, and the bronze grotesques. . . . One cannot but be struck with the marked resemblance of these carvings to early Saxon and Gothic efforts in which ignorance of the human form lead to the most ludicrous renderings of very sacred subjects. Like the Japanese, however, our early art redeems itself from evil by the thorough, hearty love for natural objects which it reveals, and the tremendous energy with which it reproduces them. In this the two styles offer a

happy contrast to the Greek, which had so few decorations outside of the human figure that one may count them on the fingers of the hands, and half of them were borrowed from Egypt besides."

77. Michael Clapper, op. cit., pp. 78–79.

78. Cited in regard to Schiller in Linda Dowling, op. cit., p. 21.

79. Linda Dowling, op. cit., p. 32; Ruskin citation in Linda Dowling, op. cit., p. 32.

80. "John Ruskin on Political Economy and Government," *New York Times*, May 15, 1867, p. 5.

81. Calvin Tomkins, op. cit., p. 46.

82. Calvin Tomkins, op. cit., p. 41. He elaborates: "At first the fee was fifty cents; it was reduced three months later to twenty-five cents, with Monday declared a free day. . . . Night openings were tried again in 1874, in response to appeals from art lovers whose business duties prevented them from attending during the day. The number of such citizens proved to be distressingly small—the average evening attendance was thirty-two souls—and the evening hours were discontinued." And Kenneth Hudson informs us that in when the museum did defy the religious organizations and open on Sunday, it opened only in the afternoon. Op. cit., p. 56. That first open Sunday afternoon brought in 12,000 people. Calvin Tomkins, op. cit., p. 78.

83. Walter M. Whitehill, op. cit., p. 40.

84. Neil Harris, op. cit., pp. 549, 552, 557.

85. *New York Times*, May 26, 1872, p. 5.

86. *New York Times*, January 15, 1874, p. 2. A letter to the editor of the *New York Times* reiterated the request that the Met open at least one evening during the week "so that those who are engaged during the day may have the opportunity of inspecting the worthy collection." And, on behalf of the "poorer working class," he further requested that the admission on that evening be free for the benefit of the working class and those who can ill afford to pay!

87. Calvin Tomkins, op. cit., p. 41.

88. See for instance, Germain Bazin, *The Museum Age*, Brussels, 1968; Kenneth Hudson, op. cit.

89. Remy Saisselin, op. cit., p. 78.

90. Alan Trachtenberg, *The Incorporation of America: Culture and Society in the Gilded Age*, Hill and Wang, New York, 1982, p. 90.

91. Ibid., p. 81; E. Digby Baltzell, *The Protestant Establishment: Aristocracy and Caste in America*, Random House, New York, 1964, pp. 110, 114.

92. Kenneth Hudson, op. cit., p. 54. Hudson was the founder of the European Museum Forum.

93. Neil Harris, op. cit., pp. 549–550.

94. Ibid., p. 55.

95. Trachtenberg, op. cit., p. 144.

96. Calvin Tomkins, op. cit., pp. 16–17.

97. Calvin Tomkins, op. cit., p. 77.

98. Calvin Tomkins, op cit., p. 29.

99. Cited in Trachtenberg, op. cit., p. 151.

100. Cited in Ibid., p. 151.

101. *The Park and the People: A History of Central Park*, by Roy Rosenzweig and Elizabeth Blackmar, Cornell University Press, Ithaca, NY, 1992. Choate was integral in fighting and terminating the Boss Tweed ring. In 1899, President McKinley made him ambassador to Great Britain, succeeding John Hay.

102. Kenneth Hudson, op. cit, p. 39.

103. Ibid., p. 54.

104. Burt, op. cit., p. 111.

105. Calvin Tomkins, op. cit., p. 69.

106. Calvin Tomkins, op. cit., pp. 16–17.

107. Reverend Henry Bellows, quoted in ibid., pp. 16–17.

108. Kenneth Hudson comments that "from about the middle of the nineteenth century onwards, men who had been successful in commerce or industry began to support the arts financially and, aided and abetted by the dealers, to influence the art market to the point at which buying outstanding examples of yesterday's art was entirely a pastime of rich individuals and rich institutions." Op. cit., p. 41.

109. Calvin Tomkins, op. cit., p. 23.

110. Whitman wrote in *Democratic Vistas*, cited in ibid, pp. 19–20.

111. Ibid.

112. Lloyd Lewis and Henry Justin Smith, *Oscar Wilde Discovers America [1882]*, Harcourt, Brace and Co., New York, 1936, p. 183.

113. Ibid, p. 30.

114. Ibid.

115. Leo Lerman, *The Museum: 100 Years and the Metropolitan Museum of Art*, Viking Press, New York, 1969, p. 14.

116. Kenneth Hudson, op. cit., p. 56.

117. Calvin Tomkins, op. cit., p. 61.

118. Leach., op. cit., p. 20.

119. Ibid., pp. 173–74.

120. Ibid., p. 16.

121. Cited in *Oscar Wilde's America: Counterculture in the Gilded Age*, by Mary Warner Blanchard, Yale University Press, New Haven, p. 289.

122. Ibid., p. 60

123. Edward Bellamy, *Looking Backward* (1887), The Modern Library, 1951; Bradford Peck, *The World a Department Store: A Story of Life Under a Cooperative System* (1900), Arno Press and The New York Times, New York, 1971.

124. Henry James, *The American Scene*, quoted in Remy Saisselin, op. cit., pp. 114–115.

125. Remy Saisselin, op. cit., p. 112.

126. Leach, op. cit., 168.

127. Robert W. Rydell, *All The World's a Fair*, University of Chicago, 1984, pp. 44–45.

128. Sarah Burns, *Inventing the Modern Artist: Art and Culture in Gilded Age America*, Yale University Press, New Haven, 1996, p. 59.

129. William Hosley, *The Japan Idea: Art and Life in Victorian America*, Wadsworth Athenaeum, Hartford, CT, 1990, pp. 48–49.

130. Roger B. Stein, "Artifact as Ideology: The Aesthetic Movement in Its American Cultural Context," in *In Pursuit of Beauty: Americans and the Aesthetic Movement*, Metropolitan Museum of Art, New York, 1987, p. 23.

131. Walter Muir Whitehill, op. cit., pp. 104–105.

132. *Boston Daily Advertiser*, November 28, 1884, p. 4.

133. "In the Way of Art the Buddhist Paintings at the Museum," *Boston Daily Advertiser*, December 11, 1894; p. 4.

134. See "High Priced Bric-a-Brac," *New York Times*, March 9, 1886, p. 5; "The Peach-Bloom Vase," *New York Times*, March 11, 1886, p. 4; "Mr. Walter's Peachblow Vase," *New York Times*, March 12, 1886, p. 5; "The Peachblow Vase," *New York Times*, March 20, 1886, p. 5; "What Mr. Walters Did Not Say," *New York Times*, March 20, 1886, p. 5; "Not Even a Peachblow," *New York Times*, March 24, 1886, p. 1; "The Rime of a Peachblow Vase," *New York Times*, March 27, 1886, p. 5; "Mrs. Morgan's Red Vase," *New York Times*, April 5, 1886, p. 5.

135. Walter Muir Whitehill, op. cit., p. 116.

136. "In the Galleries," *Boston Daily Advertiser*, November 24, 1891; p. 4.

137. Linda Dowling, op. cit., p. 37.

138. While cultural historians of art and literature debate the complexities leading from aestheticism to modernism, I am using the terms to indicate their historical relationship.

139. A. Hyatt Mayor, *Prints and People: A Social History of Printed Pictures*, The Metropolitan Museum of Art, New York, 1971. Mayor describes the practice Whistler initiated in 1887, of charging twice as much for signed lithographic sets than for the unsigned impressions, although the prints themselves were identical.

140. Calvin Tomkins, op. cit., p. 71.

141. James McNeill Whistler, *The Gentle Art of Making Enemies* (1892), Dover Publication, 1967, pp. 31–32.

142. Ibid., p. 139. The name Brummegem is derived from Brunwycheham, Birmingham's ancient name, and was used in common with Birmingham, a modification of the word signifying the home of descendants of the Saxon chief Beorm. Birmingham, England, became the marketplace for plate metal and imitation jewelry, and the word *Brummegem* came to indicate something commonplace or cheap.

143. Ibid., pp. 127–128.

144. Robert Rosenblum and H. W. Janson, *Nineteenth-Century Art*, Prentice-Hall, Upper Saddle River, NJ, 1984, p. 291.

145. James McNeill Whistler, op. cit., p. 116.

146. Alfred Werner introduction to ibid, p. xii.

147. See Whistler's *Rose and Silver: The Princess from the Land of Porcelain*, 1864, as well as *Purple and Rose: The Lange Leizen of the Six Marks*, 1864.

148. George De Maurier did a "Chinamania" series in *Punch* between 1874 and 1877.

149. Theophile Gautier, Preface to *Mademoiselle de Maupin* (1835), cited in *Art in Theory, 1815–1900: An Anthology of Changing Ideas*, edited by Charles Harrison and Paul Wood, Blackwell Publishers, 1998, p. 99.

150. James McNeill Whistler, op. cit., p. 1.

151. Calvin Tomkins, op. cit., p. 74. Charles Eliot Norton tried to stem the tide of change through word and action: in 1879 he brought in a selection of Ruskin's drawing, exhibited in Boston and New York. And in 1888 he was still fighting the new aesthetic theory, scoffing that alleged "art and morality are absolutely independent, that the relation between the Beautiful and the Good is purely external, and that it is an impertinence to ask for anything in a work of art more than it should be well executed." Stein, op. cit. pp. 231, 242. Some of Ruskin's strongest American advocates were eventually persuaded by the modernist ideas. In 1863 Russell Sturgis had been one of four founding members of the "Society for the Advancement of Truth in Art," and he wrote for their journal the *New Path*, the new path at that time being Ruskinianism. An editorial about this journal appeared in the *North American Review* in 1864, calling the *New Path* "the most interesting and noteworthy American publication concerning Art, during the past year," and commenting that the writers were "disciples of Mr. Ruskin." "They are beholden, indeed, to him, not only for quickened perceptions of natural beauty, but for understanding that truth to nature is the test of all art. . . ." Yet by the 1890s Sturgis felt dubious about his previous certitude regarding art, truth and nature, and by turn of the century, Sturgis had fully renounced his previous way of viewing art and resolved to make this abundantly clear. In the first paragraph on the first page of the introduction to his book *The Appreciation of Pictures*, he writes about the purpose of studying design: "And it may be noted at the outset of our inquiry that this is not the same standpoint as that of the lover of nature, of the lover or poetical thought and expression, of the moralist, or of the person of religions enthusiasm. It is one main purpose of these books to show how independent is the artistical standard of judgment." *The Appreciation of Pictures: A Handbook*, Baker and Taylor Company, New York, 1905, p. 11.

152. Originally hired by the Tokyo University in 1878 to teach political economy and philosophy, when Fenollosa became interested in Japanese art the Japanese government commissioned him to travel throughout Europe for a year's study of methods in art education. He subsequently became a student of Japanese art, collecting comprehensibly and voraciously, ultimately removing many important Asian works from Japan and China into the MFAB.

153. Van Wyck Brooks, *Fenollosa and His Circle: With Other Essays in Biography*, E. P. Dutton & Co., New York, 1962, p. 49.

154. Ibid.

155. William Hosley, op. cit., p. 47.

156. Alexis Krausse, *China in Decay: the Story of a Disappearing Empire*, Chapman & Hall, London, 1900, p. 305.

157. Crowther, op. cit., p. 67.

158. Walter Muir Whitehead, op. cit., pp. 83, 121.

159. Benjamin March, op. cit., p. 12.

160. The MFAB's fondness for John Singer Sargent, who was commissioned to paint the large mural at the entry way of the museum, provides a precise analogy. Sargent was renowned for his traditional subjects depicting patrons and the wealthy and famous and his use of old master techniques, but he was equally celebrated for his abstract and abbreviated, distinctly modern method of applying paint.

161. *The Metropolitan Museum of Art Handbook of a Collection of Chinese Porcelains Loaned by James A. Garland*, The Metropolitan Museum of Art, New York, 1895.
162. *Museum of Fine Arts Bulletin* III, 1 (January 1905): 5.

CHAPTER THREE. FROM CLASS TO RACE:
THE NEW YORK TIMES RECONSTRUCTS "CHINESE"

1. Quoted in bell hooks "esisting Representation," in *Outlaw Culture*, Routledge, New York, 1994, p. 33.

2. James Clifford, *The Predicament of Culture: Twentieth-Century Ethnography, Literature, and Art*, Cambridge: Harvard University Press, 1988, p. 33.

3. Many authors discuss the phenomenon of the expansion of mass communication or its consequences: in *Victorian America: Transformations in Everyday Life*, Thomas J. Schlereth explicitly places "the transformation of the content, format, and readership of the metropolitan press . . . between 1876 and 1915." p. 182. William R. Taylor's "The Evolution of Public Space in New York City," in *Consuming Visions*, discusses the growth of cities and their effect on changing the power of public opinion and creating mass culture, pp. 287–289. And in numerous texts Neil Harris emphasizes the role of the expanding print media in late-nineteenth-century America, for instance, in "The Lamp of Learning: Popular Lights and Shadows," in *The Organization of Knowledge in Modern America, 1860–1920*, he describes that "in the sixty years following the Civil War, the evolution of publishing mirrored the bewildering growth of knowledge. Because books were too static and final to serve as exclusive sources, periodicals developed which enlarged and amended, and reordered the knowledge that had appeared secure just a few months or years earlier," p. 431.

4. One popular American version of polygenesis asserted that, deriving from different "species," mixed racial offspring were weak and defective, while another version "proved" that Negroes had always been slaves of Caucasians. Although polygenesis reached greatest prominence in the years prior to the civil War, when it was supplanted by Darwinism, nevertheless, its effects were far reaching and remained long after the theory as a whole had been discarded. Richard H. Popkin, "Pre-Adamism in Nineteenth Century American Thought: 'Speculative Biology' and Racism," *Philosophia* 8, 2–3 (1978): 206, 220–224.

5. I formulated these ten characteristics before I explored that theory in greater depth.

6. E. Davis, *The History of the New York Times, 1851–1921*, Little, Ives & Co., New York, p. 7.

7. Alexander Saxton, "Problems of Class and Race in the Origins of the Mass Circulation Press," *American Quarterly* 26, 2 (Summer 1984): 211–212; Edwin Emery, *The Press and America: An Interpretative History of the Mass Media*, Prentice Hall, New York, 1974, p. 285.

8. Competition between New York newspaper owners William Randolph Hearst and Joseph Pulitzer brought the circulation of their respective newspapers to over one million. Internet, July 19, 2010, "Press Reference » Sw-Ur » United

States Press, Media, TV, Radio, Newspapers," http://www.pressreference.com/Sw-Ur/ United-States.html.

9. Priscilla Wald, *Constituting Americans: Cultural Anxiety and Narrative Form*, pp. 2, 10.

10. Edwin Emery, op. cit., p. 283.

11. Quoted in Saxton, op. cit., p. 225.

12. Quoted in Davis, op. cit., p. 7.

13. Augustus Maverick, *Henry J. Raymond and the New York Press, for Thirty Years: Progress of American Journalism from 1840 to 1870*, Nabu Press, Charleston, SC, 2010, p. 94.

14. Davis, op. cit., p. 120.

15. The fact that much of this information on the *Times* was taken from the history written by Elmer Davis, a former *Times* reporter on the editorial staff, illustrates how the *Times* saw itself and wanted to be received.

16. Wei Min She Labor Committee, *Chinese Working People in America*, United Front Publishers, San Francisco, 1974, p. 12.

17. Thomas F. McIlwraith, *North America: The Historical Geography of a Changing Continent*, Rowman & Littlefield Publishers, 2 edition, 2001, p. 286. Mary R. Coolidge, *Chinese Immigration*, Cornell University, Ithaca, NY, 2010, p. 425

18. In the *Indispensable Enemy*, University of California Press, Berkeley, 1975, Alexander Saxton details this transition from the working class to one led by politicians, especially see p. 108.

19. Andrew Gyory, *Closing the Gate: Race Politics and the Chinese Exclusion Act*, University of North Carolina Press, Chapel Hill, 1998, p. 1.

20. Elmer Clarence Sandmeyer, Roger Daniels, *The Anti-Chinese Movement in California*, University of Illinois Press, 1991, p. 64.

21. See the August 10, 1873 article, "Attack On Chinese Laborers in San Francisco." Physical acts of violence against the Chinese in California broke out as well. The *New York Times* reprinted articles from California, which reported the brutality in anguished tones. In an article from the San Francisco *Alta*, reprinted in the *New York Times* on November 3, 1870, titled "The Los Angeles Outrage. Details of the Riot—Fifteen Chinamen Hung and Many Others Wounded and Killed—In all Twenty-one Dead—Origin of the Trouble," the first line described the horrible episode: "The most terrible night Los Angeles has ever known has just been passed, corpses hung ghastly in the moonlight, while seven or eight others, mutilated, torn and crushed, lay in our streets, all of them Chinamen." The article continued: "The sad results came, first, of their own bitter feud between themselves: next of the infuriated passions of a few of their number, and lastly, of the demoniacal excitement of the lower classes of our community. Horrible beyond description has been the history of these last few hours. Chinamen, helpless, torn and mangled, more dead than alive, have been dragged by an infuriated, senseless and reckless crowd, through our peaceable streets, in the very face of the better portion of the community, to finish what little was left of their agonized existence at the end of a rope. For all this we have no apology, save that the fearful work commenced at an hour when business men, professional men and all the better classes of our community had retired to their homes, and were aroused therefrom to confront the horrible work."

The article conveys the class division over Chinese exclusion, clearly distinguishing between the lower classes capable of such savagery, and the upper-, professional class that would have, he intimates, restrained them. Despite the reporter's reassurance that such violence would be rare, anti-Chinese violence continued.

22. *The Columbia Encyclopedia*, 6th ed., Columbia University Press, New York, 2002.

23. See the August 8, 1873 article, "Strike by Chinamen." The *Times* reporter supported the Chinese, stating that "Mr. Sampson did well in introducing the Chinese, the Sunday-school teachers have done well in Christianizing them, and they will do well in demanding good pay and doing honest work."

24. Labor groups such as the Crispins discredited the Chinese by representing them all as coolies, whom it construed as a debased and inferior class; the argument asserted that the Chinese had a capacity to live unreasonably cheaply by foregoing most common enjoyments of life; therefore they must be nearly nonhuman.

25. See the July 1, 1870 article, "The Coming Coolie: Mass-Meeting in Tompkins-Square to Discuss the Chinese Labor Question—Speeches by Nelson W. Young, Mayor Hall, Alexander Troup and Others—Resolutions."

26. Abraham Oakey Hall, Mayor of New York City, 1868–1872, known as "Boss Tweed's Mayor." Hall was a front man for the infamous Tweed Ring, swindling the city of millions of dollars in one of the most corrupt administrations in the nation's history. See Melvin G. Holli's *The American Mayor: The Best & The Worst Big-City Leaders*, Pennsylvania State University Press, University Park, 1999.

27. Ronald Takiki, *Iron Cages: Race and Culture in Nineteenth-Century America*, Alfred A. Knopf, New York, 1979. Takiki discusses national attention focused on these Chinese workers, especially as their work resulted in considerable profit. Sampson's success inspired other East Coast capitalists to follow suit: three months after Sampson had hired Chinese workers, James B. Hervey hired sixty-eight Chinese in Belleville, New Jersey, to work in his Passaic Steam Laundry. Shortly after this 300 Chinese workers were employed in a laundry, and 190 hired to work for the Beaver Falls Cutlery Company in Beaver Falls, Pennsylvania. Takiki concludes: "The message of North Adams, Belleville, and Beaver Falls was clear: The Chinese constituted an enormous potential and useful source of labor in the development of American capitalism in the East," p. 235.

28. See article 11, July 1870, a letter to the editor, "The Chinese Labor Question."

29. Another level of prejudice emerges in the reporter's expression of doubt as to "whether native American working men are taking any part in the present outcry."

30. According to Takaki, the numbers of Chinese seized the American imagination more than greater numbers of other immigrant groups. Takaki quotes Henry George's well-known essay, "The Chinese on the Pacific Coast" (1869) expressing George's agitation about the image of the 100,000 Chinese on the American West Coast which, to him, represented "the fine end of the wedge which had for its base the five hundred million people of eastern Asia." Op. cit., p. 224.

31. Kenneth Burke, *A Grammar of Motives*, University of California Press, Berkeley, 1969, p. 431. Burke discusses the theory of primal hordes found in Darwin and adapted by Freud.

32. Horatio Seymour (1810–1886), governor of New York from 1853 to 1855, and again from 1863 to 1865, today is most renowned for declaring the Emancipation Proclamation unconstitutional. He ran for president against Ulysses S. Grant in 1868, and Thomas Nast depicted him in a cartoon on September 5, 1868 for *Harper's Weekly Magazine*, with the caption "This Is White Man Government," courting votes from the Confederate States and the Irish immigrants by denying the African American access to the vote. Alexander J. Wall, *A Sketch of the Life of Horatio Seymour 1810–1886*, New York Historical Soc. (1929); *Harper's Magazine*, September 1868.

33. See August 6, 1870 article, "Ex-Gov. Seymour on the Coolie question—Letter to the Working Men at Rochester."

34. The ability of conservatives to interpret American values more restrictively has been succinctly commented on by Steven Shiffrin: "Political pundits often proclaim the view that conservatives know how to tap into American values in a way that progressives do not." "For the conservative, the point is that our Constitution does not and should not provide protection for those who flout our customs and our morality." *Dissent, Injustice, and the Meanings of America*, Princeton University Press, 2000, pp. 3, 18.

35. See July 11, 1870 article, "The Chinese Labor Question."

36. Nancy Stepan described that, at the end of the nineteenth century, "census data, most of it highly unreliable," was interpreted to enable the white majority to alleviate their fears about the possible dominance of another group. Although the statistics she examined concerned African Americans, the same manipulations were applied to statistics for the Chinese. Op. cit., p. 101. The dual ability of statistics to both prove and disprove the same thing gives a fuller appreciation of the remark Mark Twain attributes in his autobiography to Benjamin Disraeli: "There are three types of lies: Lies, Damn Lies, and Statistics."

37. See January 3, 1871 article, "Statistics of Immigration. Comparisons with 1869 and Other Years—the Decline During the Last Year and the Causes."

38. See March 1, 1872 article, "John Chinaman."

39. *New York Times*, June 26, 1873.

40. See March 6, 1882 article, "The Anti-Chinese Agitation. The Hon. Montgomery Blair Approves of Senator Miller's Recent Speech."

41. George Frisbie Hoar (1826–1904), was elected to the House of Representatives in 1868 and the Senate in 1877. Richard E. Welch, *George Frisbie Hoar and the Half-Breed Republicans* Harvard University Press, Cambridge, 1971.

42. See March 7, 1882 article, "The Influx of Chinamen. More Speeches on the Anti-Immigration Bill. Senator Brown Opposes the Bill as a Breach of Faith—China in as Much Danger of Being Overrun as the United States—Mr. Teller Denounces the Chinese." Senator Joseph Emerson Brown (1821–1894), Democrat, Georgia, had been a chief justice of the supreme court of Georgia until December 1870, when he resigned and accepted the presidency of the Western and Atlantic Railroad Co, appointed and subsequently elected as a Democrat to the United States Senate from May 26, 1880, until March 3, 1891. From *Biographical Directory of the American Congress, 1774–1949*, United States Printing Office, Washington, DC, 1950.

43. See June 26, 1871 article, "A Traveler's Views on the Chinese on the Pacific Coast," and August 14, 1871 article, "The Coming Chinese: Reverend Beecher on the Chinese Question—Why They Should Be Received."

44. See, for example, June 26, 1871 article, "A Traveler's Views the Chinese on the Pacific Coast—. . . Discourse by Rev. W. H. Boole."

45. As Robert McClellan points out, though largely ignored in the West, the poem became endemic in the Eastern states, a mixture of profit and distress to Harte. Op. cit., pp. 48–52.

46. Brett Harte, "Plain Language from Truthful James," in Thomas R. Lounsbury, ed., Yale Book of American Verse, Yale Press, New Haven, 1912.

47. *New York Times*, June 16, 1874; November 4, 1877; April 23, 1878.

48. For use of the words *heathen* and *pagan*, see, for instance, September 7, 1872, "The Fate of Ah Gim"; December 21, 1872, "A Heathen Festival"; December 27, 1873, "A Chinaman the Less."

49. *New York Times*, "A Chinese Murder," February 23, 1873.

50. The murderous characteristic of Chinese immigrants appeared again in a letter to a New Orleans newspaper, reprinted in full in the *Times* on November 5, 1873, "Chinese Labor." The writer, Mr. D. Dennett, expressed indignation about the Chinese belligerence as workers in Louisiana. At their best, he found the Chinese laborers to be "slow and weak." They quickly degenerated into thieves, stealing "everything they could lay their hands on." In rapid succession Dennet itemized the violent incidents perpetrated by various groups of Chinese on different plantations: treacherous, wild, stealing, necessitating restraint, running away. He mentions incidents of wrathful violence occasioned when the Chinese voiced a complaint about bad treatment. "The planter, agent, overseer, and negroes could have no influence in restraining the wrath of the pigtails. They had to send for the city police, who subdued them with their clubs, and threatened them with six-shooters. . . . another time the overseer was compelled to shoot one of them, wounding him in the arm. The whole body of them, armed with knives, clubs, axes, and bludgeons, pursued him to the planter's house, demanded his blood, and could not be restrained by any one."

51. See May 28, 1873 article, "Small-Pox Among Chinese Immigrants at San Francisco—Know-Nothingism."

52. See July 1, 1873 article, "Chinese Leprosy." But the need for such a disclaimer indicated the ubiquity of the rumors.

53. See June 26, 1873 article (no title).

54. See February 12, 1873 article, "House of Representatives." This was a publication of a petition presented by Mr. McClelland of Pennsylvania to Congress.

55. *New York Times* (1857–1922); December 24, 1871, "Chinese Life," p. 3.

56. See February 16, 1874 article, "The Chinese New Year. Idolatry in Baxter Street—Feasting and Smoking Opium."

57. January 23, 1875, "Extensive Smuggling of Opium by Chinese." March 5, 1875, "A Chinese Banquet. How the Celestial Cigar-Makers Annually Treat Themselves in San Francisco."

58. See July 4, 1875 "Opium."

59. See June 12, 1882 article (untitled). Compare that to the article from January 10, 1870, "The Nineteenth Century in Japan," citing Professor Pumpelly's counsel against forcing opium in Japan as it had in China. This remark demonstrated the prior recognition of the role the West played in the Chinese use of opium.

60. See January 29, 1882 article, "The Chinese at Home. Some of the National Peculiarities of Moon-Eyed Celestials."

61. See July 6, 1875 article, "Chinese Customs. Their Life and Education. The Craving for Opium and Its Effects—Superstition Among Them—A Trick That Prevailed. From the *San Francisco Bulletin*."

62. See April 29, 1882 article, "Importation of Opium Prohibited."

63. See April 29, 1882 article, "Importation of Opium Prohibited," reprinted from the *San Francisco Chronicle*, April 20.

64. Ibid., p. 9. Peffer emphasizes that before the enactment of the Page Law, California had attempted exclusion laws of its own, restricting immigration of "coolies" and "prostitutes" in 1873. But the Supreme Court found these laws in violation of the Burlingame Treaty and declared them unconstitutional. Ibid., p. 8.

65. According to George Anthony Peffer in *If They Don't Bring Their Women Here: Chinese Female Immigration Before Exclusion*, the female-to-male ration in the Chinese American population in 1910 was fifty-three per thousand, a return to the of the female population to nearly the same level as in 1870; p. 25.

66. See December 17, 1874 article, "Chinese Immigration. Washington." A similar proposal was made by Mr. Hager, of California; see December 17, 1874 article, "The Chinese." Peffer also pointed out that, besides discouraging Chinese men from staying in the country, the restrictions against women also dissuaded Chinese men from asking for higher wages to support wives and children, or press for better housing or schools. Ibid., p. 9.

67. Hall, op. cit., p. 50.

68. See June 14, 1873 article, "Minor topics."

69. See July 30, 1873 article, "Auction Sale of Chinese Women."

70. See July 31, 1873 article, "The Chinese in California. Alleged Discovery of an Immoral Secret Society—Disclosures Made by the Police. San Francisco."

71. See July 25, 1875 article, "Pigeon English. A Curious Oriental Patois."

72. In 1960, Ruby Bridges, a six-year-old girl, protected by federal marshals, walked through lines of enraged white adults—the first African American child to attend a school with white children in New Orleans. See *The Story of Ruby Bridges* by Robert Coles, Scholastic, New York, 1995.

73. See April 12, 1875 article, "Chinese School Children."

74. See July 6, 1875 article, "How the Young Heathen Are Taught Their Written Language. From the *San Francisco Bulletin*."

75. See March 4, 1882 article, "Enemies of the Chinese the Senate Still Discussing Mr. Miller's Bill. Pacific Slope Senators Particularly Vehement in Their Demands—Effects of Chinese Cheap Labor—Dire Evils Predicted If Immigration Is Not Stopped." This appeared on page 1.

76. In *Orientals: Asian Americans in Popular Culture*, Robert G. Lee writes, "Against an emergent heterosexual and dimorphic order, Oriental sexuality was constructed as ambiguous, inscrutable, and hermaphroditic; the Oriental (male or

female) was constructed as a 'third sex'—Marjorie Gaber's term for a gender of imagined sexual possibility," pp. 85, 89.

77. See July 1, 1870 article, "Theories and Facts About the Chinese."

78. James Clifford, *The Predicament of Culture: Twentieth-Century Ethnography, Literature, and Art*, Harvard University Press, Cambridge, 1988, p. 6.

79. Let alone what it reveals about the desired characteristics of women at the time.

80. See December 20, 1872 article, "A Chinese Holiday."

81. See September 7, 1873 article, "The Fate of Ah Gim." And see October 4, 1973 article, "Wong Chin Foo."

82. See April 12, 1882 article, "A Murderous Chinaman. Guilty of Attempting to Kill His Uncle—A Chinese Woman in Court."

83. See April 17, 1873 article, "A Revolution in China."

84. Ibid.

85. See, for instance, July 6, 1870 article, "A New Solution of the 'Servant Girl' Question."

86. See, for instance, February 6, 1873 article, "Chinamen Shipped to Punta Arenas as 'Personal Effects.'"

87. Op. cit. July 6, 1870, "A New Solution of the 'Servant Girl' Question." This is a typical role of metaphor, which, as Eric Cheyfitz points out in *The Poetics of Imperialism: Translation and Colonization from the Tempest to Tarzan*, University of Pennsylvania Press, 1997 was defined by Aristotle in the Poetics as, "'the application of an alien name by transference either from genus to species, or from species to genus, or from species to species, or by analogy, that is, proportion.' Metaphora comes from the verb metaphero (literally, 'to carry across.')" In the above article the reporter tried to define the unfamiliar by transporting it to a familiar place.

88. M. M. Bakhtin, "The Problem of the Text," in *Speech Genres and Other Late Essays*, Caryl Emerson and Michael Holquist, eds., University of Texas Press, 1986, pp. 120–121.

89. See July 1, 1870 article, "Theories and Facts About the Chinese."

90. In April 1873, under "Minor Topics," the *Times* offered a challenge to the image of slavery. The article stated that after serving out their contract, some of the Chinese shoemakers saved enough money to rent their own stores and work for themselves. But this, too, occasioned contempt from concerned groups in California, complaining that the Chinese charged so little they made competition impossible.

91. Pierre Bourdieu, *A Social Critique of the Judgment of Taste*, Harvard University Press, 1987, pp. 12–13.

92. See December 26, 1874 article, "A New Raid on the Chinese."

93. See March 3, 1870 article, "What Shall Be Done with John Chinaman?" Nancy Stepan discusses this dislocation in "Biology: Races and Proper Places," pointing out that "As slavery was abolished . . . as industrialization brought about new social mobility and class tensions, and new anxieties about the 'proper' place of different class, national, and ethnic groups in society, racial biology provided a model for the analysis of the distances that were 'natural' between human groups. Racial 'degeneration' became a code for other social groups whose behavior and appearance seemed sufficiently different from accepted norms as to threaten traditional

social relations . . ." in *Degeneration: The Dark Side of Progress*, ed. by Chamberlin and Gilman (1985), p. 98.

94. Similarly, after professing concern for the welfare of coolies, in 1873 a *Times* article, "The New Slave Trade," followed the same pattern, claiming that coolie employment was merely a euphemism for slavery and asserted that the chief concern should be protection of the emigrant from such servitude. See May, 11, 1873 article, "The New Slave Trade."

95. Teun van Dijk, *Elite Discourse and Racism*, Sage Publications, Newbury Park, CA, 1993.

96. March 6, 1882, letter from the ex-postmaster general, Montgomery Blair, who previously had advocated restricting slavery from new territories and supported Dred Scott in the 1850s.

97. Surprisingly, an apparently effective pro-exclusion charge against anti-exclusion arguments was of sentimentality. For every attempt to address humanistic values, pro-exclusion congresspeople would cry "sentiment," effectively suppressing and eventually undermining the image of benign Chinese. In its place the Exclusionists substituted an image of demonic people, barbaric in actions and ignorance. See, for instance, the March 7, 1882, article (untitled), which stated that "Mr. Teller, of Colorado, after exhibiting his impatience 'to have at him,' literally, 'went for that heathen Chinee' with all of the reckless fervor of his own untrammeled free West. Mr. Teller is proud to say that he does not care a button for sentiment, and he rather glories in his readiness to take a scalp when occasion requires. . . ."

98. See, for instance, March 7, 1882, "The Influx of Chinamen; April 15, 1882, "Loop-Holes for Chinamen."

99. See January 27, 1882 article, "National Capital Topics: A Report Adverse to Chinese Immigration."

100. See April 27, 1882 article, "The Foes of the Chinese. Another Day Consumed by the Senate in Discussing the Anti-Immigration Bill."

101. He also observed that the same arguments had been made against Irishmen and the Indians, as well as against the Jews.

102. See March 9, 1882 article, "The Senate's Long Debate a Vote Not Yet Reached on the Anti-Chinese Bill. Another Day Wasted on Antiquated Arguments—The Ten-Year Amendment Rejected by a Tie Vote . . ."

103. April 27, 1882, 'The Foes of the Chinese. Another Day Consumed By The Senate in Discussing the Anti-Immigration Bill."

104. See March 4, 1882 article, "China in the Senate." The reporter commented: "What Mr. Maxey meant by that, he knows; nobody else does."

105. For instance, in *Oscar Wilde's America: Counterculture in the Gilded Age*, Yale University Press, New Haven, 1998, Mary W. Blanchard refers to a fiction story on aestheticism in *Peterson's* magazine titled "The Utterly Utter Boston Browns," p. 170.

106. Kenneth Burke, *A Grammar of Motives*, p. 310.

107. Mr. Dawes reading Mr. Georges speech. See March 8, article, "The War on the Chinese Another Day Spent in Talk by the Senate. Mr. Dawes Argues Against the Bill—A Reply to Mr. George's Speech—Mr. Edmunds Opposed to Chinese Immigration—A Vote Expected To-Day."

108. Quoted in Takaki, op. cit., pp. 215, 216.

109. See March 9 article, "The Senate's Long Debate. A Vote Not Yet Reached on the Anti-Chinese Bill. Another Day Wasted on Antiquated Arguments—The Ten-Year Amendment Rejected By a Tie Vote . . ."

110. See March 9, 1882 article, "Negro and Chinaman."

111. James Clifford, op. cit., p. 5.

112. See March 10, 1882 article, "The Chinese Bill Passed. A Vote of Nearly Two to One in the Affirmative. Mr. Hawley Speaks Against the Bill and Mr. Jones, af Nevada, for It."

113. In *Inventing the People*, W. W. Norton and Co., 1988, Edmund S. Morgan describes a strikingly similar response to a somewhat different circumstance in the early records of the House of Representatives (pre-1800s). After a congressional committee had determined that an election had been effected by violence toward voters by the competing party (the record states "some of the threatened to beat any person who should vote in favor of the petitioner; that one of the soldiers struck and knocked known [*sic*] a magistrate . . .") nevertheless a congressperson responded that he could not 'for his soul, discover the smallest pretence to set aside the election of Mr. Preston, nor could he comprehend or conceive upon what ground so strange a notion had been started.' He then vindicated, indeed lionized, all the associated perpetrators of violence; p. 187.

114. On January 24, 1882, introduced by Mr. Willis, a senator from Kentucky, followed two days later by a more punctilious one proposed by Mr. Page, a California congressperson.

115. See April 5, 1882 article, "The Chinese Bill Vetoed."

116. Mormon polygamy currently was an issue in Congress as well.

117. See April 29, 1882 article, "The Anti-Chinese Bill."

118. In *The Indispensable Enemy Labor and the Anti-Chinese Movement in California*, University of California Press, Berkeley, 1971. Alexander Saxton discusses a nineteenth-century strategy against the Chinese, defining Chinese as criminal. He cites an 1876 address against Chinese immigration by San Francisco's Mayor Andrew Jackson Bryant, in which he refers to the Chinese: "I think we can stop the hordes of paupers and thieves from taking possession of the city. I believe this is the best time to go to Washington," p. 106. And Takaki describes the Naturalization Law of 1790, enacted in the first US Congress, which established a probationary period for every prospective citizen, to better exclude "vagrants," "paupers," and "bad men." Op. cit., pp. 14–15. With the legislation of Exclusion, the fusion of Chinese into criminal became a fait accompli.

119. Henry Ward Beecher (1813–1887) was a brother of Rev. James Beecher, and his sister was Harriet Beecher Stowe, author of *Uncle Tom's Cabin*.

120. See March 27, 1882 article, "Beecher on the Chinese and His Poor Opinion of the Irish Immigrants." Henry Beecher's brother James had expressed similar opinions printed in the *Times* eleven years earlier; see August 14, 1871 article, ""The Coming Chinese. Rev. James Beecher on the Chinese Question—Why They Should Be Received."

121. See April 14, 1882 article, "The Union League Club. President Arthur's Veto of the Chinese Bill Commended."

122. Blaming the victim has been a successful aide in establishing racial hierarchies. As van Dijk elaborates: *"Reversal or blaming the victim is another prominent move in the overall strategy of positive self-presentation and negative other-presentation. Confronted with repeated accusations of intolerance and racism, the Right and its press systematically take recourse by reversing the charges. . . ." Elite Discourse and Racism*, p. 260.

123. See March 5, 1882 article, "The Anti-Chinese Feeling. A Holiday, and Mass-Meeting In San Francisco—Meetings In Nevada." San Francisco, March 4.

124. See April 15 article, "Denis Kearney on the Chinese Veto." Dennis Kearny had been the California leader of the anti-Chinese movement especially in violent rhetoric since 1877. See Saxton op. cit. esp. pp. 116–121.

125. Compare this call to action to the belated petitions and delayed affirmations of support for the presidential veto from the East Coast found in April 13 article, "Against the Chinese Bill," and April 14, "The Union League Club. President Arthur's Veto of the Chinese Bill Commended."

126. Van Dijk, pp. cit. pp. 253–254.

127. See April 6, 1882 article, "The Chinese Bill Veto. The Bitter Comments of the San Francisco Papers."

128. See March 4, 1882 article, "China in the Senate."

129. See March 2, 1882 article (untitled).

130. Also see similar remarks on an untitled editorial, April 27, 1882, p. 8, col. 2.

131. February 27, 1882 (no title), the last line of the article read: "Why, in the face of all these facts, the representatives of all political parties in California, commercial organizations, &c., should demand that all business should be suspended for one day, while a monster meeting gives voice to the anti-Chinese sentiment of California, is beyond comprehension."

132. Stuart C. Miller's 1966 doctoral thesis, *The Chinese Image in the Eastern United States, 1785–1882*, was one of the first articulations of the national dimension of anti-Chinese prejudice.

133. See June 16, 1873 article, "The Chinese Question. A Calm Statement of the Case from the Chinese Stand-Point."

134. Reverend Otis Gibson was the author of the 1877 book, *The Chinese in America*.

135. Braj B. Kachru, "The Alchemy of English," in *The Post-Colonial Studies Reader*, Bill Ashcroft, Gareth Griffiths, and Helen Tiffin, eds. Routledge, London, 1995, p. 292. See also *Race, Writing and Difference* by Henry Louis Gates Jr., University of Chicago Press, Chicago, 1986.

136. See March 21, 1882 article, "Protest from Christian Chinese."

137. The infrequency of newspaper articles representing the Chinese viewpoint does not reflect the actual attempts to disseminate their viewpoint. Van Dijk accentuates the underrepresentation of minority opinions in the media, and the control of public information by white individuals or corporations. In *Discourse and Discrimination*, edited by G. Smitherman-Donaldson and T. van Dijk, p. 223.

138. Carl F. Stychin gets to the heart of this malfeasance in *A Nation by Rights: National Cultures, Sexual Identity Politics and the Discourse of Rights*. Temple

University Press, Philadelphia, 1998, defining that "the constructedness of nation is apparent in the language used to describe the relationship between the immigrant and the national community. The 'foreigner' seeks 'naturalization'—to be *made* a part of the community. The term 'naturalization' highlights how the language of nation can be deeply essentialist; membership is a product, not of politics, but of nature. . . . Naturalization also suggests that the condition placed on the invitation to the outsider is that inclusion will bring normalization," p. 3.

139. Perhaps appearing as physical "proof" seemingly validating the staunch belief that Chinese could not assimilate was the different aesthetic in buildings and interior design created in Chinese immigrant communities. The physical space presented a separate place unlike any Western area, and this visual image of separateness seemed to connote a distinct nation.

140. See November 20, 1882 article, "The Anti-Chinese Bill in China."

141. Teun A. Van Dijk, op. cit., p. 254.

142. See March 10, 1882 article, "A Chinaman Wants to Be a Citizen."

143. See March 11, 1882 article, untitled.

144. See June 27, 1882 article, "Chinamen Reported Naturalized." Philadelphia, June 26.

145. Jorge Luis Borges, "The Congress," in *The Book of Sand*, Penguin Books, New York, 1980, p. 17.

CHAPTER FOUR. THE CHINESE OF THE AMERICAN IMAGINATION: NINETEENTH-CENTURY TRADE CARD IMAGES

1. T. J. Jackson Lears, *Fables of Abundance: A Cultural History of Advertising in America*, Basic Books, New York, 1994, p. 117.

2. Bernard P. Wong, *Chinatown: Economic Adaptation And Ethnic Identity of the Chinese*, Holt, Rinehart, and Winston, New York, 1982.

3. Ronald T. Takaki, *Iron Cages*, Alfred A. Knopf, New York, 1979, p. 14, describes the shoemakers brought in by the shoe manufacturer Sampson as an alternative to the conceding to the demands of the Crispin labor union. James S. Moy describes the presence of Chinese people in American circuses throughout the nineteenth century. *Marginal Sights: Staging the Chinese in America*, University of Iowa Press, Iowa City, 1993.

4. Although the East Coast tried to portray their role in voting in favor of Chinese exclusion as merely capitulating to pressure from California, its opposition to California's racism, initially indignant, became increasingly feeble over the 1870s and eroded into silence by 1882.

5. Laird, op. cit., discusses the change in products and advertising from one end of the nineteenth century to the other: "Most items offered before 1820 were traditional, generic services and goods such as foodstuffs, cloth, or ribbons. There was no need to educate the public about their uses or desirability," p. 16.

6. See Jonathon Crary's *Techniques of the Observer*, MIT Press, Cambridge, 1990, especially p. 3. Crary locates the creation of this new observer in the earlier decades of the nineteenth century—and these changes accelerated by the century's end, pp. 16–17.

7. Trade cards dominated the advertisement industry from 1876 until the early twentieth century, when magazines capitulated to the consumer's love and color and began using photographic color processes, domesticating advertising images within their pages.

8. In *The Society of the Spectacle*, Zone Books, New York, 1994, Guy Debord brings out this point, stating: "The spectacle is essentially tautological, for the simple reason that its means and its ends are identical," p. 15.

9. In *The Society of the Spectacle*, Zone Books, New York, 1994, Guy Debord clarifies this point, stating: "The spectacle is essentially tautological, for the simple reason that its means and its ends are identical," p. 15.

10. Free or inexpensive helped popularity immensely. Richard Ohmann provides statistics about the demographics of magazine circulation, pinpointing 1893 as the year in which Frank Munsey dropped his magazine prices to as low as a dime and the circulation quickly rose from 40,000 to 500,000 within a year. In *Selling Culture: Magazines, Markets and Class at the turn of the Century*, Verson, New York, 1996, p. 25.

11. In *The Trade Card in Nineteenth Century America*, University of Missouri Press, Columbia, 1987, Robert Jay proposes that the reticence on the part of magazines stemmed both from the cost of colored printing as well as a from traditional conservative aversion to commercialism in general: "In the last third of the nineteenth century, the growth in quantity of consumer products, together with much-improved means of distribution, created an unprecedented market for advertising in America. . . . Fundamentally, however, the way in which these media were used differed little from earlier in the century. . . . many publishers of newspapers and magazines remained quite conservative in their dealings with advertisers, allowing only very restricted space . . . ," p. 3.

12. Jay, op. cit., p. 3.

13. The 1891 book *Art, Society, and Accomplishments: A Treasury of Artistic Homes, Social Life and Culture*, ed. by R. Barry Blackburn, the Blackburn Company Publishers, includes the Japanese screen as an understood object of desire, asking: ". . . what is dearer to a woman's heart than her Japanese art pieces?" pp. 21–22.

14. Jay, op. cit., p. 72. Specifically, Jay refers to the trade card images of Chinese as "narrow" and as "malicious stereotypes."

15. In his analysis of trademarks, a much less complicated icon then a trade card, Casper J. Werkman itemized four possible combinations of image and word by which trademarks disseminate information: "*a.* (only or mainly) by means of content of the word. . . . *b.* (only or mainly) by means of form of the word . . . *c.* (only or mainly) by means of content of the design . . . *d.* (only or mainly) by means of form of the design . . ." and the possible relationships become more complicated after that. For the two-sided trade cards, the possibilities in relations between word and image, form and content are compounded. Casper J. Werkman, *Trademarks: Their Creation, Psychology and Perception*, J. H. De Bussy, Amsterdam, 1974, p. 67.

16. Lears, op. cit., eloquently describes this fascination with exotica: "Materialist assumptions became more overt during the latter half of the nineteenth century, but so did a vitalist countercurrent that energized the growth of primitivist and exoticist commercial iconography. Icons of lush sensuality constituted a common pool of im-

agery which melded magic elixirs with breakfast foods, cosmetics, perfumes, clothing, corsets and other products that promised bodily regeneration," p. 141.

17. Pamela Walker Laird, *Advertising Progress: American business and the Rise of Consumer Marketing*, Johns Hopkins University Press, Baltimore, 1998. Laird, discusses the selection of the image, stating that "Although printers and publishers often exerted considerable influence on an advertisement's content and style, the final determination on an advertisement always belonged to someone keenly interested in the public image of the firm and its products," and she states that advertisers held the responsibility for the message. This is crucial in regard to advertisements with virulent images of Chinese—they were chosen not to offend but to please the audience and sell the product; pp. 43, 71.

18. Ohmann, op. cit., briefly states the same point: "Ways of connecting image, text, and product that have become second nature over the decades are nonetheless not natural or inevitable. . . ." He also describes that one possible relationship between the image and the product is that of "the absurd"; pp. 194, 197.

19. Walter Benjamin who wrote more briefly about that subject in his essay "On the Mimetic Faculty" (1933) had anticipated Foucault's recognition that images had a history. Benjamin discusses the human predilection for miming what is observed, especially addressing the history of change in this faculty. "We must suppose that the gift of producing similarities—for example, in dances, whose oldest function this was—and therefore also the gift of recognizing them, have changed with historical development." He contrasts the ancient confidence that cosmic events could be manipulated through human mimesis to the modern disbelief in such correspondence between cosmic and human acts. But he finds a commonality persisting between the ancient and the modern forms of mimicry in the nonsensuous mimeses of language. Benjamin's central focus questions how the world's languages have words with no relationship to one another yet they all indicate identical objects. His premise is that "it is nonsensuous similarity that establishes the ties not only between the spoken and the signified but also between the written and the signified, and equally between the spoken and the written." Regarding trade cards, our interest is with Benjamin's relationships between the drawn and the signified, the written and the signified, and the drawn and the written. "The coherence of words or sentences is the bearer through which, like a flash, similarity appears. For its production by man—like its perception by him—is in many cases, and particularly the most important, limited to flashes. . . . It is not improbable that the rapidity of writing and reading heightens the fusion of the semiotic and the mimetic in the sphere of language." In *Reflections: Essays, Aphorisms, Autobiographical Writings*, Harcourt Brace Jovanovich, New York, 1978, pp. 333, 335.

20. For several reasons, especially costs and exorbitant newspaper taxes from 1712 until 1852, outdoor advertisement dominated the field through its use of color images. By mid-nineteenth century the number of advertisements in London newspapers increased by several hundred percent; however, the ads rarely were illustrated. Illustrated or not, though, the newspaper ads were abundant and unusual. For instance, Presbrey described the front page of the *London Times* from 1800. Within the four columns of the page were thirty-one advertisements, ranging from

somber legal notices to a conspicuous ad heading the first column, announcing the exhibition of a ten-foot rattlesnake. Presbrey, op. cit., pp. 72, 79.

21. Lears, op. cit., p. 163.

22. Jan N. Pieterse, *White on Black: Images of Africa and Blacks in Western Popular Culture*, Yale University Press, 1995, p. 233. This is reinforced by Richard Meyer's statement that: "these discourses . . . map social and sexual anxieties onto cultural and geographical differences." "Satire and Homosexual Difference," in *The Other Hogarth: Aesthetics of Difference*, ed. by Bernadette Fort, Princeton University Press, 2001, p. 169.

23. As early as the start of the twentieth century, the relationship of identity between word and image had become so naturalized that the disjunctive imagery so frequently found in the trade cards had almost completely disappeared, to be rescued at the point of its complete demise by surrealism. In works such as the 1911 *What a Life! An Autobiography*, by E. V. L. and G. M., Collins, London, 1987, which constructed an imaginary autobiography from advertisements cut out from Whiteleys's catalog, surrealism provides us with a just a hint of the abundance of possible relationships between image, word, and meaning that had populated the world previous to the twentieth century.

24. Quoted in Mary W. Blanchard's *Oscar Wilde's America*, Yale University Press, New Haven, 1998, p. 190.

25. Francois Jullien, *Detour and Access: Strategies of Meaning in China and Greece*, Zone Books, New York, 2000, p. 9.

26. Peter C. Marzio, *The Democratic Art: Chromolithography 1840–1900, Pictures for a Nineteenth-Century America*, David R. Godine, Boston, 1979, p. 28.

27. Lori E. Rotskoff, "Still-Life Chromolithography and Domestic Ideology in Nineteenth-Century America," *Journal of American Studies* 31, 1 (April 1997): 22.

28. Lears, op. cit., p. 61.

29. Quoted in Jay, op. cit., p. 2.

30. Quoted in Barbara Novak, *American Painting of the Nineteenth Century: Realism, Idealism, and the American Experience*, Harper & Row, New York, 1979, p. 83.

31. Mark Twain, *A Connecticut Yankee in King Arthur's Court* (1889), Watermill Press, Mahwah, NJ, 1980, pp. 18, 57–58.

32. Following Jean Baudrillard, Jonathan Crary describes how the controversy surrounding mimesis "is not one of aesthetics but of social power, a power founded on the capacity to produce equivalences." Jonathan Crary, *Techniques of the Observer*, MIT Press Cambridge, 1990, pp. 10–11.

33. Cited in ibid.

34. In *Modernism, Mass Culture, and the Aesthetics of Obscenity*, Cambridge University Press, 2000, Allison Pease uncovers the intriguing connection between "handable" pornographic prints and the creation of consumer culture. She confirms the vast amounts of popular pornography, describing that "Between 1834 and 1880, the Vice Society absconded more than 385,000 obscene prints and photos, 80,000 books and pamphlets, five tons of other printed matter, 28,000 sheets of obscene songs and circulars, stereoscopes, copper plates, and the like." And she states that "The limited radical audience for bawdy populism, melodrama, and libertine litera-

ture of the early nineteenth century became, through the broadening influence of the press, a mass audience in the latter half of the nineteenth century," pp. 51, 55.

35. Marzio, op. cit., pp. 210–11.

36. Miles Orvell, *The Real Thing: Imitation and Authenticity in American Culture, 1880–1940*, University of North Carolina Press, Chapel Hill, 1989, pp. 17, 37.

37. G. W. F. Hegel, *The Phenomenology of Mind*, Harper Colophon Books, New York, 1967, p. 90. See also the discussion in Gagnier, op. cit., pp. 186–187.

38. Cited by Richard Guy Wilson in "Cultural Conditions," in *The American Renaissance: 1876–1917*, The Brooklyn Museum, NY, 1980, p. 29. Starting as early as the 1830s, and growing in frequency and vigor, Americans called on art to serve nationalism. See Maura Lyons, Manuscript for *William Dunlap and the Construction of an American Art History*, p. 70.

39. Marzio, op. cit., pp. 208–209.

40. McClintock paraphrases Georg Lukacs's when she states that "the commodity lies on the threshold of culture and commerce, confusing the supposedly sacrosanct boundaries between aesthetics and economy, money and art. Anne McClintock," *Imperial Leather: Race, Gender and Sexuality in the Colonial Contest*, Routledge, New York, 1995, p. 212.

41. Charles Eastlake, *Hints on Household Taste*, written in 1868, reprint by Dover Publications, New York, 1969, p. 197.

42. Orvell, op. cit., pp. 37–38. See also Marzio, op. cit., p. 11.

43. See, for example, Hermann Melville, *The Confidence-Man: His Masquerade*, 1857.

44. Chromolithography's fall from grace occurred rapidly and quite publicly. In 1876, the Philadelphia Centennial committee had classified chromolithographs in Department IV, the Fine Arts, along with sculpture, painting, and engraving. But by the 1893 Chicago's World Columbia Exposition, against lithographer's objections chromolithographs had been reclassified, no longer placed in the fine arts but appearing in Department F: the Industrial Arts.

45. This dialectic between art and commodity, especially through the mediation of multiples, remains a source of artistic invention in contemporary culture: when it emerged in mid-twentieth century via the art of Andy Warhol it was no longer a subtext, but a provocation, and has remained so since.

46. Quoted in Regenia Gagnier, *The Insatiability of Human Wants: Economics and Aesthetics in Market Society*, University of Chicago Press, Chicago, 2000, p. 40. Nineteenth-century culture assumed that aesthetic commodities would function in a lubricant capacity.

47. Debord, op. cit., p. 17.

48. Helmut and Alison Gernshiem, *The History of Photography: 1685–1914*, McGraw-Hill, New York, 1969. Although invented simultaneously by several people in different countries, the carte des visite did not become popular until May 1859, when Napoleon III took a detour with his army as they were going to battle against Austria, stopped at Disderi's studio and had his portrait taken. This functioned brilliantly as publicity for Napoleon III, making his portrait affordable and readily available to the masses. Disderi was promptly appointed Court Photographer, p. 294.

49. Laird discusses trade card strategies to familiarize the new: ". . . the retailer John Wanamaker . . . idealized visions of the rural past even while they promoted cosmopolitanism and steam-powered presses . . . ," op. cit., pp. 13–14.

50. Ibid., p. 106.

51. Marzio, op. cit., p. 195.

52. Cited in Gregory L. Ulmer, "The Object of Post-Criticism," in *The Anti-Aesthetic: Essays on Postmodern Culture*, Bay Press, Port Townsend, 1983, p. 97. Cited in *The Sphere and the Labyrinth: Avant-Gardes and Architecture from Piranesi to the 1970s*, MIT Press, 1990, by Manfredo Tafuri, p. 56.

53. Walter Benjamin, "The Work of Art in the Age of Mechanical Reproduction" (1937) in *Illuminations*, Schocken Books, New York, 1969, pp. 226–227.

54. Marzio's conclusion that chromolithography was "a product of modern invention that was dedicated to the aesthetic values of the past," although overstated, fittingly pertains to aspects of all floating signifiers; op. cit., p. 210.

55. Hobsbawm, Introduction to *The Invention of Tradition*, ed. by E. Hobsbawm and T. Ranger, Cambridge University Press, UK, 1983, p. 14.

56. Laura K. Mills, "American Allegorical Prints: Constructing an Identity," Yale University Art Gallery, 1996, p. 5.

57. Ibid., p. 6.

58. Crary, op. cit., pp. 23–24.

59. The lack of history disturbed some Americans. In *The Divided Mind Ideology and Imagination in America 1898–1917*, Cambridge University Press, 1983, Peter Conn describes Henry James return from Europe: "What James had felt was missing from America in 1879 was a past; what he finds missing in 1905 is the possibility of America *ever* constructing a past," p. 34.

60. Trachtenberg, Marvin. *The Statue of Liberty*, Viking Press, New York, 1976, p. 65.

61. The idea of "floating" deliberately connects these markers to Baudrillard's discussion of the floatation of signs, seen especially in fashion: "Fashion is not a *drifting* of signs—it is their *flotation*, in the sense in which monetary signs are floated today." Jean Baudrillard, *Symbolic Exchange and Death*, Sage Publications, London, 1993, p. 92.

62. Jean Baudrillard, among others, finds a clear correspondence between the development of new industrial techniques and the corresponding forms of political power in the nineteenth century. Baudrillard, ibid., esp. pp. 23, 88, 90, 93.

63. Lears, op. cit. p. 54. Lears uses the term *disembodied*, stating "the proliferation of literary and monetary fictions, novels, and banknotes, allowed signifiers to float more easily, to become disembodied from specific objects like flesh or gold."

64. "Competitive democracy succeeds the endogamy of signs proper to status-based orders. With the transit of values or signs of prestige from one class to another, we simultaneously and necessarily enter into the age of the *counterfeit*." Jean Baudrillard, op. cit., pp. 50–51.

65. For a discussion of the king's body as sacred see Sara E. Melzer, Kathryn Norberg, eds., *From the Royal to the Republican Body*, University of California Press, 1998, p. 3.

66. Baudrillard, op. cit. p. 51.

67. Joseph Alsop, *The Rare Art Traditions: The history of Art Collecting and Its Linked Phenomena Wherever These Have Appeared*, Harper & Row, New York,

1976. Those cultures are Greek, Chinese, Roman, Islamic, Renaissance to the present; p. 29.

68. Ibid., p. 26.

69. Will and Ariel Durant emphasize this point, stating: "This artistic spoliation of conquered or liberated lands had scant precedent; it aroused indignation everywhere except in France, and set a model for later warriors. Most of the spoils were sent directly to the Directory, were received there with pleasure, and found their way into the Louvre. . . ." in *The Story of Civilization: Part XI, The Age of Napoleon*, Simon and Schuster, New York, 1975, p. 102. And Rene Huyghe inadvertently demonstrates the connection between such artistic usurpation and the emerging theories of aesthetics, saying: "Since Kant, we have been aware that art was one of the most characteristic expressions of culture. . . ." In *Louvre, Paris: Great Museums of the World*, Simon and Schuster, New York, 1951, p. 10.

70. Isabella Gardner, for instance, comes to mind.

71. Gagnier further indicts art collectors, giving the example of Walter Pater's "capacity to consume the treasures of the past as contributing to his own 'unique' 'personality' . . . ," op. cit., p. 91.

72. Owen Jones *The Grammar of Chinese Ornament*, 1869. Reproduced by Parkgate Books, London, 1997. The dust-cover notes on this edition raise the looting of Chinese buildings and how Jones found this fortuitous. This reinforces the connection between the sense of empire and the use of the spoils of a conquered people in western aesthetic. This also corroborates Jonathan Crary's description of the changes in visual culture being due more to the intentions with which motifs are seen then to the mere availability of those motifs. In previously centuries European countries had employed designs and patterns from Asia but not integrated into the Western canon of motifs. Rather, they prompted only a quotation of the Asian motif.

73. Debord illuminates this, stating, "The development of capitalism meant the unification of irreversible time *on a world scale*. Universal history became a reality because the entire globe was brought under the sway of this time's progression. But a history that is thus the same everywhere at once has as yet amounted to nothing more than an intrahistorical refusal of history. What appears the world over *as the same day* is merely the time of economic production—time cut up into equal abstract fragments. Unified irreversible time still belongs to the world market—and, by extension, to the world spectacle." Op. cit., p. 107.

74. William M. Ivins Jr., *Prints and Visual Communication*, MIT Press, Cambridge, 1953, pp. 2, 16.

75. This change in the Western mental mapping of geography also parallels Mircea Eliade's distinction contrasting the fixed point defined by sacred space, to profane space which has no such marker, but which "maintains the homogeneity and hence the relativity of space. No *true* orientation is now possible. . . . Properly speaking, there is no longer any world, there are only fragments of a shattered universe, an amorphous mass consisting of an infinite number of more or less neutral places in which man moves, governed and driven by the obligations of an existence incorporated into an industrial society." *The Sacred and the Profane: The Nature of Religion*, Harper & Brothers, New York, 1957, pp. 23–24. This is stated in another fashion by Marshall Berman, who sees modernism as "a struggle to make ourselves

at home in a constantly changing world. . . ." *All That Is Solid Melts into Air: The Experience of Modernity*, Penguin Books, New York, 1982, p. 6.

76. As an example, McClintock observes that numerous renderings of the popular notion of a "family of man" took the form of a tree, which naturalized the idea of evolution as it hierarchized it. She summarizes this construction: "anatomy becomes an allegory of progress and history is reproduced as a technology of the visible." Op. cit., p. 38.

77. Most distant was the time period relegated by Europeans to Africa, which Hegel asserted belonged to "no Historical part of the world . . . it has no movement or development of time in modernity, marooned and historically abandoned." Never mind that Hegel had not traveled to Africa and based his judgments, as did many Westerners, only on the bits and pieces of ephemera that arrived in the Western world. Quoted in ibid., pp. 40–41.

78. Harry Harootunian, "Forward," in Victor Segalen, *Essay on Exoticism: An Aesthetics of Diversity*, Duke University Press, Durham, NC, 2002, p. ix.

79. Perhaps the most concise definition of who had and who did not have history is found in Eric R. Wolf's preface to his *Europe and the People Without History*, University of California Press, Berkeley, 1982, in which he calls for a history of the previously excluded groups: "We thus need to uncover the history of 'the people without history'—the active histories of 'primitives,' peasantries, laborers, immigrants, and besieged minorities." One of his chapters expressly concerns the "Orient," pp. x, 232–263.

80. This supports Regenia Gagnier's thesis that after 1871 the idea of progress transformed to an idea of development. In op. cit., pp. 4–5.

81. The card describes that it is one of fifty in the pictorial series of "History of the Sports and Pastimes of All Nations."

82. Lears, op. cit., discussed the "exoticism and primitivism" of patent medicine trade cards. "Orientalist idioms preserved the ancient link between fecund sexuality and material abundance. . . ." and he quotes a 1896 pamphlet for Church's Kava-Kava Compound: "There is no doubt whatever but that many of the best botanical remedies used in medical science, have first becomes known through their use of savage or semi-barbarous people," pp. 103, 146.

83. Gagnier discusses Cora Kaplan's theory of how universalism and likeness in pre-1850 theories of race turned into intolerance of differences just as technology had brought the ability for greater equality. Op. cit., p. 106.

84. Eric Hobsbawm, "Mass-Producing Traditions: Europe, 1870–1914," in op. cit., p. 280. For Americans to clarify what it is they are, there seems to be a need for an antithetical entity symbolizing what Americans are not. This construction of dualities was challenged as early as 1958. In "Must We Mean What We Say?" Stanley Cavell discussed an alternative—an alternative for which the either/or alternatives make no sense. In *Philosophy and Linguistics*, ed. Colin Lyas, MacMillan, London, 1971, pp. 131–166.

85. McClintock coins the term *domestic degeneracy* to describe the widely used iconography of imperialism relocated into the domestic realm. Op. cit., p. 53.

86. In Hogarth's time those foreigners were most frequently Italian. Richard Meyer, op. cit., p. 169.

87. Karl Marx and Friedrich Engels, *The Communist Manifesto*, 1848, reprinted by Washington Square Press, New York, 1964, p. 63.

88. Charles Baudelaire, "The Painter of Modern Life," Phaidon Press Limited, 1964, p. 12.

89. Crary, op. cit., pp. 10–11.

90. Ibid., pp. 10–11. Crary defines modernization as "a ceaseless and self-perpetuating creation of new needs, new consumption, and new production." He links modernization with internal states: "Vision and its effects are always inseparable from the possibilities of an observing subject who is both the historical product *and* the site of certain practices, techniques, institutions, and procedures of subjectification," p. 5.

91. Benjamin "On Some Motifs in Baudelaire," in *Illuminations*, Schocken Books, New York, 1969, p. 165. In "The Object of Post-Criticism," Gregory L. Ulmer cited Stanley Mitchell, discussing Benjamin's connection of the older allegorical form to the twentieth-century innovation of the collage, and the use of collage for its sudden displacement: "Montage became for him the modern, constructive, active, unmelancholy form of allegory, namely the ability to connect dissimilars in such a way as to 'shock' people into new recognitions and understandings." Op. cit., p. 96.

92. Walter Benjamin, "Surrealism," op. cit. He writes: "In Moscow I lived in a hotel in which almost all the rooms were occupied by Tibetan lamas who had come to Moscow for a congress of Buddhist churches. I was struck by the number of doors in the corridors that were always left ajar. What had at first seemed accidental began to be disturbing. I found out that in these rooms lived members of a sect who had sworn never to occupy closed rooms. The shock I had then must be felt by the reader of *Nadja*" (a text by Andre Breton), p. 180.

93. One wonders if this isn't an oblique reference to foot-binding.

94. The Chinese dwarf appears again in another trade card this time depicted, rather than mentioned in words, appearing on a table towering above an elegant white Victorian woman.

95. Moy, op. cit., p. 12.

96. Other trade cards explicate aspects of this appearance of one world within another, showing the head of a lovely woman bursting through a newspaper, ripping the news. And in a variation of the theme of bursting in to view, one card shows a disappearance into another, safer realm. A vicious leashed dog leaps at a man who disappears over a fence. All we see of the man are his legs—his front portion has ripped through the blank space that would be read as air, now seen as a window into another place.

97. Benjamin, "Surrealism," op. cit., p. 190.

98. Allison Pease describes how "In his insistence on a purely formal art, Swinburne blazed the path for modernist critics and writers who relied on seeing aesthetic beauty as a purely formal quality in order to avoid the moral conundrums of ethically questionable and sensational subject matter." *Modernism, Mass Culture and the Aesthetics of Obscenity*, Cambridge University Press, Cambridge, UK, 2000, p. 70.

99. Karl Philipp Moritz (1756–1793), cited in ibid.

100. Karl Beckson, ed., *Oscar Wilde: The Critical Heritage*, Barnes & Noble, New York, 1970, pp. 50, 72.

101. Lloyd Lewis and Henry Justin Smith, Oscar Wilde Discovers America [1882], Harcourt, Brace and Company, New York, 1936, pp. 241–245. Interestingly, Jorge Borges agrees with the miners assessment, although he describes it in literary terms. In "About Oscar Wilde" he writes: "consider the notion that Wilde was a kind of symbolist. A great many facts support it. . . . But one important fact refutes this notion: in verse or in prose, Wilde's syntax is always very simple. . . . He was an ingenuous man who was also right." From Other Inquisitions 1937–1953, Simon and Schuster, New York, 1968, pp. 79–81.

102. See the previous discussion in chapter 3: Senator Edmunds use of the phrase "highly too utterly utter idea" in the March 4, 1882 article, "China in the Senate."

103. Oscar Wilde, *Intentions*, in Richard Ellman, ed., *The Artist as Critic: Critical Writings of Oscar Wilde*, Vintage Books, New York, 1969, pp. 393, 398.

104. Even as subtle a historical critic as Eric Hobsbawm failed to grasp that the concern of much of twentieth-century art is the friction between the desire for a democratic audience and the fundamental codedness of visual images. Writing about avant-garde painting in *Behind the Times: The Decline and Fall of the Twentieth-Century Avant-Gardes*, Thames and Hudson, New York, 1998, Eric Hobsbawm described the lack of immediate intelligibility of avant-garde art as its failure, assuming that successful art should be immediately comprehensible to a general audience; as he states, this is the core of his argument. Certainly Hobsbawm does not expect this transparency in other areas of inquiry. Hobsbawm also did not consider the role images play in establishing power or the conspicuous juggling of images along with authority in a time of political change. See especially, p. 7.

105. Gagnier subtly assesses what Wilde signified in his culture: ""he individual in the age of 'personality' in mass culture becomes a stereotype, a representative of a class. Thus Pater becomes the 'Aesthete' and his tastes 'Aestheticism,' Wilde becomes the homosexual or an 'Oscar,' . . ." op. cit., p. 91.

106. Meyer, op. cit. Meyer was speaking of a figure in Hogarth's *The Analysis of Beauty*, Plate 1, *The Sculptor's Yard*, 1753, a detail of which shows an effeminate dancing master smiling, touching a classical male nude statue; p. 171.

107. Pieterse, op. cit., p. 220.

108. An usual category of trade card images consists of white people dressed as Chinese, clearly a fascinating and transgressive crossing of boundaries.

109. Pieterse, op. cit., pp. 232–233. This antithesis is manifest in the widespread popularity of two characters: Uncle Sam and a black-face minstrel, both parts played by the popular entertainer, Dan Rice in the 1850 and 1860s. David Carlyon, *Dan Rice: The Most Famous Man You've Never Heard Of*, Public Affairs, New York, 2001, esp. pp. 51–52, 411.

110. Thanks to Nancy Ota, Professor of Law at Albany Law School, for this trade card.

CONCLUSION

1. Francois Jullien, *Detour and Access: Strategies of Meaning in China and Greece*, Zone Books, New York, 2000, p. 9.

2. Merleau-Ponty, "Eye and Mind," in *The Primacy of Perception*, Northwestern University Press, Evanston, IL, 1964, p. 166.

NAME INDEX

SUBJECT INDEX